Social Trends

No. 34

2004 edition

Editors: Carol Summerfield

Penny Babb

London: TSO

Contact points
For enquiries about this publication,
contact the Editor:
Tel: **020 7533 5778**
E-mail: **social.trends@ons.gov.uk**

To order this publication, call TSO on
0870 600 5522. See also back cover.

For general enquiries, contact the
National Statistics Customer Contact
Centre on **0845 601 3034**
(minicom: 01633 812399)
E-mail: **info@statistics.gov.uk**
Fax: 01633 652747
Letters: Room D115,
          Government Buildings,
          Cardiff Road,
          Newport NP10 8XG

You can also find National Statistics on the
internet – go to **www.statistics.gov.uk**.

About the Office for National Statistics
The Office for National Statistics (ONS) is
the government agency responsible for
compiling, analysing and disseminating
many of the United Kingdom's economic,
social and demographic statistics, including
the retail prices index, trade figures and
labour market data, as well as the periodic
census of the population and health
statistics. The Director of ONS is also the
National Statistician and the Registrar
General for England and Wales, and the
agency administers the registration of
births, marriages and deaths there.

A National Statistics publication
National Statistics are produced to high
professional standards set out in the
National Statistics Code of Practice.
They undergo regular quality assurance
reviews to ensure that they meet
customer needs. They are produced
free from any political interference.

Contents

Numbers in brackets refer to similar items appearing in Social Trends 33

Ageing and Gender: Diversity and Change	Changing demography	
	Table A.1 Proportions of older people: by sex and age, 1971 to 2001	1
	The diminishing feminisation of later life	
	Figure A.2 Sex ratios among older people: by age, 1951 to 2001	3
	Changes in marital status	
	Table A.3 Changes in marital status for people aged 65 and over, 1971 to 2021	4
	Figure A.4 Marital status of people aged 65 and over: by sex and age, 2001	4
	Gender and living arrangements	
	Table A.5 Living arrangements of people aged 65 and over: by sex and age, 2001	5
	Figure A.6 Percentage of people aged 65 and over that are living in communal establishments: by age and marital status	6
	Household poverty in later life	
	Figure A.7 Poverty rate and relative income aged 65 and over: EU comparison, 1998	7
	Figure A.8 Incomes of pensioners as a percentage of incomes of non-pensioners: selected countries	8
	Table A.9 People aged 65 and over receiving income support: by marital status, socio-economic group and age, 2001/02	9
	Diversity of income in later life	
	Table A.10 Median gross individual income of people aged 65 and over: by marital status, socio-economic group and age, 2001/02	10
	Table A.11 Private pensions receipt among those aged 65 and over: by marital status and socio-economic group, 2001/02	11
	Car ownership and transport	
	Figure A.12 People aged 50 and over with a car in the household: by sex and age, 2001	12

1: Population   Population profile

Table 1.1   Population of the United Kingdom (1.1)   16

Table 1.2   Population: by age and sex (1.2)   16

Figure 1.3   Dependent population: by age (1.3)   17

Figure 1.4   Population aged 90 years and over: by sex   17

Table 1.5   Population: by ethnic group and age, 2001 (1.5)   18

Figure 1.6   Population of working age:
                   by sex and socio-economic classification, 2003 (1.6)   18

Population change

Table 1.7   Population change (1.7)   19

Figure 1.8   Births and deaths (1.8)   19

Table 1.9   Deaths: by age and sex (1.9)   20

Geographical distribution

Map 1.10   Population aged 65 and over: by area, 2001   20

Table 1.11   Inter-regional movements within the United Kingdom, 2002   21

International migration

Table 1.12   UK nationals living in other EU states and
                   nationals of other EU states living in the UK   22

Figure 1.13   Grants of settlement: by region of origin (1.13)   22

Table 1.14   Asylum applications, including dependants:
                   EU comparison, 2002 (1.14)   23

International perspective

Table 1.15   World demographic indicators (1.16)   23

Table 1.16   European demographic indicators: EU comparison   24

2: Households and families

Household composition

Table 2.1	Households: by size (2.1)	26
Table 2.2	Households: by type of household and family (2.2)	26
Table 2.3	People in households: by type of household and family	27
Table 2.4	Percentage of dependent children living in different family types (2.4)	27
Table 2.5	Families with dependent children: by ethnic group, 2001 (2.5)	28
Map 2.6	Proportion of households which consist of one person: by area, 2001	29

Family relationships

Table 2.7	Stepfamilies with dependent children	29
Table 2.8	Adoptions: by age of child	30
Table 2.9	Adults living with their parents: by sex and age	30
Figure 2.10	Contact with relatives: by ethnic group, 2001	31

Partnerships

Figure 2.11	Marriages and divorces (2.10)	31
Table 2.12	Average age at marriage and divorce (2.12)	32
Table 2.13	Marriage and divorce rates: EU comparison, 2002 (2.11)	32
Figure 2.14	Non-married people cohabiting: by sex and age, 2001/02 (2.9)	33
Table 2.15	Attitudes towards marriage: by age, 2002	33

Family formation

Table 2.16	Fertility rates: by age of mother at childbirth	34
Table 2.17	Births outside marriage: EU comparison	34
Table 2.18	Teenage conceptions: by age at conception and outcome, 2001 (2.15)	35
Figure 2.19	Abortion rates: by age (2.17)	35
Figure 2.20	Childless women at age 25, 35 and 45: by year of birth (2.20)	36
Table 2.21	Average age of mother: by birth order (2.19)	36

3: Education

Schools

Figure 3.1	Participation rates of children aged 3–4 in maintained nursery and primary schools: by region, January 2003	38
Table 3.2	School pupils: by type of school (3.3)	38
Figure 3.3	Pupils with statements of Special Educational Needs (SEN): by type of school	39
Table 3.4	Class sizes in schools: by region, 2002/03	40
Table 3.5	Adults' attitudes towards secondary schooling, 2002	40
Table 3.6	Pupils reaching or exceeding expected standards: by Key Stage and sex, 2003 (3.7)	41
Figure 3.7	Mean score for reading achievement: G8 comparison, 2001	41
Figure 3.8	Permanent exclusion rates: by ethnic group, 2001/02	42
Table 3.9	GCSE attainment: by parents' socio-economic classification, 2002 (3.9)	42

Post-compulsory participation

Table 3.10	People working towards a qualification: by age, 2003 (3.11)	43
Table 3.11	Students in further and higher education: by type of course and sex (3.12)	44
Figure 3.12	GCE A level or equivalent entries for young people: by selected subject, 2000/01	44
Figure 3.13	Participation rates in higher education: by social class	45

Post-compulsory outcomes

Figure 3.14	Achievement at GCE A level or equivalent (3.14)	45
Table 3.15	NVQ/SVQ awards: by framework area and level, 2001/02 (3.15)	46
Figure 3.16	Graduation rates from first university degrees: EU comparison, 2001	46
Table 3.17	Highest qualification held: by sex and ethnic group, 2003	47

Adult training and learning

Figure 3.18	Employees receiving job-related training: by age and sex, 2003 (3.18)	48
Figure 3.19	People in Work Based Learning: by sex and selected area of learning, November 2002	48
Table 3.20	Enrolments on adult education courses: by age, attendance mode and sex, 2002	49

Educational resources

Table 3.21	Expenditure on education as a percentage of GDP: EU comparison, 2000 (3.22)	49
Figure 3.22	Full-time nursery & primary and secondary school teachers: by sex (3.23)	50
Figure 3.23	Non-teaching staff: by type of school (3.24)	50

4: Labour market

Economic activity

Figure 4.1	Economic activity rates: by sex (4.1)	52
Table 4.2	Economic activity: by employment status and sex, 1988 and 2003 (4.10)	53
Figure 4.3	Economic activity rates: by sex and age, 2003 (4.2)	53
Table 4.4	Economic activity status of young people: by whether in full-time education, 2003	54
Table 4.5	Economic activity status of women: by marital status and age of youngest dependent child, 2003	55
Table 4.6	Economic activity status of working age people: by sex and whether disabled, 2003 (4.4)	55
Table 4.7	Reasons for economic inactivity: by sex, 2003 (4.5)	56
Figure 4.8	Working age households: by household economic status (4.6)	57

Employment

Figure 4.9	Employment rates: by sex (4.7)	57
Figure 4.10	Employment rates: by sex, EU comparison, 2002	58
Map 4.11	Jobs density: by area, 2001	58
Table 4.12	Employment rate: by sex and highest qualification, 2003	59

Patterns of employment

Table 4.13	Employee jobs: by sex and industry (4.12)	59
Figure 4.14	People in employment who were in the higher managerial and professional group: by ethnic group, 2001–02	60
Figure 4.15	Employees: by occupation and sex, 2003 (4.13)	60
Figure 4.16	Self-employment: by industry and sex, 2003	61
Table 4.17	Distribution of usual weekly hours of work: by sex, 2003	62
Table 4.18	Employees with flexible working patterns, 2003	62

Unemployment

Figure 4.19	Unemployment: by sex (4.17)	63
Figure 4.20	Unemployment rates: by sex, EU comparison, 2002	64
Figure 4.21	Unemployment rates: by sex and age (4.19)	64
Table 4.22	Duration of unemployment: by sex and age, 2003	65

Labour market dynamics

Figure 4.23	People in employment who voluntarily left their job: by age and sex, 2002	66
Table 4.24	People entering employment through the New Deal: by age and type of employment, 1998 to 2003 (4.25)	66

The working environment

Table 4.25	Trade union membership of employees: by occupation and sex, 2002	67
Figure 4.26	Labour disputes: working days lost	67
Table 4.27	Reasons full-time employees were looking for a new job: by sex and presence of dependent children, 2003 (4.23)	68

5: Income and wealth

Household income

Figure 5.1	Real household disposable income per head and gross domestic product per head (5.1)	70
Map 5.2	Household disposable income per head: by area, 1997–1999	70
Table 5.3	Composition of household income (5.2)	71
Table 5.4	Sources of gross weekly income: by age of head of household, 2001/02	72
Table 5.5	Sources of disposable income: EU comparison, 2000	73
Figure 5.6	Median net individual income: by family type and sex, 2001/02 (5.5)	74

Earnings

Figure 5.7	Average earnings index and retail prices index	75
Figure 5.8	Gross hourly earnings: by sex and whether working full time or part time	75
Table 5.9	Distribution of hourly earnings: by industry, April 2003 (5.9)	76
Figure 5.10	Proportional effect on earnings of a degree level qualification: by sex and degree subject, 1993–2001	77

Taxes

Table 5.11	Income tax payable: by annual income, 2003/04 (5.12)	78
Table 5.12	Percentage of earnings paid in income tax and national insurance contributions: by sex and level of earnings	79
Table 5.13	Net local taxes paid by households: by region, 2001/02	80

Income distribution

Figure 5.14	Distribution of real household disposable income (5.14)	81
Table 5.15	Distribution of equivalised disposable income: by family type, 2001/02	82
Figure 5.16	Shares of equivalised disposable income, 2001/02	82
Table 5.17	Where in the income distribution individuals spent the majority of their time between 1991 and 2001	83
Table 5.18	Redistribution of income through taxes and benefits, 2001/02 (5.17)	84

Low income

Figure 5.19	Percentage of people whose income is below various fractions of median income (5.18)	85
Figure 5.20	Percentage of people with incomes below 60 per cent of the EU median: EU comparison, 2000	85
Figure 5.21	Children living in households below 60 per cent of median income (5.23)	86
Table 5.22	Individuals in households with incomes below 60 per cent of median disposable income: by ethnic group of head of household	87
Table 5.23	Individuals aged 60 and over experiencing low income: by sex, number of years worked and marital status, 1999	87

5: Income and wealth (continued)

Table 5.24	Indicators of social capital: by gross weekly household income, 2000	88

Wealth

Table 5.25	Composition of the net wealth of the household sector (5.25)	88
Table 5.26	Distribution of wealth (5.26)	89
Table 5.27	Household savings: by household type and amount, 2001/02	90

National income and expenditure

Figure 5.28	Annual growth in gross domestic product in real terms (5.28)	91
Figure 5.29	Gross domestic product per head: G7 comparison, 2001	91
Figure 5.30	Total managed expenditure as a percentage of gross domestic product	92
Table 5.31	European Union expenditure: by sector	92

6: Expenditure

Household and personal expenditure

Figure 6.1	Household expenditure index	94
Table 6.2	Household expenditure (6.2)	94
Table 6.3	Household expenditure: by socio-economic classification of household reference person, 2002/03 (6.3)	95
Table 6.4	Household expenditure: by selected family types, 2002/03	96
Figure 6.5	Students' expenditure by type, 2002/03	96
Table 6.6	Household expenditure: by age of household reference person, 2002/03	97
Table 6.7	Average weekly expenditure on selected leisure items and activities: by region, 2002/03	98
Figure 6.8	Expenditure on selected items as a percentage of total household expenditure	98

Transactions and credit

Figure 6.9	Volume of retail sales (6.8)	99
Figure 6.10	Non-cash transactions: by method of payment (6.9)	99
Table 6.11	Debit or credit card spending: by type of purchase, 2002	100
Figure 6.12	Net borrowing by consumers in real terms (6.11)	100
Figure 6.13	Number of individual insolvencies (6.12)	101

Prices

Figure 6.14	Retail prices index (6.13)	101
Figure 6.15	Percentage change in retail prices index, 2002 (6.14)	102
Table 6.16	Cost of groceries	102
Figure 6.17	Percentage change in consumer prices: EU comparison, 2002 (6.16)	103
Figure 6.18	Comparative price levels for household expenditure: G7 comparison, August 2003 (6.17)	103

7: Health   Key health indicators

Figure 7.1   Expectation of life at birth: by sex   106

Figure 7.2   Infant mortality   106

Table 7.3   Self-reported general health: by sex and age, 2001   107

Table 7.4   High blood pressure: by sex and age, 2001   108

Figure 7.5   Weekly incidence of heart attack: by sex   108

Figure 7.6   Mortality: by sex and major cause (7.11)   109

Figure 7.7   Death rates from circulatory disease: EU comparison, 1999   109

Infectious diseases

Figure 7.8   Notifications of selected infectious diseases (7.4)   110

Figure 7.9   MMR immunisation of children by their second birthday:
               by region, 2002/03   110

Figure 7.10   Influenza vaccine uptake by people aged 65 and over   111

Diet and related health

Table 7.11   Average daily portions of fruit and vegetables consumed:
               by sex and age, 2000–01   111

Figure 7.12   Obesity among adults: by sex and NS-SeC, 2001   112

Alcohol, drugs and smoking

Table 7.13   Adults exceeding daily benchmarks of alcohol:
               by sex and age, 2001/02   112

Figure 7.14   Deaths from alcohol-related diseases: by sex   113

Table 7.15   Prevalence of drug misuse by young adults in the previous year:
               by sex and drug category, 1996 and 2001/02   113

Figure 7.16   Prevalence of adult cigarette smoking: by sex (7.16)   114

Cancer

Figure 7.17   Incidence of cancer: by sex, EU comparison 2000   114

Figure 7.18   Death rates from selected cancers: by sex (7.12)   115

Table 7.19   Breast cancer screening coverage: by region (7.24)   116

Mental health

Figure 7.20   Prevalence of neurotic disorders among older people:
               by sex and gross household income, 2000   116

Table 7.21   Suicide rates: by sex and age   117

Sexual health

Table 7.22   Number of opposite sex partners in the previous three
               months: by sex and age, 1999–2001   117

Table 7.23   Use of condoms in the previous four weeks: by number
               of new sexual partners of the opposite sex, 1999–2001   118

Figure 7.24   HIV and AIDS: diagnoses and deaths in HIV infected individuals 118

8: Social protection

Carers and caring

Table 8.1	Residents in communal medical and care establishments: by age, 2001	120
Figure 8.2	Number of contact hours of home help and home care: by sector	120
Table 8.3	Informal carers who live in households: by age and sex, 2001	121
Figure 8.4	Types of help given to main person cared for: by sex of carer, 2000/01 (8.10)	122

Sick and disabled people

Table 8.5	NHS in-patient activity for sick and disabled people (8.12)	122
Table 8.6	Selected operations in NHS hospitals, 2001/02	123
Figure 8.7	Hospital and community health service expenditure: by age of recipient, 2001/02	123
Figure 8.8	Consultations with an NHS GP: by sex and age, 2001/02 (8.16)	124
Figure 8.9	Satisfaction with NHS GPs and dentists (8.17)	124
Table 8.10	Recipients of disability living allowance (DLA): by main disabling condition, 2003 (8.18)	125

Older people

Table 8.11	Use of personal social services by people aged 65 and over and living in households: by age, 2001/02	126
Table 8.12	Receipt of selected social security benefits for pensioners: by family type, 2001/02 (8.5)	126
Table 8.13	Pension provision: by selected employment status and sex, 2001/02 (8.19)	127

Families and children

Table 8.14	Receipt of selected social security benefits for families below pension age: by family type, 2001/02 (8.5)	127
Table 8.15	Informal childcare arrangements for children whose mothers are in employment, autumn 2002	128
Table 8.16	Children looked after by local authorities: by type of accommodation (8.22)	128
Figure 8.17	Children on child protection registers: by sex and category of abuse, 2002	129
Table 8.18	Calls and letters to ChildLine: by type of concern and sex, 2002/03	129
Figure 8.19	Caesarean deliveries in NHS hospitals	130

Expenditure

Figure 8.20	Expenditure on social protection benefits in real terms: by function, 1991/92 and 2001/02 (8.1)	130
Figure 8.21	Expenditure on social protection benefits per head: EU comparison, 2000 (8.2)	131
Figure 8.22	Social security benefit expenditure: by recipient group, 2002/03 (8.4)	131
Figure 8.23	Local authority personal social services expenditure: by recipient group, 2001/02 (8.6)	132

9: Crime and justice

Crime rates

Figure 9.1	British Crime Survey offences	134
Table 9.2	Recorded crime: by type of offence, 2002/03 (9.1)	134
Table 9.3	Crimes committed within last 12 months: by outcome, 2002/03 (9.3)	135
Map 9.4	Theft: by region, 2002/03	136

Offences

Table 9.5	Crimes involving firearms: by offence group	136
Table 9.6	Defendants found guilty of indictable fraud offences	137
Table 9.7	Seizures of selected drugs	137

Victims

Table 9.8	Levels of disorder	138
Table 9.9	Reasons for improving home security, 2001/02	138
Table 9.10	Concern about crime: by sex and age, 2002/03	139
Table 9.11	Victims of violent crime: by sex and age, 2002/03	139

Offenders

Table 9.12	Offenders found guilty of, or cautioned for, indictable offences: by sex, type of offence and age, 2002 (9.13)	140
Table 9.13	Offenders cautioned for indictable offences: by type of offence (9.15)	141
Figure 9.14	Prisoners reconvicted within two years of discharge in 1999: by original offence	141

Police and courts actions

Table 9.15	Reasons for stop and searches made by the police	142
Table 9.16	Detection rates for recorded crime: by type of offence, 2002/03 (9.18)	142
Table 9.17	Offenders sentenced for indictable offences: by type of offence and type of sentence, 2002 (9.16)	143
Figure 9.18	Outcome of cases at the magistrates' courts, 2001–02	144

Prisons and probation

Figure 9.19	Prison population (9.19)	144
Figure 9.20	Number of releases on temporary licence: by type of licence	145
Table 9.21	Prison population of British nationals: by ethnic grouping	145

Civil justice

Figure 9.22	Writs and summonses issued (9.21)	146
Table 9.23	Certificates issued on civil non-family proceedings, 2002/03	147
Table 9.24	Police officer strength: by rank, sex and ethnic group, at 31 March 2003 (9.24)	147

10: Housing

Housing stock and housebuilding

Figure 10.1 Dwellings and households   150

Table 10.2 Type of accommodation: by construction date, 2002/03 (10.3) 150

Figure 10.3 Housebuilding completions: by sector (10.4)   151

Table 10.4 Housebuilding completions: by number of bedrooms (10.5) 151

Tenure and accommodation

Figure 10.5 Stock of dwellings: by tenure (10.2)   152

Table 10.6 Tenure: by type of accommodation, 2001 (10.6)   152

Table 10.7 Tenure: by household composition, 2001   153

Figure 10.8 Owner-occupied dwellings: EU comparison, 2000   154

Table 10.9 Tenure: by economic activity status of household
reference person, 2001 (10.9)   154

Table 10.10 Tenure: by ethnic group, 2001 (10.11)   155

Table 10.11 Accommodation type: by household composition, 2001 (10.12) 156

Table 10.12 Accommodation type: by ethnic group, 2001   157

Homelessness

Figure 10.13 Homeless households in priority need accepted by
local authorities: by need category, 2002/03   158

Figure 10.14 Homeless households in temporary accommodation (10.13) 158

Housing condition and satisfaction with area

Figure 10.15 Households whose accommodation does not meet the
decent homes standard: by tenure, 2001   159

Table 10.16 Overcrowding and under-occupation:
by tenure, 2002/03 (10.16)   159

Table 10.17 Residents' views of problems in their neighbourhood:
by whether living in a poor or other neighbourhood, 2001   160

Housing mobility

Figure 10.18 Property transactions   160

Table 10.19 Households resident under one year:
current tenure by previous tenure, 2002/03 (10.19)   161

Figure 10.20 Sales and transfers of local authority dwellings   162

Housing costs and expenditure

Figure 10.21 Average property prices   162

Figure 10.22 New mortgages: average mortgage repayment as a
percentage of average household income   163

Figure 10.23 Mortgage loans in arrears and repossessions (10.25)   164

Figure 10.24 Median rent before housing benefit: by region, 2002/03   164

11: Environment

Pollution

Figure 11.1	Emissions of selected air pollutants (11.4)	166
Figure 11.2	Days with moderate or higher air pollution	166
Table 11.3	Water pollution incidents: by source, 2002 (11.5)	167
Table 11.4	Chemical quality of rivers and canals: by country (11.6)	168
Table 11.5	Bathing water – compliance with EC bathing water directive coliform standards: by Environment Agency region	169

Climate change

Figure 11.6	Difference in average surface temperature: comparison with 1961–1990 average (11.7)	169
Figure 11.7	Emissions of carbon dioxide: by end user (11.9)	170
Table 11.8	Electricity generated from renewable sources	170

Waste management

Table 11.9	Management of municipal waste: by method (11.17)	171
Table 11.10	Materials collected from households for recycling	171

Use of resources

Figure 11.11	Winter and summer rainfall	172
Figure 11.12	Production of primary fuels (11.21)	173
Table 11.13	Electricity generation: by fuel used, EU comparison, 2001	173
Table 11.14	Domestic energy consumption per household: by final use	174

Countryside, farming and wildlife

Table 11.15	Land by agricultural and other uses, 2002	174
Figure 11.16	Land under organic crop production	175
Figure 11.17	North Sea fish stocks	175
Figure 11.18	Woodland cover, 1980 and 2002	176
Table 11.19	Land changing to residential use: by previous use (11.13)	177
Figure 11.20	Population of wild birds	177

Environmental concerns and behaviour

Table 11.21	Frequency of visits to local green spaces or countryside, without using a car or other transport: by age, 2001	178
Table 11.22	Noise complaints received by Environmental Health Officers: by source	178

12: Transport

Overview

Figure 12.1	Passenger transport: by mode (12.1)	180
Table 12.2	Trips per person per year: by main mode and purpose, 1999–2001 (12.2)	180
Table 12.3	Trips per person per year: by car access and main mode of transport, 1999–2001	181
Figure 12.4	Average distance walked per person per year: by age	182
Figure 12.5	Goods moved by domestic freight transport: by mode (12.4)	182

Prices and expenditure

Table 12.6	Passenger transport prices (12.5)	183
Table 12.7	Household expenditure on transport in real terms (12.6)	183
Figure 12.8	Household expenditure on transport as a proportion of total household expenditure: EU comparison, 2000	184

Access to transport

Table 12.9	Full car driving licence holders: by sex and age	184
Table 12.10	Number of cars per household: by household composition, 2001	185
Map 12.11	Households without a car or van, 2001	186
Figure 12.12	Reasons for infrequent bus use, July 2002	186

Travel to work and school

| Map 12.13 | Travel to work by car or van, 2001 | 187 |
| Table 12.14 | Trips to and from school per child per year: by main mode, 1989–91 and 1999–2001 | 187 |

The roads

Table 12.15	Average daily flow of motor vehicles: by class of road (12.14)	188
Figure 12.16	Bus travel (12.15)	188
Table 12.17	Attitudes towards car and bus use, 2002	189

The railways

| Table 12.18 | Rail journeys: by operator (12.17) | 189 |
| Table 12.19 | Opinion on rail services, 2002 | 190 |

International travel

| Table 12.20 | International travel: by mode (12.19) | 190 |
| Figure 12.21 | Terminal passengers at civil airports | 191 |

Transport safety

Table 12.22	Passenger death rates: by mode of transport (12.22)	192
Figure 12.23	Average number of people killed or seriously injured in road accidents on weekdays: by road user type and time of day, 2002	192
Figure 12.24	Road deaths: EU comparison, 2001 (12.24)	193

13: Lifestyles and social participation

Everyday tasks

Figure 13.1	Time spent on main activities by full-time workers, 2000–01	196
Figure 13.2	Time spent on household tasks: by age and sex, 2000–01	196
Table 13.3	Division of household tasks: by sex, 2002	197

Leisure activities

Table 13.4	Time spent on selected free time activities of full-time workers, 2000–01	198
Table 13.5	Interest in television programme type: by age, 2002	198
Table 13.6	Share of radio listening: by station, Quarter 1 2003	199
Figure 13.7	Music sales: by age, 2002	200
Figure 13.8	VHS and DVD video rental shares: by genre, 2002	200
Table 13.9	Attendance at cultural events (13.7)	201
Figure 13.10	Cinema attendance: by age (13.9)	201
Figure 13.11	Reading preferences: by sex, 2001	202
Table 13.12	Reasons for visiting a library: by age and activity, 2000	202

e-Society and communication

Figure 13.13	Households with selected durable goods (13.13)	203
Figure 13.14	Adult mobile phone ownership or use: by age, 2001 and 2003	203
Table 13.15	Households with Internet access: by household type	204
Table 13.16	Types of goods and services bought over the Internet, July 2003	204
Figure 13.17	Security precautions taken by adults who have used the Internet, July 2003	205
Figure 13.18	Activities undertaken on the computer at home by 11–18 year olds, autumn 2002	206

Holidays and tourism

| Figure 13.19 | Visits to selected tourist attractions | 206 |
| Map 13.20 | Holidays in the United Kingdom: by destination, 2002 | 207 |

Sporting activities

| Figure 13.21 | Participation in a sport or physical activity: by age, 2000–01 | 207 |
| Table 13.22 | Participation in selected sports by young people outside lessons: by sex, 2002 | 208 |

Social participation

| Table 13.23 | Attitudes to neighbourhoods: by length of residence, 2001 | 208 |

Religion

| Table 13.24 | Belonging to a religion, 2001 | 209 |

List of contributors

Authors: Carl Bird

Ben Bradford

Simon Burtenshaw

Elaine Chamberlain

Valerie Christian

Jenny Church

Steve Howell

Kylie Lovell

Nina Mill

Matthew Richardson

Conor Shipsey

Production Manager: Kate Myers

Production Team: Lola Akinrodoye

Lisa Almqvist

Daniel Annan

John Chrzczonowicz

Sunita Dedi

Joseph Goldstein

Paul Janvier

Chris Randall

Shiva Satkunam

Review Team: Jill Barelli

David Harper

Caroline Lakin

Linda Zealey

Acknowledgements

The Editors wish to thank all their colleagues in the contributing Departments and other organisations for their generous support and helpful comments, without whom this publication would not be possible. Our thanks also go to the following for their help in the production of this volume:

Design and artwork: Tony Castro, Michelle Franco, Nick Wand, ONS Design

Publishing management: Paul Hyatt, Phil Lewin, Publications Unit

Maps: Alistair Dent, ONS Geography

Data: SARD Data Collection Team

Introduction

This is the 34th edition of *Social Trends* – one of the flagship publications from the Office for National Statistics. It draws together statistics from a wide range of government departments and other organisations to paint a broad picture of our society today, and how it has been changing. Each of the 13 chapters focuses on a different social policy area, described in tables, figures and explanatory text. This year Social Trends features an article the impact of ageing on older people today by Professor Sara Arber and Dr Jay Ginn of the University of Surrey.

Social Trends is aimed at a very wide audience: policy makers in the public and private sectors;service providers; people in local government; journalists and other commentators; academics and students; schools and the general public.

The editorial team always welcomes readers' views on how *Social Trends* could be improved. Please write to the Editors at the address shown below with your comments or suggestions.

New material and sources

To preserve topicality, half of the 313 tables and figures in the chapters of *Social Trends 34* are new compared with the previous edition, and draw on the most up-to-date available data.

In all chapters the source of the data is given below each table and figure, and where this is a major survey the name of the survey is also included. A list of contact telephone numbers, including the contact number for each chapter author, and a list of useful website addresses can be found on page 210. A list of further reading, directing readers to other relevant publications, is also given, beginning on page 218. Regional and other sub-national breakdowns of much of the information in *Social Trends* can be found in the ONS's publication *Regional Trends*.

Definitions and terms

The Appendix gives definitions and general background information, particularly on administrative and legal structures and frameworks. Anyone seeking to understand the tables and figures in detail will find it helpful to read the corresponding entries in the Appendix, as well as the footnotes on the tables and figures. An index to this edition starts on page 244.

Availability on electronic media

Social Trends 34 is available electronically as an interactive PDF via the National Statistics website, www.statistics.gov.uk/socialtrends. This PDF contains link to Excel spreadsheets giving the data for all tables, figures and maps.

Contact

Carol Summerfield
Penny Babb

Social Analysis and Reporting Division
Office for National Statistics
Room: B5/12
1 Drummond Gate
London
SW1V 2QQ

Email: social.trends@ons.gov.uk

Ageing and Gender: Diversity and Change

by Sara Arber and Jay Ginn

Centre for Research on Ageing and Gender (CRAG)

Department of Sociology, University of Surrey, Guildford, Surrey GU2 7XH, UK

Tel: 01483-689445;
Fax: 01483-689550

e-mail: S.Arber@surrey.ac.uk
         J.Ginn@surrey.ac.uk

The ageing of populations across Europe and in most parts of the world is widely discussed. There are varied reactions to the demographic 'facts' of our ageing society, ranging from concern at the assumed costs of a growing older population to celebration of greater longevity as a societal achievement.

Our article aims to complement the wealth of data presented in *Social Trends* about ageing. We first examine some implications of the changing demography of ageing, and in the second part focus on the income of older people, considering alternative approaches to measurement of poverty and the implications of current policy for income inequalities. Gender differences provide a thread running through the article. Our contribution may also help the reader navigate through the minefields of potential ageism, by considering assumptions about older people that underlie some official statistics.

Changing demography

The growth in the proportion of older people in the United Kingdom has been very modest over the last 30 years (see Table 1.2). Since 1971, the proportion of the population aged 65 and over has increased from 15.9 per cent to 18.0 per cent for women and from 10.5 per cent to 13.7 per cent for men (Table A.1). These changes represent a much slower rate of increase than in either the middle decades of the twentieth century in the United Kingdom[1] or currently in most European and other developed countries. Thus increases in the cost of

Table **A.1**

Proportions of older people: by sex and age, 1971 to 2001

United Kingdom   Percentages

	1971	1981	1991	2001	Percentage change 1971 to 2001
Males					
65–74	7.4	8.3	8.1	8.1	9
75–84	2.6	3.4	4.1	4.6	77
85 and over	0.5	0.5	0.8	1.1	120
All aged 65 and over	10.5	12.1	13.5	13.7	30
Females					
65–74	9.6	10.1	9.5	8.7	-9
75–84	5.0	6.1	6.7	6.6	32
85 and over	1.2	1.6	2.2	2.7	125
All aged 65 and over	15.9	17.8	18.4	18.0	13

Source: Office for National Statistics

retirement pensions and health care in the United Kingdom may be less than would be expected from the numerous reports in the media and from policy-makers. However, there is more rapid projected growth from 2001 to 2021 (see Table 1.2).

The modest overall increase over the last 30 years hides very substantial changes in the age composition of the older population. There has been a *declining* proportion of both men and women aged 65 to 74 since 1981 (see Table A.1). However, there has been a rapid growth in the proportion aged 85 and over, now representing 1.1 per cent of men and 2.7 per cent of women. This should be a cause for celebration that advances in public and preventive health measures and medical care, as well as the socio-economic well-being of the population, have led to this extension of life. However, it is often considered a 'mixed blessing', bringing an unsustainable increase in spending on pensions, healthcare and personal social services.

The ways in which demographic statistics are used to 'read off' additional health care or other costs has sometimes been called 'apocalyptic demography'[2]. Yet it has been suggested that people in Britain aged 70 today are healthier than 30 years ago, making chronological age a poor guide to healthcare requirements[3]. Similarly, healthcare and personal social services costs will be heavily dependent on an older person's access to informal carers, which in turn relates to their marital status and living arrangements, rather than to their chronological age.

The tendency to interpret age-related amounts of health expenditure as caused by chronological age can be misleading. Although the average per capita health care expenditure for

people aged 85 and over is much higher than for other age groups (Figure 8.7), the highest healthcare costs occur in the few months preceding death, at any age. Therefore an alternative statistic might be the healthcare expenditure in the last year of a person's life. This might show that a person dying in middle age costs on average considerably more than a person dying in their 80s.

Older people and the 'dependent population'

Terms used in official reports often contain powerful implicit messages, which may serve to devalue the lives and contributions of particular groups within society. One such term is the 'dependent population' – the proportion aged under 16 or aged 65 and over, relative to the working age population (defined as aged 16 to 64). Projections of a growing 'dependent population', as shown in Figure 1.3, could be seen to imply that this is somehow problematic, or costly, for society. It is timely to reconsider the concept of the 'dependent population'. First, these age ranges no longer reflect the actual age patterns of paid employment so that trends based on population age structure are misleading. Young people spend longer in education, with few entering the labour market at age 16, while most workers leave the labour market well before state pension age. At the same time, a larger percentage of women are in paid employment than in the past, offsetting the shorter duration of employment among men. Second, activity that benefits the economy is not confined to paid employment, as discussed below. The characterisation of all people aged 65 and over as 'dependent' may fuel the misconception that older people are a burden on society, rather than contributing to society in productive ways.

Several tables and figures in *Social Trends* demonstrate the contributions of older people. For example, Table 8.3 shows the high involvement of older people in providing unpaid informal care to family members, friends or neighbours who are 'sick, disabled or elderly'. The proportion providing care for over 50 hours per week increases with age, reaching 44 per cent among carers aged 75 to 84, and half of carers aged 85 and over. These older people are largely providing 'round the clock', intensive care for their disabled spouse. If they were not undertaking this major caring role, the cost to the health and personal services budget would be enormous. As well as being a major source of care provision for adults within the United Kingdom, older people act as carers for their grandchildren (see Table 8.15) which may support the employment of their daughters/in-law. Older people are also very active in voluntary organisations, as shown by analyses of community involvement and neighbourliness[4].

Despite the welcome evidence in *Social Trends* of ways in which older people contribute to society, statistical analyses often imply that older people are a burden, either in terms of informal care needs or of public spending on healthcare, pensions or income support. In the United Kingdom, we know little about inter-generational transfers from the older to the younger generation. Much data are collected on care flows to older people, but little on care flows from them, nor on the extent of inter-generational transfers of financial resources (eg help with housing, loans, educational fees, gifts), which research in other countries has shown flows disproportionately from the older to the middle and younger generation[5].

The diminishing feminisation of later life

Although the ageing of British society is well documented, there is less discussion about the changing gender composition of the older population. The feminisation of later life – or the numerical predominance of women – is now diminishing. The numerical balance between the sexes at different ages has a range of social and economic implications[6]. Most adults in Britain live as part of a heterosexual couple, but a numerical imbalance between the sexes in later life means fewer people are partnered, influencing household living arrangements and potential supporters should a person become sick or disabled. The sex balance in later life has implications for the social relationships of older people, as well as the provision of services and facilities.

Later life was disproportionately female throughout the latter half of the 20th century, but this situation is changing, because of a faster decline in men's than women's mortality over the last 25 years. The proportion of women to men increases with advancing age, but the magnitude of this sex ratio has varied markedly over time. In 1961 and 1971, there were 161 women for every 100 men over age 65 in England and Wales. By 2001, this had fallen to 138 women for every 100 men.

Figure A.2 shows how the sex ratio among the older population has fluctuated since 1951 for three age groups. In 2001 there were only 113 women for every 100 men aged 65 to 74 compared with 158 in 1961. There were twice as many women as men aged 75 to 84 in 1971 but only 50 per cent more by 2001. Those aged 85 and over are disproportionately female with

over three times more women than men in 1981 and 1991, but this had fallen to a sex ratio of 259 by 2001. Figure 1.4 shows that currently there are over three times more women than men over age 90 years, but this is projected to fall to twice as many women by 2021.

The high numerical predominance of women in later life during the second half of the twentieth century stemmed from two causes[6]. First, deaths of young men in the First World War led to a large numerical excess of women in the cohort aged 65 to 74 in 1961, who were aged 75 to 84 in 1971 and 85 and over in 1981. These are the years with the highest sex ratios in Figure A.2. Second, the mortality rates of men and women have changed differentially over time. From 1900 to the 1970s, there were greater reductions in women's than men's death rates, which led to a larger proportion of women at older ages. However, since 1981 there has been a more rapid fall in male than in female

mortality above age 65 (see Table 1.9), diminishing the sex ratio.

The faster reduction in male than in female mortality has diminished women's advantage in life expectancy, from 6.3 years in 1970 to 4.8 years in 2000 (see Figure 7.1). These demographic changes mean that later life is becoming *less* feminised than in the past, with implications for marital status and living arrangements, as discussed in the next sections.

Changes in marital status

Marital status and living arrangements are pivotal to an older person's financial well-being, social relationships, and access to carers should they become frail or disabled[7]. Gender differences in marital status in later life are changing.

A significant transition for many older people begins when they are widowed. Widowhood often represents the loss of a partner of 40 to 50 years, who may have

Figure A.2

Sex ratios among older people: by age, 1951 to 2001[1]

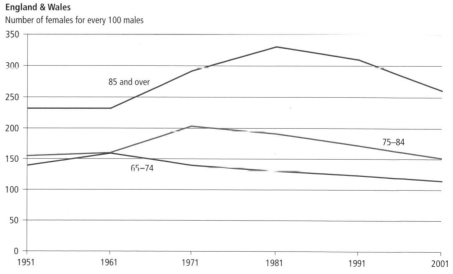

England & Wales
Number of females for every 100 males

1   Based on mid-year population estimates.
Source: Office for National Statistics

Table A.3

Changes in marital status for people aged 65 and over, 1971 to 2021[1]

England & Wales

Percentages

	1971	1986	2001	2021	Change 1971 to 2021
Males					
Married	73	73	71	66	-7
Widowed	19	18	17	13	-6
Divorced	1	2	5	13	12
Never married	7	7	7	8	1
All males (=100%) (millions)	2.5	3.1	3.5	4.8	92
Females					
Married	35	37	41	45	10
Widowed	50	50	47	35	-15
Divorced	1	3	5	14	13
Never married	14	10	7	5	-9
All females (=100%) (millions)	4.1	4.7	4.8	5.9	44

1 Mid-year population estimates by marital status for 1971 are based on the 1971 Census; those for 1986 and 2001 are based on the 2001 Census. 2021 data are based on 1996-based population projections.

Source: Office for National Statistics; Government Actuary's Department

Figure A.4

Marital status of people aged 65 and over: by sex and age, 2001

England & Wales
Percentages

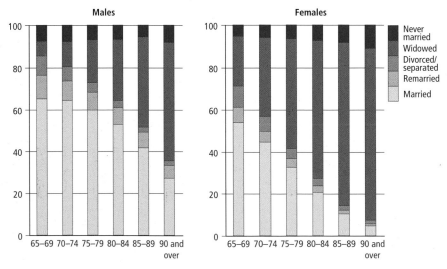

Source: Census 2001, Office for National Statistics

been the main source of companionship and support, especially for men, who frequently see their wife as their primary confidante[8]. Most older men are married and therefore have a partner for companionship, domestic service support and for care if they became physically disabled, whereas this is not the case for the majority of older women.

The distribution of older people according to marital status has changed since 1971 and is projected to change further by 2021 (Table A.3). A declining proportion of men aged 65 and over are married, due to increasing divorce, although even by 2021 two thirds of older men are projected to be married. This contrasts with older women, where the proportion married increases from 35 per cent in 1971 to a projected 45 per cent by 2021[9]. This change is due to improvements in mortality at older ages, especially among men. There is a projected sharp decline in widows between 2001 and 2021, from 47 per cent to 35 per cent of older women.

The largest proportionate change between 1971 and 2021 is the increase in older people who are divorced, rising from 1 per cent to 5 per cent between 1971 and 2001 and projected to reach over 13 per cent by 2021 (see Table A.3). Among women aged 65 to 74, there are projected to be almost as many divorcees (18 per cent) as widows (20 per cent) by 2021[9]. It is therefore important to consider the policy implications of a growing proportion of divorced older people.

Widowhood is the norm for older women, since nearly half of women aged 65 and over are widowed, reaching four fifths at ages 85 and over (Figure A.4). In contrast, over three quarters of men aged 65 to 69 are married (65 per cent in first marriages and 11 per cent remarried), falling to 60 per cent by their early 80s. Even in their late 80s, half of men are married. Remarriage is increasingly prevalent, especially among men, with older widowed or divorced men more likely to remarry later in life than comparable older women. It is notable that more men in their late 60s are divorced or separated (9 per cent) than widowed (7 per cent). Only 17 per cent of all men aged 65 and over are widowers, but this reaches 43 per cent among men in their late 80s. Although marriage is the norm for older men, this may blind us to issues facing the minority of older widowed men and the small but growing proportion who are divorced. Our research shows that older divorced men are more likely to be socially isolated from family and friends, and engage in more risky health behaviours, such as smoking and high alcohol consumption, than other groups of older men[10, 11].

Gender and living arrangements

The fact that legal marital status is an increasingly poor indicator of living arrangements among the younger population is recognised in the *Social Trends* chapter on 'Households and families'. However, the analyses of cohabitation only go up to age 59 (see Figure 2.14) because of the small numbers of older cohabitants in the General Household Survey. The 2001 Census is therefore particularly valuable in providing information on cohabitation among older, as well as younger, people[12]. Table A.5 shows that 2.5 per cent of men and 1.6 per cent of women aged 65 to 74 were cohabiting (including same-sex couples). The proportion declines with advancing age, but is still 1.4 per cent among men aged 85 and over.

The majority of older men, 70 per cent, live as part of a couple but only 40 per cent of women do so. Key issues for well-being and for service provision relate to the living arrangements of those not in a partnership. For this group, the norm is to live alone – 22 per cent of men and 44 per cent of women aged 65 and over, and this increases with advancing age (Table A.5). In addition, with advancing age, increasing proportions of older people – live with their children but have no partner (6.7 per cent of women and 3.7 per cent of men aged 85 and over). Similarly, the proportion living with others (not their children) increases with age, reaching 7.6 per cent of women and 6.1 per cent of men aged 85 and over.

Entering a residential or nursing home is usually considered a major threat to autonomy which older people resist until

Table A.5

Living arrangements of people aged 65 and over: by sex and age, 2001

England & Wales

Percentages

	Married couple family	Cohabiting couple[1]	Lone parent family	Living with others – not in family unit	Living alone	Living in communal establishment[2]	Total (=100%) (thousands)
Males							
65–74	73.9	2.5	1.9	3.2	17.5	1.0	2,045
75–84	63.0	1.8	2.5	4.0	25.7	3.1	1,168
85 and over	39.7	1.4	3.7	6.1	36.9	12.2	281
All aged 65 and over	67.5	2.2	2.2	3.7	21.8	2.6	3,494
Females							
65–74	54.7	1.6	5.4	4.0	33.2	1.1	2,322
75–84	29.6	0.8	6.2	5.7	52.5	5.2	1,765
85 and over	7.9	0.5	6.7	7.6	54.5	22.9	732
All aged 65 and over	38.4	1.2	5.9	5.2	43.5	5.9	4,819

1 A cohabiting couple family consists of two people living together as a couple but not married to each other, with or without their (unpartnered) child(ren). Cohabiting couples of the same sex are included.
2 A communal establishment is an establishment providing managed residential accommodation. Sheltered housing is treated as a communal establishment if less than half the residents possess their own cooking facilities.

Source: Census 2001, Office for National Statistics

there is no alternative. Table A.5 shows that older women are much more likely than men to live in such a 'communal' setting, reaching twice as many women as men over age 85 (23 per cent compared to 12 per cent). A somewhat smaller proportion of people over age 65 lived in a communal establishment in 2001 (2.6 per cent of men and 5.9 per cent of women) compared to 1991, when 3.0 per cent of men and 6.4 per cent of women did so[13]. However, within each marital status there is very little gender difference under age 80 (Figure A.6). Only at age 80 and above are women more likely to be communal residents than men, reflecting the higher levels of disability experienced by older women, especially at advanced ages[14].

The main reason for the higher communal residence of older women than men relates to gender differences in marital status, since the widowed and never married are far more likely to live in institutional care in later life than those who are married and these groups are disproportionately women[1, 14]. Marital status provides a proxy for the availability of family carers. In each age group, the never married are most likely to live in a communal setting (nursing, residential or other health care establishment) (Figure A.6). They are at least five times more likely than the married to be communal residents in each age group below 85. The widowed are intermediate between these two extremes (as are the divorced, who are not shown in Figure A.6). Under age 80, the widowed have less than half the level of communal residence of the never married, illustrating the role of

adult children in providing care. Under age 85, the widowed are over three times more likely to live in a residential setting than the married, demonstrating the very major role of marital partners in providing intensive care and delaying residential admissions. Thus, the changing contours of gender and marital status in later life have longer term consequences that influence the likelihood of a person spending the final part of their life in a residential setting.

Income, poverty and well-being in later life

Material resources, especially income, are crucial in influencing the quality of later life and are linked to self-assessed general health[1]. For example, older people in the lower income groups are much more likely to have poor mental health (see Table 7.20). While health and independence are most highly valued by older people as contributing to their quality of life, they see financial resources as necessary to maintain these[15]. An adequate income was described as one that provided not only physical necessities but enabled visits to kin, engagement with social networks, leisure activities and a sense of full participation in society. However, older people are over-represented among low-income households so that many remain in poverty or near-poverty.

The definition of poverty and method of measurement are complex and contentious[16]. A widely accepted definition is income below 60 per cent of the national median, but whatever level is adopted, official statistics usually adjust raw data for married or cohabiting individuals in two ways. First, the assumption is made that their combined income is shared equally. Second, income of a couple or larger

Figure **A.6**

Percentage of people aged 65 and over that are living in communal establishments[1]: by age and marital status[2]

England & Wales
Percentages

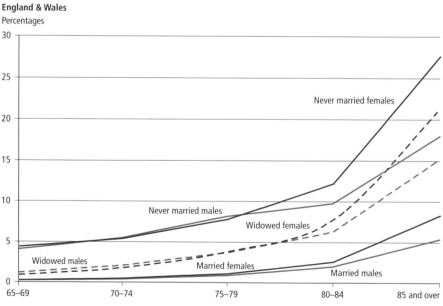

1 General hospitals, psychiatric hospitals/homes, other hospitals, nursing homes, residential care homes, other medical and care homes and other establishments.
2 Divorced and separated people have been omitted, in order to show more clearly the differences between married, widowed and never married older people.

Source: Census 2001, Office for National Statistics

household is 'equivalised', that is adjusted to take account of assumed economies of scale. In addition, incomes may be adjusted to take account of housing costs or of taxes and other mandatory reductions.

In examining gender differences in later life income, however, there are good reasons to measure individual incomes. The majority of women aged 65 and over are not married (as noted above) and those who are married can expect to outlive their husbands. Sharing between spouses or cohabiting partners may not be equal. Moreover, having one's own income is qualitatively different from income that may be transferred by a partner. Income provided at the discretion of family members or through means-tested social assistance programmes tends to be experienced as poverty, dependence and loss of autonomy[17]. For example, married women who have paid only the married woman's rate of National Insurance contributions or have worked for less than 10 years are often dismayed to discover at age 60 that they will have no state pension of their own until their husband reaches state pension age. It is therefore important in later life to examine individual income as well as household income, while bearing in mind that those who live with others benefit from economies of scale that may improve their standard of living. The main effect of assuming equal sharing and of measuring equivalised couple or household income in official statistics is to obscure the financial position of married and cohabiting women. However, because of the dominance of the household income approach, this will first be examined, before focusing on diversity in individual incomes in later life.

Household poverty in later life

The proportion of pensioners in poverty rose between 1981 and 1991 from 16 to 29 per cent but fell back to about 20 per cent by 1996 and since then has remained at roughly this level[19]. The poverty rate for the whole UK population is 17 per cent.

Poverty rates produced by Eurostat for purposes of comparison across the EU assume equal sharing in couples and use equivalised incomes, defining poverty as income below 60 per cent of national income. They are based on the European Community Household Panel Survey, a survey that uses the same concepts and definitions in each member state, though the fieldwork is undertaken by a different organisation in each country. The poverty rates for those aged 65 and above calculated by Eurostat show a rate of 21

per cent in the United Kingdom[18], (Figure A.7). This is higher than the average for EU countries. The same Eurostat data also show that the average income of UK older people relative to the rest of the population was substantially lower than the EU average (Figure A.7).

A separate cross-country comparison of pensioner incomes relative to the rest of the population was made by Disney and Johnson[20], based on eight country studies that used the family as the unit of analysis. This showed pensioners' relative income to be lower in Britain than in all the countries examined except Australia (Figure A.8). Relative incomes of pensioner couples were slightly lower in Britain than in the US, Canada and the Netherlands but substantially lower than in Germany, Italy and France. Among

Figure A.7

Poverty rate[1] and relative income[2] of people aged 65 and over: EU comparison, 1998

Percentages

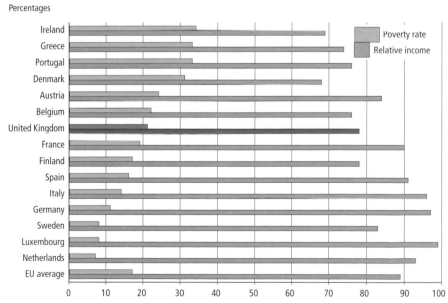

1 Percentage with income below 60 per cent of the median equivalised income of the national population.
2 Median equivalised income of those aged 65 and over as a percentage of the population aged 0 to 64.
Source: CEC from the European Household Community Panel Survey.

Figure **A.8**

Incomes of pensioners[1] as a percentage of incomes of non-pensioners: selected countries

Percentages

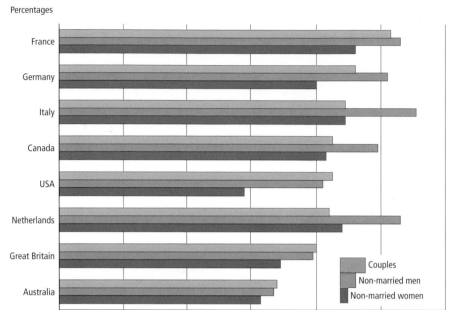

1 Pensioners are defined as all people aged 65 and over and all retired people aged 60 to 64.
 Couple incomes are equivalised using a factor of 0.7 for the second adult. Incomes are total net.

Source: Disney and Johnson, 2001 (reference 20)

non-married pensioners, relative incomes were much lower in Britain than in Canada and all the EU countries shown. Non-married women had lower incomes than similar men in all eight countries.

Another measure of pensioner poverty is the proportion receiving income support (IS). This has several drawbacks as a measure of poverty. First, the threshold for IS has no scientific basis in terms of physical or social needs and changes in the threshold over time reflect the political climate. Second, the IS threshold may be lower than the income generally seen as providing the minimum acceptable standard of living, as Parker[21] showed in the late 1990s. Third, a poverty rate based on IS receipt misses those pensioners – estimated as between one third and one quarter of all those who are eligible, or about half

a million people – who fail to claim the benefit[22]. Finally, because the means test assesses combined income and assets for married and cohabiting couples, partnered women's income, which is small on average, is not visible. For these reasons, the proportion of pensioners with a very low personal income is greater than the proportion receiving IS. Nevertheless, it is worth analysing the percentage of older people receiving IS if these caveats are borne in mind.

Among households headed by a pensioner, 6 per cent of couples were receiving income support, compared with 15 per cent of non-married men and 24 per cent of non-married women (see Table 8.12). Table A.9 shows how receipt of income support (then Minimum Income Guarantee, or MIG) varied among men and women aged 65 and over according to marital status, own previous occupation and age group in 2001/02. Among single and widowed women, a fifth received MIG but this proportion was doubled for divorced/ separated women. Among those people who had worked in routine or manual occupations 14 per cent received MIG, compared with only 3 per cent of those who had worked as professionals or managers. Women in the lowest class grouping were particularly likely to receive MIG (18 per cent). The proportion receiving MIG rose with age.

Means testing has been justified as targeting resources on the poorest pensioners. However, the persistently low take-up undermines the effectiveness of this strategy. Despite efforts by the Government to promote awareness of entitlements and to seek ways of reducing its complexity, the process of claiming is still seen as complex, intrusive and demeaning. 'The main barriers to claiming related to fears of appearing in need, losing independence and a feeling that people could manage on their own resources'[23]. Whereas pensioners see National Insurance pensions, to which they have contributed all their lives, as an entitlement they have earned and can accept with dignity, claiming means tested benefits is considered by many to signify shameful dependency. Yet many British pensioners, especially women, need income support mainly because the basic pension provides an increasingly inadequate income and they were unable to obtain a good state second pension or private pension due to their domestic roles. It remains to be seen what the impact of the recently introduced Pension Credit scheme (which subsumes the MIG scheme) will be on pensioner incomes, although the official target of 73 per cent take up suggests that many older people will not receive the help they are entitled to. We next examine how pensioner incomes vary with gender, marital status, class and ethnicity.

Diversity of income in later life

The relative contribution of private pensions, state pensions and other state benefits to older people's total income varies with a range of characteristics, including their age. Private pensions contribute 30 per cent of the income of those aged 65 to 74, but this falls to 24 per cent among those aged 85 and over. In contrast, state pensions contribute 35 per cent of income between ages 65 to 74, rising to 46 per cent among those aged 85 and over (see Table 5.4). Disability and other state benefits double from 8 to 17 per cent of income across this range of age groups.

Median individual income of those aged 65 and over varies with marital status, previous occupation and age group. Among men, the highest gross weekly

Table A.9

People aged 65 and over receiving income support[1]: by marital status, socio-economic group[2] and age, 2001/02

Great Britain   Percentages

	Males	Females	All
Marital status			
Married/cohabiting	4	1	3
Single	13	20	17
Widowed	11	20	18
Divorced/separated	23	40	34
Socio-economic group			
Professional/managerial	2	6	3
Intermediate	11	6	8
Routine and manual	10	18	14
Age			
65–69	6	5	6
70–74	6	11	8
75–79	8	18	14
80–84	8	19	15
85 and over	11	22	18
All	7	13	11

1 Respondents were asked if they were 'receiving income support in your own right: that is, where you are the named recipient'. Those married to a named recipient would therefore respond negatively, even though the benefit is intended for the couple. The data are unweighted.
2 Based on own occupation and classified according to the National Statistics Socio-economic Classification (NS-SeC). See Appendix, Part 1: NS-SeC.

Source: General Household Survey, Office for National Statistics

income was received by those who were married, but among women the never married and widowed received the highest amounts (Table A.10). The ratio of women's median income to men's, within each marital status, was highest for single women at 85 per cent and lowest for married women at only 33 per cent. The precarious financial position of older divorced women is evident; although their income was higher than that of married women, they have no prospect of inheriting a widow's pension. The risk of low income (defined as having a household equivalised disposable income in the bottom third of the distribution) among

those aged 60 and over, is very high among divorced women (see Table 5.23). Over two thirds of older divorced women who had worked for under 20 years had a low income, although the proportion reduced to half among those in paid work for over 20 years. Among widowed and never married women, about half had a low income irrespective of their number of years employed.

Older men previously employed as professionals or managers had the highest gross weekly income in later life, with a median amount over twice as high as that for men in other occupational groups. The advantage

Table A.10

Median gross individual income of people aged 65 and over: by marital status, socio-economic group[1] and age, 2001/02

Great Britain

£ per week

	Males	Females	Ratio of female to males' median income (percentages)
Marital status			
Married/cohabiting	171	56	33
Single	130	109	85
Widowed	144	112	78
Divorced/separated	125	92	74
Socio-economic group			
Professional/managerial	287	148	52
Intermediate	142	99	70
Routine and manual	136	89	65
Age			
65–69	177	90	51
70–74	168	92	55
75–79	148	92	62
80–84	143	93	65
85 and over	123	92	75
All	161	92	57

1 Based on own occupation and classified according to the National Statistics Socio-economic Classification (NS-SeC). See Appendix, Part 1: NS-SeC. The data are unweighted.

Source: General Household Survey, Office for National Statistics

conferred by a high occupational status was less marked among women – women in this occupational group had a median income only half that of similar men, whereas women in the two lower occupational groups had a median income over two thirds that of equivalent men. Among men, median income declined with age, due partly to lower private pension income in earlier cohorts, but among women this was not so.

These differences in older people's incomes reflect mainly inequalities in their ability to build private (occupational or personal) pension entitlements during the working life[1,24,25]. The gender division of labour associated with childrearing reduces women's lifetime earnings, as does the gender gap in pay. Among all working age women, only a minority are contributing to an employer's pension scheme at any one time, and their pension contributions over the working life are correspondingly reduced. The effect on state pensions is less severe, due to their redistributive features. Earnings and access to an employer's pension also depend on occupational class, with manual workers less able than non-manual to build good private pensions. Because of the low level of state pensions relative to average earnings, the presence or absence of substantial private pensions plays a pivotal role in determining pensioners position in the income distribution and whether they have an adequate retirement income.

Table A.11 shows the proportions of men and women aged 65 and over receiving private pensions and the median amounts for those with this source of income. Only 43 per cent of older women had any private pension income, including widows' pensions based on their deceased husbands' private pensions, compared with 71 per cent of men. A high proportion, 61 per cent, of single women had some private pension income and their median amount was high (£70 per week) relative to all other women and to widowers and single men. Divorced women's low total income (Table A.10) reflects the fact that only just over a third had any private pension income and the low median amount at £48 per week.

Incomes of older British individuals from minority ethnic groups are on average lower than those from the White group and reliance on means-tested income support is greater[26]. In terms of other measures of wealth – car ownership and housing tenure – older people from minority ethnic groups tend to be disadvantaged, although certain ethnic groups such as Indians and Chinese have rates of home ownership comparable with that of White people. Pakistanis and Bangladeshis have particularly high rates of poverty, measured as having an equivalised household disposable income below 60 per cent of the median (see Table 5.22). Ginn and Arber[27] examined ethnic and gender differences in individual income among the older population, showing that Asian older women are particularly disadvantaged.

Lack of private pension income among older people from minority ethnic groups reflects shorter employment records in Britain for the largely migrant older ethnic population, as well as discrimination in the labour market, limited type and availability of jobs in areas of settlement and sometimes lack of fluency in English. For migrant women, additional barriers may have prevented private pension acquisition, depending on the cultural norms surrounding women's employment, in specific ethnic groups.

Trends in later life income inequality

The distribution of pensioner incomes became more unequal between 1979 and 1996[28]. Over this period the median net income of the poorest fifth of pensioner couples before housing costs increased by 34 per cent, but that of the richest fifth grew by 80 per cent. A similar trend was evident for non-married pensioners[29]. More recent data suggest that between 1994/95 and 2001/02, growth in pensioner incomes was more evenly spread across the income distributions of both single pensioners and pensioner couples. British pension policy has contributed to these trends. Since 1980, the value of the basic state pension has declined relative to national earnings while those retiring with private occupational pensions received increasingly large amounts. Because private pension income is more closely related to lifetime earnings than income from state pensions, growing inequality in earnings during the working life (structured according to gender, educational level and occupational class) translates into a widening dispersion of later life income, with certain population groups disadvantaged. State Second Pensions,

Table A.11

Private pensions[1] receipt among those aged 65 and over: by marital status and socio-economic group[2], 2001/02

Great Britain

Percentages

	Percentage receiving		Median amount for those with private pension (£ per week)		Ratio of female to males' private pension income (percentages)
	Males	Females	Males	Females	
Marital status					
Married/cohabiting	74	28	92	34	37
Single	52	61	65	70	108
Widowed	70	56	61	46	75
Divorced/separated	57	36	78	48	62
Socio-economic group					
Professional/managerial	90	64	172	95	55
Intermediate	60	51	84	43	51
Routine and manual	62	34	50	28	56
All	71	43	83	44	53

1 Occupational or personal pension, including survivor pensions.
2 Based on own occupation and classified according to the National Statistics Socio-economic Classification (NS-SeC). See Appendix, Part 1: NS-SeC. The data are unweighted.

Source: General Household Survey, Office for National Statistics

which replaced the State Earnings-Related Pension Scheme (SERPS) in 2002, are more redistributive and may in due course help to reduce income inequality at the lower end of the distribution of pensioner incomes.

Women have been less able than men to access occupational pensions so that the gender gap in pensioners' personal incomes has widened. In the mid-1980s older women's median personal income was 71 per cent of men's, declining to 62 per cent in 1993/94 and to only 53 per cent in 1998[25]. For women, bearing and raising children is a major reason for lower pension income in later life. Motherhood reduces employment, earnings and private pension prospects for women at all educational levels but

the impact on women with mid-level qualifications, such as O levels or GCSEs, is greater than for graduate women[25,30].

The trend to longer periods in paid work for women will have only a limited effect, if any, on the gap between older men's and women's pensions as long as women's lifetime earnings remain well below men's. The modest trend of increased full-time employment among younger cohorts of women is likely to be offset by the policy of placing increased emphasis on private pensions while reducing the basic state pension relative to average earnings. The full effect of the introduction of rules in state pensions designed to compensate those who provide unpaid family care at the expense of their earnings, such as Home

Responsibilities Protection in the basic pension and the more limited carer credits in the State Second Pension, has yet to feed through fully into women's state pension receipts, and will benefit younger cohorts. However, these measures to help those with caring commitments may become less effective if the value of state pensions continues to decline relative to national earnings.

Despite projected growth in the older population, spending on state pensions is projected to remain broadly stable at 5.0 per cent of GDP between 2003 and 2050[31], a very low proportion relative to other OECD countries. Meanwhile spending on tax relief and rebates on private pension contributions is over 2.5 per cent of GDP and rising. Such tax spending is highly regressive, with half the benefit received by the top 10 per cent of taxpayers and a quarter by the top 2.5 per cent[32]. An increase in the

proportion of pensioners receiving means tested benefits is planned, changing the landscape of later life. It is expected that the introduction of the Pension Credit in October 2003 will extend entitlement to means tested income support to 'around half of all households aged over 60'[33] with a rising proportion eligible in each succeeding year as the basic state pension declines relative to average wages[34]. Compared with the Minimum Income Guarantee (MIG) which reduced benefits pound for pound, Pension Credit reduces benefits by 40p in the pound saved, although the marginal withdrawal rate may be higher for pensioners receiving other benefits. Thus a savings disincentive remains in modified form. Means testing will protect many pensioners from absolute poverty but some of the poorest will slip through this safety net because of incomplete take up.

Car ownership and transport

Having a car in the household is one aspect of quality of material life and well being for older people that depends on a certain level of income. For both men and women, having a car is a key factor in maintaining independence – the ability to shop, visit, enjoy leisure facilities, help with grandchildren, attend hospital appointments and so forth. Yet among older cohorts of women the norm was to depend on their husband for transport for social purposes, shopping, or accessing healthcare facilities. It was less usual to obtain a driving licence themselves. Thus, for women, widowhood or divorce may represent more than the loss of a breadwinner and partner – it may include the loss of mobility.

Older women are more likely than men to lack access to a car in the household. Car ownership declines with increasing age, reflecting both age and cohort effects, but falls more rapidly for women than men (see Figure A.12). Only 42 per cent of women aged 75 to 84 and 25 per cent aged 85 and over had access to a car in the household, compared to 66 per cent and 45 per cent of men in these two age groups. The absence of a household car, whether due to financial constraints or inability to drive, is a material disadvantage that may lead to more socially isolated lives[35]. However, this pattern is likely to change for cohorts of women who are now reaching retirement age. Over half (56 per cent) of women aged 60 to 69 now hold a driving licence, compared with only a quarter in the mid-1980s[36]. Three quarters of women in their fifties hold a licence, and most will continue to drive in their 60s and 70s, providing they have the financial means to do so.

Figure **A.12**

People aged 50 and over with a car in the household: by sex and age, 2001
England & Wales

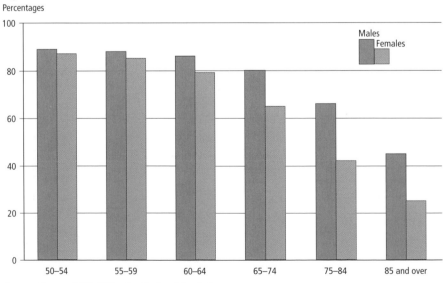

Source: Census 2001, Office for National Statistics

Travel outside the home declines with age. People aged 80 and over make about half the number of trips, and travel about a third of the distance of those aged 60 to 64. This decline is mostly accounted for by a decline in trips made as a car driver by people in their 70s, followed by a decline in trips by bus and on foot in the 80s. Over the age of 80, about half of men and two thirds of women have some kind of mobility difficulty. One in six women of this age are unable to go out on foot at all[36].

For older people without car access, public transport provides an alternative means to maintain social integration. However, its use may be prevented by frailty, disability and fear of crime, while those living in rural areas may be unable to reach the public transport network on foot. Thus public transport that is extensive, reliable, safe, affordable and adapted for impaired mobility is important, as are Dial-a-Ride schemes and subsidised taxis, especially for older women.

Conclusions

The ageing of the population is proceeding at differential rates according to gender. Greater longevity gains for men than women in recent years have led to a decline in the numerical predominance of women. This, together with rising rates of divorce and cohabitation, is changing the contours of marital status in later life. Marital status has a critical impact on older people's need for care and support from relatives or others outside their household, and from state and private services.

Older married men are the most advantaged group, both in terms of

pensions and access to carers should they become sick or disabled. This care advantage applies to the majority of older men, since 70 per cent of men aged 65 and over are married, and most remain married until they die. Widowhood is the norm for women in later life and widows have lower incomes than older men and never-married women. Divorced older women are particularly disadvantaged in terms of pensions. These findings have implications for policy on pensions, especially given the projected growth in the proportions of older people who will be divorced.

Given the low level of state pensions relative to average earnings, access to private pensions plays a central role in determining whether older people have low incomes or not, and their increased importance within the income profile of the older population has served to widen the gender gap in incomes since, historically, women have less access to them than men. Understanding the changing demographic contours of later life is essential in informing policies to maximise the financial and social well-being of older men and women.

Acknowledgements

We are grateful for the generous assistance of colleagues at the University of Surrey, in particular Debora Price for preparing some of the tables in this article and Kate Davidson who was central to our research on older men. We are also grateful to the ONS for permission to use the General Household Survey data and to the Data Archive, University of Essex, for access to the data. We appreciate the helpful comments and close attention to detail by members of ONS and other government departments in their comments on earlier drafts of this article.

The analysis and interpretation of the data is entirely the work of the authors and does not imply any endorsement by the Office for National Statistics or any other government department.

Centre for Research on Ageing and Gender (CRAG)
Department of Sociology,
University of Surrey
Guildford, Surrey, GU2 7XH

Tel: 01483 689445
Fax: 01483 689550

Email: S.Arber@surrey.ac.uk
and   J.Ginn@surrey.ac.uk

References

1   Arber, S. and Ginn, J. (1991) *Gender and Later Life: a Sociological Analysis of Resources and Constraints*, London: Sage.

2   Robertson, A. (1999) 'Beyond apocalyptic demography: toward a moral economy of interdependence', in M. Minkler and C. L. Estes (eds) *Critical Gerontology: Perspectives from Political and Moral Economy*, Amityville, NY: Baywood Publishing.

3   Hawksworth, J. (2002) *Longterm Outlook for UK Public Spending and Tax Shares of GDP*, Pricewaterhouse Coopers, July.

4   Coulthard, M., Walker, A. and Morgan, A. (2002) *People's perceptions of their neighbourhood and community involvement. Results from the social capital module of the General Household Survey 2000*, Office for National Statistics, London: The Stationery Office.

5   Arber S. and Attias-Donfut, C. (eds.) (2000) *The Myth of Generational Conflict: Family and State in Ageing Societies*, London: Routledge.

6   Britton M. and Edison N. (1986) 'The changing balance of the sexes in England and Wales, 1851–2001', *Population Trends 46*: 22-25.

7   Arber, S., Davidson, K. and Ginn, J. (eds) (2003) *Gender and Ageing: Changing Roles and Relationships*, Maidenhead: Open University Press.

8   Askham, J. (1994) 'Marriage relationships of older people', *Reviews of Clinical Gerontology*, 4: 261-268.

9   Shaw, C. (1999) '1996-based population projections by legal marital status for England and Wales', *Population Trends* 95: 23-32.

10   Arber, S., Price, D., Davidson, K. and Perren, K. (2003) 'Re-examining gender and marital status: Material well-being and social involvement' in S. Arber, K. Davidson and J. Ginn (eds.) *Gender and Ageing: Changing Roles and Relationships*, Maidenhead: Open University Press.

11   Davidson, K., Daly, T. and Arber, S. (2003) 'Exploring the social worlds of older men' in S. Arber, K. Davidson and J. Ginn (eds.) *Gender and Ageing: Changing Roles and Relationships*, Maidenhead: Open University Press.

12   ONS (2003) *Census 2001. National Report for England and Wales*, London: The Stationery Office.

13   Arber, S. and Ginn, J. (1998) 'Health and illness in later life', pp 134-152 in D. Field and S. Taylor (eds) *Sociological Perspectives on Health, Illness and Health Care*, Oxford: Blackwell Science.

14   Arber, S. and Cooper, H. (1999) 'Gender differences in health in later life: A new paradox?' *Social Science and Medicine*, 48(1): 61-76.

15   Bowling, A., Gabriel, Z., Banister, D. and Sutton, S. (2001) 'Older people's views on quality of life', *Growing Older Newsletter*, 2: 2.

16   Finch, N. and Bradshaw, J. (2003) 'Core poverty', *Journal of Social Policy*, 32(4): 513-526.

17   Sen, A. (1984) *Rights and Capabilities in Resources, Values and Development*, Oxford: Blackwell.

18   European Commission (2003) *Joint Report by the Commission and the Council on Adequate and Sustainable Pensions*, Brussels: Commission of the European Community.

19   ONS (2002) *Social Trends 32*, London: The Stationery Office.

20   Disney, R. and Johnson, P. (eds) (2001) *Pension Systems and Retirement Incomes across OECD Countries*, Cheltenham: Edward Elgar.

21   Parker, H. (ed.) (2000) *Low Cost but Acceptable Incomes for Older People. A Minimum Income Standard for Households Aged 65–74 years in the UK*. Bristol: The Policy Press.

22   Department for Work and Pensions (2003) *Income Related Benefits: Estimates of Take-up 2000/1*, London: DWP.

23   McConaghy, M., Hill, C., Kane, C., Lader, D., Costigan, P. and Thornby, M. (2003) *Entitled but not Claiming? Pensioners, the Minimum Income Guarantee and Pension Credit*, Research Report No. 197 (summary), London: DWP and www.dwp.gov.uk/asd/asd5/rrs2003.asp

24   Ginn, J. and Arber, S. (1993) 'Pension Penalties: The Gendered Division of Occupational Welfare', *Work, Employment and Society*, 7(1): 47-70.

25   Ginn, J. (2003) *Gender, Pensions and the Lifecourse*, Bristol: Policy Press.

26   Berthoud, R. (1998) *The Incomes of Ethnic Minorities*, Colchester: ISER.

27   Ginn, J. and Arber, S. (2000) 'Ethnic Inequality in Later Life: Variation in Financial Circumstances by Gender and Ethnic Group', *Education and Ageing*, 15(1): 65-83.

28   Department of Social Security (2000) *The Changing Welfare State. Pensioner Incomes,* DSS paper no. 2, London: DSS.

29   Department for Work and Pensions (2003) *Pensioners' Incomes*, www.dwp.gov.uk/asd/cqa.asp

30   Ginn, J. and Arber, S. (2000) 'Degrees of Freedom: Can Graduate Women avoid the Motherhood Gap in Pensions?' *Sociological Research On-line*, www.socresonline.org.uk/7/2/

31   DSS (1998) *A New Contract for Welfare: Partnership in Pensions*. Cm 4179. London: The Stationery Office.

32   Agulnik, P. and Le Grand, J. (1998) 'Tax Relief and Partnership Pensions', *Fiscal Studies*, 19(4): 403-28.

33   Department for Work and Pensions (2002) *United Kingdom National Strategy Report on the Future of Pension Systems*, London: DWP.

34   Clark, T. (2001) *Recent Pensions Policy and the Pension Credit*, Briefing Note No.17, London: Institute for Fiscal Studies.

35   Gilhooly, M., Hamilton, K. and O'Neill, M. (2002) *Transport and Ageing: Extending Quality of Life for Older People via Public and Private Transport*. Final End of Award report to the ESRC, Swindon: ESRC.

36   Noble, B. (2000) 'Travel characteristics of older people'. *Transport Trends 2000*. London: The Stationery Office.

Chapter 1 **Population**

Population profile

- There were 1.4 million more females than males in the United Kingdom in 2002. (Table 1.2)

- The number of children aged under 16 in the United Kingdom fell by 18 per cent between 1971 and 2002. During the same period there was a 27 per cent increase in the number of people aged 65 and over (Figure 1.3)

Population change

- There were 668,800 live births and 608,000 deaths in the United Kingdom in 2002. (Figure 1.8)

Geographical distribution

- In 2001, 19 per cent of the population living in the South West were aged 65 and over; in contrast only 12 per cent of the population living in London were aged 65 and over. (Map 1.10)

International migration

- There was a 13 per cent increase in the number of asylum applications (including dependants) to the United Kingdom between 2001 and 2002. (Page 23)

Table **1.1**

Population[1] of the United Kingdom

Millions

	1971	1981	1991	2001	2002	2011	2021
England	46.4	46.8	47.9	49.4	49.6	50.9	52.7
Wales	2.7	2.8	2.9	2.9	2.9	2.9	3.0
Scotland	5.2	5.2	5.1	5.1	5.1	5.0	4.9
Northern Ireland	1.5	1.5	1.6	1.7	1.7	1.7	1.8
United Kingdom	55.9	56.4	57.4	59.1	59.2	60.5	62.4

1 Mid-year estimates for 1971 to 2002; 2001-based projections for 2011 to 2021. See Appendix, Part 1: Population estimates and projections. Population estimates for 2001 and 2002 include provisional results from the Manchester matching exercise.

Source: Office for National Statistics; Government Actuary's Department; General Register Office for Scotland; Northern Ireland Statistics and Research Agency

Table **1.2**

Population[1]: by age and sex

United Kingdom

Percentages

	Under 16	16–24	25–34	35–44	45–54	55–64	65–74	75 and over	All ages (=100%) (millions)
Males									
1971	27	14	13	12	12	11	7	3	27.2
1981	23	15	15	12	11	11	8	4	27.4
1991	21	14	16	14	12	10	8	5	27.9
2001	21	11	15	15	13	11	8	6	28.8
2002	21	12	14	15	13	11	8	6	28.9
2011	19	12	13	14	14	12	9	7	29.5
2021	19	11	13	12	13	13	10	8	30.3
Females									
1971	24	13	12	11	12	12	10	6	28.8
1981	21	14	14	12	11	11	10	8	28.9
1991	19	13	15	13	11	10	9	9	29.5
2001	19	11	14	15	13	11	9	9	30.2
2002	19	11	14	15	13	11	9	9	30.3
2011	17	11	13	14	14	12	9	9	31.0
2021	17	10	13	12	13	13	11	10	32.1

1 Data for 1971 to 2002 are mid-year estimates; 2001-based projections for 2011 to 2021. See Appendix, Part 1: Population estimates and projections. Population estimates for 2001 and 2002 include provisional results from the Manchester matching exercise.

Source: Office for National Statistics; Government Actuary's Department; General Register Office for Scotland; Northern Ireland Statistics and Research Agency

Information on the size and structure of the population is essential in understanding aspects of society, such as the labour market and household composition. The number of births and deaths, and the number of people entering and leaving the country, all affect the size of the population. These changes in demographic patterns not only influence social structures, but also the demand for services.

Population profile

There are more people living in the United Kingdom than there have ever been – 59.2 million people in 2002 (Table 1.1). This is 3.3 million more than in 1971. The populations of England, Wales and Northern Ireland all grew between 1971 and 2002, while the population of Scotland remained fairly stable. Population projections suggest that the UK population will reach 62.4 million by 2021. Longer-term projections suggest that the UK population will peak around 2040, at almost 64 million, and will then start to fall.

The age structure of the population reflects past trends in births, deaths and migration. The number of people in any age group within the population depends on how many people are born in a particular period and how long they survive. It is also affected by the numbers and ages of migrants moving to and from the country.

Around 19,000 more boys than girls are born each year, but there are more females overall in the United Kingdom; 30.3 million females compared with 28.9 million males in 2002 (Table 1.2). By age 22 there are more women than men, this is because death rates from accidents and suicide are much higher for young men than for young women.

In 2002 there were 11.8 million children under 16 years in the United Kingdom, 18 per cent less than in 1971 (Figure 1.3). This figure is projected to fall to around 11.1 million in 2010 and then remain around this level to 2021. There were 9.4 million people aged 65 and over in the United Kingdom in 2002, a 27 per cent increase since 1971. Projections suggest that the number of people aged 65 and over will exceed the numbers aged under 16 by 2014. Information about the geographical distribution of people aged 65 and over is available in Map 1.10.

Historically the ageing of the population was largely the result of the fall in fertility that began towards the end of the 19th century. Early in the 20th century lower mortality helped increase the number of people surviving into old age. These effects were greater among younger people, offsetting the trend towards the population ageing. More recently, lower fertility rates and falls in death rates for older people have contributed to a considerable increase in the number of people living to the age of 90 and over. There were 380,000 people aged 90 and over in Great Britain in 2002, more than triple the number in 1971 (Figure 1.4). Projections suggest this trend will continue. There were over three times more women than men aged 90 and over in 2002, a similar ratio as in 1971.

The age structure of the population of the United Kingdom varies across the different ethnic groups. In general, minority ethnic groups have a younger age structure than the White group (Table 1.5 – see overleaf). In 2001, 19 per cent of the White group were aged under 16, compared with 50 per cent of the Mixed group, who had the youngest age structure. After the White group,

Figure **1.3**

Dependent population[1]: by age

United Kingdom
Millions

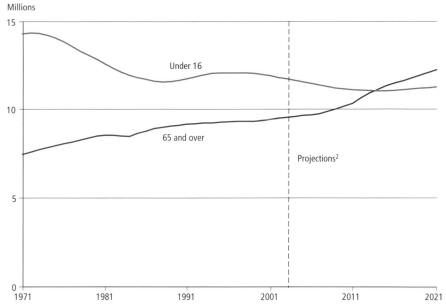

1 Population estimates for 2001 and 2002 include provisional results from the Manchester matching exercise.
2 2001-based projections.

Source: Office for National Statistics; Government Actuary's Department; General Register Office for Scotland; Northern Ireland Statistics and Research Agency

Figure **1.4**

Population aged 90 years and over: by sex

Great Britain
Thousands

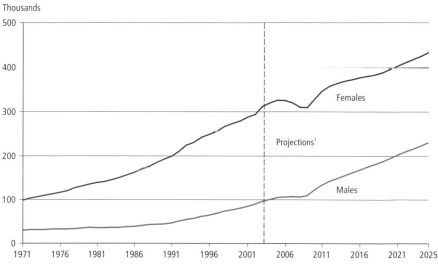

1 2001-based projections for the United Kingdom.

Source: Office for National Statistics; Government Actuary's Department

Table **1.5**

Population: by ethnic group and age, 2001

Great Britain   Percentages

	Under 16	16–64	65 and over	All people (=100%) (thousands)
White	19	64	17	52,481
Mixed	50	47	3	674
Asian or Asian British				
Indian	23	71	7	1,052
Pakistani	35	61	4	747
Bangladeshi	38	58	3	283
Other Asian	24	71	5	247
All Asian or Asian British	29	66	5	2,329
Black or Black British				
Black Caribbean	20	69	11	566
Black African	30	68	2	485
Other Black	38	59	3	97
All Black or Black British	26	68	6	1,148
Chinese	19	76	5	243
Other ethnic groups	19	78	3	229
All ethnic groups	20	64	16	57,104

1 See Appendix, Part 1: Classification of ethnic groups.

Source: Census 2001, Office for National Statistics; Census 2001, General Register Office for Scotland

Figure **1.6**

Population of working age: by sex and socio-economic classification, 2003[1]

United Kingdom
Percentages

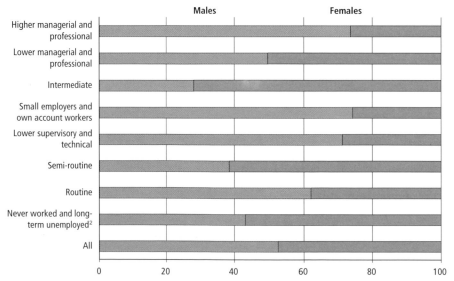

1 At spring. Males aged 16 to 64, females aged 16 to 59. See Appendix, Part 1: National Statistics Socio-economic Classification. These estimates are not seasonally adjusted and have not been adjusted to take account of the 2001 Census results. See Appendix, Part 4: LFS reweighting.
2 People unemployed for less than 1 year are classified according to their previous occupation. Includes those not classified elsewhere.

Black Caribbeans have the oldest age structure, with 20 per cent under 16, and 11 per cent aged 65 and over. These patterns are influenced by past immigration to the United Kingdom. In the 1950s and 1960s, better job opportunities led to the arrival of Caribbean immigrant workers, particularly men, while immigration from India, Pakistan and Bangladesh peaked in the late 1960s and early 1970s. Much of the recent growth in the UK's minority ethnic population has been through children born in the United Kingdom. The differences in age structure across ethnic groups are expected to disappear over time.

Using the Labour Force Survey it is possible to analyse the adult household population by socio-economic status. There are considerable differences in the socio-economic structure of men and women across the United Kingdom. In spring 2003, higher managers and professionals (which includes lawyers and engineers), the small employers and own account workers class (which contains the self-employed), and the lower supervisory and technical class (which includes traffic wardens and bakers) were all more likely to be male (Figure 1.6). Around 7 out of 10 people in each of these classes were male. Women were more likely than men to be in the 'intermediate' class (including receptionists and dental nurses): more than 7 out of 10 people in this class were female.

There were also variations in the proportions in each socio-economic classification across the regions. In spring 2003 the proportions of people who worked in managerial and professional occupations was highest in the South East and lowest in the North East.

Population change

The rate of population change over time depends upon the net natural change – the difference between the numbers of births and deaths – and the net effect of people migrating to and from the country. Natural change is an important factor in population growth in the United Kingdom, although since the 1980s net migration has had an increased influence (Table 1.7). Projections suggest that this trend will continue, with net migration accounting for over half of the population change by 2021.

There were 668,800 live births in the United Kingdom in 2002, 37 per cent fewer than in 1901 (Figure 1.8). The two world wars had a major impact on births. There was a fall in the numbers of births during the First World War, followed by a post-war 'baby boom', with births peaking at 1.1 million in 1920. The numbers of births then decreased and remained low during the inter-war years and the Second World War. A second baby boom followed the Second World War, with a further baby boom in the 1960s when women born in the baby boom after the Second World War reached childbearing ages. In the mid-1970s the number of births fell to similar levels as the number of deaths. There was a mini boom in births in the 1980s and early 1990s before numbers began falling again. Projections suggest that the number of births will remain relatively constant over the next 40 years, ranging from 660,000 to 710,000.

The number of deaths has fluctuated around the 600,000 level over the last century with 608,000 deaths registered in 2002. It is projected that the number of deaths will increase as the number of people born in the baby boom after the Second World War begin to reach

Table **1.7**

Population change[1]

United Kingdom

Thousands

	Population at start of period	Annual averages				
		Live births	Deaths	Net natural change	Net migration & other	Overall change
1901–1911	38,237	1,091	624	467	–82	385
1951–1961	50,287	839	593	246	6	252
1971–1981	55,928	736	666	69	–27	42
1981–1991	56,357	757	655	103	43	146
1991–2002	57,439	725	628	96	66	163
2002–2011	59,207	681	612	69	100	169
2011–2021	60,524	704	617	86	100	186

1 Data are census enumerated for 1901 to 1911; mid–year estimates for 1951 to 2002; 2001–based projections for 2002 to 2021. See Appendix, Part 1: Population estimates and projections. Population estimates for 2002 include provisional results from the Manchester matching exercise.

Source: Office for National Statistics; Government Actuary's Department; General Register Office for Scotland; Northern Ireland Statistics and Research Agency

Figure **1.8**

Births[1,2] and deaths[1]

United Kingdom
Millions

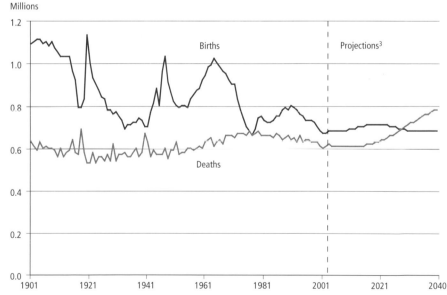

1 Data for 1901 to 1921 exclude Ireland which was constitutionally a part of the United Kingdom during this period.
2 Data from 1981 exclude the non-residents of Northern Ireland.
3 2001-based.

Source: Office for National Statistics; Government Actuary's Department; General Register Office for Scotland; Northern Ireland Statistics and Research Agency

Table **1.9**

Deaths: by age and sex

United Kingdom

Death rates per 1,000 in each age group

	Under 1[1]	1–15	16–34	35–54	55–64	65–74	75 and over	All ages	All deaths (thousands)
Males									
1971	20.2	0.5	1.0	4.8	20.4	51.1	131.4	12.1	329
1981	12.7	0.4	1.0	4.0	18.1	46.4	122.2	12.0	329
1991	8.3	0.3	0.9	3.1	14.2	38.7	111.2	11.3	314
2001	6.0	0.2	0.9	2.8	10.4	28.8	96.7	10.0	288
2002	6.0	0.2	0.9	2.7	10.1	28.0	96.2	10.0	289
2011[2]	4.2	0.2	0.8	2.6	10.0	24.3	86.5	10.1	296
2021[2]	3.6	0.1	0.8	2.4	8.7	23.0	79.3	10.7	324
Females									
1971	15.5	0.4	0.5	3.1	10.3	26.6	96.6	11.0	317
1981	9.5	0.3	0.4	2.5	9.8	24.7	90.2	11.4	329
1991	6.3	0.2	0.4	1.9	8.4	22.3	85.0	11.2	332
2001	5.0	0.1	0.4	1.8	6.4	17.9	81.7	10.5	316
2002	4.6	0.1	0.4	1.7	6.2	17.5	82.7	10.5	319
2011[2]	3.7	0.1	0.4	1.7	6.1	15.8	78.9	10.1	312
2021[2]	3.1	0.1	0.3	1.6	5.0	14.6	69.5	9.7	312

1 Rate per 1,000 live births.
2 2001-based projections.

Source: Office for National Statistics; Government Actuary's Department; General Register Office for Scotland; Northern Ireland Statistics and Research Agency

Map **1.10**

Population aged 65 and over: by area[1], 2001

Percentages

- 25.0 and over
- 20.0–24.9
- 15.0–19.9
- Under 15.0

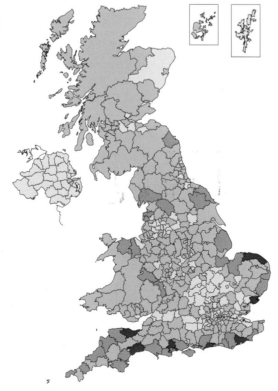

1 Unitary and local authorities.

Source: Census 2001, Office for National Statistics; Census 2001, General Register Office for Scotland; Census 2001, Northern Ireland Statistics and Research Agency

advanced ages. The number of deaths is expected to exceed the number of births from around 2029.

Although the number of deaths each year over the last century remained relatively stable, death rates fell considerably. Rising standards of living and developments in medical technology and practice help to explain the decline in the death rates. Between 1971 and 2002 the death rate for all males fell by 17 per cent, while the death rate for all females fell by 4 per cent (Table 1.9). Infant mortality rates fell by 70 per cent during this period.

Geographical distribution

People aged 65 and over are unevenly distributed across the country. In 2001 nearly 16 per cent of the population in England and Wales were aged 65 and over. In the South West 19 per cent

Table 1.11

Inter-regional movements[1] within the United Kingdom, 2002

Thousands

					Origin								
	United Kingdom	England	North East	North West	Yorkshire & the Humber	East Midlands	West Midlands	East	London	South East	South West	Wales	Scotland	Northern Ireland
Destination														
United Kingdom	.	119	41	108	95	97	103	130	262	220	111	50	48	11
England	101	.	36	87	86	90	89	120	247	199	94	48	45	9
North East	43	37	.	6	9	3	3	3	5	5	2	1	4	1
North West	109	91	6	.	18	10	13	8	14	14	8	9	7	2
Yorkshire & the Humber	100	91	9	18	.	17	8	9	11	13	6	3	5	1
East Midlands	120	113	3	10	18	.	17	20	15	22	8	3	3	1
West Midlands	99	87	3	12	8	14	.	8	13	16	13	8	3	1
East	150	142	3	7	7	13	7	.	66	28	9	3	4	1
London	155	142	5	12	10	10	11	28	.	51	15	5	7	1
South East	229	213	4	12	9	14	14	29	98	.	33	8	7	1
South West	146	132	2	9	6	9	16	14	25	50	.	9	4	1
Wales	64	62	1	11	3	3	10	4	6	11	12	.	2	-
Scotland	53	49	4	8	5	3	3	5	7	9	4	2	.	2
Northern Ireland	11	8	-	1	1	1	1	1	2	1	1	-	2	.

1 Based on patients re-registering with NHS doctors in other parts of the United Kingdom. Moves where the origin and destination lie within the same region do not appear in the table. Figures may be revised in the light of the 2001 Census. See Appendix, Part 1: Internal migration estimates.

Source: Office for National Statistics; General Register Office for Scotland; Northern Ireland Statistics and Research Agency

were aged 65 years and over, and the proportion ranged from almost 14 per cent in Swindon UA, to almost 30 per cent in Christchurch (Map 1.10). In London 12 per cent were aged 65 years and over. Older people are particularly concentrated along the South coast.

Migration flows influence the size, growth and profile of the population. Regional populations are affected by people relocating within the United Kingdom, as well as births, deaths and by international migration flows. During

the last century there was a movement of people from the coal, ship building and steel industry areas in the north of England, Scotland and Wales to the south of England and the Midlands, where many light industries and service industries are based.

In 2002 Wales gained 14,000 people from migration within the United Kingdom and Scotland gained over 4,000 people, while England experienced a net loss of more than 18,000 people (Table 1.11). Within the

regions of England, the greatest net loss due to internal migration in 2002 occurred in London, where nearly 108,000 more people moved from the capital to other parts of the United Kingdom than moved into London. Over a third of people leaving London for elsewhere in the United Kingdom moved to the South East region and a quarter to the East of England. The South West experienced the highest net gain (35,000 people), with 34 per cent moving from the South East and a further 17 per cent moving from London.

Table **1.12**

UK nationals living in other EU states and nationals of other EU states living in the UK

Thousands

	UK nationals living in other EU states 2002[1]	EU nationals living in the UK 2000
Germany	115.2	62.1
Spain	107.3	46.6
Ireland	77.3	411.8
France	75.3	85.6
Netherlands	43.6	28.8
Belgium	26.4	8.2
Italy	24.6	97.2
Portugal	15.0	33.9
Sweden	13.8	20.4
Greece	13.2	26.3
Denmark	12.8	16.7
Austria	5.4	6.0
Luxembourg	4.3	0.5
Finland	2.4	12.0
All	524.5	856.2

1 2001 data for Italy, Greece, Luxembourg and Austria. 1999 data for France.

Souce: Eurostat

Figure **1.13**

Grants of settlement: by region of origin

United Kingdom
Thousands

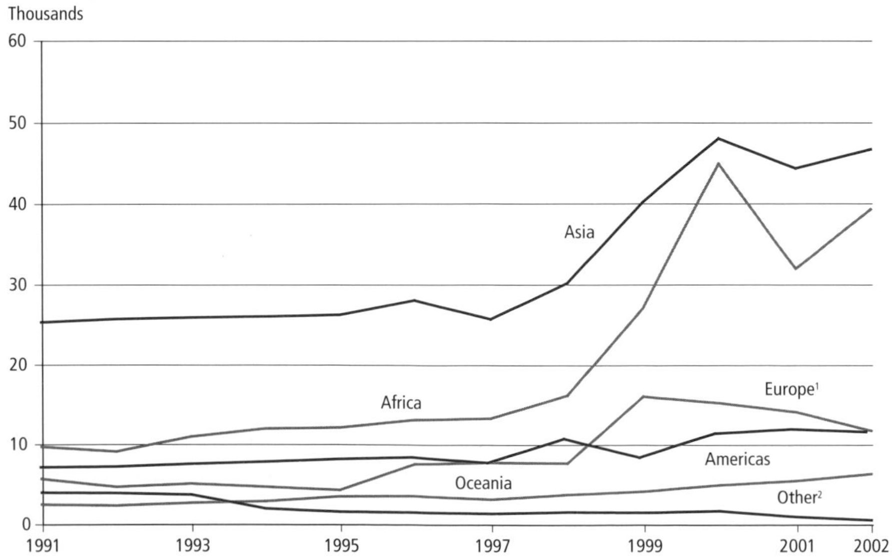

1 European Economic Area (EEA) nationals may apply for settlement, but are not obliged to do so. The figures do not represent the total number of Europeans eligible to stay indefinitely in the UK. Data on EEA nationals granted settlement have not been recorded since 1998.
2 Includes British Overseas citizens, those whose nationality was unknown and, up to 1993, acceptances where the nationality was not separately identified; from 1994 these nationalities have been included in the relevant geographical area.

Source: Home Office

Young adults are the most mobile age group. Many people in their twenties leave their home area to study or seek employment. In 2002 London experienced the largest net increase of people aged 16 to 24 due to migration within the United Kingdom (10,000 people) but experienced a net loss in all other age groups, especially those associated with young families: the under 15s and people aged 25 to 44. The West Midlands experienced the biggest net loss of 16 to 24 year olds, of over 4,000.

International migration

The pattern of people entering and leaving the United Kingdom has changed over the 20th century. There was a net loss due to international migration during the first four decades of the 20th century. However, since 1983 there has generally been net migration into the United Kingdom.

In 2002 an estimated 153,000 more people arrived to live in the United Kingdom for at least a year, than left to live elsewhere. The number of in-migrants to the United Kingdom increased from 480,000 in 2001 to 513,000 in 2002. There were 359,000 out-migrants in 2002, 51,000 more than in 2001. Net international in-migration is projected to remain at a relatively high level in the near future.

In 2000 there were nearly 412,000 Irish nationals living in the United Kingdom, accounting for just under half of all the other EU nationals living here, while nationals from Italy and from France each accounted for around 1 in 10 (Table 1.12). There were nearly 525,000 UK nationals living outside the United Kingdom but still within the EU in 2002. Over 1 in 5 of these UK nationals lived in Germany, with almost as many living in Spain.

Nationals of the European Economic Area (EU plus Iceland, Liechtenstein, and Norway) have the right to reside in the United Kingdom provided they are working or are able to support themselves financially. Nearly all other overseas nationals wishing to live permanently in the United Kingdom require Home Office acceptance for settlement. The number of people accepted for settlement in the United Kingdom increased by 7,600 to 116,000 between 2001 and 2002 (Figure 1.13).

Asylum-related settlement grants rose sharply in 1999 and 2000 due to a change in the rules reducing the qualifying periods for people granted asylum and exceptional leave to remain, and effectively increasing the number of people eligible for settlement. Forty per cent of grants of settlement in 2002 were granted to Asian nationals, and a further 34 per cent to African nationals.

The fall in grants in 2001 was mainly due to a fall in acceptances of African nationals – these fell by 29 per cent from 2000, and then rose by 23 per cent in 2002. The number of people seeking asylum in the United Kingdom varies from year to year, although the total number of asylum applications, including dependants, to EU countries remained relatively steady between 1999 and 2002. In 2002 the United Kingdom received 103,100 applications, 11,500 more than in 2001 – a rise of 13 per cent (Table 1.14). Belgium, Denmark, Germany, Italy, Spain and the Netherlands each recorded a fall in applications between 2001 and 2002. When the relative size of the countries' populations are taken into account, the United Kingdom ranked sixth in 2002, one place higher than in 2001, with a rate of 1.7 asylum seekers per 1,000 population. Austria had the highest rate at 4.9 per 1,000 population, an increase of 32 per cent since 2001.

The countries from which people arrive to claim asylum in the United Kingdom vary with world events. Iraqi asylum applications increased from nearly 6,700 in 2001 to over 14,500 in 2002. Large numbers of asylum seekers in 2002 also came from Afghanistan, Somalia and Zimbabwe, areas that have seen escalations in conflict.

International perspective

In 2003 the world's population exceeded 6.3 billion people (Table 1.15). Nearly 61 per cent of the population lived in Asia, 13 per cent in Africa and 12 per cent in Europe. World population growth was at its highest between 1965 and 1970, when the annual growth rate was 2 per cent. Since 1970 the world population has been growing at a slower rate. The projected average population growth rate for 2000 to 2005 is 1.2 per cent.

In 2002 Western Sahara had the lowest population density in the world with 1 person per square kilometre, while Singapore had the highest density with 6,502 people per square kilometre. In contrast there were 244 people per square mile in the United Kingdom.

In 2001 almost half of the world's population lived in urban areas. However there was wide variability between areas: 38 per cent of people in Asia and Africa lived in urban areas compared with 78 per cent of those in North America. Africa had a high infant mortality rate,

Table **1.14**

Asylum applications, including dependants: EU comparison, 2002

	Number of asylum seekers[1]	Asylum seekers per 1,000 population
Austria	39,400	4.9
Sweden	33,000	3.7
Ireland	11,600	3.1
Belgium	21,400	2.1
Luxembourg	1,000	2.1
United Kingdom	103,100	1.7
Netherlands	18,700	1.2
Denmark	5,900	1.1
France	58,100	1.0
Germany	71,100	0.9
Finland	3,400	0.6
Greece	5,700	0.5
Spain	6,200	0.1
Italy	7,300	0.1
Portugal	200	-
All applications to EU	386,100	1.0

1 Figures rounded to the nearest 100.

Source: Home Office

Table **1.15**

World demographic indicators

	Population (millions) 2003	Percentage in urban areas 2001	Infant mortality rate[1]	Total fertility rate[2]	Life expectancy at birth (years)	
					Males	Females
Asia	3,823	38	53	2.6	66	69
Africa	851	38	89	4.9	48	50
Europe	726	74	9	1.4	70	78
Latin America & Caribbean	543	76	32	2.5	67	74
North America	326	78	7	2.1	75	80
Oceania	32	74	26	2.3	72	77
World	6,302	48	56	2.7	63	68

1 Per 1,000 live births.
2 Data are for 2000–05. Total fertility rate is the number of children that would be born to a woman if current patterns of fertility persisted throughout her childbearing life.

Source: United Nations

Table **1.16**

European demographic indicators: EU comparison

	Population (millions) 2002	Infant mortality rate[1]	Total fertility rate[2]	Life expectancy at birth (years) Males	Females
Germany	82.4	4.3	1.4	74.8	80.8
France	59.3	4.5	1.9	75.6	82.9
United Kingdom[3]	59.2	5.3	1.6	75.7	80.4
Italy[4]	57.0	4.7	1.3	76.8	82.9
Spain	40.4	3.4	1.3	75.7	83.1
Netherlands	16.1	5.1	1.7	75.9	80.6
Greece[4]	11.0	5.9	1.3	75.4	80.7
Portugal	10.3	5.0	1.4	73.4	80.4
Belgium[3]	10.3	4.9	1.6	74.5	80.8
Sweden	8.9	2.8	1.7	77.7	82.1
Austria	8.0	4.1	1.4	75.6	81.6
Denmark	5.4	4.4	1.7	74.7	79.2
Finland	5.2	3.0	1.7	74.9	81.5
Ireland	3.9	5.1	2.0	73.0	78.5
Luxembourg[3]	0.4	5.1	1.6	75.3	80.1

1 Per 1,000 live births.
2 Total fertility rate is the number of children that would be born to a woman if current patterns of fertility persisted throughout her childbearing life.
3 Life expectancy data are for 2001.
4 Population data are based on the latest population census.

Source: Eurostat

the expectancy for a 20 year old was 40 years, meaning that those children born in Africa who survive to their twenties can expect to live till they are around 60 years old. The difference in Europe is much less pronounced at 74 years at birth and 55 years at age 20.

Differences also exist in fertility and mortality rates across the EU. In 2002 there were 5.9 infant deaths per 1,000 live births in Greece, while in Sweden the rate was 2.8 (Table 1.16). The total fertility rate was fairly low throughout Europe: Ireland had the highest rate with 2.0 children per woman, Italy, Spain and Greece had the lowest rates, with around 1.3 children per woman. There were also differences in life expectancy: in Sweden, life expectancy at birth was 82.1 years for females and 77.7 for males in 2002, whereas in Ireland life expectancy at birth was 78.5 years for females and 73.0 for males.

There was greater variability across the candidate countries (countries that will become part of the EU). In Turkey in 2002 there were 38.7 infant deaths per 1,000 live births, compared with 3.9 infant deaths per 1,000 live births in Slovenia. The total fertility rate was also lower in most candidate countries, compared with the rates in the EU countries. The lowest was in the Czech Republic, which had a total fertility rate of 1.2 children per woman. However the highest total fertility rate occurred in Turkey with 2.5 children per woman. Life expectancy ranged from 70.9 years for females and 66.2 for males in Turkey, to 81.0 years for females and 76.1 for males in Cyprus.

at 89 infant deaths per 1,000 live births in 2002, while the rates in North America and Europe were less than 9 and 7 infant deaths per 1,000 live births, respectively. The total fertility rate was also high in Africa, at 4.9 children per woman, while Europe had a rate of 1.4. There was also a wide variability in life expectancy; life expectancy at birth in Africa was 49, but

Chapter 2 **Households and Families**

Household composition

- The proportion of one-person households in Great Britain increased from 18 to 29 per cent between 1971 and spring 2003. (Table 2.1)

- In 2001 around half of Black Caribbean and Other Black families with dependent children in Great Britain were headed by a lone parent. (Table 2.5)

Family relationships

- In England, 56 per cent of men, and 37 per cent of women aged 20 to 24 lived at home with their parents in spring 2003. (Table 2.9)

Partnerships

- Since 1971, the number of people marrying in the United Kingdom has fallen by 38 per cent to over 286,000 in 2001. (Page 31)

- Among non-married women, those aged 25 to 29 were most likely to cohabit, whereas among non-married men, those aged 30 to 34 years old were most likely to cohabit in Great Britain in 2001/02. (Figure 2.14)

Family formation

- In 2002 almost 41 per cent of all children were born outside marriage in the United Kingdom, compared with 56 per cent in Sweden and 4 per cent in Greece. (Table 2.17)

Table 2.1

Households[1]: by size

Great Britain   Percentages

	1971	1981	1991	2001[2]	2003[2]
One person	18	22	27	29	29
Two people	32	32	34	35	35
Three people	19	17	16	16	15
Four people	17	18	16	14	14
Five people	8	7	5	5	5
Six or more people	6	4	2	2	2
All households (=100%) (millions)	18.6	20.2	22.4	24.2	24.5
Average household size (number of people)	2.9	2.7	2.5	2.4	2.4

1 See Appendix, Part 2: Households.
2 At spring. These estimates are not seasonally adjusted and have not been adjusted to take account of the Census 2001 results. See Appendix, Part 4: LFS reweighting.

Source: Census, Labour Force Survey, Office for National Statistics

Table 2.2

Households[1]: by type of household and family

Great Britain   Percentages

	1971	1981	1991	2001[2]	2003[2]
One person					
Under state pension age	6	8	11	14	15
Over state pension age	12	14	16	15	14
Two or more unrelated adults	4	5	3	8	8
One family households					
Couple[3]					
No children	27	26	28	28	28
1–2 dependent children[4]	26	25	20	19	18
3 or more dependent children[4]	9	6	5	4	4
Non-dependent children only	8	8	8	6	6
Lone parent[3]					
Dependent children[4]	3	5	6	5	5
Non-dependent children only	4	4	4	3	3
Multi-family households	1	1	1	1	1
All households (=100%) (millions)	18.6	20.2	22.4	24.2	24.5

1 See Appendix, Part 2: Households and families.
2 At spring. These estimates are not seasonally adjusted and have not been adjusted to take account of the 2001 Census results. See Appendix, Part 4: LFS reweighting.
3 Other individuals who were not family members may also be included.
4 May also include non-dependent children.

Source: Census, Labour Force Survey, Office for National Statistics

The types of households and families that people live in are becoming more diverse, reflecting changes in partnership formation and dissolution. People live in a variety of household types over their lifetime. They may leave their parental home, form partnerships, marry and have children. They may also experience separation and divorce, lone-parenthood, and the formation of new partnerships, leading to new households and second families. People are also spending more time living on their own, either before forming relationships, or after a relationship has broken down.

Household composition

There were 24.5 million households in Great Britain in 2003 (Table 2.1). Although the population has been increasing, the number of households has increased faster. The population of the United Kingdom grew by 6 per cent between 1971 and 2002, while the number of households increased by 31 per cent. Trends towards smaller household sizes have also contributed to the increase in the number of households. The Labour Force survey (LFS) estimates used in this chapter have not been adjusted to take account of the 2001 Census results. The Office for National Statistics is producing reweighted LFS estimates based on the findings of the 2001 Census, which will be available from spring 2004.

There has been a decrease in the proportion of households containing the traditional family unit – couple families with dependent children – and an increase in the proportion of lone-parent families (Table 2.2). The proportion of households in Great Britain comprising a couple with dependent children fell from around a third in 1971 to a just over fifth in spring

2003. Over the same period, the proportion of lone-parent households with dependent children almost doubled, and accounted for 5 per cent of households in spring 2003.

While Table 2.2 shows that over half of households were headed by a couple in spring 2003, Table 2.3 is based on people. It shows that almost three quarters of people living in private households lived in couple family households. The 'traditional' family household of a couple with dependent children was the most common household type. However, since 1971 the proportion of people living in such households has fallen from just over a half to just under two fifths and the proportion of people living in couple family households with no children has increased from almost a fifth of people to a quarter. One in eight people lived in a lone-parent household in spring 2003, three times the proportion in 1971.

There have also been changes in the proportions of children living in different family types (Table 2.4). Since the early 1970s, there has been a decrease in the percentage of children living in families headed by a couple and an increase in those living in lone-parent families. In spring 2003, 78 per cent of children lived in a family unit headed by a couple. The proportion of children living in lone-parent families increased from 7 per cent in 1972 to 23 per cent in spring 2003. Lone mothers head around 9 out of 10 lone-parent families. The rise in the proportion of divorced mothers contributed to most of the increase up to the mid-1980s, while more recently the proportion of single lone mothers has grown at a faster rate because of a growth in the proportion of births outside marriage. The proportion of children living in lone-

Table **2.3**

People in households[1]: by type of household and family

Great Britain   Percentages

	1971	1981	1991	2001[2]	2003[2]
One family households					
Living alone	6	8	11	12	13
Couple					
No children	19	20	23	25	25
Dependent children[3]	52	47	41	39	38
Non-dependent children only	10	10	11	8	8
Lone parent	4	6	10	12	12
Other households	9	9	4	4	5
All people in private households (=100%) (millions)	53.4	53.9	55.4	..	..
People not in private households (millions)	0.9	0.8	0.8	..	..
Total population (millions)[4]	54.4	54.8	56.2	57.4	57.6

1 See Appendix, Part 2: Households and families.
2 At spring. These estimates are not seasonally adjusted and have not been adjusted to take account of the Census 2001 results. See Appendix, Part 4: LFS reweighting.
3 May also include non-dependent children.
4 Data for 1971 to 1991 are census enumerated. Data for 2001 and 2002 are mid-year estimates.

Source: Census, Labour Force Survey, Office for National Statistics

Table **2.4**

Percentage of dependent children[1] living in different family types

Great Britain   Percentages

	1972	1981	1992[2]	2001[2]	2003[2]
Couple families					
1 child	16	18	18	17	17
2 children	35	41	39	38	37
3 or more children	41	29	27	25	24
Lone mother families					
1 child	2	3	4	6	6
2 children	2	4	5	7	8
3 or more children	2	3	4	5	6
Lone father families					
1 child	-	1	1	1	2
2 or more children	1	1	1	1	1
All children[3]	100	100	100	100	100

1 See Appendix, Part 2: Families.
2 At spring. These estimates are not seasonally adjusted and have not been adjusted to take account of the Census 2001 results. See Appendix, Part 4: LFS reweighting.
3 Excludes cases where the dependent child is a family unit, for example, a foster child.

Source: General Household Survey, Census, Labour Force Survey, Office for National Statistics

parent families headed by a father has tripled since 1972.

The pattern of family types with dependent children varies across different ethnic groups (Table 2.5). In 2001 among families with dependent children in Great Britain, those headed by people from the Asian group were the least likely to be lone parents. Households headed by people from White, Mixed and Black Caribbean ethnic groups were most likely to contain cohabiting couples, and those households where the head was from the Chinese or Indian ethnic group were most likely to contain married couples.

There are differences between ethnic groups in their views about ideal family size. Such differences in attitude are reflected in part in the patterns of actual family size. Pakistani and Bangladeshi households tend to be larger than those of other ethnic groups, while Indian households tend to be smaller than Pakistani and Bangladeshi households, but they are larger than those of other ethnic groups. The average household size in 2001 was 4.46 people for Bangladeshi households and 4.11 for Pakistani households. Asian households may contain three generations, with grandparents living with a married couple and their children. In comparison, the average size for all households was 2.35, with White Irish and Black Caribbeans, having the smallest households at 2.15 and 2.26 people respectively in 2001.

One of the most notable changes in household composition since 1971 has been the increase in the number of one-person households. The proportion of one-person households in Great Britain increased from 18 per cent in 1971 to 29 per cent in 2003. The rate of change has not been uniform across all categories of those living alone. The largest increase has occurred among men under age 65. The proportion of one-person households comprising men aged under 65, at nearly 11 per cent in 2002, was more than three times the proportion in 1971. The proportion of households consisting of women aged 65 and over living alone was around 9 per cent in 2002. This proportion has remained fairly stable since the beginning of the 1970s. Over the same period, the proportion of households comprising of women aged under 65 living alone has increased by over 2 percentage points. The increases, in part, reflect the decline in marriage and the rise in separation

Table **2.5**

Families with dependent children: by ethnic group[1], 2001

Great Britain   Percentages

	One family households			Other households with dependent children	All
	Married couple families	Cohabiting couple familes	Lone parent families		
White	60	12	22	6	100
Mixed	38	11	39	12	100
Asian or Asian British					
Indian	68	2	10	21	100
Pakistani	61	2	13	24	100
Bangladeshi	63	2	12	23	100
Other Asian	66	3	12	19	100
All Asian or Asian British	65	2	11	22	100
Black or Black British					
Black Caribbean	29	11	48	12	100
Black African	38	7	36	19	100
Other Black	24	9	52	15	100
All Black or Black British	32	9	43	15	100
Chinese	69	3	15	13	100
Other ethnic group	67	3	18	12	100
All ethnic groups	60	11	22	7	100

1 Of household reference person.

Source: Census 2001, Office for National Statistics; Census 2001, General Register Office for Scotland

and divorce, as well as the increase in the age at which people first marry.

The 2001 Census showed that the proportion of people living alone varies geographically with the highest proportions occurring in Westminster and Kensington and Chelsea (Map 2.6). Nearly half of all people in these areas lived alone. Outside of London, the highest proportions (nearly two fifths) were in Glasgow city, Brighton and Hove UA and Manchester. In contrast, Hart in Hampshire and Magherafelt and Limavady in Northern Ireland had the lowest proportions of the population living in one-person households at just over a fifth. In Scotland, almost 33 per cent of the population lived alone, compared with 27 per cent in Northern Ireland. In England and Wales 30 per cent of the population lived alone.

Family relationships

There have been considerable changes to the family environment since the early 1970s. Children are living in an increasing variety of different structures. Due to changes in cohabitation, marriage and divorce patterns, children may experience a range of different family structures during their lives. Parents separating can result in lone-parent families, and new relationships can create stepfamilies.

Stepfamilies are formed when parents with children remarry or cohabit with their new partners (Table 2.7). In 2001/02 the vast majority (83 per cent) of stepfamilies in Great Britain consisted of a stepfather and natural mother. This is explained partly by the tendency for children to stay with their mother following the break-up of a partnership. The number of children aged under 16 in England and Wales who experienced the divorce of their parents peaked at almost 176,000 in 1993. The number fell

Map **2.6**

Proportion of households which consist of one person: by area[1], 2001

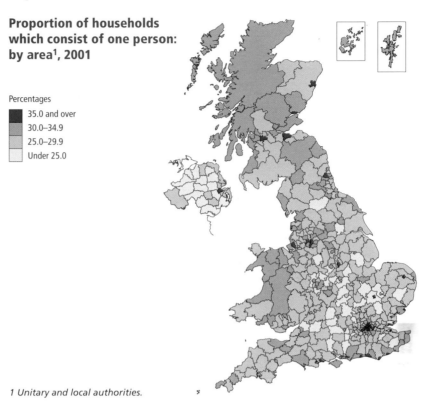

Percentages
- 35.0 and over
- 30.0–34.9
- 25.0–29.9
- Under 25.0

1 Unitary and local authorities.

Source: Census 2001, Office for National Statistics; Census 2001, General Register Office for Scotland; Census 2001, Northern Ireland Statistics and Research Agency

Table **2.7**

Stepfamilies[1] with dependent children[2]

Great Britain — Percentages

	1991/92	1996/97	2000/01	2001/02
Child(ren) from the woman's previous marriage/cohabitation	86	84	88	83
Child(ren) from the man's previous marriage/cohabitation	6	12	9	9
Child(ren) from both partners' previous marriage/cohabitation	6	4	3	8
Lone parent with child(ren) from a former partner's previous marriage	1	-	-	-
All	100	100	100	100

1 Family head aged 16–59.
2 Dependent children are persons under 16, or aged 16–18 and in full-time education, in the family unit, and living in the household.

Source: General Household Survey, Office for National Statistics

Table **2.8**

Adoptions[1]: by age of child

United Kingdom

Percentages

	1981[2]	1991[2]	1996	2000	2001	2002
Under 1	26	12	5	5	4	5
1–4	20	29	26	40	44	44
5–9	30	34	39	32	31	31
10–14	20	19	24	19	17	16
15–17	4	6	6	4	4	4
All ages (=100%) (thousands)	10.4	8.0	6.7	5.5	6.6	6.2

1 By date of entry into adopted children register.
2 Data for 1981 to 1995 are for Great Britain.

Source: Office for National Statistics; General Register Office for Scotland

Table **2.9**

Adults living with their parents: by sex and age

England

Percentages

	1991	2000–01	2002[1]	2003[1]
Males				
20–24	50	56	56	56
25–29	19	25	20	21
30–34	9	9	8	8
Females				
20–24	32	39	37	37
25–29	9	11	10	10
30–34	5	4	2	3

1 At spring. These estimates are not seasonally adjusted and have not been adjusted to take account of the Census 2001 results. See Appendix, Part 4: LFS reweighting.

Source: National Dwelling and Household Survey and Survey of English Housing, Office of the Deputy Prime Minister; Labour Force Survey, Office for National Statistics

to 149,000 in 2002 when nearly one in four children affected by divorce was under five and just over two in three were aged ten or under.

Another way in which people form families is through adoption. In 2001/02 there were 6,200 adoptions in the United Kingdom, with 44 per cent aged between 1 and 4 years (Table 2.8). One in four children adopted were aged under 1 in 1981, compared with one in twenty in 2002. Increased use of contraception, new abortion laws and changed attitudes towards lone motherhood have meant that fewer children are put up for adoption than 20 years ago. In England and Wales the number of adoptions decreased from 21,500 in 1971 to 5,700 in 2002. There was a rapid decline in the number of children available for adoption following the introduction of legal abortion in the *Abortion Act 1967* and after the

implementation of the *Children Act 1975*. This required courts dealing with adoption applications for children of divorced parents to dismiss these applications where a legal custody order was in the child's best interests. Despite these changes, children born outside marriage have formed the majority of children adopted since 1981, and accounted for 72 per cent of children adopted in 2002 in England and Wales.

Another recent change in family structure and relationships has been the increase in the number of adults who live with their parents (Table 2.9). Some young people may be delaying leaving home because of economic necessity, such as difficulties entering the housing market. Others may simply choose to continue living with their parents. The later age at marriage may also be a factor. In spring 2003 nearly three fifths of men aged 20 to 24 lived with their parents, compared with half in 1991. For women the proportion of 20 to 24 year olds living with their parents increased from a third to nearly two fifths.

Families continue to play an important role in people's lives and regular contact with close relatives living elsewhere is common. According to the Home Office Citizenship Survey in 2001, there was some variability across ethnic groups in England and Wales in the frequency in which adults kept in touch with their relatives. More than two thirds of all adults kept in regular contact with their relatives (at least once a month either through visiting, telephoning, emailing or writing a letter) (Figure 2.10). Over four fifths of Asian adults, and nearly three quarters of Black adults, who had a cousin, aunt, uncle, niece, or nephew kept in regular contact with them, compared with less than half of White adults. White adults tended to keep in touch with just their closest relatives, while Asian adults kept in regular contact with their extended relatives, which suggests that they may have more close-knit families. There was also a similar pattern across ethnic groups receiving help from relatives with around one in seven White adults receiving help from their cousin, aunt, uncle, niece or nephew, compared with nearly one in three Black and Asian adults.

Partnerships

The pattern of partnership formation has changed since the early 1970s, but despite the decrease in the overall numbers of people marrying, it is still the most common form of partnership for men and women. Since 1971, the number of marriages in the United Kingdom has fallen from around 459,000 to just over 286,000 in 2001 (Figure 2.11). The number of divorces increased from just under 80,000 in 1971 and peaked in 1993 at 180,000. The number of divorces then fell by 13 per cent to 157,000 in 2001. In 2001 around half of the UK population were married.

In England and Wales the average age at first marriage has also increased (Table 2.12 – see overleaf). In 2001 it was 30.6 years for men and 28.4 years for women, compared with 24.6 years for men and 22.6 years for women in 1971. In 2001, 6 per cent of women aged 45 and over, compared with 9 per cent of men aged 45 and over remained never married. The average age at divorce has also increased. In 2002 the average age was 41.9 years for men and 39.4 years for women.

Figure **2.10**

Contact with relatives[1]: by ethnic group, 2001
England & Wales
Percentages

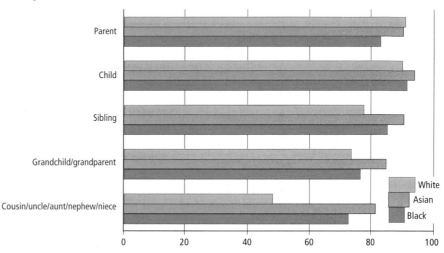

1 Of adults aged 16 and over who had that relative type.
Source: Citizenship Survey, Home Office

Figure **2.11**

Marriages and divorces[1]
United Kingdom
Thousands

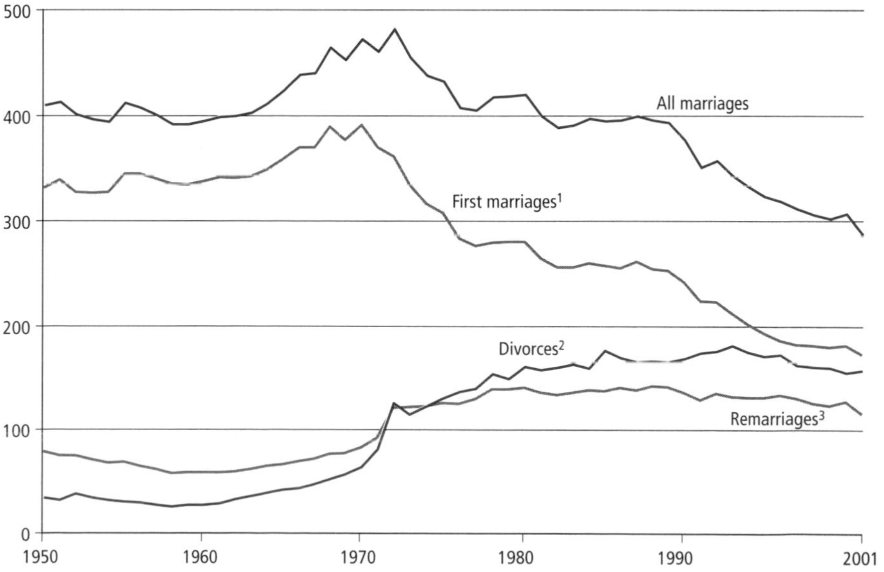

1 For both partners.
2 Includes annulments. Data for 1950 to 1970 are for Great Britain only.
3 For one or both partners.

Source: Office for National Statistics; General Register Office for Scotland; Northern Ireland Statistics and Research Agency

Table 2.12

Average age at marriage and divorce

England & Wales

Mean age (years)

	First marriage		Divorce	
	Males	Females	Males	Females
1971	24.6	22.6	39.4	36.8
1981	25.4	23.1	37.7	35.2
1991	27.5	25.5	38.6	36.0
2001	30.6	28.4	41.5	39.1

Source: Office for National Statistics

Table 2.13

Marriage and divorce rates: EU comparison, 2002

Rates per 1,000 population

	Marriages[1]	Divorces[2]
Denmark	6.9	2.8
Netherlands	5.5	2.1
Portugal	5.4	2.6
Greece	5.2	1.1
Finland	5.2	2.6
Ireland	5.1	0.7
Spain	5.1	0.9
United Kingdom	4.8	2.7
Germany	4.7	2.4
France	4.7	1.9
Italy	4.7	0.7
Austria	4.5	2.4
Luxembourg	4.5	2.4
Sweden	4.3	2.4
Belgium	3.9	3.0
EU average	4.8	1.9

1 2001 data for Spain.
2 2001 data for Ireland, Spain, Germany, France, Italy and EU average.

Source: Eurostat

The same trends in marriage and marital breakdown are evident across Europe, with the majority of countries in the EU reporting a fall in the number of marriages in 2002. This trend started in Northern Europe, but has since spread throughout Western and most of Southern Europe. In 2002 Denmark had the highest marriage rate at 6.9 marriages per 1,000 people, whereas Belgium had the lowest rate at 3.9 per 1,000 people (Table 2.13). The EU average age at which people first marry is also increasing. In 2001, the average age for women was 28.4 years and 30.6 years for men. This was nearly five years older for women and over four years older for men than in 1971. In 2002 Belgium had the highest divorce rate at 3.0 per 1,000 married people. Italy and Ireland had the lowest divorce rates both at 0.7 per 1,000 married people.

There has been an increase in cohabitation in Great Britain. Among non-married women aged under 60, the proportion cohabiting more than doubled from 13 per cent in 1986, which is the first year data are available on a consistent basis, to 28 per cent in 2001/02. For men it also more than doubled over the same period from 12 per cent to 25 per cent. In 2001/02 the prevalence of cohabitation was highest for women aged 25 to 29; for men it was highest for those aged 30 to 34 (Figure 2.14).

Higher proportions of divorced people in Great Britain cohabit compared with other marital statuses: 34 per cent of divorced men and 30 per cent of divorced women lived in a cohabiting relationship in 2001/02. Women who cohabit tend to be divorced or single. Cohabitation may be transitional for some, leading to marriage, and most cohabiting couples go on to (or expect to) get married. However, in 2001/02, 13 per cent of people aged 16 to 59 had had a least one cohabiting relationship that did not lead to marriage; this was more likely among those aged 25 to 39 than the rest of the population.

Attitudes towards partnerships also differ with age. According to the British Social Attitudes survey in 2002, the proportion who agreed or strongly agreed that 'married people are generally happier than unmarried people', generally increased with age (Table 2.15). Over four fifths of 18 to 44 year olds agreed or strongly agreed that 'it is alright for a couple to live together without intending to get married'; this was double the proportion of those aged 65 and over. However, the proportions who agreed or strongly agreed that 'divorce is usually the best solution when a couple can't seem to work out their problems', increased with age.

Family formation

Fertility patterns influence the size of households and families, and also affect the age structure of the population. There was a downward trend in the fertility rate in the United Kingdom during the 20th century. It was 57 live births per 1,000 women aged 15–44 at the end of the century, compared with 115 live births per 1,000 women aged 15–44 at the start of the century.

Fertility patterns also vary by age. In general, fertility rates for women aged 30 and over have increased since the 1980s while those for women aged under 30 have declined (Table 2.16 – see overleaf). In 2002 the fertility rate for women aged 25 to 29 was still the highest but only slightly greater than the rate for the 30 to 34 age group

Figure **2.14**

Non-married people[1] cohabiting: by sex and age, 2001/02

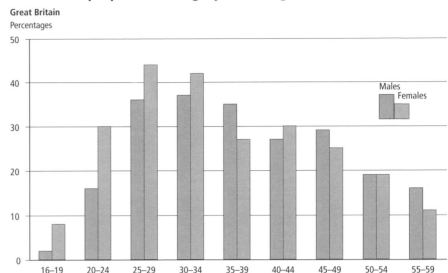

Great Britain
Percentages

1 Males and females aged 16–59. Includes those respondents describing themselves as separated.
Source: General Household Survey, Office for National Statistics

Table **2.15**

Attitudes[1] towards marriage: by age, 2002

Great Britain   Percentages

	18–24	25–44	45–64	65 and over	All aged 18 and over
Married people are generally happier than unmarried people	14	14	25	43	23
It is alright for a couple to live together without intending to get married	88	83	61	40	68
Divorce is usually the best solution when a couple can't seem to work out their marriage problems	44	53	62	72	59

1 Respondents who said they 'strongly agreed' or 'agreed' with each statement.
Source: British Social Attitudes Survey, National Centre for Social Research

Table **2.16**

Fertility rates: by age of mother at childbirth

United Kingdom   Live births per 1,000 women

	1971	1981	1991	2001	2002
Under 20[1]	50.0	28.3	32.9	27.9	26.9
20–24	154.4	106.8	88.9	68.2	68.2
25–29	154.6	130.4	119.9	91.7	91.3
30–34	79.4	69.5	86.5	88.2	89.8
35–39	34.3	22.4	32.0	41.4	42.8
40 and over[2]	9.2	5.0	5.3	8.2	8.9
All ages[3]	84.3	62.1	63.6	54.5	54.3
Total births[4] (thousands)	901.6	730.7	792.3	669.1	668.8

1 Live births per 1,000 women aged 15 to 19.
2 Live births per 1,000 women aged 40 to 44.
3 Total live births per 1,000 women aged 15 to 44.
4 Including 'not stated' in Scotland.

Source: Office for National Statistics

Table **2.17**

Births outside marriage: EU comparison

                                                                                      Percentages

	1980	1990	2000	2002[1]
Sweden	40	47	55	56
Denmark	33	46	45	45
France	11	30	43	44
United Kingdom	12	28	40	41
Finland	13	25	39	40
Austria	18	24	31	34
Ireland	5	15	32	31
Netherlands	4	11	25	29
Belgium	4	12	26	28
Portugal	9	15	22	26
Germany	12	15	23	25
Luxembourg	6	13	22	23
Spain	4	10	18	19
Italy	4	7	10	10
Greece	2	2	4	4
EU average	10	20	29	29

1 Data for Belgium, Spain, Italy, and EU average are for 2001.

Source: Eurostat

which, since 1992, has exceeded that for those aged 20 to 24. Increased female participation in education and the labour market, and the greater choice and effectiveness of contraception, have encouraged the trend towards later childbearing, and smaller families.

Although most children are born to married couples, there has been substantial rise in the proportion of births occurring outside marriage. In 1980 nearly 12 per cent of all births in the United Kingdom were outside marriage; by 2002 this figure was 41 per cent (Table 2.17). In 2002 the United Kingdom was among the EU countries with the highest levels of births outside marriage, together with Sweden, Denmark, France and Finland. The highest proportion was in Sweden with 56 per cent of births occurring outside marriage, while the lowest proportion was in Greece at 4 per cent.

The proportion of births occurring outside marriage differs across regions of the United Kingdom. In 2001 the North East at 51 per cent, had the highest proportion of all births outside marriage, 16 percentage points higher than the South East, which had the lowest rate at 35 per cent. Most of the increase in the number of births outside marriage since the late 1980s in the United Kingdom has been to cohabiting couples. In 2002 nearly 64 per cent of all live births outside marriage were jointly registered by parents living at the same address; more than twice the proportion in 1986.

Despite the overall trend towards later childbearing, the proportion of teenage girls in England and Wales becoming pregnant rose in the 1980s, but then fell slightly in the 1990s. There were almost 96,000 conceptions to girls aged under 20 in 2001 (Table 2.18). This is around

2,000 fewer than in 2000. There were nearly 8,000 conceptions among girls under the age of 16 in 2001, less than a tenth of the total number of conceptions to teenagers, and 200 fewer than in 2000. Of these conceptions in 2001, almost 400 were to girls under the age of 14, under half of which led to maternities. There was also a variation across age in the number of legal abortions. In 2002, 61 per cent of conceptions to 14 year olds resulted in legal abortions, this was 6 percentage points higher than the 15 year old group which was the next highest.

Throughout most of Western Europe, teenage birth rates have fallen rapidly since the 1970s. In the United Kingdom the rates have remained at the 1980s level or above. In 2001 the United Kingdom had the highest rate of live births to teenage girls in the EU, with an average of 29 live births per 1,000 girls aged 15–19. This was nearly 44 per cent higher than Portugal, the country with the next highest rate. Sweden and Italy had the lowest rates at around 7 live births per 1,000 girls aged 15–19.

Trends in abortion rates also vary by the age of the woman (Figure 2.19). Since 1969, following the introduction of the *Abortion Act 1967,* the abortion rates have risen, particularly for women aged 16 to 34. In 2002 the highest rate, of 30.3 per 1,000 women, occurred among 20 to 24 year olds. Women under 16 and women aged 35 and over have far lower rates than those in other age groups. In 2002, the abortion rate for women under 16 was 3.5 per 1,000 women; for women aged 35 and over it was 6.7 per 1,000 women.

During the early 1990s the abortion rate among young women fell slightly, but then rose again between 1995 and

Table **2.18**

Teenage conceptions[1]: by age at conception and outcome, 2001

England & Wales

	Number of conceptions		Rates per 1,000 women[2]	
	Leading to maternities	Leading to abortions	Leading to maternities	Leading to abortions
Under 14	179	219	0.5	0.7
14	729	1,154	2.2	3.5
15	2,585	3,025	8.0	9.4
All aged under 16	3,493	4,398	3.5	4.5
16	7,110	5,993	22.0	18.5
17	11,649	8,323	37.3	26.6
18	16,065	9,666	52.3	31.4
19	18,904	10,312	61.2	33.4
All aged under 20	57,221	38,693	36.3	24.6

1 See Appendix, Part 2: Conceptions.
2 Rates for girls aged under 14, under 16 and under 20 are based on the population of girls aged 13, 13–15, and 15–19, respectively.

Source: Office for National Statistics

Figure **2.19**

Abortion rates[1]: by age

England & Wales
Rates per 1,000 women

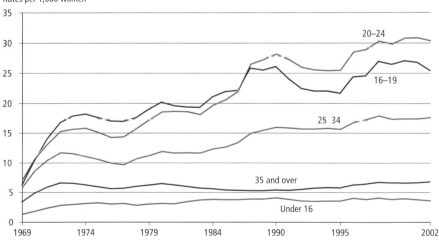

1 The rates for girls aged under 16 are based on the population of girls aged 13–15. The rates for females aged 35 and over are based on the population of females aged 35–44.

Source: Office for National Statistics; Department of Health

Figure **2.20**

Childless women at age 25, 35 and 45[1]: by year of birth

England & Wales
Percentages

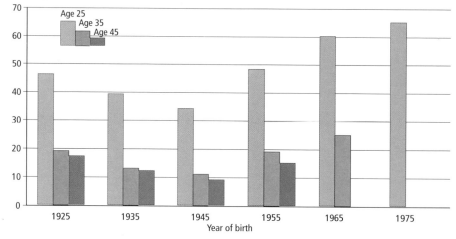

1 Includes births at ages over 45. Data for women aged 35 born in 1975 and for those aged 45 born since 1965 are not available.

Source: Office for National Statistics

Table **2.21**

Average age of mother[1]: by birth order[2]

England & Wales

Average age (years)

	1971	1981	1991	2001	2002
1st child	23.7	24.8	25.6	26.5	26.7
2nd child	26.4	27.3	28.2	29.3	29.5
3rd child	29.0	29.2	29.9	30.7	30.7
4th child	30.9	30.9	31.2	31.7	31.8
5th child and higher	33.6	33.8	33.3	34.1	34.1
All births	26.6	27.0	27.7	28.6	28.7

1 The average ages presented here have been standardised to take account of the changing population distribution of women.
2 See Appendix, Part 2: True birth order.

Source: Office for National Statistics

1996. This increase is thought to have been the result of a pill scare. In 1995 the Committee on Safety of Medicines warned that several brands of the contraceptive pill carried an increased risk of thrombosis. This warning is believed to have contributed to an increase in conceptions and a related increase in abortions in 1996, particularly among young women as they were more likely to have been using the pill. Following this pill scare the abortion rates did not fall back to the 1995 level but continued to rise.

Related to the trend of delaying childbirth, is the growth in the number of women remaining childless (Figure 2.20). Successive cohorts of women in England and Wales born since the Second World War have waited longer before starting a family. Eleven per cent of women born in 1925 were still childless at age 35; this increased to 25 per cent for women aged 35 born in 1965. It is expected that this trend will continue.

The average age of mothers at childbirth has increased by just over two years since 1971 when it was 26.6 years (Table 2.21). In 2002 the average age for first births was 26.7 years, three years older than in 1971. Women giving birth outside marriage tend to do so earlier than those giving birth inside marriage: 26.8 and 31.0 years respectively.

Although the average age of all mothers at childbirth is increasing, the average number of children women think they will have is still around two children per woman. Over time there has been a fall in the average intended family size for women aged 21 to 23 from 2.23 in 1979-81 to 2.14 at the turn of the 20th century.

Chapter 3 **Education and Training**

Schools

- In 2002/03, the average class size in Great Britain was 25 pupils for Key Stage 1 (5 to 7 year olds) and 27 pupils for Key Stage 2 (8 to 11 year olds). (Table 3.4)

- The highest exclusion rates in England were among Black Caribbean and Other Black pupils, with 42 and 36 exclusions, respectively, for every 10,000 pupils of compulsory school age in 2001/02. (Figure 3.8).

- In 2001/02, 53 per cent of pupils in the United Kingdom gained five or more GCSEs (or equivalent) at grades A* to C, compared with 46 per cent in 1995/96. (Page 42).

Post-compulsory outcomes

- In the United Kingdom, the proportion of young women who achieve two or more GCE A levels (or equivalent) has increased from 20 per cent in 1992/93 to 43 per cent in 2001/02. For young men over the same period, the increase has been from 18 per cent to 34 per cent. (Figure 3.14).

Educational resources

- The number of full-time qualified teachers within public sector mainstream schools in the United Kingdom has decreased by 11 per cent to 438,000 between 1981/82 and 2001/02, although numbers have been rising since 1998/99. (Figure 3.22).

- The number of non-teaching staff in England who provide additional learning support within the classroom increased by 91 per cent since 1996, to nearly 175,000 in 2003. (Table 3.23).

Figure **3.1**

Participation rates[1] of children aged 3–4[2] in maintained nursery and primary schools: by region, January 2003

Percentages

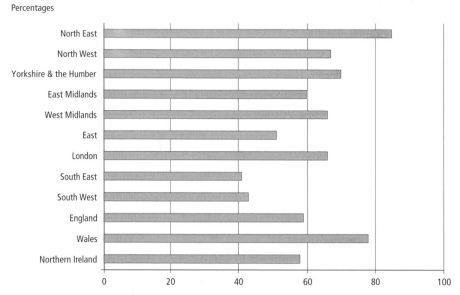

1 Number of three and four year olds attending provider expressed as a percentage of all three and four year olds. See Appendix, Part 3: Foundation stage.
2 Headcounts of children aged three and four may include some two year olds, and any child attending more than one provider may have been counted twice.

Source: Department for Education and Skills; National Assembly for Wales; Northern Ireland Department of Education

Table **3.2**

School pupils[1]: by type of school[2]

United Kingdom   Thousands

	1970/71	1980/81	1990/91	2000/01	2001/02	2002/03
Public sector schools						
Nursery	50	89	105	152	149	154
Primary	5,902	5,171	4,955	5,298	5,245	5,178
Secondary						
Comprehensive	1,313	3,730	2,925	3,340	3,390	3,434
Grammar	673	149	156	205	209	213
Modern	1,164	233	94	112	103	106
Other	403	434	298	260	247	242
All public sector schools	9,507	9,806	8,533	9,367	9,344	9,327
Non-maintained schools	621	619	613	626	635	644
Special schools	103	148	114	113	112	112
Pupil referral units	.	.	.	10	10	12
All schools	10,230	10,572	9,260	10,116	10,102	10,095

1 Headcounts.
2 See Appendix, Part 3: Main categories of educational establishments and Stages of education.

Source: Department for Education and Skills; National Assembly for Wales; Scottish Executive; Northern Ireland Department of Education

For increasing numbers of people, experience of education is no longer confined to compulsory schooling. Early learning and participation in pre-school education is seen as being important for building a foundation for future learning, and most people continue in full-time education beyond school-leaving age.

Many people return to education later in their lives, and qualifications attained at school are increasingly supplemented by further education and training to equip them with the skills required by a modern labour market.

Schools

There has been a major expansion in pre-school education over the last 30 years. The proportion of three and four year olds enrolled in schools in the United Kingdom rose from 26 per cent in 1972/73 to 65 per cent in 2002/03. This is due both to the expanding provision of places – there were around 3,800 state nursery schools in 2002/03, more than double the number in 1990/91 – and a fall in the three and four year old population in recent years. In 2002/03, 34 per cent were enrolled in other settings offering early education such as playgroups, either in addition to, or instead of, their school place. The pattern of participation varies regionally. Participation in maintained nursery and primary schools is generally higher in the north of England and Wales than in the south, where more children are enrolled with private and voluntary providers. Around twice the proportion of three and four year olds attended maintained nursery and primary schools in the North East compared with the South East and South West of England (Figure 3.1).

The number of children of school age in the United Kingdom has fluctuated due to factors such as changes in the birth rate (see Chapter 1, Population), and the raising of the school-leaving age in 1972. The declining birth rates during the late 1970s led to a fall in pupil numbers in the 1980s and early 1990s. Pupil numbers increased to 2000/01, but have declined since then, and are still below the peak level of the mid-1970s.

In 2002/03 there were over 34,500 schools in the United Kingdom, accommodating over 10 million pupils (Table 3.2). Public sector schools (not including special schools) were attended by over 9 million or 92 per cent of all pupils. Six per cent of pupils attended one of the 2,400 non-maintained schools. This proportion has remained unchanged since the mid-1990s, although there has been a rise in the number of pupils. One per cent of pupils attended one of the 1,500 special schools in 2002/03, and there were nearly 400 pupil referral units (PRUs), catering for 12,000 pupils. PRUs provide suitable alternative education on a temporary basis for pupils who may not be able to attend a mainstream school.

Most pupils who attend special schools have special educational needs (SEN), that is, they have significantly greater difficulty in learning than other children of the same age, or have a disability which makes it difficult to use normal educational facilities. Approximately 1.4 million pupils with SEN were identified in the United Kingdom in 2002/03. If an education authority or board believes that it should determine the education for a child with SEN, it must draw up a formal statement of those needs and the action it intends to take to meet them. Almost 300,000 pupils had these statements (called a Record of Needs in Scotland). In England, the number of

Figure **3.3**

Pupils with statements of Special Educational Needs (SEN): by type of school[1]

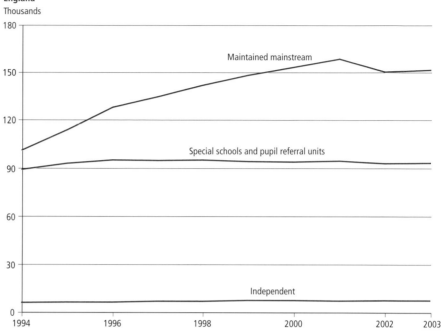

England
Thousands

1 Pupil referral units did not exist prior to 1995. Estimates were made for 2001 because the SEN data were known to be incomplete.

Source: Department for Education and Skills

pupils with statements of SEN increased from around 195,000 in 1994 to a peak of nearly 260,000 in 2001 (although data for that year are estimated). Numbers declined in 2002, and levelled off to around 250,000 in 2003, though the number of children for whom a statement is issued for the first time has decreased. While the number of pupils in special schools has remained fairly constant, the number of pupils with statements of SEN in mainstream maintained schools has increased by around 50 per cent from 1994, to 151,000 pupils in 2003 (Figure 3.3). In 2003, 60 per cent of pupils with statements of SEN were in maintained mainstream schools, 37 per cent were in special schools or pupil referral units and 3 per cent were in mainstream independent schools.

For several years, reductions have been made in class sizes in the drive to improve standards, particularly in the size of primary classes. In 2002/03, the average class size in Great Britain was 25 pupils for Key Stage 1 (5 to 7 year olds) and 27 pupils for Key Stage 2 (8 to 11 year olds) (Table 3.4 – see overleaf). Key Stage 2 pupils were far more likely to be in classes of more than 30 pupils than Key Stage 1 pupils, 22 per cent and 2 per cent, respectively. These proportions have fallen from 28 per cent and 4 per cent respectively, in 2000/01. Across the country, nearly 30 per cent of Key Stage 2 classes in the North West, East Midlands and South West had 31 or more pupils in 2002/03 compared with around one in ten in Northern Ireland and London. Average class sizes in Key Stages 3 and 4 (11 to

Table **3.4**

Class sizes in schools[1]: by region, 2002/03

	Key Stage 1[2]		Key Stage 2[2]		Key Stages 3 and 4	
	Average number in class	Percentage of classes with 31 or more pupils	Average number in class	Percentage of classes with 31 or more pupils	Average number in class	Percentage of classes with 31 or more pupils
Great Britain	25.3	1.7	27.1	22.4	21.9	..
England	25.6	1.7	27.4	23.5	21.9	8.2
North East	24.6	1.2	26.5	19.7	21.8	7.8
North West	25.0	1.3	27.5	28.8	21.8	8.9
Yorkshire & the Humber	25.5	2.4	27.4	24.6	22.1	8.4
East Midlands	24.9	1.9	27.7	28.2	22.0	8.0
West Midlands	25.7	1.8	27.3	22.9	21.9	8.7
East	25.4	2.2	27.4	21.9	21.6	7.7
London	27.0	1.5	27.4	12.7	22.1	6.6
South East	25.6	1.4	27.5	25.3	21.8	7.3
South West	25.5	1.3	27.3	27.9	22.3	10.5
Wales[3]	24.2	2.6	25.9	17.5	21.2	..
Scotland[3]	23.6	1.5	25.3	16.1	..	..
Northern Ireland	22.9	1.7	24.1	8.0	..	..

1 Maintained schools only. Figures relate to all classes - not just those taught by one teacher. In Northern Ireland a class is defined as a group of pupils normally under the control of one teacher.
2 Pupils in composite classes which overlap Key Stage 1 and Key Stage 2 are not included. In Scotland primary P1–P3 is interpreted to be Key Stage 1 and P4–P7, Key Stage 2.
3 Data for Wales and Scotland refer to 2001/02.

Source: Department for Education and Skills; National Assembly for Wales; Scottish Executive; Northern Ireland Department of Education

Table **3.5**

Adults' attitudes towards secondary schooling, 2002

Great Britain   Percentages

	Agree strongly	Agree	Neither agree nor disagree	Disagree	Disagree strongly	All[1]
Formal exams are the best way to judge pupils	5	43	20	27	3	100
On the whole pupils are too young when they have to decide which subjects to specialise in	10	53	20	14	1	100
The present law allows pupils to leave school when they are too young	4	25	30	37	3	100
So much attention is given to exam results that a pupil's everyday classroom work counts for too little	13	51	20	13	1	100

1 Includes respondents who did not answer.

Source: British Social Attitudes Survey, National Centre for Social Research

16 year olds) in England were around 22 pupils per class, despite there being far more pupils per secondary school than per primary school. This is in part because students choose different subjects in preparation for formal exams at the end of their compulsory secondary schooling.

The British Social Attitudes survey in 2002 asked adults aged 18 and over in Great Britain about their attitudes towards various aspects of secondary schooling. Nearly two thirds of those that gave a response felt that, on the whole, pupils are too young when they have to decide which subjects to specialise in (Table 3.5). This is mirrored by changes being introduced across the United Kingdom to post-primary education, such as the Welsh Baccalaureate in Wales and changes to the educational options for 14 to 19 year olds in England. However, while around half of those who responded believed that formal exams were the best way to judge pupils, nearly two thirds believed that the attention given to exam results meant that pupils' everyday classroom work counts for too little. Teacher assessment has become increasingly important, and is used to formally evaluate progress made against Key Stages in the National Curriculum.

The Key Stages form part of the National Curriculum in England and Wales, more details of which can be found in Appendix, Part 3: The National Curriculum. Scotland and Northern Ireland have their own schemes. In 2003, the proportion of boys in England reaching the required standard for English at all Key Stages was lower than that for girls, particularly at Key Stages 2 and 3 (Table 3.6). The difference between the proportions of boys and girls reaching the expected level in tests and teacher assessments for mathematics and science was less pronounced. The proportion of pupils achieving the expected level generally declined with age for both boys and girls. At Key Stage 1, 81 per cent of boys and 89 per cent of girls achieved the expected level in teacher assessments in English. By Key Stage 3, this had fallen to 60 per cent of boys and 75 per cent of girls. In science teacher assessments, 88 per cent of boys and 91 per cent of girls at Key Stage 1 reached the expected level, compared with 68 per cent and 70 per cent, respectively, at Key Stage 3.

Patterns of achievement at Key Stages 1 to 3 in Wales and teacher assessments in Northern Ireland in 2001/02 were similar to those in England, with the percentage of pupils achieving the expected level or above declining with age, and girls generally doing better than boys. In Scotland in 2001/02, the proportion of pupils achieving the expected levels set out in national guidelines also fell with age. In 2001/02, in the primary year 3 group (children aged around 7), 95 per cent of pupils attained the required standard or above in mathematics, while 87 per cent did so in reading and 85 per cent in writing. By the secondary year 2 group (children aged around 13), these percentages had dropped to 54, 59 and 50 per cent, respectively.

In 2001 the International Association for the Evaluation of Educational Achievement co-ordinated the Progress in International Reading Literacy Study (PIRLS). It assessed the reading abilities of over 150,000 ten year old pupils in 35 countries. Pupils in both England and Scotland were ranked above the standardised international average score of 500 (Figure 3.7), with English pupils ranked third in the countries taking part, behind Sweden and the Netherlands. In England, boys had the third highest

Table 3.6

Pupils reaching or exceeding expected standards[1]: by Key Stage and sex, 2003

England   Percentages

	Teacher assessment		Tests	
	Males	Females	Males	Females
Key Stage 1				
English	81	89	.	.
Reading	81	89	80	88
Writing	78	87	76	87
Mathematics	87	90	89	91
Science	88	91	.	.
Key Stage 2				
English	67	78	70	80
Mathematics	74	75	73	72
Science	81	83	86	87
Key Stage 3				
English	60	75	61	75
Mathematics	70	74	69	72
Science	68	70	68	68

1 See Appendix, Part 3: The National Curriculum.
Source: Department for Education and Skills

Figure 3.7

Mean score for reading achievement: G8 comparison[1], 2001

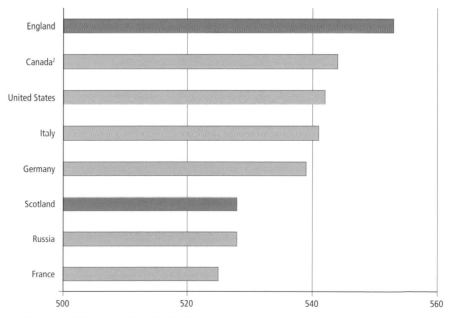

1 All pupils had four years formal schooling prior to test except in England and Scotland with five years and in Russia where some had three years. The countries shown are those that are members of the G8, excluding Japan who did not take part.
2 Ontario and Quebec only.
Source: Progress in International Reading Literacy Study; National Foundation for Educational Research

Figure **3.8**

Permanent exclusion rates[1]: by ethnic group, 2001/02

England
Rate per 10,000 pupils

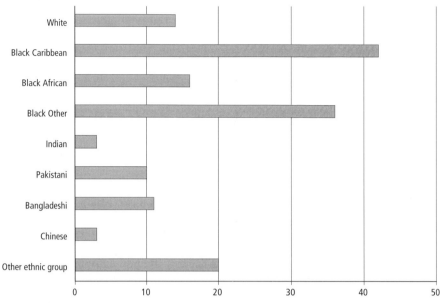

1 The number of permanent exclusions per 10,000 pupils (headcount) in each ethnic group in primary, secondary and special schools (excluding dually registered pupils in special schools) for compulsory school age.

Source: Department for Education and Skills

Table **3.9**

GCSE attainment[1]: by parents' socio-economic classification[2], 2002

England & Wales   Percentages

	5 or more GCSE grades A*–C	1–4 GCSE grades A*–C[3]	5 or more GCSE grades D–G	1–4 GCSE grades D–G	None reported	All
Higher professional	77	13	6	..	3	100
Lower professional	64	21	11	2	2	100
Intermediate	52	25	17	2	4	100
Lower supervisory	35	30	27	4	4	100
Routine	32	32	25	5	6	100
Other	32	29	26	4	9	100

1 For pupils in year 11. Includes equivalent GNVQ qualifications achieved in year 11.
2 See Appendix, Part 1: National Statistics Socio-economic Classification.
3 Consists of those with 1–4 GCSE grades A*–C and any number of other grades.

Source: Youth Cohort Study, Department for Education and Skills

score (541), behind those in Sweden and the Netherlands, and girls had the second highest score (564), exceeded only by Sweden. Scores in Scotland were 537 for girls and 519 for boys. In common with all other countries participating, in both England and Scotland the performance of girls was significantly better than that of boys.

There has been growing awareness and concern over the number of children outside the education system. Some have been excluded from schools, while others truant. In 2001/02, over 10,000 children in Great Britain were permanently excluded from schools. This was around 4 per cent higher than in the previous year, but still lower than in 1996/97, when over 13,000 children were permanently excluded. The number of boys permanently excluded again outnumbered girls by nearly five to one in 2001/02.

Exclusion rates vary by ethnic group. In 2001/02 the highest permanent exclusion rates in England were among Black Caribbean and Other Black pupils, with rates of 42 and 36 exclusions per 10,000 pupils of compulsory school age, respectively (Figure 3.8). These were nearly half the rates in 1996/97 – 78 and 71 pupils per 10,000, respectively. Rates were lowest for Indian and Chinese pupils. Exclusions were most common among those aged 13 and 14; pupils of these ages accounted for half of all permanent exclusions.

In England, Wales and Northern Ireland, young people aged 15 and 16 sit GCSEs, while Standard Grades are taken in Scotland. In 2001/02, 53 per cent of pupils in the United Kingdom gained five or more GCSEs (or equivalent) at grades A*–C, compared with 46 per cent in 1995/96. Pass rates have risen over the last few years for both sexes but again girls continue to outperform boys. In 2001/02, 58 per cent of girls gained five or more GCSEs at grades A*–C (or equivalent), compared with 47 per cent of boys.

The socio-economic status and educational attainment of parents can have a significant impact on the GCSE attainment of their children. In England and Wales, over three quarters of pupils whose parents were in the higher professional group achieved five or more GCSEs at grades A*–C (or the GNVQ equivalent) in 2002 (Table 3.9). Of those pupils whose parents were in the routine group, just a third achieved the same level. Furthermore, 71 per cent of young people whose parents were qualified to degree level and 60 per cent whose parents' highest qualification was a GCE A level achieved five or more GCSEs at grades A*–C, compared with 40 per cent with parents whose highest qualification was below GCE A level.

Post-compulsory participation

Following compulsory education, at the age of 16 young people can choose to continue in full-time education, go into training or seek employment. However, not everyone working towards a qualification beyond the age of 16 will have worked their way continuously through the various levels of education. Table 3.10 shows that while half of people of working age who were studying towards a qualification in the United Kingdom in spring 2003 were aged between 16 and 24, a fifth were aged 40 and over. These Labour Force Survey (LFS) estimates, and others used in the chapter, are not seasonally adjusted and have not been adjusted to take account of the Census 2001 results (see Appendix, Part 4: LFS reweighting).

Table **3.10**

People working towards a qualification[1]: by age, 2003[2]

United Kingdom

Percentages

	Degree or higher or equivalent	Higher education[3]	GCE A level or equivalent	GCSE or equivalent	Other qualification[4]	All studying
16–19	15	14	71	66	11	32
20–24	41	23	10	7	12	20
25–29	13	14	3	4	14	10
30–39	17	23	8	13	27	18
40–49	10	20	6	7	22	13
50–59/64	4	6	2	4	13	6
All aged 16–59/64[5]	100	100	100	100	100	100

1 For those working towards more than one qualification, the highest is recorded. See Appendix, Part 3: Qualifications.
2 At spring. These estimates are not seasonally adjusted and have not been adjusted to take account of the Census 2001 results. See Appendix, Part 4: LFS reweighting.
3 Below degree level but including NVQ level 4.
4 Includes those who did not state which qualifications.
5 Of working age population, defined as men aged 16–64 and women aged 16–59.

Source: Labour Force Survey, Office for National Statistics

The age distribution varies according to the level of qualification being undertaken. In spring 2003, around a fifth of people of working age studying towards a GCE A level or equivalent were over 25, compared with nearly half of those studying for a degree or equivalent.

There were nearly 5.4 million students in further education in the United Kingdom in 2001/02, 58 per cent of whom were female (Table 3.11 – see overleaf). There were more than four times as many female further education students as in 1970/71, but only around twice as many male students. Part-time students form the majority of those in further education, with 79 per cent of students studying in this way. Slightly more men study full-time than women, but far more women than men study part-time.

Table **3.11**

Students[1] in further and higher education: by type of course and sex

United Kingdom

Thousands

	Males				Females			
	1970/71	1980/81	1990/91	2001/02	1970/71	1980/81	1990/91	2001/02
Further education[2]								
Full-time	116	154	219	569	95	196	261	559
Part-time	891	697	768	1,665	630	624	986	2,562
All further education	1,007	851	987	2,234	725	820	1,247	3,121
Higher education[2]								
Undergraduate								
Full-time	241	277	345	519	173	196	319	620
Part-time	127	176	193	263	19	71	148	412
Postgraduate								
Full-time	33	41	50	94	10	21	34	93
Part-time	15	32	50	133	3	13	36	153
All higher education[3]	416	526	638	1,009	205	301	537	1,279

1 Home and overseas students.
2 See Appendix, Part 3: Stages of education.
3 Figures for 2001/02 include a number of higher education students for which details are not available by level.

Source: Department for Education and Skills; National Assembly for Wales; Scottish Executive; Northern Ireland Department for Employment and Learning; Higher Education Statistics Agency

Figure **3.12**

GCE A level or equivalent entries for young people[1]: by selected subject, 2001/02

United Kingdom
Percentages

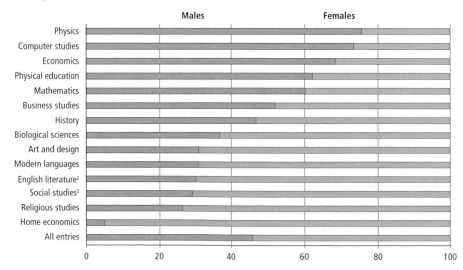

1 Pupils in schools and students in further education institutions aged 16-18 at the start of the academic year in England and in Northern Ireland, and aged 17 in Wales. Pupils in Scotland generally sit Highers one year earlier and the figures relate to the result of pupils in Year S5/S6.
2 England and Wales only.

Source: Department for Education and Skills; National Assembly for Wales; Scottish Executive; Northern Ireland Department of Education

There have also been substantial increases in the number of students in higher education over the last 30 years. In 2001/02 there were nearly 2.3 million students in higher education, 56 per cent of whom were female. For women, there were six times as many students in higher education in 2001/02 as in 1970/71. For men, there were nearly two and a half times as many students in 2001/02 as in 1970/71.

There is a wide variety of subjects available for those who continue with their education, although gender differences in subject choice do exist (Figure 3.12). In 2001/02, around 75 per cent of young people aged around 16 to 18 who entered for GCE A level (or equivalent) physics and computer studies in the United Kingdom, and 60 per cent of those entered for mathematics, were men. In comparison, around 70 per cent of entries for social studies and English literature, and 95 per cent of entries for home economics, were women. However, a predominance of one sex does not indicate the likelihood of achieving a high grade in a given subject. For example, 75 per cent of women achieved grades A–C in physics, compared with 65 per cent of men.

Young people in manual social classes remain under-represented in higher education in Great Britain. Despite increasing from a participation rate of 11 per cent in 1991/92 to 19 per cent in 2001/02, participation remains well below that of the non-manual social classes. Participation rates for the non-manual social classes increased from 35 per cent to 50 per cent over the same period (Figure 3.13).

The percentage of students from minority ethnic groups accepted to higher education institutions in the United Kingdom through the Universities and Colleges Admissions Service (UCAS) has also increased. Students of Indian origin continued to make up the largest proportion of non-White undergraduates – 4.2 per cent of all undergraduates in 2002/03 compared with 3.8 per cent in 1990/91 and 4.8 per cent in 2001/02. Students of Black African origin, however, have seen the largest increase since 1990/91, up from 0.7 per cent to 1.9 per cent.

Post-compulsory outcomes

The GCE A level is usually taken after GCSEs and a further two years of study in a sixth form or equivalent in England, Scotland and Northern Ireland. In Scotland, Higher and Advanced Higher qualifications are usually taken at ages 17 and 18, as part of the National Qualifications framework. The proportion

Figure **3.13**

Participation rates in higher education: by social class[1]

Great Britain
Percentages

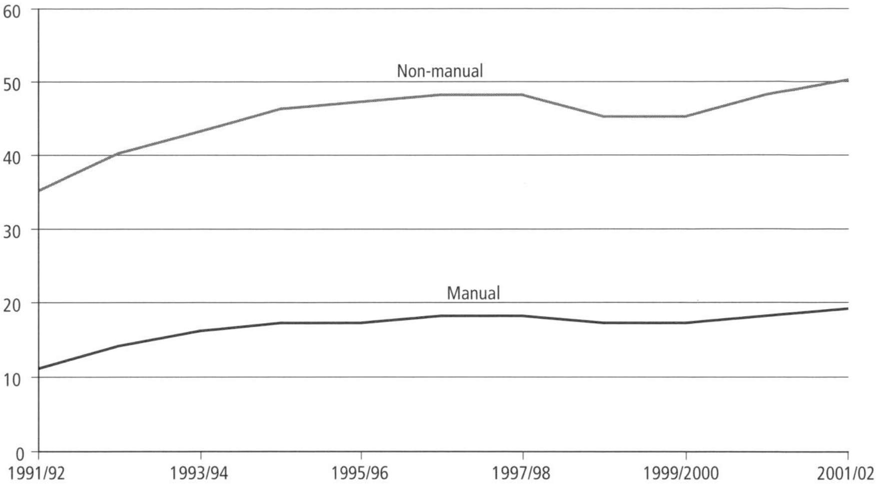

Chart showing Non-manual and Manual participation rates from 1991/92 to 2001/02. Non-manual rises from 35 to 50 per cent. Manual rises from 11 to 19 per cent.

1   See Appendix, Part 3: Social class.
Source: Department for Education and Skills

of pupils in the United Kingdom gaining two or more GCE A levels (or equivalent) has increased from 30 per cent in 1995/96 to 39 per cent in 2001/02. The proportion of young women who achieve this has increased from 20 per cent in 1992/93 to 43 per cent in 2001/02 (Figure 3.14). For young men over the same period, the increase has been from 18 per cent to 34 per cent. This performance gap between the sexes has widened to 9 percentage points, from just under 2 percentage points in 1992/93.

An alternative to the more traditional and academic GCE A levels (or equivalent) are National Vocational Qualifications (NVQs). Since their introduction in 1987, over 4 million NVQs and Scottish Vocational Qualifications (SVQs) had been awarded in the United Kingdom by September 2002. In 2001/02, 408,000 NVQs and SVQs were awarded, 5 per cent

Figure **3.14**

Achievement at GCE A level[1] or equivalent

United Kingdom
Percentages

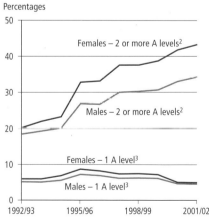

Chart showing Females – 2 or more A levels[2], Males – 2 or more A levels[2], Females – 1 A level[3], and Males – 1 A level[3] from 1992/93 to 2001/02.

1   2 AS levels count as 1 A level pass. Data from 2000/01 are not on the same basis as earlier years, and data prior to 1995/96 refer to school pupils only.
2   Equivalent to 3 or more Highers.
3   Equivalent to 1 or 2 Highers. Includes those with 1.5 A levels.

Source: Department for Education and Skills; National Assembly for Wales; Scottish Executive; Northern Ireland Department of Education

Table **3.15**

NVQ/SVQ awards[1]: by framework area and level, 2001/02

United Kingdom   Thousands

	Level 1	Level 2	Level 3	Level 4 & 5	Total
Providing goods and services	26.2	71.5	17.3	..	115.1
Providing business services	5.0	51.9	32.0	11.2	100.0
Providing health, social and protective services	..	32.2	29.1	2.6	64.5
Constructing	5.0	25.6	13.0	..	43.8
Engineering	2.7	15.8	14.1	..	32.7
Manufacturing	4.4	19.9	1.2	1.0	26.5
Tending animals, plants and land	2.8	6.3	1.7	..	10.8
Other[2]	..	7.5	4.5	1.1	14.2
Total	47.0	231.4	113.5	16.6	408.4

1 Missing figures were less than 1,000. See Appendix, Part 3: Qualifications.
2 Includes transporting, developing and extending skill and knowledge, extracting and providing natural resources, communicating and other not classified.

Source: Department for Education and Skills, from the National Information System for Vocational Qualifications

Figure **3.16**

Graduation rates from first university degrees: EU comparison[1], 2001

Percentages

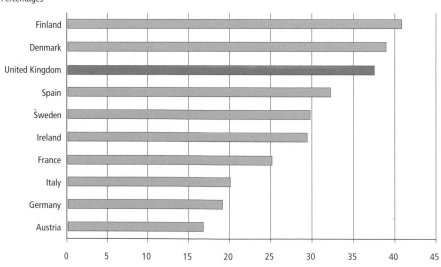

1 Data are not available for Belgium, Greece, Luxembourg, Netherlands and Portugal.

Source: Organisation for Economic Co-operation and Development

fewer than in the previous year (Table 3.15). The majority awarded were at level 2, accounting for 57 per cent of such qualifications. Over a quarter of NVQs and SVQs were in areas providing goods and services (such as catering and tourism). A further quarter in areas providing business services (such as management studies). Around 14,000 NVQ and SVQ awards were in other areas such as transporting, extracting and providing natural resources, and communicating.

Graduation rates from university vary across the European Union (EU). In 2001 the United Kingdom had the third highest graduation rate from first university degrees at 37 per cent, behind Finland and Denmark (Figure 3.16). The graduation rate in Austria, at 17 per cent, was lower than in any other EU country for which data were available. A possible explanation for the difference in graduation rates across the countries is the variation in provision of non-university education. Alternative vocational education and apprenticeships for example, may reduce the perceived need of some students to enrol in formal university-level studies as preparation for work.

In spring 2003, 18 per cent of men, and 15 per cent of women of working age in Great Britain held a degree or equivalent. This, however, is influenced by historic social effects, as the proportion of working age men aged 55 and over with a degree or equivalent is nearly double that of women.

The highest qualification held varies between the different ethnic groups. The ethnic group with the largest proportion of men holding a qualification above GCSE grade A*–C (or equivalent) in spring 2003 was White (57 per cent), whereas for women it was Chinese (49 per cent) (Table 3.17). The ethnic groups with the lowest proportions holding

Table **3.17**

Highest qualification held[1]: by sex and ethnic group, 2003[2]

Great Britain

Percentages

	Degree or equivalent	Higher education qualification[3]	GCE A level or equivalent	GCSE grades A*–C or equivalent	Other qualification	No qualification	All
Males							
White	18	8	31	18	12	13	100
Mixed	14	7	21	22	17	17	100
Asian or Asian British	20	6	17	11	24	20	100
Black or Black British	19	7	21	16	23	12	100
Chinese	29	4	19	9	28	10	100
Other ethnic group[4]	23	6	11	7	36	18	100
All	18	8	29	17	14	13	100
Females							
White	15	10	18	27	13	16	100
Mixed	21	9	17	21	15	17	100
Asian or Asian British	14	6	13	17	25	24	100
Black or Black British	13	12	16	21	24	13	100
Chinese	26	9	14	10	30	11	100
Other ethnic group[4]	14	9	11	10	34	22	100
All	15	10	18	26	14	16	100

1 Males aged 16 to 64, females aged 16 to 59.
2 At spring. These estimates are not seasonally adjusted and have not been adjusted to take account of the Census 2001 results. See Appendix, Part 4: LFS reweighting.
3 Below degree level.
4 Includes those who did not state their ethnic group.

Source: Department for Education and Skills, from the Labour Force Survey

these qualifications were 'Other' for men (40 per cent) and Asian or Asian British for women (33 per cent). The Asian or Asian British group were the most likely to hold no qualifications for both men and women.

Adult training and learning

Learning throughout working life is becoming increasingly necessary because of the pace of change within the labour market, and many people receive training in the workplace. Training is seen by a large number of employers as an essential investment for the future, and in 2002, 90 per cent of employers in England reported providing job-related training in the previous 12 months. In spring 2003, nearly 16 per cent of employees of working age in the United Kingdom had received some

job-related training in the four weeks prior to interview in the LFS, about the same as for the last ten years. In general, greater proportions of women than men received such training, and the proportion declined as the age of the employees increased. Men aged 16 to 17 and women aged 18 to 24 were the most likely to have received job-related training (Figure 3.18 – see overleaf).

There are various education and training options available to young people who decide not to continue in full-time education, including a number of government-supported training initiatives. In England and Wales, Work-based Training for Young People (WBTYP) – now known as Work-based Learning for Young People (WBLYP) in England – was introduced in 1998 (replacing Youth Training) with the aim of ensuring that

Figure **3.18**

Employees[1] receiving job-related training[2]: by age and sex, 2003[3]

United Kingdom
Percentages

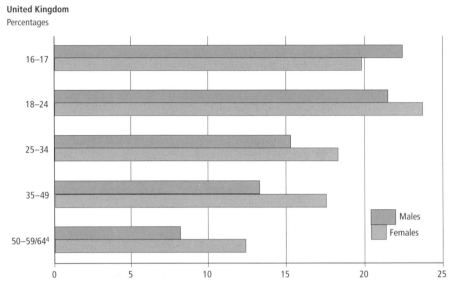

1 Employees are those in employment excluding the self-employed, unpaid family workers and those on government programmes.
2 Percentage who received job-related training in the four weeks before interview.
3 At spring. These estimates are not seasonally adjusted and have not been adjusted to take account of the Census 2001 results. See Appendix, Part 4: LFS reweighting.
4 Males aged 50–64, females aged 50–59.

Source: Department for Education and Skills, from the Labour Force Survey

Figure **3.19**

People in Work Based Learning[1]: by sex and selected area of learning, November 2002

England
Percentages

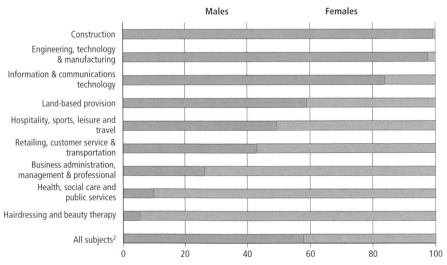

1 Work Based Learning includes Advanced Modern Apprenticeships, Foundation Modern Apprenticeships, NVQ Learning, Life Skills, Preparatory Training and Entry to Employment (E2E) Pathfinders.
2 Includes science and mathematics, visual and performing arts and media, and people whose area of learning is not known.

Source: Learning and Skills Council

all young people have access to post-compulsory education or training. Included within this initiative are Advanced Modern Apprenticeships (AMAs) and Foundation Modern Apprenticeships (FMAs) – AMAs and FMAs are called Modern Apprenticeships and National Traineeships in Wales. AMAs are aimed at developing technical, supervisory and craft-level skills among 16 to 24 year olds. In November 2002 there were 284,000 young people on Work Based Learning Schemes in England.

Some Work Based Learning areas contain a much greater proportion of one sex than the other. In November 2002, almost all participants in England in the areas of construction, and engineering, technology and manufacturing were men (Figure 3.19). In contrast, women greatly outnumbered men in health, social care and public services, and hairdressing and beauty therapy.

Many adults continue their education outside the work environment, either for enjoyment or to develop new skills. In November 2002, there were 1.1 million enrolments on adult education courses in England and Wales, around three quarters of whom were women (Table 3.20). In England, enrolments in daytime classes increased from 514,000 in November 1995 to 580,000 in November 2002. Evening and open distance learning course enrolments decreased from 639,000 to 461,000 over the same period. Over a third of enrolments were for courses that usually lead to a qualification (known as former Schedule 2 courses). The rest were for courses such as physical education, sports and fitness, or practical crafts, although these courses have seen a 20 per cent decrease in the number of enrolments since 1995.

Educational resources

Spending on education varies across the EU. According to the Organisation for Economic Co-operation and Development, the United Kingdom spent 5.3 per cent of Gross Domestic Product (GDP) on education in 2000 (Table 3.21). Most of this, 4.5 per cent of GDP, came from public sources. The United Kingdom was ranked towards the middle of the range of EU countries for such expenditure. Denmark spent the most on education at all levels as a proportion of GDP at 6.7 per cent and Greece the least at 4.0 per cent. Spending as a proportion of GDP increased between 1999 and 2000 in the United Kingdom, but was still below that in 1995.

In 2002/03, recurrent expenditure by central and local government on schools in England was an estimated £27.8 billion, 64 per cent of all education spending. This was an overall increase of 34 per cent in real terms since 1997/98, with spending on under 5s, primary and secondary schools increasing by 59 per cent, 25 per cent and 29 per cent, respectively. Secondary schools accounted for the greatest percentage of expenditure (43 per cent in 2002/03), despite there being many more primary school pupils. In 2001/02 in LEA maintained schools in England, expenditure per full-time equivalent pupil at 2001/02 prices was £2,540 in nursery and primary schools and £3,120 in secondary schools.

Within nursery and primary, and secondary public sector mainstream schools in the United Kingdom the numbers of full-time qualified teachers decreased by around 54,000 between 1981/82 and 2001/02 to 438,000, although they have been rising since 1998/99. The number of full-time female teachers in these schools

Table 3.20

Enrolments on adult education courses[1]: by age, attendance mode and sex, 2002

England & Wales

Thousands

	Under 19	19 to 59	60 and over	All ages[2]
Daytime				
Males	11.7	79.5	50.2	147.1
Females	19.1	280.6	147.2	462.3
Other[3]				
Males	6.3	105.7	27.2	145.0
Females	11.7	271.7	47.2	343.1
All				
Males	18.0	185.2	77.4	292.1
Females	30.8	552.3	194.4	805.3
All enrolments	48.7	737.5	271.8	1,097.5

1 Enrolments based on a snapshot as at 1 November in England, and leavers enrolled in the week of 1 December in Wales.
2 Includes figures for Wales which are not available by age and sex.
3 Includes evening courses, open distance learning and link students (school pupils in regular daytime attendance at a further education college).

Source: Department for Education and Skills; National Assembly for Wales

Table 3.21

Expenditure on education[1] as a percentage of GDP: EU comparison, 2000

Percentages

	Primary and secondary education	Higher education	All levels[2]
Denmark	4.2	1.6	6.7
Sweden	4.4	1.7	6.5
France	4.3	1.1	6.1
Austria	3.9	1.2	5.7
Portugal	4.1	1.1	5.7
Finland	3.5	1.7	5.6
Belgium	3.6	1.3	5.5
United Kingdom	3.8	1.0	5.3
Germany	3.6	1.0	5.3
Spain	3.3	1.2	4.9
Italy	3.3	0.9	4.9
Netherlands	3.1	1.2	4.7
Ireland	3.0	1.5	4.6
Greece	3.0	0.9	4.0
Luxembourg	..	..	..

1 Direct expenditure for institutions and public subsidies to students, eg for tuition fees and living costs.
2 Includes expenditure for early childhood education and other miscellaneous expenditure.

Source: Organisation for Economic Co-operation and Development

Figure **3.22**

Full-time nursery & primary and secondary school teachers[1]: by sex

United Kingdom
Thousands

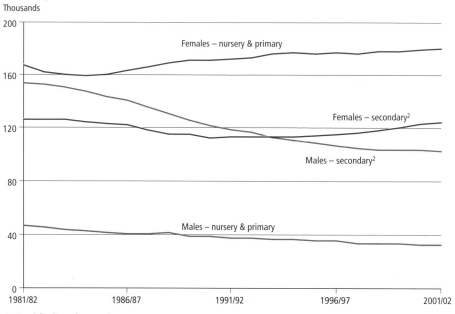

1 Qualified teachers only.
2 From 1993/94 data exclude sixth form colleges in England and Wales which were reclassified as further education colleges on 1 April 1993.

Source: Department for Education and Skills; Scottish Executive; Northern Ireland Department of Education

Figure **3.23**

Non-teaching staff[1]: by type of school

England
Thousands

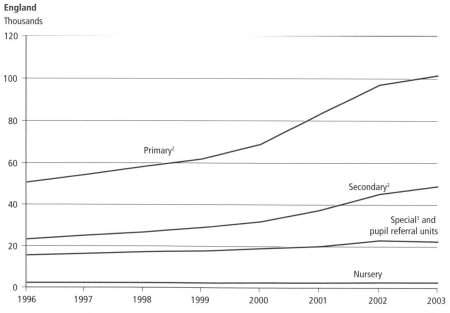

1 In maintained schools. Includes teaching assistants, technicians and other non-teaching staff but excludes administrative staff. Includes both full-time and the full-time equivalent of part-time non-teaching staff.
2 Includes middle schools as deemed.
3 Includes non-maintained special schools.

Source: Department for Education and Skills

increased by 4 per cent to 304,000 over the 20 year period, while the number of male teachers fell by 33 per cent to 134,000 (Figure 3.22). Overall, women represented the majority of full-time teachers – in nursery and primary schools 85 per cent were female in 2001/02, while for secondary schools it was more balanced, with females comprising 55 per cent.

An evaluation of the impact of teaching assistants in primary schools found that teachers value their support and appreciate the benefits of having another adult in the classroom. The number of non-teaching staff in England who provide additional learning support within the classroom increased by 91 per cent between 1996 and 2003, to nearly 175,000 (Figure 3.23). An increase in the number of non-teaching staff occurred in all types of school, but the largest percentage increase was in secondary schools, where the numbers more than doubled. However, most non-teaching staff are found in primary schools, accounting for the placement of nearly three fifths of these staff in 2003.

Financial support for students in higher education has changed considerably in recent years. In 2002/03, 82 per cent of eligible students in the United Kingdom took out a loan to support them through higher education, averaging just over £3,100. The average loan value has increased as the maintenance grant has decreased. In England and Wales in 2002/03, the maximum amount available for all those receiving student support through the full-year loan and basic mandatory grant was 3 per cent higher in real terms than in 1990/91, at £3,905.

Chapter 4 **Labour Market**

Economic activity

- In the United Kingdom the economic activity rate for working age males fell from 89 per cent in 1984 to 84 per cent in 2003, while the rate for working age females rose, from 67 per cent to 73 per cent. (Figure 4.1)

- In spring 2003 there were 28.1 million people in employment in the United Kingdom, the highest number since records began. (Table 4.2)

Employment

- Ninety per cent of working age men and 85 per cent of working age women in the United Kingdom, who had a degree or the equivalent, were in employment in spring 2003. This compares with 57 per cent of working age men and 44 per cent of working age women who did not have any qualifications. (Table 4.12)

Patterns of employment

- In Great Britain in 2001–02 around one in five of Pakistani and Chinese people in employment were self-employed, compared with around one in ten White British people and less than one in ten Black people. (Page 61)

- Around 21 per cent of employees working full time in the United Kingdom and 25 per cent of those working part time had some type of flexible working arrangement in spring 2003. (Table 4.18)

Unemployment

- In 2001 unemployment in the United Kingdom was 1.44 million, its lowest level since 1990. Unemployment increased slightly to 1.53 million people in spring 2002, but then fell slightly again by spring 2003 to 1.48 million. (Figure 4.19)

Figure **4.1**

Economic activity rates[1]: by sex

United Kingdom
Percentages

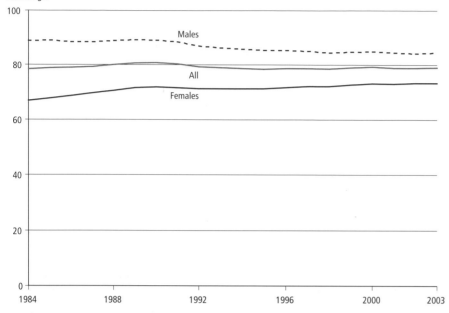

1 Males aged 16 to 64, females aged 16 to 59. The percentage of the population that is in the labour force. At spring. Data are seasonally adjusted, and have been adjusted to take account of the Census 2001 results. See Appendix, Part 4: LFS reweighting.

Source: Labour Force Survey, Office for National Statistics

Labour Force Survey (LFS) data

The results from the 2001 Census, published in September 2002, showed that previous estimates of the total UK population were around one million too high. As a result, ONS published interim revised estimates of the population for the years 1982 to 2001 which are consistent with the 2001 Census findings. Interim national LFS estimates consistent with the latest population data have now been produced. Initial analysis work conducted by the ONS has shown that revisions to the LFS census-adjusted data have a greater impact on levels data than on rates. Generally, revisions to rates are within sampling variability, while those for levels are not. This chapter uses adjusted data where possible, however where adjusted data are not available only rates have been used. For more information, see Appendix, Part 4: Labour Force Survey (LFS) reweighting.

Most people spend a large part of their lives in the labour force, and so their experience of the world of work has an important impact on their lives and attitudes. The proportion of time in the labour force has been falling. Young people are remaining longer in education and older people, due to the increase in longevity, are spending more years in retirement. More women than ever before are in paid employment, and employment in service industries continues to increase while employment in manufacturing continues to fall.

Economic activity

People are considered to be economically active, or in the labour force, if they are aged 16 and over and are either in work or actively looking for work. In the United Kingdom, the proportion of economically active men has fallen and the proportion of economically active women has increased over the long term. The male economic activity rate fell from 89 per cent in 1984 to 84 per cent in 2003 (Figure 4.1). The female economic activity rate on the other hand rose steadily, from 67 per cent in 1984 to 73 per cent in 2003. The gap between economic activity rates for men and women has halved from 22 percentage points in 1984 to 11 percentage points in 2003. As the economically active include those who are unemployed (see Glossary on page 54), the rates are less liable to be affected by the economic cycle than employment rates.

In spring 2003 there were 28.1 million people in employment in the United Kingdom (Table 4.2). This is the highest number of people in employment on record. Comparing the labour market in spring 2003 with that in spring 1988, data from the Labour Force Survey (LFS) show that the number of people in employment has risen by over 2 million, as more people are working full time or part time, or are self-employed, and fewer people are unemployed. Twenty six per cent of employees were working part time in spring 2003, when 81 per cent of part-time workers were women. The number of part-time workers has increased by almost a third since 1988. Two and a half times as many men as women were self-employed (2.4 million compared with 0.9 million).

Economic activity rates in the United Kingdom differ with age. In spring 2003, rates were highest for 25 to 34 and 35 to 49 year old men at around 92 per cent, while for women the rate was highest for 35 to 49 year olds at 78 per cent (Figure 4.3). People over the state retirement age (65 for men and 60 for women) can also be economically active, although the rates are low: 9 per cent for both men over 65 and women over 60.

Although economic activity rates for men have fallen over the last 10 years while the rates for women have risen, there have been different trends for men and women of different ages. The largest decrease in the economic activity rate between spring 1993 and spring 2003 was for 18 to 24 year old men (5 percentage points). The largest increase was for 50 to 59 year old women (7 percentage points).

Employment rates of young people (aged 16 to 24) are affected by whether or not they are in full-time education. Rates are far higher for those not in full-time education. Among those not in full-time education young men were more likely than young women to be in employment (79 per cent compared with 69 per cent) and also to be

Table **4.2**

Economic activity: by employment status and sex, 1988 and 2003[1]

United Kingdom   Millions

	1988			2003		
	Males	Females	All	Males	Females	All
Economically active						
In employment						
Full-time employees	11.4	5.8	17.2	11.5	6.7	18.3
Part-time employees	0.6	4.3	4.8	1.2	5.1	6.3
Self-employed	2.4	0.8	3.2	2.4	0.9	3.3
Others in employment[2]	0.3	0.2	0.6	0.1	0.1	0.2
All in employment	14.7	11.1	25.8	15.2	12.9	28.1
Unemployed[3]	1.5	1.0	2.5	0.9	0.6	1.5
All economically active	16.2	12.1	28.3	16.1	13.5	29.6
Economically inactive	5.2	11.1	16.2	6.5	10.8	17.3

1 At spring each year. Data are seasonally adjusted and have been adjusted to take account of the Census 2001 results. See Appendix, Part 4: LFS reweighting.
2 Those on government-supported training and employment programmes, and, for 2003, also unpaid family workers.
3 See Appendix, Part 4: Unemployment.

Source: Labour Force Survey, Office for National Statistics

Figure **4.3**

Economic activity rates[1]: by sex and age, 2003[2]

United Kingdom
Percentages

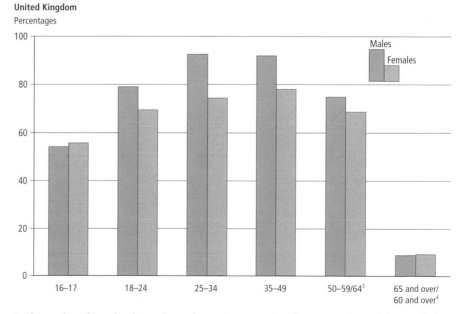

1 The number of people who are in employment or unemployed as a percentage of the population.
2 At spring. Data are seasonally adjusted and have been adjusted to take account of the Census 2001 results. See Appendix, Part 4: LFS reweighting.
3 Males aged 50–64, females aged 50–59.
4 Males aged 65 and over, females aged 60 and over.

Source: Labour Force Survey, Office for National Statistics

Table **4.4**

Economic activity status of young people[1]: by whether in full-time education, 2003[2]

United Kingdom   Percentages

	In full-time education		Not in full-time education		
	Males	Females	Males	Females	All
Economically active					
In employment	35	43	79	69	61
Unemployed	6	6	13	8	9
All economically active	41	49	92	77	70
Economically inactive	59	51	8	23	30
All (=100%) (thousands)	1,211	1,273	2,101	2,004	6,588

1 Aged 16 to 24.
2 At spring. Data are seasonally adjusted and have been adjusted to take account of the Census 2001 results. See Appendix, Part 4: LFS reweighting.

Source: Labour Force Survey, Office for National Statistics

unemployed (13 per cent compared with 8 per cent) (Table 4.4). Conversely, for those in full-time education young women have higher employment rates than young men (43 per cent compared with 35 per cent). The employment rates for both young men and young women in full-time education fluctuated in the early 1990s and peaked at 41 per cent in spring 2000.

One of the main themes in this chapter is the increased participation of women in the labour market over the last three decades. The labour market participation patterns of women without dependent children are fairly similar whether they are married or cohabiting, or neither (Table 4.5). However, the likelihood of women

Glossary of terms

Employees (Labour Force Survey measure) – a measure, obtained from household surveys, of people aged 16 and over who regard themselves as paid employees. People with two or more jobs are counted only once.

Self-employed – a measure, obtained from household surveys, of people aged 16 and over who regard themselves as self-employed, that is, who in their main employment work on their own account, whether or not they have employees.

In employment – a measure, obtained from household surveys and censuses, of employees, self-employed people, participants in government employment and training programmes, and people doing unpaid family work.

Government employment and training programmes – a measure, obtained from household surveys, of those who said they were participants on Youth Training, Training for Work, Employment Action or Community Industry or a programme organised by the Learning and Skills Council (LSC) in England and the National Council for Education and Training for Wales (ELWa), together with LECs in Scotland.

Unemployment – the measure based on International Labour Organisation (ILO) guidelines, and used in the Labour Force Survey, which counts as unemployed those aged 16 and over who are without a job, are available to start work in the next two weeks, who have been seeking a job in the last four weeks or are waiting to start a job already obtained.

Economically active (labour force) – those in employment plus those unemployed.

Unemployment rate – the percentage of the economically active who are unemployed.

Economically inactive – people who are neither in employment nor unemployment. For example, all people under 16, those looking after a home or retired, or those permanently unable to work.

Economic activity rate – the percentage of the population in a given age group which is economically active.

Working age household – a household that includes at least one person of working age.

Workless household – a household that includes at least one person of working age where no-one is in employment.

being economically active varies considerably according to whether or not they have dependent children. For both lone mothers and for those with a partner, economic activity rates are lowest when they have a child under five. However, lone mothers with a pre-school child are less likely to be working than mothers with a partner (33 per cent compared with 58 per cent). This differential decreases with the age of the child, so that for mothers whose youngest child is aged 16 to 18, 72 per cent of lone mothers work, compared with 80 per cent of mothers with a partner.

Another factor which can affect labour market participation patterns is whether or not a person is disabled. In spring 2003 there were about 7 million people of working age with long-term disabilities in the United Kingdom, of whom just under half were in employment (Table 4.6). People without a disability were much more likely to be in employment than those who had a disability (81 per cent compared with 49 per cent). Disabled people were much more likely to be economically inactive than people without a disability (47 per cent compared with 15 per cent). This difference was greater for men than for women. Among the economically inactive, those with disabilities were more likely than non-disabled people to want a job – this was the case for both men and women.

People can be economically inactive for a number of reasons: some do not want a job, while others want a job but are either not available for, or are not seeking, work. In spring 2003 there were 7.7 million people of working age who were economically inactive in the United Kingdom. Approximately three quarters did not want a job while just under a quarter wanted a job but had

Table **4.5**

Economic activity status of women[1]: by marital status and age of youngest dependent child, 2003

United Kingdom — Percentages

	Age of youngest dependent child				No dependent children	All women
	Under 5	5–10	11–15	16–18[2]		
Not married/cohabiting[3]						
Working full time	10	21	35	46	46	40
Working part time	23	31	32	26	21	23
Unemployed[4]	5	7	5	6	5	5
Economically inactive	62	40	28	22	28	33
All	100	100	100	100	100	100
Married/cohabiting						
Working full time	19	28	39	41	52	40
Working part time	39	48	42	39	25	34
Unemployed[4]	2	2	1	1	2	2
Economically inactive	40	22	17	19	20	24
All	100	100	100	100	100	100

1 Aged 16 to 59. At spring. These estimates are not seasonally adjusted and have not been adjusted to take account of the Census 2001 results. See Appendix, Part 4: LFS reweighting.
2 Those in full-time education.
3 Includes single, widowed, separated or divorced.
4 See Appendix, Part 4: Unemployment.

Source: Labour Force Survey, Office for National Statistics

Table **4.6**

Economic activity status of working age people[1]: by sex and whether disabled[2], 2003[3]

United Kingdom — Percentages

	Men		Women		All	
	Disabled	Not disabled	Disabled	Not disabled	Disabled	Not disabled
Economically active						
In employment	51	86	46	75	49	81
Unemployed	5	4	3	3	4	4
All economically active	57	90	49	78	53	85
Economically inactive						
Wants a job	15	2	15	5	15	4
Does not want a job	28	7	36	17	32	12
All economically inactive	43	10	51	22	47	15

1 Males aged 16 to 64, females aged 16 to 59.
2 Current long-term health problem or disability.
3 At spring. Data are not seasonally adjusted and have not been adjusted to take account of the Census 2001 results. See Appendix, Part 4: LFS reweighting.

Source: Labour Force Survey, Office for National Statistics

Table **4.7**

Reasons for economic inactivity[1]: by sex, 2003[2]

United Kingdom

Percentages

	Males	Females	All
Does not want a job			
Looking after family or home	4	35	23
Long-term sick or disabled	24	14	18
Student	24	15	18
Other	19	10	14
All	70	74	73
Wants a job but not seeking in last four weeks			
Looking after family or home	2	10	7
Long-term sick or disabled	14	6	9
Student	4	3	3
Discouraged worker[3]	1	-	-
Other	5	4	4
All	26	23	24
Wants a job and seeking work but not available to start[4]	4	2	3
All reasons	100	100	100

1 Males aged 16 to 64, females aged 16 to 59.
2 At spring. Data are not seasonally adjusted and have not been adjusted to take account of the Census 2001 results. See Appendix, Part 4: LFS reweighting.
3 People who believed no jobs were available.
4 Not available for work in the next two weeks. Includes those who did not state whether or not they were available.

Source: Labour Force Survey, Office for National Statistics

not sought work in the last four weeks (Table 4.7). We have already seen that looking after a family is a major factor in women's labour market participation and this was the reason given by about half the women who said they did not want a job. For men, long-term sickness or disability and being a student were the major reasons for not wanting a job.

There are now more people in the United Kingdom in employment than at any other time in the post-war period, and most working age households are work-rich – that is, households which include at least one person of working age and where all the people of working age are in employment. There were 11 million work-rich households in spring 2003, an increase of just over 800,000 since spring 1998. Work-rich households, as a proportion of all working age households, have risen from 50 per cent in 1992 to level off at 58 per cent in 2001 to 2003 (Figure 4.8). In spring 2003 around 16 per cent of working age households were workless – that is, households where at least one person is of working age but no-one is in employment. Although this proportion was virtually the same as in 1984, during the early 1990s it rose to peak at 19 per cent in spring 1996, but has since been decreasing gradually. Among lone-parent households with dependent children, the proportion who are workless is much higher, at 43 per cent in spring 2003. This proportion peaked in the early 1990s, at 54 per cent.

Employment

The proportion of the working age population in employment remained fairly stable during the 1960s and 1970s. However trends in the overall rate masked large differences for men and women with the rate for men falling and the rate for women rising. While the economic cycle has affected the rates, over the period as a whole there is no sign of a long-run change in employment rates.

Data from the LFS shows that the trend in employment rates for men has fluctuated between 78 per cent in 1984 and 79 per cent in 2003 with a peak in 1990 of 82 per cent, followed by a low in 1993 of 75 per cent after the recession (Figure 4.9). For women employment rates have generally been rising from 59 per cent in 1984 to 70 per cent in 2003. As with men the proportion of women in employment has followed the economic cycle, but for them such effects have generally been less marked. For example, between 1990 and 1993 the female employment rate fell less sharply than the male rate. However, since 1993 it has risen at virtually the same rate as the male employment rate. As with economic activity rates (see Figure 4.1) the difference in the employment rates of males and females is narrowing, from 19 percentage points in 1984 to 10 percentage points in 2003.

In March 2000 the Lisbon European Council agreed an aim to achieve an overall EU employment rate as close as possible to 70 per cent by 2010 and, for women, an employment rate of more than 60 per cent. In 2002 the overall employment rate in the EU was 64 per cent and the United Kingdom was one of only four out of the 15 member states with employment rates above the 2010 overall target. Indeed, the United Kingdom had one of the highest employment rates across the EU, after Denmark, the Netherlands and Sweden. The range in employment rates across the EU differed greatly between men and women. For men, the Netherlands had the highest employment rate, at 83

Figure **4.8**

Working age households[1]: by household economic status

United Kingdom
Percentages

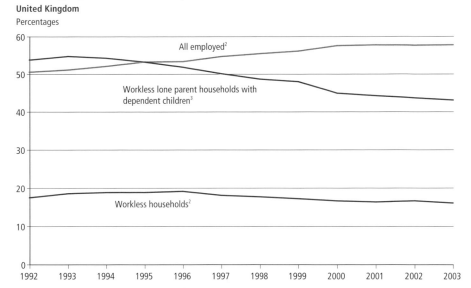

1 Percentages have been adjusted to include estimates for households with unknown economic activity and are for spring each year. A working age household is a household that includes at least one female between 16 and 59 or a male aged between 16 and 64. These estimates are not seasonally adjusted and have not been adjusted to take account of the Census 2001 results. See Appendix, Part 4: LFS reweighting.
2 As a percentage of working age households.
3 As a percentage of working age lone parent households with dependent children.

Source: Labour Force Survey, Office for National Statistics

Figure **4.9**

Employment rates[1]: by sex

United Kingdom
Percentages

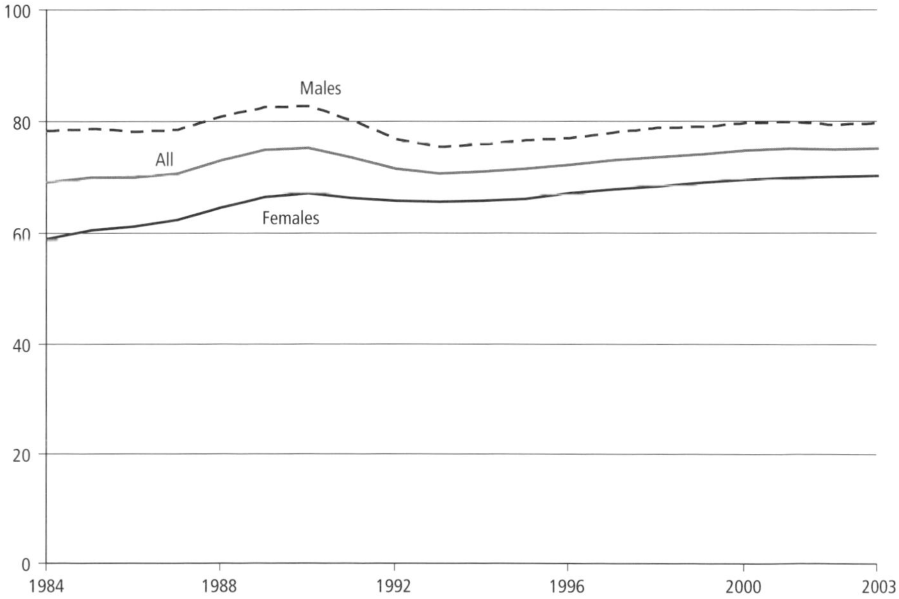

1 Males aged 16 to 64, females aged 16 to 59. The percentage of the population that is in employment. At spring. Data are seasonally adjusted and have been adjusted to take account of the Census 2001 results. See Appendix, Part 4: LFS reweighting.

Source: Labour Force Survey, Office for National Statistics

Figure **4.10**

Employment rates[1]: by sex, EU comparison, 2002

Percentages

1 People aged 15–64, except for the United Kingdom where data refer to those aged 16–64.

Source: Labour Force surveys, Eurostat

Map **4.11**

Jobs density[1]: by area[2], 2001[3]

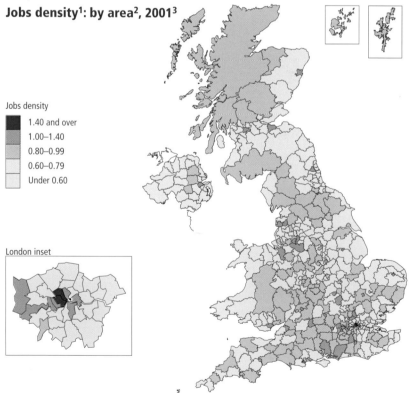

Jobs density

- 1.40 and over
- 1.00–1.40
- 0.80–0.99
- 0.60–0.79
- Under 0.60

London inset

1 The total number of filled jobs in an area divided by the resident population of working age in that area. See Appendix Part 4: Jobs densities for local areas.
2 Unitary and local authorities.
3 Data are not seasonally adjusted. Includes data on self-employment jobs from the Labour Force Survey which have not been adjusted to take account of the Census 2001 results. See Appendix, Part 4: LFS reweighting.
Source: Office for National Statistics

per cent it was 15 percentage points higher than Belgium, the country with the lowest rate (Figure 4.10). The range of employment rates for women was more than double that of men, from 73 per cent in Denmark and Sweden to 42 per cent in Italy. Although Finland had one of the lowest employment rates for males it had the third highest rate for females. The United Kingdom had the third highest male rate and fifth highest female rate in the EU.

A new local area labour market indicator – jobs density – has been developed. It is an indicator of labour demand and is defined as the total number of filled jobs in an area divided by the resident population of working age in that area (see also Appendix, Part 4: Jobs densities for local areas). The overall UK figure in 2001 was just over 0.8 jobs per person of working age. Around 50 local authority areas had a jobs density of 1.0 or more, that is at least one job for every resident of working age, but all bar three of these authorities had rates below 1.4 (Map 4.11). The three authorities are all in Central London – City of London (60.1), Westminster (4.6) and Camden (2.1). East Renfrewshire had the lowest jobs density of 0.4 jobs per person of working age, which may be explained by high outward commuting to nearby Glasgow. Large isolated rural areas, such as the highlands and islands of Scotland tend to have relatively high jobs densities, as workers are less likely to travel outside the area.

Employment rates also vary by the qualifications people have obtained. For both sexes employment rates increase with the level of qualifications (Table 4.12). Ninety per cent of men and 85 per cent of women who had a degree or the equivalent were in employment in spring 2003. This compares with 57 per cent of men and 44 per cent of women who did not have any qualifications.

Skills requirements within occupations have led to training beyond formal education. The Learning and Training at Work survey for the Department for Education and Skills (DfES) found that in 2002. Overall information technology was the most common course offered by employers in England. Ninety per cent of employers had provided some job-related training to their employees in the 12 months prior to interview.

Patterns of employment

The UK economy experienced structural change in the post-war period, with a decline in the manufacturing sector and an increase in service industries. In 1983 29 per cent of male employee jobs were in manufacturing but by 2003 this had fallen to 20 per cent (Table 4.13). The proportion of female employee jobs in the manufacturing sector also fell over the period, from 16 per cent to 7 per cent. The largest increase in both male and female jobs over the last 20 years has been in financial and business services, which accounted for about one in five of both male and female jobs in June 2003. The total number of jobs done by women is now virtually the same as the number done by men – 12.8 million compared with 13.0 million – whereas in 1983 there were 2.5 million more male than female employee jobs. Note that this table is based on jobs rather than people – one person may have more than one job, and jobs may vary in the number of hours' work they involve.

Certain ethnic groups are concentrated in particular industries. In 2001–02, two thirds of Bangladeshi and half of Chinese men in employment worked in the distribution, hotel and restaurant industry compared with just 16 per cent

Table 4.12

Employment rate[1]: by sex and highest qualification, 2003[2]

United Kingdom   Percentages

	Males	Females	All
Degree or equivalent	90	85	88
Higher education	87	84	86
GCE A level or equivalent	81	73	78
GCSE grades A–C or equivalent	80	73	76
Other qualifications	78	65	71
No qualification	57	44	50
All	79	70	75

1 The percentage of the working age population in employment.
2 At spring. Data are not seasonally adjusted and have not been adjusted to take account of the Census 2001 results. See Appendix, Part 4: LFS reweighting.

Source: Labour Force Survey, Office for National Statistics

Table 4.13

Employee jobs[1]: by sex and industry

United Kingdom   Percentages

	Males			Females		
	1983	1993	2003	1983	1993	2003
Distribution, hotels, catering and repairs	17	20	22	26	26	26
Manufacturing	29	24	20	16	11	7
Financial and business services	12	17	20	14	17	19
Transport and communication	10	10	8	2	2	4
Construction	8	7	8	2	1	1
Agriculture	2	2	1	1	1	–
Energy and water supply	4	2	1	1	1	–
Other services[2]	17	19	20	39	41	42
All employee jobs (=100%) (millions)	12.4	11.3	13.0	9.9	11.5	12.8

1 Data are at June each year and are not seasonally adjusted.
2 Public administration, education, health and other community, social and personal service activities.

Source: Short-term Turnover and Employment Survey, Office for National Statistics

Figure **4.14**

People in employment who were in the higher managerial and professional group[1]: by ethnic group[2], 2001–02[3]

Great Britain
Percentages

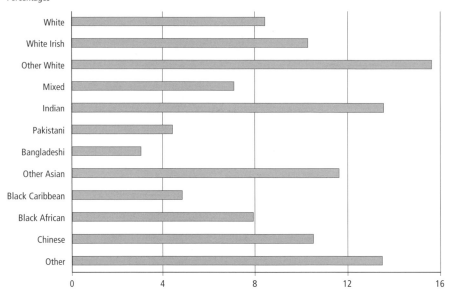

1 See Appendix, Part 1: National Statistics Socio-economic Classification.
2 Sample too small for reliable estimates for the Other Black group.
3 See Appendix, Part 4: Annual Local Area Labour Force Survey.

Source: Annual Local Area Labour Force Survey, Office for National Statistics

Figure **4.15**

Employees: by occupation and sex, 2003[1]

United Kingdom
Percentages

	Males	Females
Managers and senior officials		
Professional		
Associate professional and technical		
Administrative and secretarial		
Skilled trades		
Personal service		
Sales and customer service		
Process plant and machine operatives		
Elementary		
All		

1 At spring. Data are not seasonally adjusted and have not been adjusted to take account of the Census 2001 results. See Appendix, Part 4: LFS reweighting.

Source: Labour Force Survey, Office for National Statistics

of their White British counterparts. White Irish men were more likely than other men to work in the construction industry – 21 per cent compared with 12 per cent overall. Bangladeshi and Chinese women were also concentrated in the distribution, hotel and restaurant industry while half of Black Caribbean women worked in the public administration, education or health sector – the highest proportion for any ethnic group.

There were also variations in the socio-economic group of those in employment from different ethnic groups. Bangladeshis, Pakistanis and Black Caribbeans were those least likely to be in the highest socio-economic group, that is higher managers and professionals – 3 per cent, 4 per cent and 5 per cent respectively (Figure 4.14). This was in contrast to men and women from the Other White (16), Indian (14), Other Asian (12), and Chinese (11 per cent) groups. This compared with 8 per cent of White British group.

The pattern of occupations followed by men and women is quite different (Figure 4.15). In spring 2003, 91 per cent of employees who worked in the skilled trades were male. These occupations, together with work as process plant and machine operatives (84 per cent), were those that men accounted for a higher proportion of employees than women. Employees who were managers and senior officials were also more likely to be male than female (69 per cent compared with 31 per cent). This was also the case with professional occupations, but to a lesser degree, with 58 per cent of professional employees being male and 42 per cent female. Occupations where employees were most likely to be female were personal service (83 per cent), administrative (79 per cent) and sales and customer service (70 per cent).

The self-employed also form an important part of the labour force. Just over 3.3 million people were self-employed in the United Kingdom in spring 2003 (see Table 4.2), representing 12 per cent of all in employment. Self-employment is more common among men than women – 16 per cent of men in employment were self-employed in spring 2003 compared with 7 per cent of women.

Men and women also vary considerably in the type of self-employed work they undertake. Almost a third of self-employed men work in the construction industry but very few women do (Figure 4.16). On the other hand, 23 per cent of self-employed women work in 'other services' – for example community, social and personal services – and a further 22 per cent are in public administration, education and health, areas where self-employed men are comparatively under-represented. The biggest changes over the last 10 years in the type of self-employed work undertaken were the increase in the proportion of women in the banking, finance and insurance sector, which accounted for 14 per cent of self-employed women in 1993, and a corresponding fall in the proportion working in distribution, hotels and restaurants.

In Great Britain in 2001–02 people from Pakistani and Chinese groups were more likely to be self-employed than those in other ethnic groups. Around one fifth of Pakistani (22 per cent) and Chinese (19 per cent) people in employment were self-employed compared with around one in ten White British people and less than one in ten Black people.

Table 4.2 showed that there were 6.3 million people working part time in the United Kingdom in spring 2003, of whom 5.1 million were women. However

Figure **4.16**

Self-employment: by industry and sex, 2003[1]

United Kingdom
Percentages

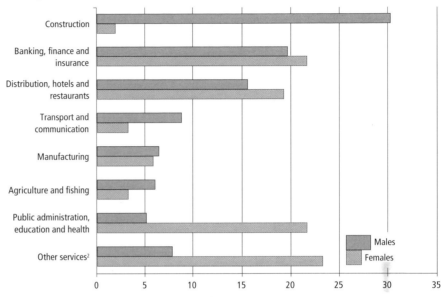

1 At spring. Data are not seasonally adjusted and have not been adjusted to take account of the Census 2001 results. See Appendix, Part 4: LFS reweighting.
2 Community, social and personal services including sanitation, dry cleaning, personal care, and recreational, cultural and sporting activities.

Source: Labour Force Survey, Office for National Statistics

to distinguish only between full time and part time masks a variety of working patterns. Table 4.17 (see overleaf) shows the distribution of usual weekly hours of work, including regular paid and unpaid overtime, for both men and women in spring 2003. The most common length of working week for both male and female employees was between 31 and 45 hours. The next most common length for male employees was over 45 hours, whereas for female employees it was between 16 and 30 hours. Female employees were more likely to work shorter hours – approximately 4 in 10

Table **4.17**

Distribution of usual weekly hours of work[1]: by sex, 2003[2]

United Kingdom   Percentages

	Less than 6 hours	6 up to 15 hours	16 up to 30 hours	31 up to 45 hours	Over 45 hours	Total (=100%) (millions)
Males						
Employees	1	3	6	59	32	12.7
Self-employed	1	4	12	40	43	2.4
All males[3]	1	3	7	56	33	15.2
Females						
Employees	2	12	29	48	9	11.9
Self-employed	6	19	30	27	17	0.9
All females[3]	2	13	29	46	10	12.9

1 Time rounded to the nearest hour respondents worked on their main job.
2 At spring. Data are seasonally adjusted and have been adjusted to take account of the Census 2001 results. See Appendix, Part 4: LFS reweighting.
3 Includes those on government-supported training and employment programmes and unpaid family workers.

Source: Labour Force Survey, Office for National Statistics

Table **4.18**

Employees with flexible working patterns[1], 2003[2]

United Kingdom   Percentages

	Males	Females	All employees
Full-time employees			
Flexible working hours	9.7	14.9	11.6
Annualised working hours	4.9	5.1	5.0
Four and a half day week	1.8	1.1	1.5
Term-time working	1.2	5.8	2.9
Nine day fortnight	0.4	0.3	0.3
Any flexible working pattern[3]	18.0	26.7	21.1
Part-time employees			
Flexible working hours	6.6	8.4	8.0
Annualised working hours	3.4	4.2	4.0
Term-time working	3.9	11.2	9.8
Job sharing	1.2	3.5	3.1
Any flexible working pattern[3]	16.9	26.7	24.8

1 Percentages are based on totals which exclude people who did not state whether or not they had a flexible working arrangement. Respondents could give more than one answer.
2 At spring. Data are not seasonally adjusted and have not been adjusted to take account of the Census 2001 results. See Appendix, Part 4: LFS reweighting.
3 Includes other categories of flexible working not separately identified.

Source: Labour Force Survey, Office for National Statistics

female employees worked up to 30 hours a week compared with around 1 in 10 male employees. For women who were self-employed there were also different work patterns – a higher proportion of the self-employed than employed worked less than 16 hours. Similarly a higher proportion of the self-employed worked longer hours with 43 per cent of self-employed males working over 45 hours compared with 32 per cent of male employees. Although a higher proportion of self-employed females than employees also worked over 45 hours (17 per cent compared with 9 per cent), this was a smaller proportion than for males. Self-employed females were most likely to work from 16 up to 30 hours.

Men also work longer hours than women across the EU. The EU average for men working full time was 42 hours in 2002, compared with 38 hours for women. The United Kingdom has the fourth highest number of hours worked overall in the EU at 42 hours. This was one hour less than the countries with the highest. People working full time in Italy worked 37 hours per week, the lowest in the EU.

Government policy over recent years has stressed the importance of maintaining a healthy work-life balance. One initiative cited as important in this is the availability of flexible working. A fifth of employees working full time and a quarter of those working part time had some type of flexible working arrangement in spring 2003 (Table 4.18). Flexible working hours was the most common form of flexible working for full-time employees from both sexes. It was also the most common arrangement for men who worked part time, whereas term-time working was the most common arrangement for women who worked part time. In spring 2003 over half of all term-time workers in the UK were school teachers, post-compulsory education teachers or teaching assistants.

Caring for somebody can sometimes lead to a change in working arrangements, or even giving up work. The British Social Attitudes survey in 2002 found that 26 per cent of males and 47 per cent of females, who had ever been in paid employment, had at some point changed their hours or working arrangements to look after someone (mainly children). It also found that 9 per cent of males and 33 per cent of females had given up work (excluding maternity leave) to enable them to do this.

Unemployment

The number of unemployed people is linked to the economic cycle, albeit with a time lag. Broadly speaking, as the country experiences economic growth so the number of jobs grows and unemployment falls, though any mismatches between the skill needs of the new jobs and the skills of those available for work may slow this process. Conversely as the economy slows and goes into recession so unemployment tends to rise. The latest peak in unemployment occurred in 1993, when it reached nearly 3 million (Figure 4.19). This recession had a much greater effect on unemployment among men than among women. In 2001 the number of people unemployed fell to its lowest level since 1990. More recently, however, unemployment increased slightly to 1.53 million people in spring 2002, but then fell slightly again to 1.48 million by spring 2003.

The measure of unemployment shown in Figure 4.19 is based on LFS estimates of the number of people without a job who are seeking work. It is based on

Figure **4.19**

Unemployment[1,2]: by sex

United Kingdom
Millions

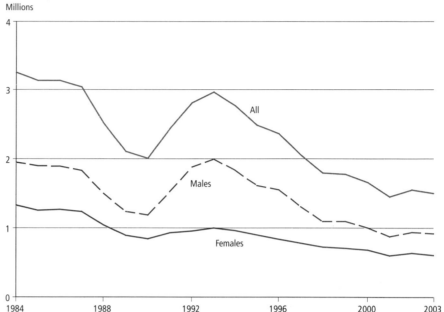

1 See Appendix, Part 4: Unemployment.
2 At spring each year. Data are seasonally adjusted and have been adjusted to take account of the Census 2001 results. See Appendix, Part 4: LFS reweighting.

Source: Labour Force Survey, Office for National Statistics

internationally agreed definitions and is the official measure of unemployment. A complementary alternative indicator of unemployment is the claimant count which is a count of the number of people claiming unemployment-related benefits. For more information on the differences between both measures see the appendix (Part 4: Claimant count).

Within the United Kingdom, unemployment rates in spring 2003 were 5.0 per cent in England, 4.4 per cent in Wales, 5.6 per cent in Scotland, and 5.3 per cent in Northern Ireland. London and the North East regions of England had the highest unemployment rates, at 7.0 per cent and 6.5 per cent, respectively. The lowest unemployment rates were in the South East and South West, both at 3.8 per cent.

Figure **4.20**

Unemployment rates[1]: by sex, EU comparison, 2002

Percentages

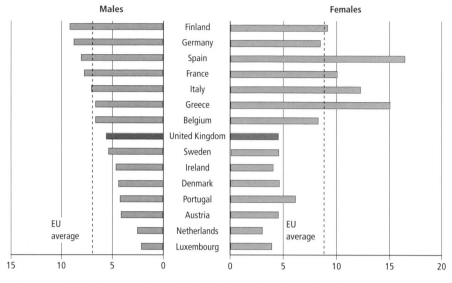

1 People aged 15 to 64, except for the United Kingdom where data refer to those aged 16 to 64.

Source: Labour Force surveys, Eurostat

Figure **4.21**

Unemployment rates[1,2]: by sex and age

United Kingdom
Percentages

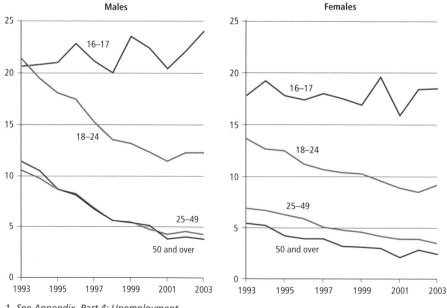

1 See Appendix, Part 4: Unemployment.
2 At spring each year. Data are seasonally adjusted and have been adjusted to take account of the
   Census 2001 results. See Appendix, Part 4: LFS reweighting.

Source: Labour Force Survey, Office for National Statistics

Across the EU, unemployment rates in 2002 varied from 11 per cent in Spain to 3 per cent in Luxembourg and the Netherlands. Figure 4.20 shows that among men unemployment was highest in Finland and Germany (9 per cent each) and lowest in Luxembourg (2 per cent). For women the highest rate was in Spain (16 per cent) and the lowest rate was in the Netherlands (3 per cent).

A higher proportion of men than women are unemployed in the United Kingdom and a higher proportion of young people than older people are unemployed. Unemployment rates peaked in 1993 and have since declined across almost all age groups, although there have been slight increases in some age groups over the last two years. The largest decline was for those aged 18 to 24, with a fall of 9 percentage points for men and nearly 5 percentage points for women between spring 1993 and spring 2003 (Figure 4.21). For those aged 16 to 17, unemployment rates have fluctuated over the past decade between around 20 and 24 per cent for young men and around 17 to 20 per cent for young women. The lowest unemployment rates in spring 2003 were among men and women over 50, at 3.7 per cent for men and 2.3 per cent for women.

Age and sex also influence the length of time that people spend unemployed. Young unemployed people are less likely to have been so for a long period than older people, and women are less likely than men to have been unemployed for a long period (Table 4.22). In spring 2003, half of unemployed women aged between 16 and 29 had been out of work for less than three months, and less than one in ten had been unemployed for a year or more. However, around one in ten unemployed men in their thirties had been unemployed for three years or more and this rose to nearly one in five among those aged 50 to 64.

Labour market dynamics

In spring 2002 one in ten employees of working age in the United Kingdom had been in their job for less than six months and about one in three had been with same employer for more than 10 years. In spring 2002 twice as many employees left their job voluntarily (2.9 per cent) as involuntarily (1.4 per cent). Younger employees in particular were more likely to leave their jobs voluntarily than older employees (Figure 4.23 – see overleaf). This could be because young people may act on the qualifications their education brings or they may undertake seasonal or temporary work while studying. Similarly young employees, new to the labour market, often voluntarily transfer from job to job until they feel their skills are being used and expectations realised. As people grow older their financial responsibilities usually grow, so they may be less inclined to take on the risks involved in changing jobs. The rate at which people voluntarily leave their job also varies by their occupation. The lowest rates were for professionals (1.4 per cent) and those in the associate professional and technical sector (1.9 per cent). The highest rates were in sales and customer service (4.0 per cent), followed by elementary occupations (3.6 per cent).

Participation in the Government's New Deal scheme is mandatory for 18 to 24 year olds who have claimed Jobseeker's Allowance continuously for six months. Initially there is a gateway period which includes intensive careers advice and guidance, and help with job search skills. The aim is to find unsubsidised jobs for

Table **4.22**

Duration of unemployment[1]: by sex and age, 2003[2]

United Kingdom   Percentages

	Less than 3 months	3 months but less than 6 months	6 months but less than 1 year	1 year but less than 2 years	2 years but less than 3 years	3 years or more	All durations
Males							
16–19	43	25	20	8	..	..	100
20–29	48	22	12	10	..	6	100
30–39	37	17	13	14	8	11	100
40–49	33	19	13	15	..	14	100
50–64	30	17	15	16	..	18	100
All aged 16 and over[3]	39	20	14	12	5	9	100
Females							
16–19	51	25	15	8	..	..	100
20–29	55	19	14	7	..	..	100
30–39	47	20	14	11	..	..	100
40–49	42	21	14	14	..	..	100
50–59	39	..	17	18	..	..	100
All aged 16 and over[3]	48	20	14	10	3	4	100

1 Excludes those who did not state their duration of unemployment. See Appendix, Part 4: Unemployment.
2 At spring. Data are not seasonally adjusted and have not been adjusted to take account of the Census 2001 results. See Appendix, Part 4: LFS reweighting.
3 Includes males aged 65 and over and females aged 60 and over.

Source: Labour Force Survey, Office for National Statistics

Figure **4.23**

People in employment who voluntarily left their job[1]: by age and sex, 2002[2]

United Kingdom
Percentages

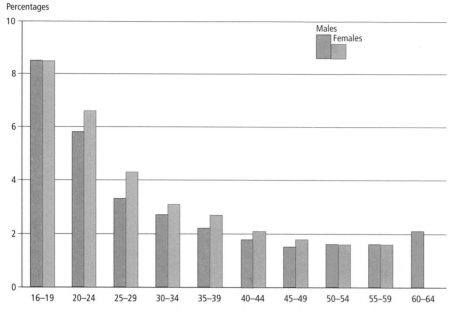

1 People of working age who left a paid job in the three months before interview. See Appendix, Part 4: Job separations.

2 At spring. Data are not seasonally adjusted and have not been adjusted to take account of the Census 2001 results. See Appendix, Part 4: LFS reweighting.

Source: Labour Force Survey, Office for National Statistics

Table **4.24**

People entering employment through the New Deal: by age and type of employment, 1998 to 2003[1]

Great Britain   Thousands

	18–24	25 and over	All aged 18 and over
Sustained employment	367	130	497
Other employment[2]	96	35	130
All entering employment	463	165	628
Those entering sustained employment as a percentage of all leavers	*39*	*25*	*36*

1 Data for those aged 18–24 are for January 1998 to September 2003. Data for those aged 25 and over are for July 1998 to September 2003.

2 Employment lasting less than 13 weeks.

Source: Department for Work and Pensions

as many as possible. Those who do not find a job then move onto one of a number of options: subsidised employment; work experience with a voluntary organisation or on an environmental task force, both with training; or full-time education. For those reaching the end of their option without keeping or finding work, there is a follow-through period of support and further training if needed. The New Deal scheme also covers other groups, including people with disabilities, the long-term unemployed, those over 50 and lone parents. Of those young people in Great Britain leaving the New Deal during the period January 1998 to September 2003, 39 per cent went into sustained employment (lasting 13 weeks or more) (Table 4.24). Among those aged 25 and over leaving during the period July 1998 to September 2003, 25 per cent went into sustained employment.

The working environment

In autumn 2002 there were 7.3 million trade union members in the United Kingdom, a decrease of 0.8 million since 1995 (when the LFS began collecting trade union membership data for the United Kingdom). There has been a general decrease in membership over the last 20 years – in 1979 membership in Great Britain was just over 13 million. In 2002 union density (union membership as a proportion of all in employment) for both men and women was 29 per cent. There were however variations between occupations. Membership was highest for men who worked as process, plant and machinery operatives, in personal services, or in associate professional and technical occupations (Table 4.25). Membership for women was highest among those in professional occupations. For both sexes, sales and customer service occupations had the lowest trade union membership.

There were also variations by age and by type of employment. Over a third of those aged 50 and over were union members compared with a quarter of those aged 25 to 34, while the proportion of full-time employees belonging to a union stood at 32 per cent compared with 21 per cent for those working part time.

Work-related issues such as labour disputes provide further insight into the state of the labour market. The largest number of working days lost through stoppages in one year in the United Kingdom was during the General Strike in 1926 when just over 160 million working days were lost – the coal industry alone accounted for 146 million of these days. Further periods of high industrial dispute occurred in 1972, 1979 and 1984. In 1972, a miners' strike accounted for 45 per cent of the 24 million days lost and a strike by the engineering workers in 1979 resulted in just over half of the 29 million days lost. Another miners' strike in 1984 was responsible for over 80 per cent of the 27 million days lost in that year. The 2002 total of 1.3 million working days lost through labour disputes was the highest calendar year total since 1990 (Figure 4.26). It is also more than double the figure for both 2000 and 2001 (0.5 million). The 2002 total is double the average number of working days lost per year in the 1990s (0.7 million), yet is considerably lower than the average for both the 1980s (7.2 million) and the 1970s (12.9 million).

The British Social Attitudes survey in 2002 asked those in employment how satisfied they were with their jobs. The

Table **4.25**

Trade union membership[1] of employees: by occupation and sex, 2002[2]

United Kingdom		Percentages
	Males	Females
Managers & senior officials	16	22
Professional	36	60
Associate professional & technical	37	46
Adminstrative & secretarial	31	23
Skilled trades	30	25
Personal service	37	30
Sales & customer service	13	13
Process, plant & machine operatives	38	27
Elementary	26	17
All occupations[3]	29	29

1 Includes organisations described as staff associations. Percentages are based on totals that exclude people who did not state whether or not they were a member of a trade union.
2 At autumn. Data are not seasonally adjusted and have not been adjusted to take account of the Census 2001 results. See Appendix, Part 4: LFS reweighting.
3 Includes those who did not state their occupation.

Source: Labour Force Survey, Office for National Statistics

Figure **4.26**

Labour disputes[1]: working days lost

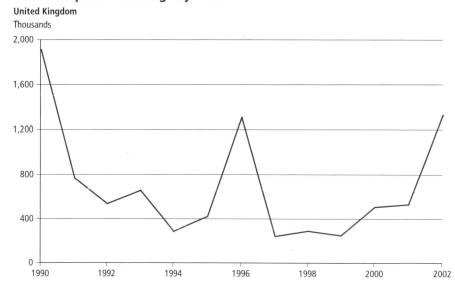

United Kingdom
Thousands

1 See Appendix, Part 4: Labour disputes.
Source: Office for National Statistics

Table **4.27**

Reasons[1] full-time employees were looking for a new job: by sex and presence of dependent children, 2003[2]

United Kingdom
Percentages

	Males	Females With dependent children	Females Without dependent children	All females	All persons
Pay unsatisfactory in present job	31	26	28	27	30
Present job may come to an end	15	17	16	16	15
In present job to fill time before finding another	10	..	8	6	9
Wants shorter hours than in present job	7	..	5	6	7
Journey unsatisfactory in present job	7	..	6	7	7
Other aspects of present job unsatisfactory	37	39	34	35	37
Percentage of full-time employees looking for a new job	6	5	6	5	6

1 More than one reason could be given.
2 At spring. Data are not seasonally adjusted and have not been adjusted to take account of the Census 2001 results. See Appendix, Part 4: LFS reweighting.

Source: Labour Force Survey, Office for National Statistics

answers can be interpreted as a summary assessment by the individual of all the different characteristics of their job. Overall, 77 per cent of those who answered were completely, very or fairly satisfied with their job. Women had slightly higher levels of job satisfaction than men (80 per cent compared with 74 per cent).

Most people who want to move jobs are dissatisfied with aspects of their current job (Table 4.27). In spring 2003, 6 per cent of male, and 5 per cent of female, full-time employees in the United Kingdom were looking for a new job. For almost a third of men and over a quarter of women who were looking for a new job, unsatisfactory pay in their current job was a trigger for looking for another one. Around 15 per cent of both men and women were looking for a new job because their present job may come to an end, while around 7 per cent said they wanted shorter hours or that the journey was unsatisfactory.

Chapter 5 **Income and Wealth**

Household income

- Between 2001 and 2002, real household disposable income grew by 1.1 per cent, slightly less than the growth in GDP per head in the United Kingdom (Figure 5.1)

- In 2001/02, the median net income of women was 57 per cent that of men, and the gap was largest between women and men living in couples with children or in pensioner couples in Great Britain (Figure 5.6)

Taxes

- Between 1981/82 and 2003/04, a single man with no dependent children on average earnings would have experienced a decrease in the proportion of their earnings paid out in income tax, from 24 per cent to 17 per cent in the United Kingdom. (Table 5.12)

Income distribution

- During the first half of the 1990s, the distribution of disposable household income was relatively stable, but since about 1994/95 there appears to have been a small increase in inequality in the United Kingdom. (Figure 5.14)

Low incomes

- In 2001/02, over half of people living in households headed by a Pakistani or Bangladeshi person had household disposable income below 60 per cent of the median, compared with an estimated 16 per cent of people in households headed by a White person in Great Britain. (Table 5.22)

Wealth

- In 2001/02, 28 per cent of households in Great Britain reported having no savings – working age lone parent households were the most likely to have none (67 per cent). (Table 5.27)

Figure **5.1**

Real household disposable income per head[1] and gross domestic product per head[2]

United Kingdom
Index (1971=100)

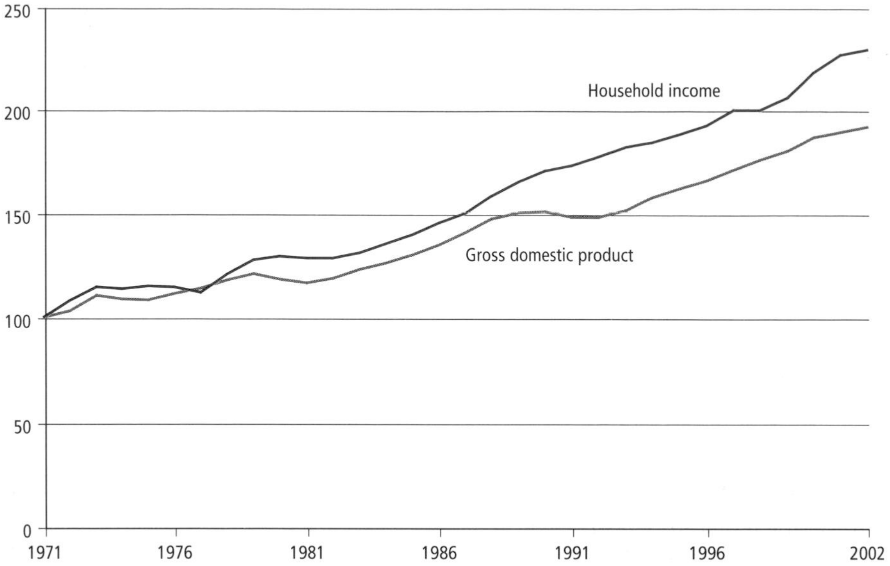

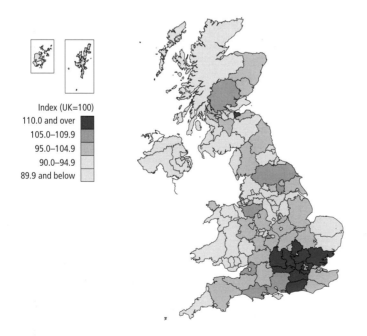

1 Adjusted to real terms using the expenditure deflator for the household sector. See also Appendix, Part 5: Household sector.
2 Adjusted to real terms using the GDP deflator.

Source: Office for National Statistics

Map **5.2**

Household disposable income per head: by area[1], 1997–1999

Index (UK=100)
- 110.0 and over
- 105.0–109.9
- 95.0–104.9
- 90.0–94.9
- 89.9 and below

1 See Appendix, Part 5: 'Local areas' for statistical purposes.

Source: Office for National Statistics

People's income determines how much they are able to spend and save and therefore the access that they have to goods and services for which payment is required. Thus although income is primarily an economic concept, it also has an important influence on social well-being. Income levels depend on the level of activity within the economy as a whole each year – the national income – and on the way in which national income is distributed. Wealth, on the other hand, represents the ownership of assets valued at a point in time.

Household income

Gross domestic product (GDP) is the most commonly used measure of overall economic activity, sometimes also referred to as the amount of 'value added' generated within the economy of a country. The total income generated is divided between individuals, companies and other organisations (for example, in the form of profits retained for investment), and government (in the form of taxes on production). If GDP is growing in real terms this means that the economy is expanding and there is more 'cake' available for distribution. Household disposable income per head represents the amount of this 'cake' which ends up in people's pockets – in other words it is the amount they have available to spend or save. Analysis of the trends in UK GDP may be found in the final section of this chapter.

Household income is derived not only directly from economic activity in the form of wages and salaries and self-employment income but also through transfers such as social security benefits. It is then subject to a number of deductions such as income tax, local taxes, and contributions towards pensions and national insurance. The amount of income remaining is referred to as household disposable income – the amount people actually have available to spend or save – and it is this measure which is commonly used to describe people's 'economic well-being'.

Household disposable income per head, adjusted for inflation, increased more than one and a quarter times between 1971 and 2002 (Figure 5.1). During the 1970s and early 1980s growth was somewhat erratic, and in some years there were small year-on-year falls, such as in 1974, 1976, 1977, 1981 and 1982. However, since then there has been growth each year. Over the period since 1971, a comparison of the patterns of growth of household disposable income and GDP per head shows that there has been a small shift between the shares of households and organisations in GDP in favour of households. However, between 2001 and 2002, real household disposable income per head grew by 1.1 per cent, slightly less than the GDP per head growth of 1.4 per cent.

Household disposable income differs considerably across the United Kingdom. In 1999, the London region had disposable income per head that was 20 per cent above the UK average, while in Wales it was only 87 per cent of the UK average. However, there are often greater income differences between the local areas within regions than between regions (Map 5.2). For example, averaged over the years 1997 to 1999, within the London region, Inner London–West had household disposable income per head 64 per cent above the UK average – the highest of all 129 areas shown in the map.

However, Inner London–East was only 6 per cent above the UK average. In general, the highest household incomes were recorded in and around London and the South East of England, though

values 10 per cent or more above the UK average were also recorded in the City of Edinburgh and in Sefton in Merseyside.

The North of Northern Ireland area had the lowest household disposable income per head of all the areas shown, at 72 per cent of the UK average. There were 42 areas out of 129 with disposable income per head lower than 90 per cent of the UK average, spread across virtually all regions within the United Kingdom though with concentrations in Wales, Northern Ireland, Scotland and the major conurbations of England outside London.

People derive their income from a number of sources and Table 5.3 illustrates how the shares of the various components of household income have changed since 1987. There was a fall in the proportion

derived from wages and salaries from 52 per cent to 47 per cent in 1996, but since then a gradual rise to 50 per cent in 2002. The proportion of income derived from social benefits has remained at around 21 per cent since 1996.

Taxes on income as a proportion of household income have remained stable since 1987 at around 11 per cent. Social contributions (that is, employees' national insurance contributions) have also remained stable at 8 per cent of household income, though there was a slight fall to 7 per cent in 2002. More information on taxes may be found in the Taxes section (see page 77).

The data in Figure 5.1 and Map 5.2 and Table 5.3 are derived from the UK national and regional accounts (see

Table 5.3

Composition of household income

United Kingdom — Percentages

	1987	1991	1996	2000	2001	2002
Source of income						
Wages and salaries[1]	52	50	47	49	49	50
Operating income[2]	11	11	12	12	12	13
Net property income	15	16	14	14	14	12
Social benefits[3]	19	19	21	21	21	21
Other current transfers[4]	3	4	5	4	4	4
Total household income (=100%) (£ billion at 2002 prices[5])	669	769	850	993	1,025	1,041
Taxes etc as a percentage of total household income						
Taxes on income	11	11	10	11	11	11
Social contributions[1]	9	8	8	8	8	7
Other current taxes	2	2	2	2	2	2
Other current transfers	2	3	4	3	2	3
Total household disposable income (=100%) (£ billion at 2002 prices[5])	452	527	592	678	710	720

1 Excludes employers' social contributions.
2 Includes self-employment income for sole-traders and rental income.
3 Comprises pensions and benefits.
4 Mostly other government grants, but including transfers from abroad and non-profit making bodies.
5 Adjusted to 2002 prices using the expenditure deflator for the household sector.

Source: Office for National Statistics

Appendix, Part 5: Household sector). In the national and regional accounts, households are combined with the non-profit making institutions such as universities, charities and clubs, and it is not at present possible to separate the two sectors. Non-profit making bodies receive income mainly in the form of property income (that is, investment income) and of other current receipts. Thus if it were possible to separate the two sectors, receipts of these two types of income by households alone would be lower than that shown in Table 5.3.

The household sector also includes people living in institutions such as nursing homes, as well as people living in private households. In most of the remainder of this chapter, the tables and charts are derived directly from surveys of households (such as the Family Resources Survey, the Expenditure and Food Survey, the Labour Force Survey, the European Community Household Panel Survey and the British Household Panel Survey) and surveys of businesses

(such as the New Earnings Survey). Data from these surveys cover the population living in households and some cover certain parts of the population living in institutions, but all exclude non-profit making institutions. Surveys can be used to analyse the distribution of household income between different sub-groups of the population, such as pensioners.

Survey sources differ from the national accounts not only in their population coverage but also in the way that household income is defined. One of the main differences is that the national accounts include the value of national insurance and pension contributions made on behalf of employees by their employer as part of total household income, whereas survey sources do not. Also, receipts of investment income are usually expressed net of repayments of loans in the national accounts. However, household income in Table 5.3 has been re-defined to exclude employers' social contributions and to include gross receipts of investment income. This

means that the data are not comparable with those in national accounts publications nor with those in *Social Trends 32* and earlier editions, but they are more consistent with the definition of income used for most income surveys.

Survey sources are also subject to under-reporting and non-response bias. In the case of household income surveys, investment income is commonly underestimated, as is income from self-employment. All these factors mean that the survey data on income used in the rest of this chapter are not entirely consistent with the national accounts household sector data.

The main sources of household income identified in Table 5.3 differ considerably in their importance between different types of households. During their working lives, earnings are the main source of income for most people: in 2001/02 they formed over three quarters of the total weekly income of households in Great Britain whose head was aged between 25 and 54 (Table 5.4).

Table **5.4**

Sources of gross weekly income: by age of head of household, 2001/02

United Kingdom   Percentages

	Wages & salaries	Self-employment income	Investment income	Tax credits	Retirement pensions	Private pensions	Disability benefits	Other benefits	Other income
16–24	69	2	1	1	-	-	-	11	15
25–34	81	7	1	1	-	-	1	7	2
35–44	78	11	1	1	-	-	1	6	2
45–54	77	11	2	-	-	3	2	4	2
55–59	57	21	3	-	1	9	3	4	2
60–64	34	25	4	-	7	18	5	5	2
65–74	12	6	6	-	35	30	3	5	2
75–84	5	1	8	-	43	27	5	8	3
85 or over	3	1	7	0	46	24	7	10	2
All households	64	11	2	1	6	7	2	5	2

Source: Family Resources Survey, Department for Work and Pensions

They gradually decline in importance once the head of household passes their mid-fifties, when first private pensions and then state retirement pensions become more important. Income from self-employment also forms an important part of the income of households with heads aged between 55 and 64. Higher proportions of income are derived from investments as the head of household gets older, reflecting the fact they have been able to build up savings through their working lives. 'Other income' sources are important for households where the head is aged between 16 and 24: these are mainly student loans and other forms of student support.

Income composition also varies according to ethnic group. In 2001/02, households in Great Britain whose head was of Mixed ethnic origin derived a much higher proportion of their income from self-employment (33 per cent) and a corresponding lower proportion from wages and salaries (52 per cent) compared with the average (64 per cent from wages and salaries). Compared with the White group, all other ethnic groups derived lower than average proportions from pensions, reflecting at least in part the younger age structure of the minority ethnic populations compared with the White population – see Table 1.5 in Chapter 1. Disability benefits formed about the same proportion of income for all ethnic groups, but the minority ethnic groups had above average proportions of income from other social security benefits, ranging from 8 per cent for the Mixed ethnic group to 13 per cent for the Black/Black British group.

The average income of pensioner couples after deduction of tax was £322 per week in 2001/02, just under twice that of single

Table 5.5

Sources of disposable income: EU comparison, 2000

Percentages

	Income from work[1]	Private income[2]	Social transfers[3]	Total income
Ireland	79	2	19	100
Portugal	77	2	21	100
Denmark	76	3	21	100
Spain	75	4	21	100
Greece	72	6	22	100
Netherlands	72	2	26	100
Austria	70	3	26	100
France	70	4	27	100
United Kingdom	70	7	24	100
Finland	69	4	27	100
Italy	68	4	27	100
Luxembourg	68	5	27	100
Belgium	67	8	26	100
Germany	66	4	29	100
Sweden	66	2	32	100
EU average	70	4	26	100

1 Wages and salaries and self employment.
2 Investment income and private transfers.
3 Includes private pensions.

Source: European Community Household Panel, Eurostat

pensioners (£167 per week). Average income after tax for all pensioner families grew in real terms (that is, deflated by the all items retail prices index less council tax/rates) by around 23 per cent between 1994/95 and 2001/02, an average annual growth rate of about 3.0 per cent. Over the same period average earnings in the whole economy grew by 12 per cent in real terms. Thus not only did average pensioner incomes grow in real terms between 1994/95 and 2001/02, but they grew almost twice as fast as earnings. However, it should be noted that changes in average income do not just reflect the changes experienced by individual pensioners but also reflect changes in the composition of the pensioner group, for example

as new retirees with higher incomes join the group.

The European Community Household Panel Survey is a longitudinal household income and resources survey that uses the same concepts and definitions in each member state, though the fieldwork is undertaken by a different organisation in each country. Table 5.5 shows that averaged over the European Union, income from employment and self-employment formed 70 per cent of household disposable income in 2000. However, this proportion varied between 66 per cent in Germany and Sweden to 79 per cent in Ireland. Generally speaking, where the proportion of income derived from employment was below the EU average, social transfers formed an above average proportion of income – for example, in Sweden they accounted for 32 per cent. In the United Kingdom, Luxembourg, Greece and Belgium, the proportion of income from private sources – mainly investment income – was above the EU average.

The information presented in this section so far has been in terms of household or family income, since these are generally considered to be the units across which resources are shared. Thus total household income can be taken as representing the (potential) standard of living of each of its members. The assumption of equal sharing of resources between each member of the household is very difficult to test. Using certain assumptions it is possible to use household survey data to derive estimates of the income accruing to individuals, but it is not possible to infer their living standards from these.

The results of such an exercise are shown in Figure 5.6 which compares the median net incomes of men and women

by family type. See Appendix Part 5: Individual income for details of how these estimates were derived, and the Box on page 80 for explanation of median. Note also that, as explained further in the Appendix, the term net income is used in place of disposable income because the term disposable income for this series has a different definition from elsewhere in this chapter.

On average, men's incomes exceeded those of women in 2001/02, irrespective of the type of family in which they were living. Taken over all family types the median net income of women was 58 per cent of that of men. However, the gap was largest for couples with children and pensioner couples, where the median net income of women was 43 per cent and 38 per cent of men, respectively. Among couples with children this is a result of the propensity of women to work part time or to leave the labour force entirely while bringing up children. For pensioner couples it is the result mainly of historic factors leading to lower entitlements among

wives both for state and occupational pensions. The gap was smallest for single people without children and single pensioners.

Earnings

Income from employment is the most important component of household income overall (see Tables 5.3 and 5.4). The average earnings index (AEI), a monthly measure of the pay of a representative sample of all employees across all sectors of the economy, is one of the indicators used to judge the state of the UK economy. If the index rises rapidly, this may indicate that the labour market is under-supplied with employees in the right numbers and with the right skills to meet the level of demand within the economy. In addition, a rapid rise may indicate that wage settlements are higher than the rate of economic growth can sustain and thus create inflationary pressures. A fall in the index may be a reflection of reduced demand within the economy and may presage a fall in GDP and an increase in unemployment. The relationship between the AEI and the retail prices index (RPI) is also of importance. If the AEI rises faster than the RPI, this means that employees' pay is increasing faster than the prices they have to pay for goods and services and that, therefore, all things being equal, their purchasing power will rise and they will feel 'better off'.

During the two decades from 1971, the AEI and RPI showed similar patterns of change, but with the RPI generally showing slower growth (Figure 5.7). For example, the peak in earnings growth over this period occurred in February 1975 when it reached an annual rate of 32 per cent. The peak in the RPI occurred in August that year at 27 per cent. During

Figure **5.6**

Median net individual income[1]: by family type and sex, 2001/02
Great Britain

£ per week

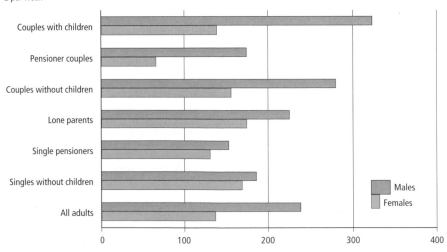

1 See Appendix, Part 5: Individual income.

Source: Individual Income, Department for Work and Pensions

most of the 1990s, the AEI outpaced the RPI. This was made possible mainly through increases in productivity, enabling employers to pay higher wages while not increasing their prices to the same extent to finance their wage bill. The periods during which prices have risen faster than earnings – for example in the latter half of 1995 – have been times of economic downturn when a fall in demand for labour depressed earnings growth. Although the RPI did not overtake the AEI in the period January to August 2003, the gap between the two narrowed appreciably, with the indices recording the same values of 3.2 per cent in February 2003 and not being more than 0.5 percentage points from then on.

In April 2003, average gross weekly pay of full-time employees in Great Britain was £476. However, a wide variety of factors influence the level of earnings received by each individual employee such as their skills and experience, their occupation, the economic sector in which they work, the hours they work, and so on. The area of the country in which they work and their gender may also have an impact. The remainder of this section explores some of these factors. However, it should be borne in mind that they are all very much interlinked, and it is not possible here to disentangle the effect that any single factor may have.

Government legislation may also have an effect on wages. The *Equal Pay Act 1970* and subsequent revisions, together with the *Sex Discrimination Act 1975*, established the principle of equal pay for work which can be established to be of equal value to that done by a member of the opposite sex, employed by the same employer, under common terms and conditions of employment. As Figure 5.8

Figure 5.7

Average earnings index[1,2] and retail prices index[3]

Percentage change over 12 months

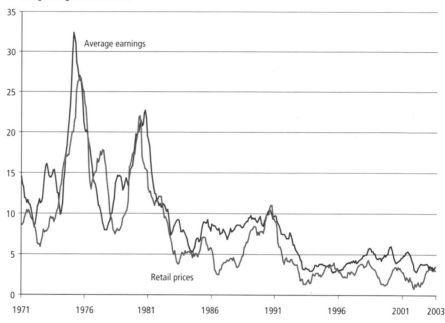

1 Data are for Great Britain.
2 Whole economy, seasonally adjusted, headline rate.
3 Data are for United Kingdom.

Source: Office for National Statistics

Figure 5.8

Gross hourly earnings[1]: by sex and whether working full time or part time

Great Britain

£ per hour

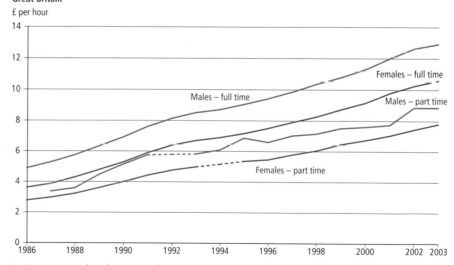

1 Average gross hourly earnings for employees on adult rates at April each year. Data are not available for male part-time earnings for 1986 and 1992, nor for female part-time earnings for 1994.

Source: New Earnings Survey, Office for National Statistics

shows, the impact of this legislation, together with other important factors such as the opening up of higher paid work to women, has been to narrow the differential between the hourly earnings of men and women, even though in absolute terms the gap has widened. In 1986, the hourly earnings of women working full time in Great Britain were 74 per cent of those of men, whereas in 2003 they had risen to 82 per cent. On average, part-time employees receive lower hourly earnings than full-time employees, and the differential between men and women working part time is smaller. For example women's hourly earnings were 88 per cent of those of men in 2003. However, this proportion fluctuates from year to year and shows no clear trend over the 17 years shown in the chart. It should be noted that coverage of part-time employees by the New Earnings Survey (NES) is not comprehensive because many employees with earnings below the income tax threshold are excluded, and the extent to which they are included or excluded in each survey contributes to the volatility of the data.

Although average hourly pay provides a useful comparison between the earnings of men and women, it does not reveal differences in rates of pay for comparable jobs. This is because such averages do not reflect the different employment characteristics of men and women, such as the proportions in different occupations and their length of time in jobs.

Wage rates can vary considerably between industrial sectors. Agriculture has traditionally been a relatively low-paid sector and this is still the case, with 38 per cent of employees in Great Britain on wage rates of less than £6 per hour in April 2003 (Table 5.9). However, the hotel and restaurant sector is the lowest paid industry, with 64 per cent earning less than £6 per hour. The wholesale and retail trade is also relatively low paid with 41 per cent earning less than £6 per hour. At the other end of the scale, 46 per cent of those in financial intermediation earned at least £12 per hour. Averaged over all industries, 22 per cent of employees earned less than £6 per hour compared to 30 per cent earning more than £12 per hour.

The broad industrial groupings shown in Table 5.9 can mask considerable variation within the sectors and the NES data allows more detailed industrial analyses. These reveal that in addition to employees within the financial intermediation sector, full-time employees on the highest weekly pay in April 2003 included those involved in 'other computer related activities' (£768), software consultancy and supply (£754), and radio and television activities (£691). Various branches of the hotel and restaurant and manufacturing sectors made up much of the ten lowest paid industries. Full-time employees in hotels were the lowest paid of all, with average earnings of £288 per week.

One major factor that can influence the wage rate of an individual is their educational level. Research using pooled Labour Force Survey data for the period 1993 to 2001 for England and Wales

Table **5.9**

Distribution of hourly earnings[1]: by industry, April 2003

Great Britain   Percentages

	Less than £6	£6 but less than £8	£8 but less than £10	£10 but less than £12	£12 and over
Hotels and restaurants	64	18	8	4	6
Wholesale and retail trade	41	24	12	7	16
Agriculture, hunting, forestry and fishing	38	37	12	5	7
Health and social work	22	23	15	13	28
Real estate, renting and business activities	22	18	13	9	37
Construction	8	23	23	16	29
Education	20	18	13	9	39
Manufacturing	13	22	20	14	31
Transport, storage and communication	10	28	23	12	27
Public administration and defence	7	22	19	16	36
Financial intermediation	5	20	18	11	46
Mining, quarrying, electricity, gas and water supplies	4	15	17	19	44
Other services	28	23	15	9	25
All industries[2]	22	22	16	11	30

1 Both full-and part-time employees on adult rates, including overtime payments, whose gross hourly earnings were less than £100 and whose pay for the survey period was unaffected by absence.
2 Includes employees with no industry code.
Source: New Earnings Survey, Office for National Statistics

indicates that there is a high financial return to education. This analysis factors out the variance in wages that arises from differences in age, region of residence, year, decade of birth, having a work-limiting health problem, being from a non-White ethnic group, being a union member and marital status – see Appendix Part 5: Earnings and education. Separate analyses were carried out for women and men. Both men and women appear to experience a 50 per cent wage increase as the length of education rises from leaving full-time education at 16 to leaving at 21.

The research also examined the returns to a first degree qualification compared with two A levels, by degree subject (Figure 5.10). There are large differences in the returns to different degree subjects, with returns for health, law, economics and business studies, and mathematics considerably higher than those for arts, education, languages and other social sciences. For example, graduates in mathematics, economics, law and health had earnings that were on average nearly 30 per cent higher for men and around 40 per cent higher for women than for employees with 2 or more A levels only, over the period 1993 to 2001. It should be noted that these estimates do not control for A level score, and this may explain some of the cross-subject differences since different subjects demand different A level scores to gain admission.

Taxes

Table 5.3 showed that in 2002, 11 per cent of household income was paid out in taxes on income and 7 per cent in social contributions. Every taxpayer is entitled to a personal allowance and those with income below this do not pay any tax. In 2003/04 the personal

Figure **5.10**

Proportional effect[1] on earnings of a degree level qualification: by sex and degree subject, 1993–2001[2]

England & Wales
Percentages

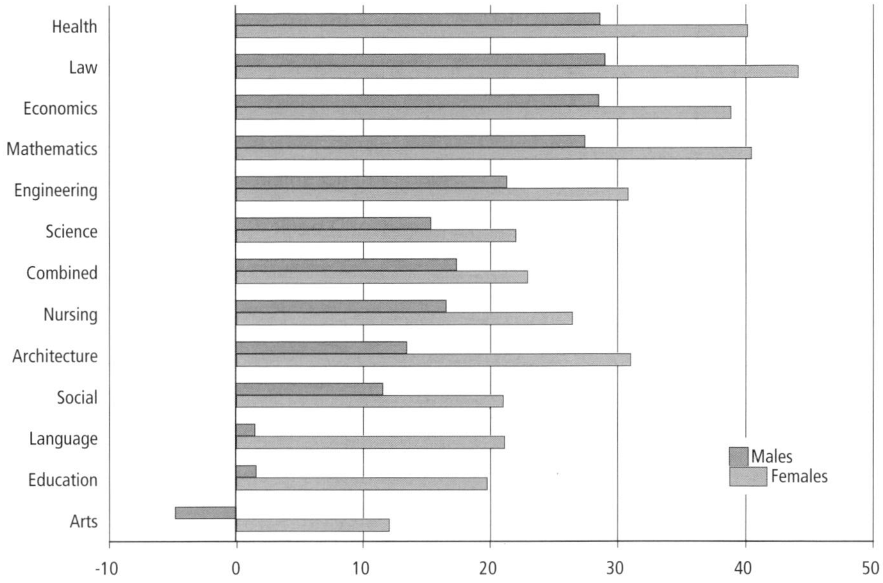

1 Compared with the average earnings for those with at least 2 A levels.
2 Data from 1993 to 2001 have been pooled. See Appendix, Part 5: Earnings and education.
Source: Department of Economics, University of Warwick, from Labour Force Survey

allowance is £4,615 for those aged under 65, with further allowances for people aged over 65. The income tax regime for 2003/04 includes three different rates of tax. Taxable income of up to £1,960 (that is, after the deduction of allowances and any other tax relief to which the individual may be entitled) is charged at 10 per cent. Taxable income above £1,960 but less than £30,500 is charged at 22 per cent, while income above this level is charged at 40 per cent. Special rates apply to savings income.

The Inland Revenue estimates that in 2003/04 there will be around 30.7 million taxpayers in the United Kingdom

Table **5.11**

Income tax payable: by annual income[1], 2003/04[2]

United Kingdom

	Number of taxpayers (millions)	Total tax payable (£ million)	Average rate of tax payable (percentages)	Average amount of tax payable (£)
£4,615–£4,999	0.5	10	0.4	20
£5,000–£7,499	3.3	510	2.5	160
£7,500–£9,999	3.8	1,990	6.0	520
£10,000–£14,999	6.5	8,270	10.3	1,280
£15,000–£19,999	5.1	11,660	13.3	2,310
£20,000–£29,999	6.3	23,670	15.5	3,780
£30,000–£49,999	3.7	25,220	18.3	6,790
£50,000–£99,999	1.3	21,950	25.9	17,210
£100,000 and over	0.4	30,810	34.0	76,080
All incomes	30.7	124,090	18.0	4,040

1 Total income of the individual for income tax purposes including earned and investment income. Figures relate to taxpayers only.
2 Based on projections in line with the April 2003 Budget.

Source: Inland Revenue

(Table 5.11). Because of the progressive nature of the income tax system, the amount of tax payable increases both in cash terms and as a proportion of income as income increases, averaging £160 per year for taxpayers with taxable incomes between £5,000 and £7,499 and £76,080 for those with incomes of £100,000 and above.

National insurance (NI) contributions are paid according to an individual's earnings rather than their total income, and for employees, payments are made both by the individual and by their employer. Employees' contributions tend to be slightly smaller as a proportion of earnings for those on higher weekly earnings compared with those on lower earnings because there was a ceiling on contributions before 2003/04. In 2003/04 contributions are

levied at 11 per cent on the first £595 of weekly earnings and at 1 per cent on weekly earnings above £595.

Table 5.12 uses modelled data to show the impact of income tax and national insurance contributions on men and women at different earnings levels. This illustrates how income tax liabilities increase as a proportion of earnings as earnings increase, whereas NI contributions decrease once an employee crosses the level of earnings at which the ceiling on contributions applies. Women on average earnings pay a lower proportion of their earnings in income and NI contributions compared with men, because their average earnings are lower than those of men.

Between 1981/82 and 2003/04, a single man on average or half male average earnings each year would have experienced a decrease of about a third in the proportion of their earnings paid out in income tax – for example, from 24 per cent to 17 per cent for a man on average earnings. A man on twice average earnings would also have experienced a decrease, but a much smaller one. (Note that prior to 2000/01, married people were able to claim an additional married couple's allowance which would have reduced the tax liabilities shown in the table.) NI contributions as a proportion of earnings showed a less clear pattern over time. There was a fall between 1989/90 and 1990/91 when the rates of contributions fell, followed by a period of stability until a slight increase in 2003/04 when the percentage rate at which contributions are levied was increased.

In addition to direct taxes such as income tax, households also pay indirect taxes through their expenditure. Indirect taxes include value added tax (VAT), customs duties and excise duties and are included in the prices of consumer goods and services. These taxes are specific to particular commodities: for example, in 2000/01 VAT was payable on most consumer goods at 17.5 per cent of their value, though not on most foods or on books and newspapers or on children's clothing and at a reduced rate on heating and lighting. Customs and excise duties on the other hand tend to vary by the volume rather than value of goods purchased. Because high income households are more likely to devote a larger proportion of their income to investments or repaying loans, and low income households may be funding their expenditure through taking out loans or drawing down savings, the proportion of income paid in indirect taxes tends to be higher for those on low incomes than for those on high incomes.

A further means of raising revenue from households is through local taxes, comprising council tax in Great Britain and domestic rates in Northern Ireland. These taxes are raised by local authorities to part-fund the services they provide. For both council tax and domestic rates, the amount payable by a household depends on the value of the property they occupy. However, for those on low incomes, assistance is available in the form of council tax benefits (rates rebates in Northern Ireland). In 2001/02, estimates from the Expenditure and Food Survey indicate the average council tax/rates payable was £880 per household, after taking into account the relevant benefit payments (Table 5.13 – see overleaf). Net local council tax varied from £960 per year in Scotland and the South East to £770 in the North East. Net domestic rates in Northern Ireland, which are based on a quite different valuation system, averaged £420,

Table **5.12**

Percentage of earnings paid in income tax and national insurance contributions[1]: by sex and level of earnings[2]

United Kingdom

Percentages

	1981/82	1991/92	1996/97	2001/02	2002/03	2003/04
Single man						
Half average earnings						
Tax	18.7	15.1	13.6	12.4	12.7	12.8
NIC	7.8	6.7	7.5	6.5	6.5	7.3
Average earnings						
Tax	24.4	20.0	18.8	17.2	17.3	17.4
NIC	7.8	7.9	8.8	8.2	8.3	9.1
Twice average earnings						
Tax	28.5	25.3	25.9	25.6	26.0	26.1
NIC	5.5	4.9	5.2	5.0	4.8	5.7
Single woman						
Half average earnings						
Tax	12.6	10.8	9.8	9.2	9.5	9.9
NIC	7.8	5.7	6.6	5.3	5.4	6.1
Average earnings						
Tax	21.3	17.9	16.8	15.6	15.8	15.9
NIC	7.8	7.4	8.3	7.6	7.7	8.5
Twice average earnings						
Tax	25.7	21.4	20.5	20.8	21.3	21.6
NIC	7.8	7.1	7.2	6.7	6.5	7.3

1 Employee's contributions. Assumes contributions at Class 1, contracted in, standard rate.
2 Average earnings for full-time male/female employees at the start of each financial year in all occupations working a full week on adult rates.

Source: Inland Revenue

Table **5.13**

Net local taxes paid by households: by region, 2001/02

	Net local taxes[1] (£ per year)	Net local taxes as a percentage of gross household income
United Kingdom	880	3.0
North East	770	3.0
North West	880	3.6
Yorkshire & the Humber	780	3.3
East Midlands	870	3.2
West Midlands	830	3.2
East	940	3.1
London	900	2.3
South East	960	2.7
South West	940	3.5
England	890	3.0
Wales	780	3.2
Scotland	960	3.9
Northern Ireland	420	1.8

1 Council tax net of council tax benefit in Great Britain; domestic rates net of rates rebate in Northern Ireland.

Source: Office for National Statistics

Equivalisation – in analysing the distribution of income, household disposable income is usually adjusted to take account of the size and composition of the household. This is in recognition of the fact that, for example, to achieve the same standard of living a household of five would require a higher income than would a single person. This process is known as equivalisation (see Appendix, Part 5: Equivalisation scales).

Quintile and decile groups – the main method of analysing income distribution used in this chapter is to rank units (households, individuals or adults) by a given income measure, and then to divide the ranked units into groups of equal size. Groups containing 20 per cent of units are referred to as 'quintile groups' or 'fifths'. Thus the 'bottom quintile group' is the 20 per cent of units with the lowest incomes. Similarly, groups containing 10 per cent of units are referred to as 'decile groups' or 'tenths'.

Percentiles – an alternative method also used in the chapter is to present the income level above or below which a certain proportion of units fall. Thus the ninetieth percentile is the income level above which only 10 per cent of units fall when ranked by a given income measure. The median is then the midpoint of the distribution above and below which 50 per cent of units fall.

representing 1.8 per cent of gross income. Within Great Britain, council tax as a percentage of gross household income varied from 2.3 per cent in London to 3.9 per cent in Scotland.

Income distribution

The first section of this chapter demonstrated how the various components of income differ in importance for different household types and how the levels of earnings vary between individuals. The result is an uneven distribution of total income between households, though the inequality is reduced to some extent by the deduction of taxes and social contributions and their redistribution to households in the form of social security benefits and other payments from government. The analysis of income distribution is therefore usually based on household disposable income, that is total income less payments of income tax and social contributions. However, in the analysis of Households Below Average Income carried out by the Department for Work and Pensions (on which most of the items in this and the next section are based), disposable income is presented both before and after the further deduction of housing costs. It can be argued that the costs of housing faced by different households at a given time may or may not reflect the true value of the housing that they actually enjoy. For example, the housing costs faced by someone renting a property in London may be much higher than they would have to pay for a property of similar quality outside London. Equally, a retired person living in a property which they own outright will enjoy the same level of housing as their younger neighbour in an identical property but owned with a mortgage, but their housing costs will be very different. Thus estimates are presented on both bases to take into account variations in housing costs that do not correspond to comparable variations in the quality of housing. Neither is given pre-eminence over the other. For more details, see Appendix, Part 5: Households Below Average Income.

During the 1970s there was relatively little change in the distribution of disposable income among households (Figure 5.14). However, although household disposable income grew in real terms across the distribution as a whole over the 1980s, this decade was characterised by a large increase in inequality. Between 1981 and 1989 average (median) income rose by 27 per cent when adjusted for inflation, whereas income at the ninetieth percentile rose by 38 per cent and that at the tenth percentile rose by only 7 per cent. During the first half of the 1990s, the income distribution appeared to stabilise, but in the most recent period there appears to have been a further small increase in inequality even though incomes have continued to grow in real terms.

The Institute for Fiscal Studies has investigated some of the possible explanations for the changes in inequality seen over the last two decades, and in particular why the trends are different over the economic cycles of the 1980s and 1990s. They found that wage growth played a part: inequality tends to rise during periods of rapid wage growth because the poorest households are the most likely to contain non-working individuals. The economic recovery in the 1980s was characterised by large increases in wages in each of the years from 1984 to 1988 matching the period when inequality increased rapidly. In contrast wage growth was very slow to return in

Figure **5.14**

Distribution of real[1] household disposable income[2]

United Kingdom
£ per week

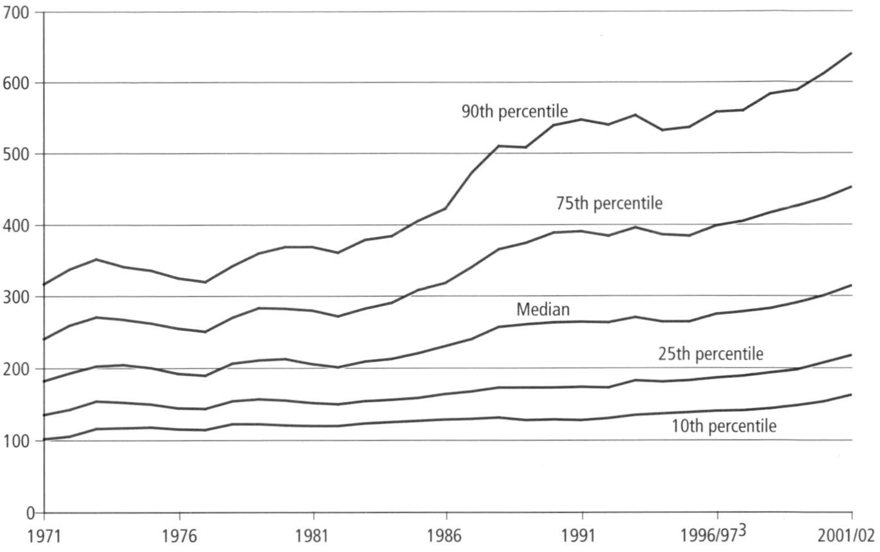

1 Data adjusted to 2001/02 prices using the retail prices index less local taxes.
2 Equivalised household disposable income before housing costs. See Appendix, Part 5: Households Below Average Income, and Equivalisation scales.
3 Data from 1993/94 onwards are for financial years; data for 1994/95 onwards exclude Northern Ireland.

Source: Institute for Fiscal Studies

the recovery of the early to mid-1990s – a time of stable or falling inequality. Growth in self-employment income and in unemployment were also found to be associated with periods of increased inequality. It would appear that demographic factors such as the growth in one person households make a relatively unimportant contribution compared with labour market changes. However, they have found that changes in the tax and benefit system have an impact in accordance with what economic theory would suggest: the income tax cuts of the 1970s and late 1980s worked to increase income inequality while direct tax rises in the early 1980s and 1990s – together with the increases in means-tested benefits in the late 1990s – produced the opposite effect. The recent small

increase in inequality appears to be driven by changes at the very top and possibly also at the very bottom of the income distribution: across most of the income distribution income growth has been very even.

People in couple families under state pension age and without children were nearly twice as likely as the population as a whole to be in the top quintile group of disposable income in 2001/02 (Table 5.15 – see overleaf). Also over-represented in the top quintile group were single people under pension age without children, though this group along with couple families with children were relatively evenly spread across the income distribution. At the other end of the distribution, people under pension age living in single person families with

Table **5.15**

Distribution of equivalised disposable income[1]: by family type, 2001/02

Great Britain

Percentages

	Bottom fifth	Next fifth	Middle fifth	Next fifth	Top fifth	All (=100%) (millions)
Before deduction of housing costs						
Pensioner couple	26	26	20	15	12	6.9
Single pensioner	26	33	21	14	7	4.1
Couple with children	18	20	23	21	18	19.8
Couple without children	10	10	16	27	38	10.5
Single adult with children	40	33	16	8	3	4.9
Single adult without children	18	15	19	23	24	10.7
All individuals	20	20	20	20	20	57.0
After deduction of housing costs						
Pensioner couple	20	27	21	18	15	6.9
Single pensioner	18	34	22	16	10	4.1
Couple with children	18	21	24	20	16	19.8
Couple without children	10	10	16	27	37	10.5
Single adult with children	49	26	14	7	3	4.9
Single adult without children	20	15	18	22	25	10.7
All individuals	20	20	20	20	20	57.0

1 Equivalised household disposable income has been used for ranking the individuals. See Appendix, Part 5: Households Below Average Income, and Equivalisation scales.

Source: Households Below Average Income, Department for Work and Pensions

Figure **5.16**

Shares of equivalised disposable income[1], 2001/02

Great Britain

Percentages

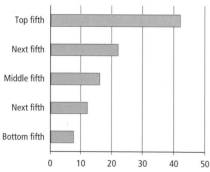

1 Equivalised household disposable income before housing costs has been used to rank individuals. See Appendix, Part 5: Households Below Average Income, and Equivalisation scales.

Source: Households Below Average Income, Department for Work and Pensions

children were twice as likely as the population as a whole to be in the bottom quintile group, and there were very small proportions of such individuals in the top quintile group. The section of this chapter on low incomes which begins on page 83 examines the characteristics of those at the lower end of the income distribution in more depth.

An alternative approach to the analysis of income distribution is to compare the share of total income received by each quintile group: if income were evenly distributed across all individuals each of these shares would be 20 per cent. Figure 5.16 shows the shares of disposable income received by each quintile group of individuals in Great

Britain in 2001/02. The ratio of the share of the bottom quintile group (7.5 per cent) to that of the top quintile group (42 per cent) was 5.6, slightly higher than the ratio of 5.2 in 1994/95 indicating a slight increase in inequality. However, these results are sensitive to data at the extremes of the income distribution that may be less reliable than other data. Between 1994/95 and 2001/02, median disposable income before the deduction of housing costs rose by 19 per cent in real terms (25 per cent after deduction of housing costs). Growth in median income within both the top and bottom quintile groups was very similar to this level.

The Department for Work and Pension's Households Below Average Income analysis from which Figure 5.16 and Table 5.17 are derived, provides an annual cross-sectional snapshot of the distribution of income based on the Family Resources Survey. The British Household Panel Survey (BHPS) complements this by providing longitudinal information about how the incomes of a fixed sample of individuals change from year to year. This enables us to track how people move through the income distribution over time, and to identify the factors associated with changes in their position in the distribution.

One of the major factors contributing to changes in an individual's position in the income distribution is change in the composition of the family in which they live. For women over the period 1991 to 1999, setting up home with a male partner was more than twice as likely to result in an increase in household income of one or more quintile groups as it was to result in a fall of one or more quintile groups. Conversely, when they separated from a male partner about half experienced a fall of one or more quintiles whereas only about one fifth experienced a rise. For men, joining with a female partner is more likely to result in a fall in household income than it is to result in a rise, whereas separating from them is more likely to result in a rise. In general, changes in family composition have less effect on men's position in the income distribution than on the position of women. These results reflect the higher individual incomes of men compared to women (see Figure 5.8).

Around 17 per cent of those adults in the top quintile group of gross income in 1991 remained in the same group throughout the period 1991 to 2001 (Table 5.17). A much lower proportion of people (8 per cent) remained in the bottom quintile group throughout the eleven year period. The majority of people (94 per cent) moved between quintile groups at least once over the period. There is more movement in and out of the three middle quintile groups, simply because it is possible to move out of these groups through either an increase or a decrease in income. Movement out of the top group generally only occurs if income falls – an individual will remain in the group however great an increase in income is experienced. The converse is true at the bottom of the distribution. Nevertheless, the table shows that there is considerable mobility within the income distribution.

As discussed earlier in this chapter, households initially receive income from various sources such as employment, occupational pensions, investments, and transfers from other households. The state then intervenes both to raise taxes and national insurance contributions from individuals and to redistribute the revenue thus raised in the form of cash benefits to

households and in the provision of services which are free or provided at a subsidised price at the point of use. Some households will pay more in tax than they receive in benefits, while others will benefit more than they are taxed. Overall, this process results in a redistribution of income from households with higher incomes to those on lower incomes.

The average taxes paid and benefits received by each quintile group in 2001/02 are set out in Table 5.18 – see overleaf. The distribution of 'original' income – before any state intervention – is highly unequal, with the average income of the top quintile group about 18 times greater than that of the bottom quintile group. Payment of cash benefits reduces this disparity so that the ratio of gross income in the top group compared with the bottom is 7:1, and deduction of direct and local taxes reduces the ratio further to around 6:1. Based on people's

expenditure patterns it is then possible to calculate an estimated payment of indirect taxes such as VAT and excise duties, which are deducted to produce a measure of post-tax income. Finally, an estimate is made for the value of the benefit they receive from government expenditure on services such as education and health. (It is not possible to estimate the benefit to households of some items of government expenditure, for example defence and road-building.) Addition of these estimates gives a household's final income. The ratio of average final income in the top quintile group to that in the bottom quintile group is 4:1. In this analysis, around 57 per cent of general government expenditure is allocated to households in the form of benefits.

Low incomes

The definition of 'low' income has always been a source of debate and to some

Table **5.17**

Where in the income distribution individuals spent the majority of their time between 1991 and 2001

Great Britain   Percentages

	Original quintile group in 1991					
	Bottom fifth	Second fifth	Third fifth	Fourth fifth	Top fifth	All individuals
All years in the same quintile as 1991	8	2	1	1	17	6
Majority of years in same quintile as 1991[1]	46	32	27	33	43	36
Majority of years above 1991 quintile	46	34	28	14	..	24
Majority of years below 1991 quintile	..	14	27	34	40	23
None of the above[2]	..	18	18	17	..	11
All individuals	100	100	100	100	100	100

1 Six or more years out of eleven in the same quintile as 1991 but excluding those in the 'All years in same quintile' row.
2 These individuals have neither remained in the same quintile as the original, nor been in a higher or lower quintile for six of the eleven years between 1991 and 2001.

Source: Department for Work and Pensions from British Household Panel Survey, Institute of Economic and Social Research

Table **5.18**

Redistribution of income through taxes and benefits[1], 2001/02

United Kingdom   £ per year

	Quintile group of households[2]					
	Bottom fifth	Next fifth	Middle fifth	Next fifth	Top fifth	All house-holds
Average per household						
Wages and salaries	2,040	6,400	15,160	26,100	46,920	19,320
Imputed income from benefits in kind	30	50	190	410	1,170	370
Self-employment income	390	800	970	1,840	7,830	2,360
Occupational pensions, annuities	530	1,330	2,240	2,500	2,790	1,880
Investment income	240	400	490	920	3,070	1,020
Other income	180	160	200	230	310	220
Total original income	3,410	9,140	19,240	32,000	62,080	25,180
plus Benefits in cash						
Contributory	2,590	2,880	2,040	1,280	720	1,900
Non-contributory	2,900	2,810	1,970	950	420	1,810
Gross income	8,910	14,820	23,260	34,230	63,230	28,890
less Income tax[3] and NIC[4]	390	1,380	3,320	6,280	14,070	5,090
less Local taxes[5] (net)	650	710	890	1,010	1,130	880
Disposable income	7,870	12,730	19,050	26,950	48,030	22,930
less Indirect taxes	2,710	2,940	4,150	5,200	6,660	4,330
Post-tax income	5,160	9,790	14,910	21,750	41,370	18,600
plus Benefits in kind						
Education	2,250	1,630	1,650	1,410	770	1,540
National Health Service	2,770	2,740	2,330	2,150	1,790	2,360
Housing subsidy	80	80	40	20	10	50
Travel subsidies	60	60	50	60	80	60
School meals and welfare milk	70	30	10	-	-	20
Final income	10,410	14,320	18,990	25,390	44,020	22,620

1 See Appendix, Part 5: Redistribution of income.
2 Equivalised disposable income has been used for ranking the households. See Appendix, Part 5: Equivalisation scales.
3 After tax relief at source on life assurance premiums.
4 Employees' national insurance contributions.
5 Council tax net of council tax benefits, rates and water charges. Rates net of rebates in Northern Ireland.

Source: Office for National Statistics

extent has to be arbitrary. Only in countries at a very low level of economic development is it sensible to take an absolutist, 'basic needs' approach, which costs the bare essentials to maintain human life and uses this as the yardstick against which incomes are measured. All other approaches are to a greater or lesser extent relative: 'low' income is defined in terms of what is generally considered adequate to maintain an acceptable standard of living given the norms of a particular society at a particular time. With such approaches, it is possible and indeed perfectly acceptable for 'low' income to differ both temporally and spatially. So for example, while in one country the possession of sufficient income to pay for central heating might be considered a necessity, this might not have been the case in the same country a generation ago and nor might it be so for a different country today.

In this section, the threshold generally adopted to define low income is 60 per cent of median equivalised household disposable income. This is one of a set of indicators in the *Opportunity For All* report used to monitor the Government's strategy to tackle poverty and social exclusion. It has also been agreed by the Statistical Programme Committee of the European Union as the basis for making international comparisons of numbers of people on low incomes.

The Institute for Fiscal Studies estimates that in 2001/02 17 per cent of the population in Great Britain lived in households with income below this level, the same proportion as in 2000/01 (Figure 5.19). This proportion was fairly static during the 1960s, 1970s and early 1980s, fluctuating between 10 and 15 per cent. It then rose steeply from 1985 to reach a peak of 21 per cent in 1992. During the 1990s the proportion declined in most years, with the exception of 1996/97, though it remained well above the pre-1985 level. This pattern is also reflected in the proportion of people with incomes less than 50 per cent of the median.

The European Community Household Panel Survey allows us to compare the proportions of people on low incomes in each European Union (EU) member state. Overall, Eurostat estimates that 17 per cent of EU households had incomes below 60 per cent of the EU median equivalised disposable income in 2000 (Figure 5.20). However, only 1 per cent of households in Luxembourg, which had the highest GDP per head in the EU, fell below this income threshold compared with 49 per cent of households in Portugal and 41 per cent in Greece. In the United Kingdom, 15 per cent of households fell below the threshold, a similar proportion to Finland, France and Sweden.

Children are disproportionately present in low-income households: 21 per cent of children (2.7 million) were living in households with below 60 per cent of median income (before deduction of housing costs) in Great Britain in 2001/02 (Figure 5.21 – see overleaf). This proportion rose steeply between 1979 and 1981 from 12 per cent to 18 per cent and continued to rise to reach a peak of 27 per cent in 1991/92 and 1992/93. It fell back during the first half of the 1990s but then rose again to 25 per cent in 1996/97 and 1997/98, since when there has again been a gradual fall. If housing costs are deducted from income, the pattern of annual change during the 1990s is much the same, but at a level around 10 percentage points higher, resulting in 3.8 million children living in low-income households in 2001/02 on this basis. This is principally

Figure 5.19

Percentage of people whose income is below various fractions of median income[1,2]

United Kingdom
Percentages

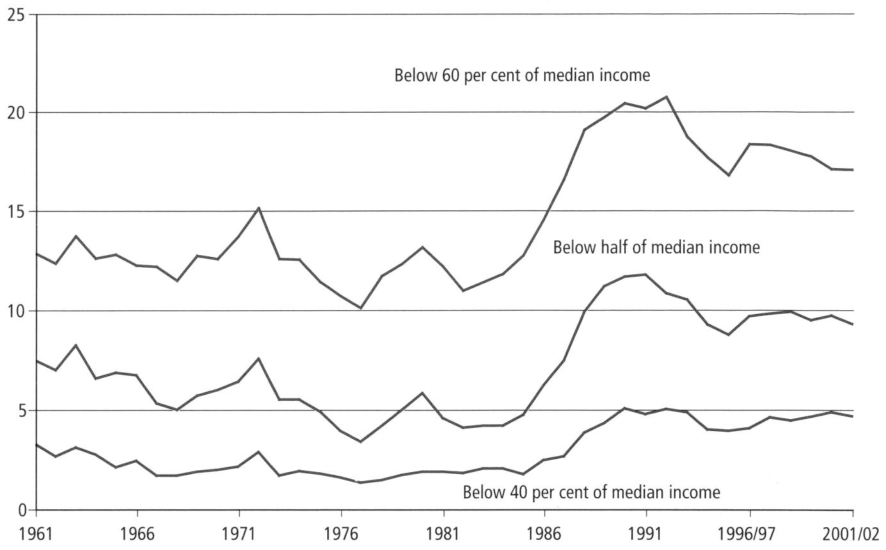

Below 60 per cent of median income

Below half of median income

Below 40 per cent of median income

1961 1966 1971 1976 1981 1986 1991 1996/97 2001/02

1 Equivalised household disposable income before housing costs. See Appendix, Part 5: Households Below Average Income, and Equivalisation scales.
2 Data from 1993/94 onwards are for financial years; data for 1994/95 onwards exclude Northern Ireland.

Source: Institute for Fiscal Studies

Figure 5.20

Percentage of people with incomes[1] below 60 per cent of the EU median: EU comparison, 2000

Percentages

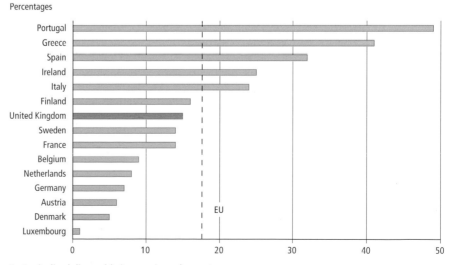

1 Equivalised disposable income in each country.

Source: European Community Household Panel, Eurostat

because housing costs for low-income households are large in relation to their income as a whole. This relationship applies not only to the results in Figure 5.21 but those in Table 5.22 as well.

Children living in workless families or households have a much higher risk of low income than those in families with one or more adults in full-time work. Around half of children in workless lone-parent families and around two thirds of children in workless couple families in 2001/02 were living in households with below 60 per cent of median income (before deduction of housing costs). If housing costs are deducted, these proportions rise to around three quarters for children in both workless couple and lone parent families. Other risk factors include being part of a large family, having one or more disabled adults in the family, and

being in a family where the head of household comes from a minority ethnic group, particularly if of Pakistani or Bangladeshi origin.

Indeed, people from minority ethnic groups are over-represented among low income households in Great Britain whatever their age (Table 5.22). Over half of people living in households headed by a Pakistani or Bangladeshi person had household disposable income below 60 per cent of the median before deduction of housing costs in 2000/01. This compares with between 21 and 29 per cent of those from other minority ethnic groups, but only 16 per cent of people in households headed by a White person. These proportions are higher after housing costs are deducted, for the reason explained above.

For some people, for example students and those unemployed for only a brief

period, the experience of low income may be a relatively transient one, whereas for others it may be a more or less permanent state through their life times. The British Household Panel Survey (BHPS) provides longitudinal data which allow income mobility and the persistence of low income to be analysed. Although around half of individuals had had at least one year living in households with income below 60 per cent of the median over the period 1991 to 2001, only 1 per cent were on low incomes throughout the period. This finding corroborates academic research that has examined different types of low-income trajectories and found that a considerable proportion of the population were 'blipping' in and out of low income or experiencing repeated spells of low income.

The Department for Work and Pensions analysis of Households Below Average Income, on which Figure 5.21 and Table 5.22 are based, shows also that pensioners (people living in families headed by someone of state pension age or above) are skewed towards the lower end of the income distribution. Overall, 22 per cent of pensioners were living in households with income less than 60 per cent of the median in 2001/02, compared with 17 per cent of the population as a whole. It seems reasonable to suppose that people's experience of low income after retirement will depend at least in part on their work history, since this will determine their entitlement to state, occupational and private pensions, together with the accumulation of other financial assets on which they can draw in retirement.

Using work history data collected as part of the BHPS, researchers at the Institute of Social and Economic Research have investigated the relationship between having a low income in later life and

Figure 5.21

Children living in households below 60 per cent of median income[1]

Great Britain
Percentages

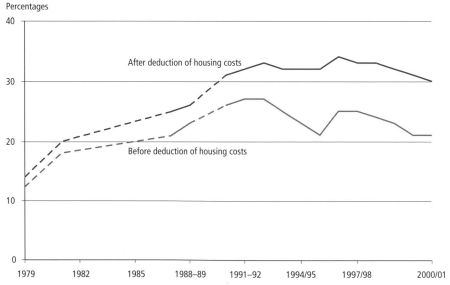

1 Equivalised household disposable income. See Appendix, Part 5: Households Below Average Income, and Equivalisation scales. Data are not available for 1980 and 1982 to 1986. Data from 1979 to 1993/94 are for United Kingdom from the Family Expenditure Survey. FES figures are single calendar years from 1979 to 1987, two combined calendar years from 1988–89 to 1992–93 and two financial years combined from 1993/94. From 1994/95 onwards data are for single financial years from the Family Resources Survey for Great Britain.

Source: Households Below Average Income, Department for Work and Pensions

people's lifetime employment history. They found that spending more years in paid work between the ages of 20 and 60 did not necessarily lower the risk of having a low income after the age of 60. Table 5.23 shows that although men who had spent fewer than 35 years in work between the ages of 20 and 60 had the highest rates of low income, the rates for men and women who worked at least 38 years out of 40 were higher than those who worked 35 to 37 years. (Note that this table uses a different definition of low income from that in the rest of this section.) In fact the effect depended on the occupational group in which an individual worked. A reduction in the risk of low income was associated with more years of paid work for men in the professional and personal and protective services occupations, and for women in managerial, professional, technical and clerical occupations. The table also shows that marital status is an important determinant of low income in later life for women but not for men. Women aged 60 and over living without

Table 5.22

Individuals in households with incomes below 60 per cent of median disposable income[1,2]: by ethnic group of head of household

Great Britain[1]   Percentages[2]

	1995/96	1999/2000	2000/01
Income before deduction of housing costs			
White	17	16	16
Black Caribbean	23	21	21
Black non-Caribbean	29	31	29
Indian	25	26	25
Pakistani/Bangladeshi	63	58	58
Other	29	26	26
All	18	18	17
Income after deduction of housing costs			
White	22	22	21
Black Caribbean	37	32	31
Black non-Caribbean	51	51	48
Indian	33	30	30
Pakistani/Bangladeshi	72	65	65
Other	45	39	37
All	24	23	23

1 Equivalised household disposable income. See Appendix, Part 5: Households Below Average Income and Equivalisation scales.
2 Estimates for each year are shown as three-year averages. For example the percentage of individuals in low income in 2000/01 is calculated from the unweighted raw estimates of 1999/2000, 2000/01 and 2001/02.

Source: Households Below Average Income, Department for Work and Pensions

Table 5.23

Individuals aged 60 and over experiencing low income[1]: by sex, number of years worked[2] and marital status, 1999

Great Britain   Percentages

	Males, number of years in work			Females, number of years in work				
	0–34	35–37	38–40	0	1–19	20–34	35–37	38–40
Single								
Widowed	39	22	33	45	53	52	51	49
Divorced	45	26	22	72	65	44	52	69
Never married	24	38	30	42	55	25	32	45
Married								
Partner employed	8	4	9	9	15	5	2	2
Partner not employed	36	23	29	44	34	27	30	21
All aged 60 and over	34	21	25	45	42	37	35	39

1 An individual was defined as having low income if his or her household equivalised disposable income averaged over the last three years was in the bottom third of the income distribution among all persons aged 60 and over.
2 Years worked between the ages of 20 and 59.

Source: British Household Panel Survey, Institute of Social and Economic Research

Table **5.24**

Indicators of social capital[1]: by gross weekly household income, 2000

Great Britain   Percentages

	Household income less than £250 per week	All other Households
Positive indicators		
High reciprocity	49	54
High neighbourliness	36	32
Satisfactory friendship network	66	66
Satisfactory relatives network	58	49
Enjoys living in area	83	88
Feels safe after dark	41	62
Feels civically engaged	17	19
Negative indicators		
Low social support	25	15
Low local facilities	35	33
High local problems	39	32
Been a victim of crime	14	15

1 See Appendix, Part 5: Indicators of social capital.

Source: General Household Survey, Office for National Statistics

Table **5.25**

Composition of the net wealth[1] of the household sector

United Kingdom   £ billion at 2002[2] prices

	1991	1996	2000	2001	2002
Non-financial assets	1,897	1,651	2,463	2,586	3,078
Financial assets					
Life assurance and pension funds	817	1,211	1,741	1,628	1,377
Securities and shares	340	498	780	584	451
Currency and deposits	511	556	665	701	743
Other assets	86	82	93	94	91
Total assets	3,651	3,998	5,742	5,594	5,740
Financial liabilities					
Loans secured on dwellings	424	458	555	598	669
Other loans	114	106	153	170	186
Other liabilities	60	57	61	61	63
Total liabilities	597	621	768	830	919
Total net wealth	3,054	3,377	4,974	4,765	4,821

1 See Appendix, Part 5: Net wealth of the household sector.
2 Adjusted to 2002 prices using the expenditure deflator for the household sector.

Source: Office for National Statistics

a partner, particularly those who were divorced, had a substantially higher risk of low income even if they had worked for much of their life.

Having a low income is usually seen as synonymous with being disadvantaged, and thus 'excluded' from many of the opportunities available to the average citizen. While low income is clearly central to poverty and social exclusion, it is now widely accepted that there is a wide range of other factors which are important. People can experience poverty of education, of training, of health, and of environment, as well as poverty in purely cash terms. It is therefore of interest to see how such factors are related to cash poverty. One such factor is social capital, the main aspects of which are citizenship, neighbourliness, trust and shared values, community involvement, volunteering, social networks and civic and political participation. See Appendix, Part 5: Indicators of social capital for descriptions of the indicators used in this table.

Table 5.24 indicates that lower income is not necessarily related to low levels of social capital. (Note that low income is defined here as gross weekly household income of £250 or less – in the General Household Survey from which these data are drawn, 39 per cent of households had incomes below this level, equivalent to the two lowest quintile groups). High neighbourliness and a satisfactory relatives network were in fact more prevalent among households with incomes less than £250 per week compared with those with incomes above that level. However, the lower income households were considerably less likely to give and receive favours from neighbours (high reciprocity), to enjoy living in their areas, and to feel safe after dark, though their likelihood of having been a victim of crime was not very different. Lower income households were also rather more likely to report low social support and high local problems.

Wealth

Although the terms 'wealthy' and 'high income' are often used interchangeably, in fact they relate to quite distinct concepts. 'Income' represents a flow of resources over a period, received either in cash or in kind. 'Wealth' on the other hand describes the ownership of assets valued at a particular point in time. These assets may provide the owner with a flow of income, for example interest payments on a building society account, or they may not, for example the ownership of works of art – unless of course the asset is sold. However, not all assets can be sold and their value realised. In particular, an individual's stake in an occupational pension scheme often cannot be 'cashed in'. The distinction is therefore usually made between 'marketable wealth' which the owner can sell if they so desire, and 'non-marketable wealth'. Wealth may be accumulated either by the acquisition of new assets, or by the increase in value of existing assets.

The wealth of the household sector in the United Kingdom, net of any loans outstanding on the purchase of assets such as housing, showed strong growth during the 1990s, increasing by nearly two thirds between 1991 and 2000 after adjusting for inflation (Table 5.25). Wealth then fell in real terms between 2000 and 2001, due mainly to falls in the value of holdings in life assurance and pension funds and in securities and shares, by 6 per cent and 25 per cent, respectively, reflecting the fall in stock market values. These elements of wealth fell again in value between 2001 and 2002, by a further 15 per cent and 23

Table **5.26**

Distribution of wealth[1]

United Kingdom

Percentages

	1991	1996	1999	2000	2001
Marketable wealth					
Percentage of wealth owned by[2]					
Most wealthy 1%	17	20	23	22	23
Most wealthy 5%	35	40	43	42	43
Most wealthy 10%	47	52	55	55	56
Most wealthy 25%	71	74	74	74	75
Most wealthy 50%	92	93	94	94	95
Total marketable wealth (£ billion)	1,711	2,092	2,842	3,093	3,363
Marketable wealth less value of dwellings					
Percentage of wealth owned by[2]					
Most wealthy 1%	29	26	34	32	33
Most wealthy 5%	51	49	59	58	58
Most wealthy 10%	64	63	72	72	72
Most wealthy 25%	80	81	86	88	86
Most wealthy 50%	93	94	98	98	97

1 See Appendix, Part 5: Distribution of personal wealth. Estimates for individual years should be treated with caution as they are affected by sampling error and the particular pattern of deaths in that year.
2 Adults aged 18 and over.

Source: Inland Revenue

per cent, respectively. However, growth in the value of the stock of non-financial assets such as residential dwellings was 19 per cent between 2001 and 2002, reflecting the buoyant state of the housing market, and meant that net wealth rose overall.

Non-financial assets formed the most important component of the wealth of the household sector in 2002, though the largest category of liability was loans secured on dwellings. The second most important component of household sector wealth in 2002 was holdings in life assurance and pension funds. The strong growth in this component of wealth over the last 10 years or so until recently has resulted both from increases in the contributions paid into occupational pension schemes as well as increased take-up of personal pension provision. Table 8.13 in

Chapter 8, Social Protection on page 119 shows how pension provision for those of working age varies between the sexes and type of work. Note that Table 5.25, like charts and tables at the beginning of this chapter, is drawn from the national accounts and therefore households are combined with the non-profit making institutions.

Wealth is considerably less evenly distributed than income. Life cycle effects mean that this will almost always be so: people build up assets during the course of their working lives and then draw them down during the years of retirement with the residue passing to others at their death. It is estimated that the most wealthy 1 per cent of individuals owned between a sixth and a quarter of the total wealth of the household sector over the last decade (Table 5.26). In contrast, half

Table **5.27**

Household savings: by household type and amount, 2001/02

Great Britain

Percentages

	No savings	Less than £1,500	£1,500 but less than £10,000	£10,000 but less than £20,000	£20,000 or more	All households (=100%) (millions)
One adult over pensionable age, no children	28	19	27	10	16	3.7
Two adults, one or both over pensionable age, no children	17	14	25	14	30	4.0
Two adults under pensionable age						
No children	19	22	30	12	17	4.5
One or more children	30	26	26	8	9	5.3
One adult under pensionable age						
No children	37	22	26	8	8	3.6
One or more children	67	23	7	1	2	1.9
Other households	21	23	29	12	15	2.3
All households	28	21	26	10	15	25.3

Source: Family Resources Survey, Department for Work and Pensions

the population shared between them only 5 per cent of total wealth in 2001. If the value of housing is omitted from the wealth estimates, the resulting distribution is even more skewed indicating that this form of wealth is rather more evenly distributed than the remainder.

This analysis of the aggregate data available on the distribution of wealth is borne out by information available from the Family Resources Survey based on individuals' own estimates of their savings. In 2001/02, 28 per cent of households in Great Britain reported having no savings at all (Table 5.27). Savings patterns vary with household type. Couples where one or both partner were over state retirement pension age are the most likely to have substantial savings – three in ten had savings of £20,000 or more, twice the proportion in the population as a whole.

This is perhaps not surprising since they may have had the opportunity to build up their savings over their working lives, though the pattern of savings of single pensioner households is very similar to that of the population as a whole. Single people with children were the most likely to have no savings at all.

The term 'financial exclusion' has been coined to describe those people who do not use financial services at all. Data from the Family Resources Survey indicate that in 2001/02, nearly one in ten benefit units did not have any kind of current account (including Post Office account) or investments such as savings accounts or premium bonds. This proportion rose to one in four of lone parent families. Since the options for operating a household budget without mainstream financial services are more expensive and often unregulated, this is of policy concern.

National income and expenditure

Gross domestic product (GDP) measures the level of income generated by economic activity in the United Kingdom in accordance with international conventions. Figure 5.1 at the beginning of this chapter showed that, when adjusted for inflation, the trend in GDP per head since 1971 has generally been one of steady growth. However, within this long term trend the United Kingdom is nevertheless subject to cycles of weaker and stronger growth, usually referred to as the economic or business cycle.

The year on year growth rates for total GDP, adjusted to remove the effects of inflation, shown in Figure 5.28 suggest that the UK economy contracted in the mid-1970s, at the time of the OPEC oil crisis, and again in the early 1980s and early 1990s. However, growth has exceeded 4 per cent per year ten times in the post-war period, most recently in 1994. The long term average annual growth rate was 2.5 per cent between 1948 and 2002, but growth between 2001 and 2002 fell to 1.7 per cent, the lowest rate since 1992. In 2000, the base year for these figures, over two thirds of gross value added was from the services sector, compared to under a quarter from the production sector. Agriculture accounted for about 1 per cent, and construction for about 5 per cent.

The major industrialised countries, often known as the G7, all had GDP per head in excess of US$26,000 in 2001, measured in current prices and making adjustments for the relative purchasing power of national currencies (Figure 5.29). The level of economic activity in the United States was by far the highest within this grouping, around a third higher than the United Kingdom, Japan, France, Germany and Italy all of whom

Figure 5.28

Annual growth in gross domestic product in real terms[1]

United Kingdom
Percentages

1 Chain linked volume measure of GDP.
Source: Office for National Statistics

clustered between US$26,000 and US$27,000 per head.

The World Bank publishes estimates of gross national income (GNI) per head for virtually all the countries of the world, on a slightly different basis from those of OECD shown in Figure 5.29. For 2002 the World Bank estimates that the countries with lowest GNI per head in the world were the Democratic Republic of the Congo, Ethiopia and Burundi, with GNI of US$100 per head or less. Of the 25 poorest countries, 22 were in sub-Saharan Africa and all had GNI per head of less than US$300.

Government receives income primarily through transfers from individuals, companies and other organisations in the form of taxes, national insurance contributions and other payments, though they may also engage in economic activity from which income is derived. This revenue is then spent on the provision of goods and services such as healthcare and education, on servicing government debt, and on transfer payments such as

Figure 5.29

Gross domestic product per head: G7 comparison, 2001

US$ (thousands)[1]

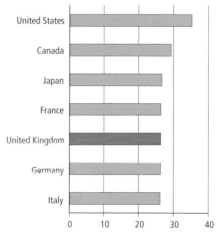

1 Based on current purchasing power parities.
Source: Organisation for Economic Co-operation and Development

Figure **5.30**

Total managed expenditure as a percentage of gross domestic product

United Kingdom
Percentages

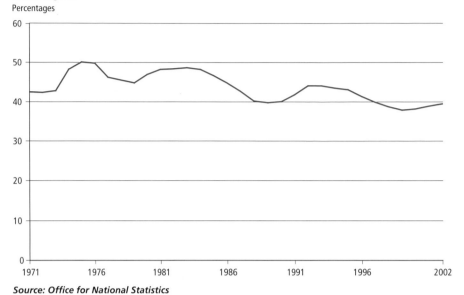

Source: Office for National Statistics

Table **5.31**

European Union expenditure[1]: by sector

Percentages

	1981	1986	1991	1996	2000	2001	2002
Agricultural Guarantee	62	64	58	51	46	47	46
Structural funds							
Agricultural guidance	3	2	4	4	4	3	3
Regional policy	14	7	12	14	16	15	15
Social policy	3	7	8	8	9	9	9
Other	.	.	3	6	7	6	6
All structural funds	20	16	26	32	36	34	34
Research	2	2	3	4	4	4	4
External action	4	3	4	5	6	7	8
Administration	5	4	5	5	5	5	5
Other	6	10	4	3	2	2	2
All expenditure (=100%) (€ billion)	17.7	34.7	53.5	77.0	89.4	93.8	95.7

1 At current prices.

Source: European Commission

social security benefits. The present Government's main measure of public expenditure is however total managed expenditure (TME).

TME rose as a proportion of GDP during the economic downturn in the first half of the 1970s, in particular between 1973 and 1974, and reached nearly 50 per cent in 1975 and 1976 (Figure 5.30). Between 1983 and 1989 the proportion fell, but there was a slight rise in the early 1990s during another period of economic downturn. From 1993 to 1999, it fell again to reach 38 per cent, the lowest figure since the early 1960s, but it has since risen to 39 per cent in 2002.

As well as expenditure for purely domestic purposes, total managed expenditure also includes the contributions made by the United Kingdom to the EC budget. In 2002, the United Kingdom contributed €10.2 billion and had receipts amounting to €6.2 billion. Germany was the largest net contributor, with contributions exceeding receipts by €5.9 billion, while Finland, Belgium, Luxembourg, Ireland, Portugal, Greece and Spain were net recipients from the EC budget in 2002.

Of total EC expenditure in 2002, just under half was budgeted to be spent in support of agriculture in the form of Agricultural Guarantee (Table 5.31). Although still substantial, this proportion has fallen by 16 percentage points since 1981, while structural funds expenditure has risen in importance. Structural funds aim to reduce regional disparities and thus to achieve a more even social and economic balance across the EU. The areas within the United Kingdom currently eligible for EU structural funds include Cornwall, West Wales and the Valleys, South Yorkshire and Merseyside.

Chapter 6 **Expenditure**

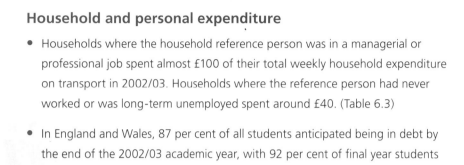

Household and personal expenditure

- Households where the household reference person was in a managerial or professional job spent almost £100 of their total weekly household expenditure on transport in 2002/03. Households where the reference person had never worked or was long-term unemployed spent around £40. (Table 6.3)

- In England and Wales, 87 per cent of all students anticipated being in debt by the end of the 2002/03 academic year, with 92 per cent of final year students anticipating being in debt by the time they left university. (Page 97)

Transactions and credit

- Transactions by credit and debit cards in the United Kingdom continued to grow with total purchases by credit card of around £100 billion and total purchases by debit card just under £110 billion in 2002. (Table 6.11)

- Net consumer borrowing continues to be high, and was £5 billion in the second quarter of 2003. (Figure 6.12)

Prices

- In 2003, relative regional consumer price levels were published for the first time and showed London prices to be over 7 per cent above the national average and those in the North East over 8 per cent below the national average. (Page 102)

- A visitor from the United Kingdom would have found only one G7 country, Japan, more expensive than the United Kingdom in the summer of 2003. (Figure 6.18)

Figure **6.1**

Household expenditure index[1]

United Kingdom
Indices[1] (1971=100)

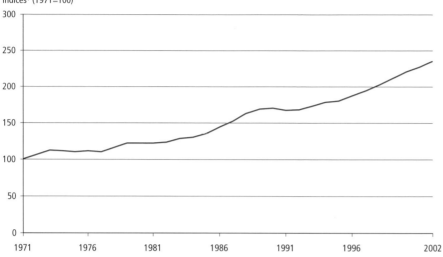

1 See Appendix, Part 6: Household expenditure index.

Source: Office for National Statistics

Table **6.2**

Household expenditure[1]

United Kingdom   Indices[1] (1971=100)

	1971	1981	1991	.. 2001	2002	£ billion (current prices) 2002
Housing, water and fuel	100	117	138	152	154	118.4
Transport	100	128	181	242	251	98.3
Recreation and culture	100	161	283	545	570	79.5
Restaurants and hotels[2]	100	126	167	194	199	76.6
Food and non-alcoholic drink	100	105	117	137	138	60.8
Household goods and services	100	117	160	268	296	43.3
Clothing and footwear	100	120	187	340	371	37.8
Alcohol and tobacco	100	99	92	89	91	26.3
Communication	100	190	306	790	828	15.0
Health	100	125	182	175	179	10.1
Education	100	160	199	250	218	8.4
Miscellaneous	100	119	230	280	290	82.0
Less expenditure by foreign tourists, etc	100	152	187	210	219	-14.3
Household expenditure abroad	100	193	298	669	715	24.6
All household expenditure	100	122	167	227	235	666.9

1 See Appendix, Part 6: Household expenditure. Classified to COICOP ESA95 (Classification Of
   Individual Consumption by Purpose).
2 Includes purchase of alcoholic drink.

Source: Office for National Statistics

The types of goods and services people choose to spend their income on have changed considerably over the past 30 years. Such personal spending allows insights into both people and society – being an indication of a person's standard of living and material well being, as well as a reflection of changes in society, consumer preference, and the growth in choices available to the consumer.

Household and personal expenditure

There has been a steady increase in household expenditure over the last 30 years in the United Kingdom (Figure 6.1). This represents an average increase in expenditure of 2.8 per cent a year, in real terms, that is after allowing for the effects of inflation. There were periods (most notably in the mid-1970s and early 1990s) when household expenditure, in real terms, fell as a result of general economic downturns. In contrast, more recent economic and other world-wide uncertainties related to events in 2001 have had smaller impacts. The rate of increase in household expenditure slowed between 2000 and 2001 to 3.1 per cent but then recovered to 3.6 per cent in 2002.

Since 1971, household spending has increased for all of the broad categories of expenditure, with the exception of alcohol and tobacco (Table 6.2). The latter fall could be partly due to under-reporting and the fact that personal imports are separately identified in the survey. In 2002, household expenditure on certain non-essentials including communication, spending abroad, and recreation and culture, has risen far more sharply than for the more essential items. This reflects higher levels of disposable income (see Figure 5.1) which allow increased spending on such non-essentials, with proportionally less spent on items such as food.

Levels of expenditure vary among different groups in the population. This is evident when household spending is considered in relation to the social economic classification (NS-SeC) of the household reference person. The detailed NS-SeC classification can be reduced to four broad classes. The classes are defined as managerial and professional; intermediate; routine and manual; and never worked and long-term unemployed (Table 6.3). Total expenditure in 2002/03 was highest for those households where the reference person was in the managerial and professional group and was almost double the expenditure for households in the never worked and long-term unemployed group. Indeed, the managerial and professional group had the highest level of spending on most expenditure categories, with spending on health and household goods and services being almost four times greater than spending on these categories by never worked and long-term unemployed households.

Total expenditure for the routine and manual group and the intermediate group was substantially below that for the managerial and professional group. Although the group of those who had never worked and long term unemployed had by far the lowest level of overall expenditure, they spent more than the other groups on education, housing, fuel and power (excluding mortgage interest payments, water charges, council tax and domestic rates in Northern Ireland) and communication. This is likely to be due to the inclusion of students in this group, who are known to have high levels of spending on these

categories. Of all groups, however, those in routine and manual occupations spent most on alcohol and tobacco and the least on education.

The size and composition of a household influences the expenditure patterns within that household. Larger households tend to have higher expenditure, with the presence or

absence of children having a great influence on household size and therefore on expenditure. However, when weekly household expenditure for a particular category of goods or services is analysed as a percentage of overall household expenditure, the variations between family types are fairly marginal (Table 6.4 – see overleaf) Such similarity in proportions spent is

Table **6.3**

Household expenditure: by socio-economic classification[1] of household reference person, 2002/03

United Kingdom   £ per week

	Occupations			Never worked[2] and long-term unemployed
	Managerial and professional	Intermediate	Routine and manual	
Transport	98.40	72.10	57.70	37.80
Recreation and culture	86.30	59.20	57.20	44.00
Food and non-alcoholic drink	52.60	44.90	43.40	30.90
Housing, fuel and power[3]	47.00	39.40	38.30	67.20
Restaurant and hotels	58.90	38.10	35.50	42.90
Household goods and services	49.50	29.70	26.80	13.90
Clothing and footwear	33.60	25.30	24.10	24.50
Alcohol and tobacco	13.50	11.60	13.80	9.00
Communication	13.80	12.40	11.40	17.10
Education	13.20	5.10	2.10	14.80
Health	7.30	4.50	3.10	2.00
Miscellaneous goods and services	53.30	35.40	30.10	18.20
Other expenditure items	109.70	69.70	52.70	17.70
All household expenditure	637.00	447.50	396.10	340.00

1 See Appendix, Part 6: Household expenditure, and National Statistics Socio-economic Classification. Expenditure rounded to the nearest 10 pence.
2 Includes students.
3 Excludes mortgage interest payments, water charges, council tax and domestic rates in Northern Ireland. See 'Other expenditure items' for spending on these.

Source: Expenditure and Food Survey, Office for National Statistics

Table 6.4

Household expenditure[1]: by selected family types, 2002/03

United Kingdom | Percentages

| | Couple | | Single | | | | |
	With children	No children	With children	No children	Pensioner couple	Single pensioner	All households
Transport	14	16	11	14	12	9	15
Recreation and culture	14	14	13	13	16	12	14
Food and non-alcoholic drink	10	9	12	7	16	15	11
Housing, fuel and power[2]	7	8	12	12	10	17	9
Restaurants and hotels	8	9	8	9	7	5	9
Household goods and services	7	7	6	7	8	9	7
Clothing and footwear	6	5	8	4	4	4	6
Alcohol and tobacco	2	3	3	3	3	3	3
Communication	2	2	4	3	2	3	3
Education	3	1	1	1	1	0	1
Health	1	1	1	1	3	2	1
Miscellaneous goods and services	9	8	9	7	9	9	8
Other expenditure items	16	17	14	20	10	11	14
All household expenditure (=100%) (£ per week)	587.40	502.10	328.10	292.80	286.00	142.30	406.60

1 See Appendix, Part 6: Household expenditure. Expenditure rounded to the nearest 10 pence.
2 Excludes mortgage interest payments, water charges, council tax and domestic rates in Northern Ireland. See 'Other expenditure items' for spending on these.

Source: Expenditure and Food Survey, Office for National Statistics

Figure 6.5

Students' expenditure by type, 2002/03

England & Wales
Percentages

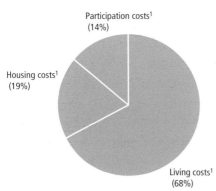

Participation costs[1] (14%)

Housing costs[1] (19%)

Living costs[1] (68%)

Total mean expenditure: £6,897

1 See Appendix, Part 6: Student expenditure.

Source: Student Income and Expenditure Survey, South Bank University

also evident when data are analysed according to income groups, with the highest and lowest groups spending similar proportions of their household incomes on many categories. However, single pensioners – most often women living alone – spent far more (17 per cent) on housing, fuel and power (excluding mortgage interest payments, water charges, council tax and domestic rates in Northern Ireland) than did couple pensioners (10 per cent).

The number of students pursuing higher education in the United Kingdom has almost doubled over the last decade (see Table 3.11), and more than half of all such students are in full-time education. Recent analyses for the Department for Education and Skills investigated the spending patterns of full-time university students in England and Wales (Figure 6.5). Ninety per cent of the students surveyed were between 17 and 20 years old at the start of their courses with the remaining 10 per cent between 21 and 24 years old. In the 2002/03 academic year total average expenditure per student was almost £7,000, representing an increase of 28 per cent from four years earlier, with living costs accounting for around two thirds of all expenditure in both periods.

Table **6.6**

Household expenditure: by age of household reference person, 2002/03

United Kingdom
£ per week

	Under 30	30-49	50-64	65-74	75 and over	All households
Transport	58.60	72.90	72.40	35.10	15.60	59.20
Recreation and culture	51.40	67.20	65.60	42.10	23.00	56.40
Food and non-alcoholic beverages	30.90	48.20	47.80	38.90	29.40	42.70
Housing, water, electricity, gas and other fuels[1]	55.80	38.90	35.30	29.30	25.90	36.90
Restaurants and hotels	43.80	44.00	38.50	20.10	11.50	35.40
Furnishings, household equipment and routine maintenance of the house	22.70	35.60	36.90	22.00	14.90	30.20
Clothing and footwear	23.00	29.20	24.00	11.60	7.80	22.30
Alcoholic beverages and tobacco	11.20	13.00	13.40	8.50	5.10	11.40
Communication	13.30	12.80	10.60	6.90	5.10	10.60
Education	4.80	7.40	6.40	1.00	0.60	5.20
Health	2.40	4.60	6.30	5.90	3.50	4.80
Miscellaneous goods and services	31.80	41.20	34.70	22.20	16.90	33.10
Other expenditure items	50.60	82.50	59.70	27.90	18.00	58.30
All household expenditure	400.40	497.40	451.70	271.50	177.40	406.60

1 *Excludes mortgage interest payments, water charges, council tax and domestic rates in Northern Ireland. See 'Other expenditure items' for spending on these.*

Source: Expenditure and Food Survey, Office for National Statistics

Large variations in total annual expenditure were observed, with a student's age and region of study being the two most important factors contributing to these variations. These factors also interacted, as there were more older students in London. Students who were over 21 years old when they started their course spent around £1,500 more than younger students and those in London spent around £1,000 more than students outside the capital. While older students spent more on each of the three categories of expenditure shown in Figure 6.5, it was students living at home and in London who incurred particularly high travel costs. Indeed, most of the variation in all

students' participation costs can be accounted for by their travel costs. Other expenses covered in participation costs included books, equipment, and personal contributions towards fees.

In the 2002/03 academic year, students' average expenditure exceeded their average income by about £1,400. The most marked overspend was among older male London-based students. Eighty seven per cent of all students anticipated being in debt by the end of the 2002/03 academic year, with an average debt of around £5,000. Among final year students, 92 per cent anticipated leaving university with debts. All final year students anticipated

graduating with an average debt of around £9,000.

Household expenditure varies by the age of the household reference person (Table 6.6). In 2002/03, total weekly household expenditure was highest, at around £500, for the age group 30 to 49 years, after which it generally fell for each successive age group to under £180 for those aged 75 years and over. Overall, total household expenditure by the highest spending group (with a household reference person from 30 to 49 years old) is almost three times higher than for the oldest age group (which has a smaller household size on average).

Table **6.7**

Average weekly household expenditure on selected leisure items and activities[1]: by region, 2002/03

United Kingdom

£ per week

	Games, toys & hobbies[1]	Package holidays	Holiday accommodation (UK & abroad)	Restaurant & café meals	Alcoholic drinks (away from home)
United Kingdom	3.30	12.70	4.90	11.30	8.90
England	3.40	13.00	5.20	11.60	9.00
North East	3.60	8.40	2.20	9.30	10.30
North West	3.70	12.80	4.00	10.20	10.10
Yorkshire & the Humber	2.90	13.80	3.40	9.80	8.90
East Midlands	3.10	10.50	5.50	11.00	8.70
West Midlands	3.00	12.80	4.80	9.00	8.10
East	3.30	11.70	5.80	12.70	7.60
London	3.60	13.30	6.30	15.30	9.60
South East	3.70	15.70	6.80	12.80	9.70
South West	2.90	13.20	5.20	11.10	7.90
Wales	2.90	11.60	3.60	8.70	8.20
Scotland	2.70	11.50	4.40	9.90	8.00
Northern Ireland	3.30	9.00	2.10	10.60	8.70

1 Includes computer software and games.

Source: Expenditure and Food Survey, Office for National Statistics

Figure **6.8**

Expenditure on selected items as a percentage of total household expenditure[1]

United Kingdom
Percentages

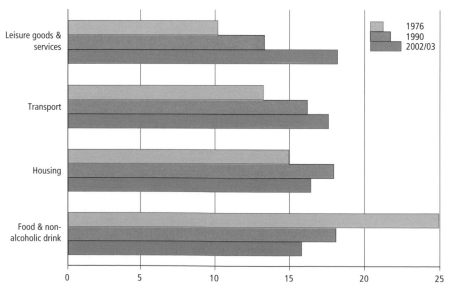

1 Figures for 1976 and 1990 are based on unweighted, adult-only data. Figures for 2002/03 are based on weighted data, including children's expenditure, with commodities and services based on COICOP codes broadly mapped to FES codes.

Source: Family Expenditure Survey and Expenditure and Food Survey, Office for National Statistics

Household expenditure also varies across both the regions of England and the four countries of the United Kingdom. Table 6.7 shows that households in Wales, Scotland and Northern Ireland consistently spent below UK averages for each of the selected leisure items and activities in 2002/03, with those in England spending more than any of the other parts of the United Kingdom. Those in the South East of England spent the most on package holidays and holiday accommodation. Households in London spent the most on restaurant and café meals.

As household incomes have grown during the last 26 years, the proportion of spending on some non-essential items has increased. Spending on food and non-alcoholic drink, as a percentage of total expenditure, has reduced from 25 per cent in 1976 to 16 per cent in 2002/03 (Figure 6.8). Over the same period spending on leisure goods and services has increased from 10 per cent to 18 per cent. Spending on transport also increased over this period, from 13 per cent to 18 per cent, reflecting changing patterns in car ownership and the volume of travel undertaken (see also Chapter 12, Transport – Figure 12.7). There have also been notable changes in spending on telephone communication. For example, between 1998/99 and 2002/03, spending on call charges for mobiles as a proportion of total account payments increased from 19 to 36 per cent, with payments for fixed phones dropping from 81 to 64 per cent.

The number of people shopping through the Internet has continued to increase. The Expenditure and Food Survey reported that in the third quarter of 2003, 48 per cent of UK households had Internet access at home. The Omnibus

Survey in October 2003 showed that almost 31 per cent of all adults in Great Britain had ordered tickets, goods or services over the Internet. This represented 53 per cent of all those who had ever accessed the Internet (see also Chapter 13, Lifestyles and social participation – Table 13.16).

Transactions and credit

The volume of retail sales in Great Britain has increased steadily over the last decade (Figure 6.9), despite the slowdown in the rate of increase in gross domestic product. Within any given year, retail sales show a strong seasonal pattern, peaking in December.

A standard indicator for measuring the changes in levels of retail sales is the percentage change in the volume of these sales compared with the same twelve month period a year earlier. This measure has increased in each of the last four years, from 2.9 per cent in 1998 to 6.2 per cent in 2002. The twelve-month increase between 2001 and 2002 is the largest in the last decade.

The manner in which transactions are undertaken in the United Kingdom continues to show an increase towards methods which do not involve cash. The value of transactions by credit and debit cards continue to grow, while the use of personal cheques continues to fall (Figure 6.10). With these changes there has, however, been an increase in card-related crime and new cards are being issued to combat such fraud. These cards will have a chip which can store information more securely than a magnetic strip, with consumers verifying a transaction by keying in a four-digit personal identification number (PIN), rather than signing a receipt. By 2005, the majority of face-to-face plastic card transactions will be made in such a way.

Figure **6.9**

Volume of retail sales
Great Britain
Index (2000=100)

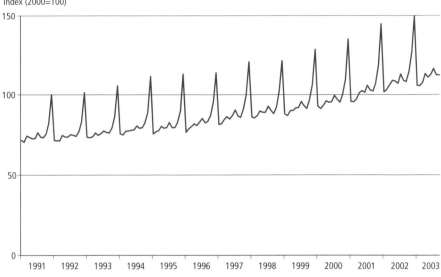

Source: Office for National Statistics

Figure **6.10**

Non-cash transactions[1]: by method of payment
United Kingdom
Billions

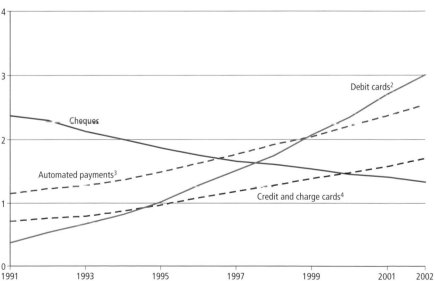

1 Figures are for payments only, cheque encashments and cash withdrawals from ATMs and branch counters using credit/charge and debit cards are not included.
2 Visa Debit and Switch cards in all years; includes Electron cards from 1996 and Solo cards from 1997.
3 Includes direct debits, standing orders, direct credits, inter-branch automated items.
4 Visa, MasterCard, travel/entertainment cards and store cards.

Source: Association for Payment Clearing Services

Table **6.11**

Debit[1] or credit[2] card spending: by type of purchase, 2002

United Kingdom   £ billions

	Debit cards	Credit cards
Food and drink	30.93	11.94
Motoring	13.92	11.51
Household	9.61	12.95
Clothing	7.07	5.42
Mixed business	6.52	7.04
Travel	5.99	11.70
Entertainment	5.07	6.23
Financial	1.32	0.60
Hotels	1.16	4.23
Other services	12.84	13.27
Other retail	12.59	16.89
Total	107.00	101.77

1 Visa and Switch cards only.
2 MasterCard and Visa cards only.

Source: Credit Card Research Group

Figures from the Credit Card Research Group (CCRG) indicate that spending patterns differ for credit and debit cards (Figure 6.11). Spending by debit card is greatest on purchases from retailers of food and drink, such as supermarkets, off licences, and general food stores. Such use of debit cards accounted for approximately £31 billion in 2002, up from £24 billion in 2000, and is more than double that spent with credit cards in such outlets. By comparison, credit card spending is higher than debit card spending for hotels and travel, and from household retailers (including DIY stores, furniture shops, garden centres, household appliance and electrical goods stores) and 'other' retailers. This suggests that the use of credit cards is preferred for larger, less routine items.

The single greatest use of credit cards was for goods from other retailers, which include book shops, record stores, pharmacies, jewellers and computer shops, and accounted for spending of around £17 billion.

Continuing high levels of retail sales have also been matched by high levels of consumer borrowing (Figure 6.12). Consumer borrowing in real terms increased each year between 1992 and 1998, from £0.6 billion to £15.6 billion, and then remained fairly level to 2000. That levelling was followed by sharp increases in 2001 and 2002. Mortgage Equity Withdrawal, that part of borrowing secured on dwellings that is not invested in the housing market, has also been strong in recent years.

Such high, generally continuous levels of borrowing can result in people being unable to meet their debt repayments. An individual may be officially declared bankrupt if a court is satisfied that there is no prospect of the debt being paid. However, in many cases, the courts encourage a voluntary arrangement to be agreed between the debtor and their creditors. Annual figures of individual insolvencies show a steady increase since 1999 (Figure 6.13). The number of voluntary arrangements has dropped since 2000 but this has been more than offset by an increase in bankruptcies.

Prices

How people and households choose to spend their money is affected by the price of the goods and services that they want to buy. The retail prices index (RPI) is the most familiar general purpose measure of inflation in the United Kingdom. It measures the average change, from month to month, in the prices of the goods and services purchased by most households in the United Kingdom.

Figure **6.12**

Net borrowing[1] by consumers in real terms[2]

United Kingdom
£ billion at 2002 prices[3]

1 Excludes lending secured on dwellings.
2 Adjusted to 2002 prices using RPI deflator.
3 Quarterly data, seasonally adjusted.

Source: Bank of England; Office for National Statistics

The RPI monitors the cost of a representative shopping basket of around 650 goods and services which are bought by a typical household. The price movements of these are measured in around 150 areas throughout the United Kingdom, with prices for around 100 goods and services collected centrally by the Office for National Statistics (ONS). A small number of changes are made each year to the basket to ensure the RPI continues to reflect consumer spending patterns. In 2003, around 30 new items were added to this representative basket, and a similar number dropped. The changes reflected increasing use of takeaways and convenience foods plus the growth of high street coffee shops. Prices for diet drink powder and slimming clubs are also now tracked as people continue to increase spending on trying to lose weight. For the first time, a specific price index for air fares was introduced, and the new London congestion charge was added.

There have been periods of both high and low inflation over the last 40 years, with peaks exceeding 20 per cent during some periods in 1975, 1976, 1980 (Figure 6.14). Inflation rates were generally below 5 per cent throughout most of the 1960s and again through the 1990s. In 2003, however, inflation has been generally higher than at any time since 1998. Inflation rates fluctuating between 2.8 and 3.2 per cent between January and September 2003, were consistently at levels above the same 12-month periods a year earlier. The movement of the inflation rate reflects the price movements of the goods and services of which the RPI is composed. Figure 6.15 (see overleaf) shows the annual percentage change for selected groups of purchases in the RPI between 2001 and 2002. The greatest change

Figure 6.13

Number of individual insolvencies

England & Wales
Thousands

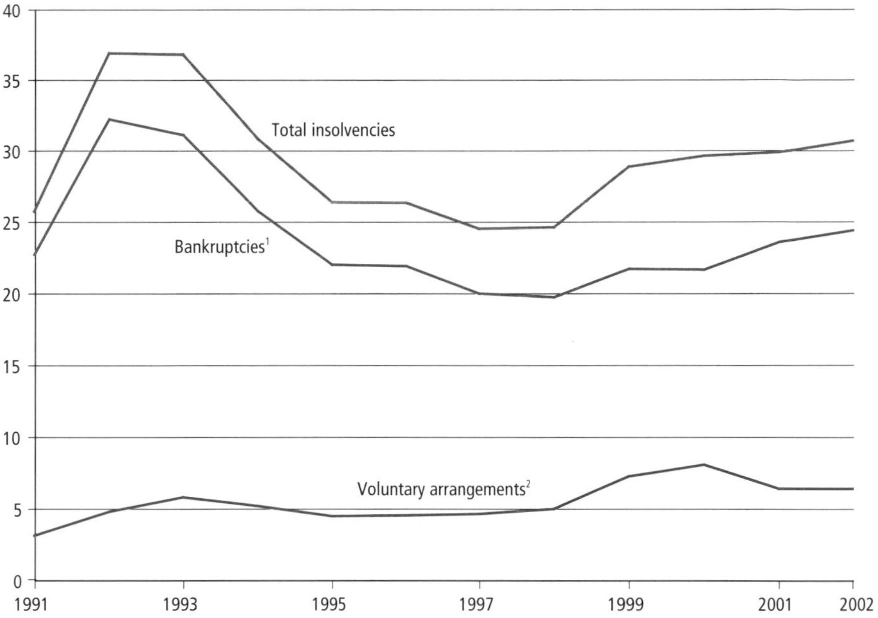

1 Individuals declared bankrupt by a court.
2 Individuals who make a voluntary agreement with their creditors.
Source: Department of Trade and Industry

Figure 6.14

Retail prices index[1]

United Kingdom
Percentage change over 12 months

1 See Appendix, Part 6: Retail prices index.
Source: Office for National Statistics

occurred in prices for leisure services, which increased by 8 per cent, while price changes for household services and catering both increased by 4 per cent. Three categories decreased in price with the largest reduction being for clothing and footwear at almost 5 per cent.

The prices of food items can fluctuate up or down due to production and supply levels which, in turn, can be affected by factors out of the producers' direct control. Such factors may include weather conditions, local or international agricultural policies, and disruptions to supplies.

Table 6.16 shows the average cost of selected groceries between 1971 and 2002. While many prices for grocery items such as bacon, cheese and eggs have consistently increased over this time, those for some, such as granulated sugar and white sliced bread, have fluctuated with prices decreasing between 1991 and 2001.

It is recognised that prices of items in the RPI may vary across the country. The ONS is currently considering how regional variations to prices and inflation may be accurately estimated. So far, experimental work has been undertaken and regional consumer price levels for 2003 published. These show that prices in London are over 7 per cent above the national average, while those in the North East are over 8 per cent below average. Work will continue to ensure that increasingly accurate regional estimates are developed in the future.

The United Kingdom Consumer Price Index (CPI) is the main domestic measure of inflation for macroeconomic purposes. From 10 December 2003, this index replaced the all items RPI excluding mortgage interest payment (RPIX) as the target measure of inflation. Prior to 10 December 2003 this index was published in the UK as the Harmonised Index of Consumer Prices (HICP). The CPI is constructed using the same principles as the RPI but differs in a number of ways, including the coverage of goods and services. For example, the RPI index for new cars is imputed from movements in second hand car prices, whereas the CPI uses a quality adjusted index based on published prices of new cars. Additionally, the CPI includes series for university accommodation fees while the RPI does not. There is also an

Figure **6.15**

Percentage change in retail prices index, 2002[1]

United Kingdom
Percentages

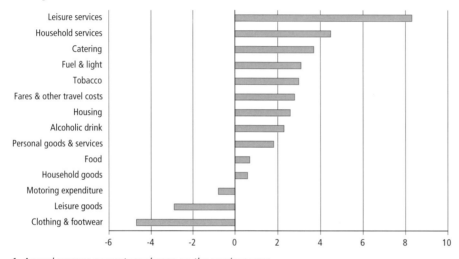

1 Annual average percentage change on the previous year.

Source: Office for National Statistics

Table **6.16**

Cost of groceries

United Kingdom

Pence

	1971	1981	1991	1996	2001	2002
500g back bacon	41	144	243	295	343	350
250g cheddar cheese	14	58	86	115	128	131
500g margarine	14	37	45	73	80	80
250g butter (UK produced)	15	51	62	82	79	77
Half dozen eggs (size 2)	11	39	59	79	86	86
125g loose tea	9	28	59	63	83	..
250g tea bags	..	..	..	134	146	153
1 kg granulated sugar	19	39	66	76	57	62
800g white sliced bread	10	37	53	55	51	57
1 kg old potatoes	4	15	35	62	89	85
1 pint pasteurised milk	6	19	32	36	37	36

Source: Office for National Statistics

important methodological difference between the two indices in the way in which individual prices are combined at the most basic level. The CPI uses the geometric mean, whereas the RPI uses the arithmetic mean. This lowers the CPI inflation rate relative to the RPI.

Figure 6.17 shows the changes in consumer prices across EU countries which are based on the 12 month change in the HICP at December 2002. Within the European Union (EU), the United Kingdom continued to experience a low inflation rate, which, at 1.7 per cent, was below the EU average of 2.2 per cent. Only Germany and Belgium, at 1.1 per cent and 1.3 per cent, respectively, had lower inflation rates than the United Kingdom. The highest rates were in Ireland, Portugal and Spain. All had inflation rates in 2002 of 4 per cent or above.

The world-wide spending power of the pound sterling depends on the relative price levels of goods and services and the exchange rates between countries. comparative price levels (CPLs) are used to indicate whether another country will appear cheaper or more expensive to a UK visitor in a given year. Figure 6.18 gives CPLs for each G7 country relative to the United Kingdom (CPL=100). In August 2003, Japan was the only country of this group to have appeared more expensive to a UK visitor, while all the others seemed cheaper. Canada would have seemed the least expensive of all G7 countries to the UK visitor in 2003. Although useful indicators of a current situation, these comparative differences are likely to fluctuate significantly from year to year due to fluctuations in exchange rates.

Figure 6.17

Percentage change in consumer prices[1]: EU comparison, 2002

Percentage change over 12 months

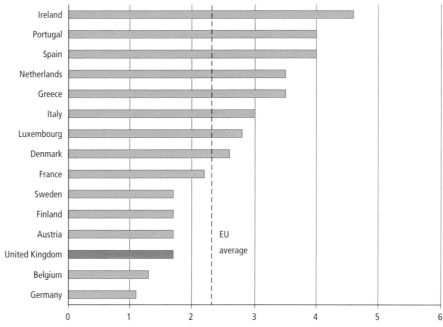

1 As measured by the harmonised index of consumer prices. See Appendix, Part 6: Harmonised Index of Consumer Prices.

Source: Office for National Statistics; Eurostat

Figure 6.18

Comparative price levels[1] for household expenditure: G7 comparison, August 2003

Indices (UK=100)

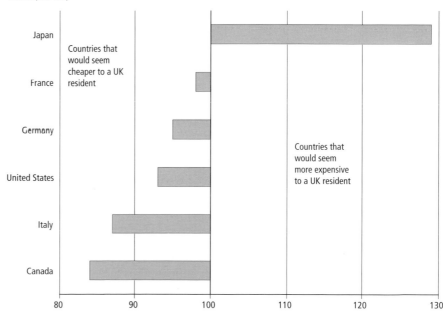

1 Price level indices for private consumption – the ratio of purchasing power parities to exchange rates.

Source: OECD

Chapter 7 **Health**

Key health indicators

- In 2002 life expectancy at birth in the United Kingdom was almost 76 years for males and just over 80 years for females, around 30 years longer than for those born in 1901. (Figure 7.1)

- There was a steep decline in the weekly incidence of heart attack in England and Wales between 1981 and 2001, from 5.6 to 1.6 per 100,000 in men and from 3.1 to 1.0 per 100,000 in women. (Figure 7.5)

Diet and related health

- In 2000/01, 13 per cent of men and 15 per cent of women (aged 19 to 64) in Great Britain consumed the recommended five or more portions of fruit and vegetables on an average daily basis. (Table 7.11).

Alcohol, drugs and smoking

- Deaths related to alcohol consumption have been rising in England and Wales for many years, and particularly since 1980 – the number of alcohol related deaths rose by 115 per cent from 2,575 in 1980 to 5,543 in 2000. (Figure 7.14)

Cancer

- In 2001/02, three quarters of women in the target population in the United Kingdom underwent screening for breast cancer. In most regions and countries of the United Kingdom coverage was between 70 and 77 per cent, but in London it was 57 per cent. (Table 7.19)

Sexual health

- In the period 1999 to 2001 those aged between 18 and 24 years in Great Britain were the most likely age group to have had more than one sexual partner in the previous three months. Among each age group around twice as many men than women had had more than one sexual partner during this period. (Table 7.22)

Figure **7.1**

Expectation of life[1] at birth: by sex

United Kingdom
Years

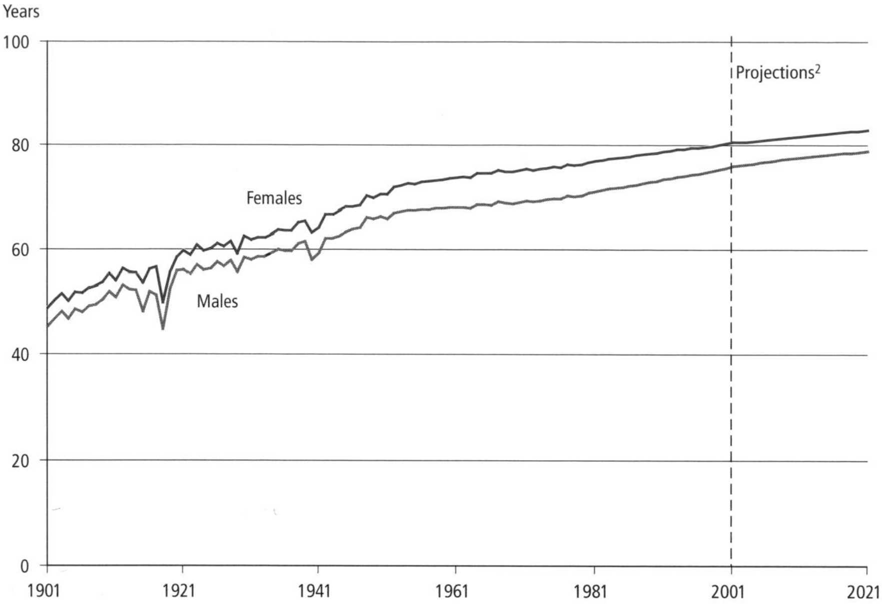

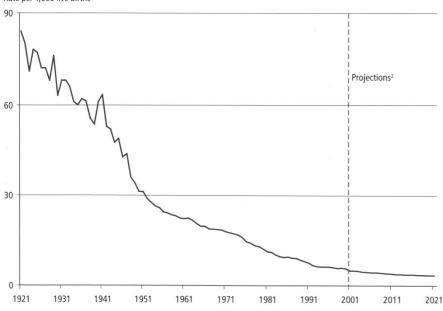

1 See Appendix, Part 7: Expectation of life. The average number of years a new-born baby would
   survive if he or she experienced age-specific mortality rates for that time period throughout his
   or her life.
2 2001-based projections.

Source: Government Actuary's Department

Figure **7.2**

Infant mortality[1]

United Kingdom
Rate per 1,000 live births

1 Deaths within one year of birth.
2 2001-based projections.

**Source: Office for National Statistics; General Register Office for Scotland; Northern Ireland
Statistics and Research Agency; Government Actuary's Department**

The health of a nation provides some of the most revealing indications of its social and economic characteristics. Over the past century improved nutrition and housing, advances in medicine and technology, and the development of health services which are freely available to all have led to progressive improvements in health in the United Kingdom. However, the same developments also play a part in raising our knowledge of new and existing health problems.

Key health indicators

Life expectancy is a widely used indicator of the state of the nation's health. Large improvements in expectancy of life at birth have been seen over the past century for both males and females. In 1901 males born in the United Kingdom could expect to live to around 45 years of age and females to around 49 (Figure 7.1). By 2002 male life expectancy at birth had risen to almost 76 years and for females to just over 80 years. It was not, however, until the latter part of the 20th century that life expectancy for adults showed any significant improvement, and in recent years it has been the increase in life expectancy among older adults that has been particularly dramatic. For example, life expectancy for men aged 60 increased by 4.5 years between 1971 and 2001 compared with an increase of only 1.6 years between 1911 and 1971.

Despite its use as a general indicator of health, life expectancy takes no account of the quality of life. Recent research into healthy life expectancy has shown that since 1981 healthy life expectancy has increased in Great Britain. However, the rise has not been as much as for overall life expectancy. The result of this difference is that as people have been living longer, there has also been an increase in the number of years spent in poor health. While women live longer on average than men, they also spend more years in poor health than men.

The reduction in the infant mortality rate has been one of the major factors contributing to an overall increase in life expectancy over the past century (Figure 7.2). In 1921, 84.0 children per 1,000 live births in the United Kingdom died before the age of one; by 2002 the rate was 4.8 per 1,000 live births. Despite the significant decline in infant mortality, notable socio-economic inequalities still exist. In England and Wales the infant mortality rate in 2002 among babies born inside marriage whose fathers were in semi-routine occupations was 7.5 per 1,000 live births, almost three times the rate of 2.7 per 1,000 live births of those whose fathers were in higher managerial occupations.

The 2001 Census was the first to include a question on general health. Overall a greater proportion of males than females reported good health (Table 7.3). However, among those reporting that their health was 'not good', the proportions were similar between the sexes.

The 2001 Census also asked about people's experience of long-term illnesses or disabilities which limited their daily activities or work. Over 90 per cent of young people (aged under 16) without a limiting long-term illness or disability reported that they were in good health. While this proportion falls with age, over half of such people aged 75 and over were in good health and around 5 per cent reported that their health was not good.

For those with a limiting long-term illness or disability the proportions in good health were lower: just under half of young people (aged under 16) with a

limiting long-term illness or disability reported being in good health, while just under a fifth reported that their health was not good. Age had less of an impact for this group, with similar levels of good health reported by people aged 45 or over with a limiting long-term illness or disability. Around half of people aged 45 to 64 with a limiting long-term illness or disability reported that their health was not good. This was slightly higher than for those aged 65 and over – just over two fifths. Although this pattern may seem surprising, it is most likely explained by higher survival rates among those who have reached the age of 65 and over in good health.

High blood pressure is a risk factor for a number of conditions including cardiovascular disease. Many people

with high blood pressure go undetected and so remain at increased risk. High blood pressure can be successfully treated both by drugs and changes to diet, alcohol intake and levels of exercise. However, 8–9 per cent of men and women continue to have high blood pressure despite receiving treatment. Men are more likely than women to have high blood pressure at younger ages, whereas there is little difference between the sexes at age 65 and over (Table 7.4 – see overleaf). High blood pressure increases with age in both sexes. In 2001, around 4 per cent of men and women in England aged 16 and over had normal blood pressure as a result of treatment. However, 29 per cent of men and 22 per cent of women had untreated high blood pressure.

Table **7.3**

Self-reported general health[1]: by sex and age, 2001

England & Wales   Percentages

	Good	Fairly good	Not good	All
Males				
0–15	91	8	1	100
16–24	86	12	2	100
25–44	77	17	5	100
45–64	60	27	14	100
65 74	42	39	19	100
75 and over	31	43	26	100
All ages	71	20	8	100
Females				
0–15	91	8	1	100
16–24	80	17	3	100
25–44	73	21	6	100
45–64	56	30	14	100
65–74	39	42	19	100
75 and over	28	44	29	100
All ages	66	24	10	100

1 Refers to health over the 12 months prior to Census day (29 April 2001).

Source: Census 2001, Office for National Statistics

Table 7.4

High blood pressure[1]: by sex and age, 2001

England   Percentages

	16–44	45–54	55–64	65–74	75 and over	All aged 16 and over
Males						
Treated	1	6	15	20	20	8
Untreated	19	32	37	41	42	29
Females						
Treated	1	6	13	23	28	9
Untreated	8	24	33	41	44	22

1 See Appendix, Part 7: Blood pressure level.

Source: Health Survey for England, Department of Health

Figure 7.5

Weekly incidence[1] of heart attack[2]: by sex

England & Wales
Rate per 100,000 population

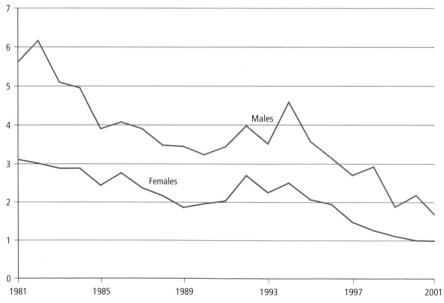

1 Data recorded are from all practices reporting to the Weekly Returns Service and in the period
  1994 to 1998 included practices whose data extraction routines were not fully automated.
2 Acute myocardial infarction (ICD 410).

Source: Royal College of General Practitioners

As with high blood pressure, the incidence of heart attack rises sharply with age, being most common in both men and women aged 65 and over. There has been a steep decline in the weekly incidence of heart attack in England and Wales since the early 1980s (Figure 7.5). Between 1981 and 2001 the rate among men of all ages fell from 5.6 to 1.6 per 100,000. Among women of all ages, the rate fell from 3.1 to 1.0 per 100,000 over the same period. The trend in heart attack prevalence among older men in particular can be linked to the fall in cigarette smoking (see Figure 7.16).

In the United Kingdom over the past 30 years, while circulatory diseases (which includes heart disease and stroke) have remained the most common cause of death among males and females of all ages, they have also shown by far the greatest decline (Figure 7.6). In 1972, death rates from circulatory diseases were 7,100 per million males and 4,400 per million females. By 2002 the death rates had fallen by over half for both sexes to 3,200 per million males and 2,000 per million females.

Cancers are the second most common cause of death among both sexes, but over the past 30 years have shown different trends for males and females. Among males the death rate from cancers showed a downward trend since the early 1980s and by 2002 had fallen to 2,400 per million males. Although during this period cancer death rates among females were consistently lower than those for males, they did not reach a peak until the late 1980s, since when they have fallen gradually from 1,900 per million in 1989 to 1,700 per million in 2002.

Although all-age death rates from infections such as tuberculosis (TB) and measles, and respiratory diseases such as pneumonia, have been much lower than those for cancer and circulatory disease over the past 30 years, they have not followed the same trends. Among males the death rate from infections fell from 89 per million in 1972 to just 40 per million in 1983. However, since this time there has been an increase in the death rate which by 2002 was 72 per million males. There was a similar trend among females, with the death rate from infections falling from 48 to 27 per million between 1972 and 1983, before increasing during the 1990s to reach 51 per million females in 2002. Since 1972 death rates from respiratory diseases followed an overall downward trend among both sexes. The sharp falls seen in 1984 and 1994 are artefacts of changes in the rules involving deaths from pneumonia (see Appendix, Part 7: International Classification of Diseases).

The United Kingdom had death rates from circulatory diseases among both males and females were around the EU average in 1999 (Figure 7.7). France had the lowest death rates for both males and females at 230 and 133 per 100,000 population, respectively. Ireland had the highest death rate among males at 422 per 100,000 and third highest among females at 258 per 100,000 population. In all EU countries death rates from circulatory diseases were higher among males than females. Of the other major causes of death the United Kingdom had below EU average death rates for cancer for both men and women. For death rates from respiratory diseases, the United Kingdom had the second highest rates for both men and women; Ireland had the highest rates in the EU for both sexes.

Figure **7.6**

Mortality[1]: by sex and major cause

United Kingdom[2]

Rates per million population

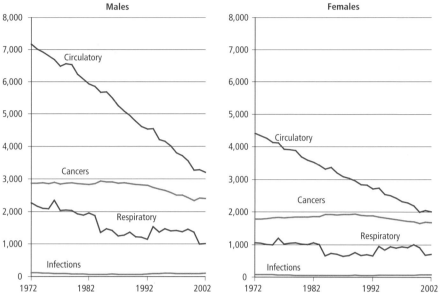

1 Data are for all ages and have been age standardised using the European standard population. See Appendix, Part 7: Standardised rates, and International Classification of Diseases.
2 Data for 2000 are for England and Wales only.

Source: Office for National Statistics

Figure **7.7**

Death rates from circulatory disease: EU comparison, 1999[1]

Rates per 100,000 population

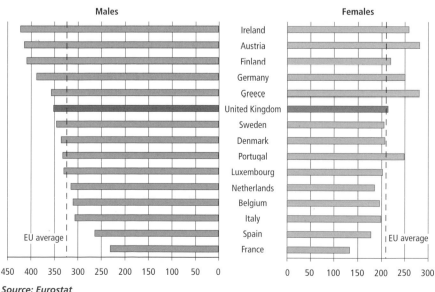

Source: Eurostat

Figure **7.8**

Notifications of selected infectious diseases

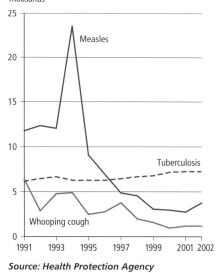

United Kingdom
Thousands

Source: Health Protection Agency

Infectious diseases

In the past ten years there have been contrasting trends in the most commonly diagnosed infectious diseases in the United Kingdom. Figure 7.8 shows an epidemic of measles in 1994 before it resumed its underlying downward trend in 1995. In contrast the number of notifications of TB has increased since the early 1990s and is now more common than either measles or whooping cough. In 2002 there were around 7,200 cases of TB compared with around 6,100 in 1991. The rise has been particularly noticeable in London, with a TB notification rate of 39 per 100,000 population in 2002. This was two and a half times higher than in the West Midlands, which had the next highest rate, and almost ten times higher than in Northern Ireland, which had the lowest notification rate in the United Kingdom at 4 per 100,000 population.

Over the past 50 years a key factor in the reduction of infectious diseases and associated morbidity and mortality has been the development of childhood vaccination programmes. Nearly all children in the United Kingdom are now immunised against tetanus, diphtheria, polio, whooping cough, haemophilus influenzae b, meningitis C and measles, mumps and rubella. Current government immunisation targets are for 95 per cent of children to be immunised against these diseases by the age of two.

The measles/mumps/rubella (MMR) vaccine was introduced in 1988. Notifications of measles fell to their lowest recorded annual total of under 3,000 in 2001 (see Figure 7.8). However, in recent years, concerns by some over the safety of the MMR combined vaccine has led to a fall in the proportion of children immunised against MMR by their second birthday. In 2002/03, 82 per cent of children in the United Kingdom had received the vaccine compared to 91 per cent in 1991/92. The regional variations were generally small, ranging from 81 to 87 per cent in most regions, with the exception of London at 72 per cent (Figure 7.9).

Vaccination against influenza is intended primarily for persons in high risk groups, which include those with chronic heart disease, lung disease (including asthma), renal disease or diabetes. Older people are particularly vulnerable to the effects of influenza, and from 2000/01 free NHS vaccination was extended to people aged 65 and over who are not in a high risk group. The extension of free vaccination and a national advertising campaign have been major factors in the increased uptake among this group. The Government target for 2002 was for 70 per cent of those aged 65 and over to

Figure **7.9**

MMR immunisation[1] of children by their second birthday: by region, 2002/03[2]

Percentages

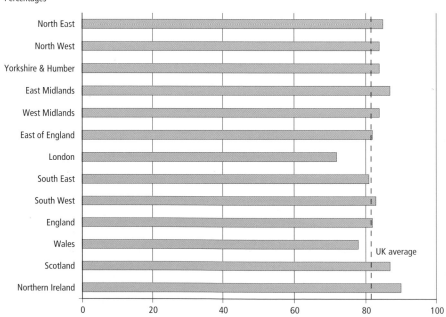

1 See Appendix, Part 7: Immunisation.
2 Data for Scotland are for 2002.

Source: Department of Health; National Assembly for Wales; National Health Service in Scotland; Department of Health, Social Services and Public Safety, Northern Ireland

be immunised against influenza. Between 1990/91 and 2000/01 the proportion of those aged 65 and over who received the vaccine rose from 27 per cent to 65 per cent (Figure 7.10). By 2002/03 this proportion had risen to 69 per cent, just below the Government target.

Diet and related health

A key feature of the Government's strategy for reducing premature deaths from coronary heart disease and cancer (see Figure 7.6), and reducing health inequalities among the general population, is to improve access to, and increase the consumption of, fruit and vegetables. The Department of Health (DH) recommends that a healthy diet should include at least five portions of a variety of fruit and vegetables (excluding potatoes) a day. Data from the 2000–01 National Diet and Nutrition Survey showed that overall 13 per cent of men and 15 per cent of women aged 19 to 64 in Great Britain had consumed this amount on an average daily basis (Table 7.11). The proportion of men and women eating five or more portions a day increased with age. Less than 5 per cent of men and women aged 19 to 24 had consumed an average five or more portions a day, compared with 24 per cent of men and 22 per cent of women aged 50 to 64.

Obesity is a major risk factor linked to heart disease, diabetes and premature death. The body mass index (BMI, see Appendix 7, Part 7: Body Mass Index) is a common measure for assessing an individual's weight relative to their height, and a BMI score of over 30 is taken as the definition of obesity. In recent years the proportion of the population who are obese or overweight has been rising. In 2001 over a fifth of males and females

aged 16 and over in England were classified as obese, and a further half of men and third of women were classified as overweight. Obesity is linked to social class, being more common among those in the routine or semi-routine occupational groups than the managerial and professional groups (Figure 7.12 – see overleaf). The link is stronger among women. In 2001, 30 per cent of women in routine occupations were classified as obese compared with 16 per cent in higher managerial and professional occupations. Among those who had never worked and the long-term unemployed, 25 per cent of women were classified as obese, compared with 16 per cent of men. Men in the higher managerial and professional and intermediate

Figure **7.10**

Influenza vaccine uptake by people aged 65 and over

Great Britain[1]
Percentages

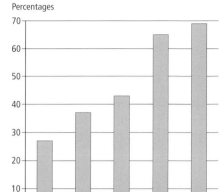

1 Data for 2000/01 onwards are for England only.

Source: Department of Health; Medicines & Healthcare Regulatory Agency

Table **7.11**

Average daily portions of fruit and vegetables consumed[1]: by sex and age, 2000–01[2]

Great Britain
Percentages

		Average number of portions per day				
	None	Above 0 but less than 1	1 but less than 3	3 but less than 5	5 or more	All
Males						
19–24	6	32	57	5	0	100
25–34	1	26	49	17	7	100
35–49	0	14	45	27	14	100
50–64	1	6	38	31	24	100
All males aged 19–64	1	17	46	23	13	100
Females						
19–24	2	34	47	13	4	100
25–34	1	18	52	20	9	100
35–49	1	15	45	22	17	100
50–64	0	7	37	34	22	100
All females aged 19–64	1	15	45	24	15	100

1 Fruit and vegetables including composite dishes (all fruit juice counted as one portion; all baked beans and other pulses counted as one portion).
2 July 2000 to June 2001.

Source: National Diet and Nutrition Survey, Office for National Statistics

Figure **7.12**

Obesity[1] among adults: by sex and NS-SeC[2], 2001

England
Percentages

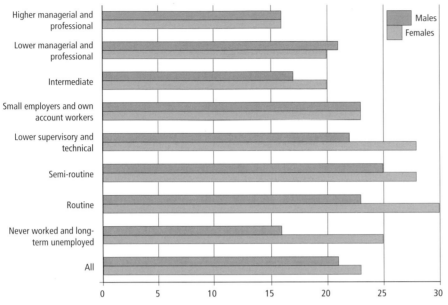

1 Using the body mass index (BMI) for people aged 16 and over. See Appendix, Part 7: Body
mass index.
2 See Appendix, Part 1: National Statistics Socio-economic Classification.

Source: Health Survey for England, Department of Health

Table **7.13**

Adults exceeding daily benchmarks[1] of alcohol: by sex and age, 2001/02

Great Britain   Percentages

	Males	Females
16–24	49	39
25–44	46	30
45–64	36	19
65 and over	18	5
All aged 16 and over	39	22

1 On heaviest drinking day in last week.
Current Department of Health advice is that
consumption of between 3 and 4 units a day
for men and 2 to 3 units a day for women
should not lead to significant health risks.

**Source: General Household Survey, Office for
National Statistics**

occupations, as well as those who had
never worked or were long-term
unemployed, had the lowest proportion
of obesity. Results from the National
Diet and Nutrition Survey show that in
2000–01 women aged 19 to 64 (24 per
cent) were more than twice as likely as
men of this age group (10 per cent) to
be dieting to lose weight. Women aged
25 to 34 were the most likely to be
dieting (28 per cent).

Alcohol, drugs and smoking

The consumption of alcohol in excessive
amounts can lead to ill health, with an
increased likelihood of problems such as
high blood pressure, cancer and cirrhosis
of the liver. The current DH advice on
alcohol is that consumption of between
three and four units a day for men and

between two and three units a day for
women should not lead to significant
health risks. Consistently drinking more
is not advised because of the associated
health risks. Data from the 2001/02
General Household Survey (GHS) show
that although young people drink alcohol
less frequently than older people, men
and women aged 16 to 24 were more
likely to have exceeded the recommended
number of daily units on at least one day
in the previous week (Table 7.13). Half of
men and two fifths of women in this age
group had done so in the previous week,
compared with only two fifths of all
men and one fifth of all women. Similar
patterns were evident for heavy drinking,
defined as more than eight units for
men and six units for women on their
heaviest drinking day in the past week.

Mortality rates for deaths related to
alcohol consumption have been rising in
England and Wales for many years with
the number of alcohol-related deaths
rising from just under 2,600 in 1980 to
just over 5,500 in 2000 (See Appendix,
Part 7: Alcohol-related deaths). Of the
total number of alcohol-related deaths in
2000, 85 per cent were due to chronic
liver disease and cirrhosis, with 15 per
cent due to other alcohol-related causes.
Marked increases in death rates have
been observed since the early 1980s.
Between 1980 and 2000 the death rate
from alcohol-related diseases among
males more than doubled from 6 to 13
deaths per 100,000 population (Figure
7.14). Rates were lower for females, but
rose from 4 to 7 deaths per 100,000
population over the same period.

Among males there was an upward
trend in alcohol-related death rates in all
age groups above 15 to 24. The most
marked increase occurred among those
aged 25 to 44, with the death rate
increasing from 4 deaths per 100,000 in

1980 to a peak of 10 per 100,000 in 1998. Among females in this age group the death rate also increased from 2 to 5 per 100,000 between 1980 and 2000. From 1996 onwards the highest alcohol-related death rates occurred in men aged 45 to 64. Between 1980 and 1995, however, the highest death rates for males were among those aged 65 and over. Among females, the highest death rate from 1980 to 2000 was consistently among those aged 65 and over, although by the end of this period the death rate for those aged 45 to 64 almost equalled that for older women.

The misuse of drugs, such as heroin, cocaine and amphetamines, is a serious social and health problem. Results from the 2001/02 British Crime Survey indicate that 15 per cent of men and 9 per cent of women aged 16 to 24 in England and Wales had taken an illicit drug in the previous year. Young people are more likely to use drugs than older people. Of those aged 16 to 24, 35 per cent of men and 24 per cent of women had done so in the previous year (Table 7.15). The most commonly used drug in 2001/02 by this age group was cannabis, which had been used by 33 per cent of men and 21 per cent of women in the previous year. Ecstasy was the most commonly used Class A drug, with higher use among the 16 to 24 year olds than those aged 25 to 59. In 2001/02, 9 per cent of men and 4 per cent of women aged 16 to 24 had used ecstasy in the previous year. Since 1996 there has been an increase in the use of cocaine among young people, especially among young men. In contrast the use of amphetamines and LSD has declined.

Over the past 30 years there has been a substantial decline in the proportion of adults who smoke cigarettes. In 1974, 51 per cent of men and 41 per cent of

Figure **7.14**

Death rates[1] from alcohol-related diseases[2]: by sex
England & Wales
Rate per 1,000 population

1 Age-standardised death rates. See Appendix, Part 7: Standardised rates.
2 See Appendix, Part 7: Alcohol-related deaths.

Source: Office for National Statistics

Table **7.15**

Prevalence of drug misuse by young adults[1] in the previous year: by sex and drug category, 1996 and 2001/02

England & Wales   Percentages

	Males		Females	
	1996	2001/02	1996	2001/02
Cannabis	30	33	22	21
Amphetamines	15	7	9	3
Ecstasy	9	9	4	4
Magic mushrooms or LSD	9	3	2	1
Cocaine	2	7	-	2
All Class A drugs[2]	13	12	6	5
Any drug	34	35	25	24

1 Those aged 16 to 24 years.
2 Include heroin, cocaine (both cocaine powder and 'crack'), ecstasy, magic mushrooms, LSD and unprescribed use of methadone.

Source: British Crime Survey, Home Office

Figure **7.16**

Prevalence of adult[1] cigarette smoking[2]: by sex

Great Britain
Percentages

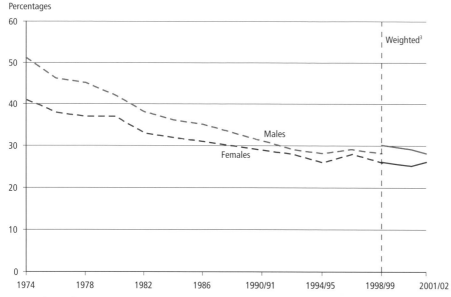

1 People aged 16 and over.
2 From 1988 data are for financial years. Between 1974 and 2000/01 the surveys were run every two years.
3 From 2000/01 data are weighted to compensate for non-response and to match known population distributions. Weighted and unweighted data for 1998 are shown for comparison.

Source: General Household Survey, Office for National Statistics

Figure **7.17**

Incidence of cancer[1]: by sex, EU comparison, 2000

Rates per 100,000 population

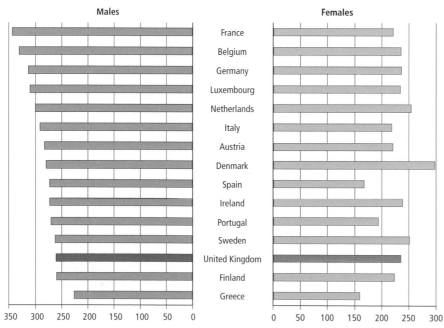

1 All malignant cancers excluding non-melanoma skin cancer. Data are age standardised using the World standard population. See Appendix, Part 7: Standardised rates.

Source: International Agency for Research on Cancer

women aged 16 and over in Great Britain reported that they were regular cigarette smokers. By 2001/02 these proportions had fallen to 28 per cent and 26 per cent, respectively, although these data were weighted to take account of survey non-response (Figure 7.16). The biggest declines have been among older men: among those aged 60 and over, 44 per cent were smokers in 1974 compared with 16 per cent in 2001/02. However, more recent trends in smoking indicate a levelling off although smoking has risen over the last ten years among women aged 16 to 19, from 25 per cent in 1992 to 31 per cent in 2001/02. In contrast the prevalence of smoking among men in this age group fell from 29 per cent in 1992 to 25 per cent in 2001/02. Smoking is a major health risk associated with cardiovascular disease (linked to intake of carbon monoxide and nicotine), and lung cancer (linked to tar). There are several other cancers which are more common among smokers than non-smokers, including cancers of the oesophagus, pancreas, cervix, bladder and kidney.

Cancer

About a third of the population develop cancer at some time in their lives and in its various forms cancer is responsible for around a quarter of all deaths in the United Kingdom (see Figures 7.6 and 7.18). In 2000 the United Kingdom had the third lowest male incidence rate for all cancer (excluding non-melanoma skin cancer) in all EU countries at 260 per 100,000 (Figure 7.17). Among females the UK incidence rate of 234 per 100,000 was the seventh highest in the EU. In all countries, except Denmark, cancer incidence was higher among men than women.

Since the mid-1970s there has been a steep decline in the death rate for lung cancer among males (Figure 7.18). This can be closely linked to the proportion of the population who smoke (see Figure 7.16). In 1974 the death rate among all males in the United Kingdom from lung cancer was 110 per 100,000. By 2002 it had declined to 58 per 100,000. In contrast, the lung cancer death rate among females reached its peak of 31 per 100,000 in 1988. Since then the rate has declined very little, and in 2002 it was half that of men. Breast cancer is the most common cause of cancer death among women. Death rates from this form of cancer peaked in the late 1980s at around 42 per 100,000 but have since fallen steadily to a rate of around 30 per 100,000 in 2002. This can be linked to advances in treatment and to the introduction of a national screening programme (see Figure 7.19).

Colorectal cancer is the third most common cause of cancer death among both males and females. The death rates have gradually declined since the mid-1970s from 34 per 100,000 males and 26 per 100,000 females in 1976 to 25 and 15 per 100,000, respectively in 2002. These represented falls of 26 per cent among males and 42 per cent among females. For prostate cancer, which only affects men, the death rate peaked at 30 per 100,000 in 1992. The rate has since declined and by 2002 it was 27 per 100,000.

Cancer patient survival is a key indicator of the effectiveness of cancer control in the population. Survival rates from lung cancer are very low compared with the other most common cancers. For those diagnosed with lung cancer in England and Wales in the period 1996 to 1999, the five year survival rate (adjusted for overall levels of mortality from other causes in the general population) for

Figure 7.18

Death rates from selected cancers[1]: by sex

United Kingdom
Rates per 100,000 population

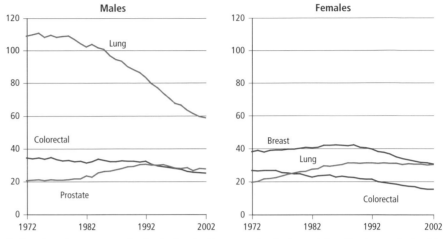

1 Data have been age standardised using the European standard population. See Appendix, Part 7: Standardised rates, and International Classification of Diseases.

Source: Office for National Statistics

both men and women was around 6 per cent. In contrast, five year survival rates for colon cancer were around 47 per cent for men and 48 per cent for women. Survival rates for those forms of cancer where screening is available were even higher. The five year survival rate was 65 per cent for prostate cancer and 78 per cent for female breast cancer.

National Health Service (NHS) screening programmes aim to prevent deaths from breast cancer and lower the incidence of cervical cancer. At present, breast screening is offered to all women aged 50 to 64, and to women aged 65 and over on request. By 2004, this will be extended to women in England aged 65 to 70, and to women over 70 on request. In Scotland, the extension to women aged 65 to 70 began on a phased basis in 2003 and is being

implemented over a three year round of screening. In Wales, an extension to women aged 65 to 67 was piloted in certain areas in 2003. Following review of the pilots, it is intended to extend the screening programme to all women in Wales up to the age of 70. In 2001/02, three quarters of women in the target population in the United Kingdom underwent screening for breast cancer (Table 7.19 – see overleaf). Some regional variation does exist, however; while the proportion screened in 2001/02 in most regions and countries of the United Kingdom was between 70 and 77 per cent, in London it was only 57 per cent. In recent years the proportion of the target population who have undergone breast screening has been rising in most regions and countries of the United Kingdom.

Table **7.19**

Breast cancer screening coverage[1]: by region

United Kingdom

Percentages

	1996/97	1998/99	2000/01	2001/02
United Kingdom	72	72	73	73
England	66	68	70	70
Northern and Yorkshire	67	67	70	72
North West	67	66	70	71
Trent	71	70	74	74
West Midlands	68	70	74	73
Eastern	66	70	72	71
London	53	57	58	57
South East	67	71	71	70
South West	67	68	74	72
Wales	78	77	77	77
Scotland	72	74	73	75
Northern Ireland	71	71	73	71

1 As a percentage of women aged 50 to 64 eligible for screening. See Appendix, Part 7: Breast cancer and cervical screening programmes.

Source: Department of Health; National Assembly for Wales; National Health Service in Scotland; Department of Health, Social Services and Public Safety, Northern Ireland

Figure **7.20**

Prevalence of neurotic disorders[1] among older people[2]: by sex and gross household income, 2000

Great Britain
Percentages

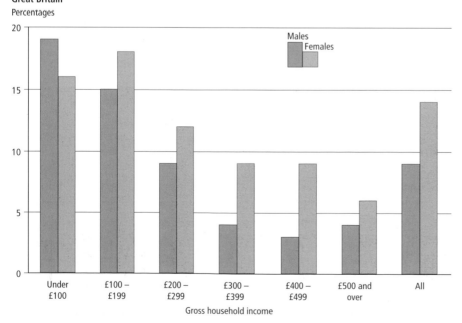

1 Includes depression, anxiety, obsessive compulsive disorder, panic disorder and phobias.
2 Those aged 60 to 74 years living in private households.

Source: Psychiatric Morbidity Survey, Office for National Statistics

Between 1996/97 and 2001/02, the proportion increased by 5 percentage points in the Northern and Yorkshire, the West Midlands, Eastern and South West regions. During the same period coverage rose by 3 percentage points in the Trent region, with the highest coverage in England. In 2001/02 Wales had the highest coverage in the United Kingdom at 77 per cent.

The national policy for cervical screening is that women aged 20 to 64 (20 to 59 in Scotland) should be screened every three to five years. The test identifies a pre-cancerous stage which after a long developmental period may sometimes proceed to invasive cancer. In 2002/03, 82 per cent of the target population in the United Kingdom had been screened, the same proportion as in the previous year.

Mental health

As with many other illnesses, mental health problems are associated with socio-economic disadvantage. Results from the 2000 Psychiatric Morbidity Survey of people living in private households in Great Britain found that, among those aged 60 to 74, the likelihood of having a neurotic disorder increased in both sexes as household income fell (Figure 7.20). Among women in this age group, the prevalence of neurotic disorder, such as anxiety or depression, was around three times as common among those with a weekly household income of under £200 (16 to 18 per cent) as it was among those women with a weekly household income of £500 or more (6 per cent). There was a similar finding when comparing men in these two income groups, although overall there was a lower prevalence of neurotic disorder among men than women.

Men are far more likely to commit suicide than women. Since the 1970s suicide rates have risen in men and fallen in women (Table 7.21). During this period there was an overall increase in suicide rates among young men, although the rates have fallen since the late 1990s. There was an overall decrease among women of all ages and among older men. The likelihood of committing suicide will depend to some extent on the ease of access to, and knowledge of, effective means. In 2001 in England and Wales, the main methods of suicide in men were: hanging, strangulation and suffocation (44 per cent), drug-related poisoning (20 per cent), and 'other poisoning' (10 per cent), which mainly comprised poisoning by motor vehicle exhaust gas. Among women the most common methods of suicide were: drug-related poisoning (46 per cent), and hanging, stranqulation and suffocation (27 per cent).

Sexual health

The prevalence of diseases that can be sexually transmitted has been increasing in recent years, especially among young people. Data from the 2000 National Survey of Sexual Attitudes and Lifestyles among people aged 16 to 44 showed that those aged 18 to 24 were more likely than older or younger people to have had more than one sexual partner of the opposite sex in the previous three months (Table 7.22). Among each age group, around twice as many men as women had had more than one sexual partner of the opposite sex during this period. Those aged 25 and over were the most likely to have had one sexual partner and also least likely to have had none. Those reporting more than one sexual partner in the previous three months tended not to be married or cohabiting. Of single, divorced and separated, and widowed

Table **7.21**

Suicide rates[1]: by sex and age

United Kingdom					Rates per 100,000 population	
	1976	1981	1986	1991	1996	2002
Males						
15–24	9.8	10.8	12.8	15.8	15.0	13.3
25–44	15.1	19.6	20.4	24.8	23.9	24.1
45–64	20.9	23.0	22.6	20.4	17.3	17.9
65 and over	24.0	24.1	26.3	18.7	17.3	13.5
Females						
15–24	4.6	3.4	3.3	3.9	4.2	3.7
25–44	9.1	7.9	6.6	5.9	6.2	6.4
45–64	14.1	14.9	11.8	8.3	6.4	6.4
65 and over	15.1	15.7	13.7	8.5	6.7	5.8

1 Includes deaths with a verdict of undetermined intent (open verdict).
2 Rates for 2002 are coded to ICD-10. Rates are age-standardised to the European standard population. See Appendix, Part 7: Standardised rates, and International Classification of Diseases.

Source: Office for National Statistics; General Register Office for Scotland; Northern Ireland Statistics and Research Agency

Table **7.22**

Number of opposite sex partners in the previous three months: by sex and age, 1999–2001

Great Britain					Percentages
	16–17	18–19	20–24	25–34	35–44
Males					
0 partners	61	33	24	15	14
1 partner	28	47	58	76	81
2 or more partners	11	20	18	9	5
All aged 16–44	100	100	100	100	100
Females					
0 partners	56	25	17	11	14
1 partner	38	64	75	86	83
2 or more partners	6	11	9	4	3
All aged 16–44	100	100	100	100	100

Source: National Survey of Sexual Attitudes and Lifestyles 2000, National Centre for Social Research, Royal Free and University College London Medical School and London School of Hygiene and Tropical Medicine

Table **7.23**

Use of condoms in the previous four weeks: by number of new partners of the opposite sex[1], 1999–2001

Great Britain		Percentages
	Number of new partners	
	None[2]	1 or more
Males		
Used on every occasion	20	46
Used on some occasions	9	17
Not used at all	70	38
All	100	100
Females		
Used on every occasion	17	37
Used on some occasions	8	16
Not used at all	76	48
All	100	100

1 See Appendix, Part 7: Use of condoms.
2 Existing partners only.

Source: National Survey of Sexual Attitudes and Lifestyles 2000, National Centre for Social Research, Royal Free and University College London Medical School and the London School of Hygiene and Tropical Medicine

Figure **7.24**

HIV and AIDS: diagnoses[1] and deaths in HIV-infected individuals

United Kingdom
Thousands

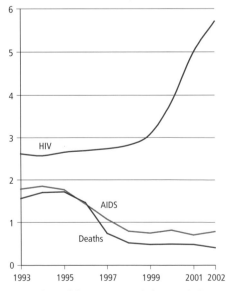

1 Numbers of diagnoses recorded, particularly for recent years, will rise as further reports are received.

Source: Health Protection Agency

people, 16 per cent of men and 9 per cent of women had had more than one sexual partner in the previous three months. Less than 10 per cent of married and cohabiting men and women had had more than one sexual partner in the previous three months.

People can take action to protect their own health and that of others by using condoms, reducing the risk of contracting sexually transmitted diseases. Data from the National Survey of Sexual Attitudes and Lifestyles 2000 showed that the use of condoms among heterosexual partners was twice as common among those who had had one or more new sexual partners in the previous four weeks than among those who had had no new partners (Table 7.23). Men with one or more new sexual partners in the previous four weeks were more likely than women to have used a condom on every occasion. Men and women aged 16 to 17 were the most likely to have used a condom on every occasion. Those who do not use a condom place themselves at increased risk of contracting a sexually transmitted disease. Overall, 38 per cent of men and 48 per cent of women who had had one or more sexual partners in the previous four weeks had not used a condom at all.

By the end of 2002 the estimated number of people living with HIV in the United Kingdom was estimated at 49,500, an increase of 20 per cent compared with 2001. In 2002, 5,700 new HIV cases were diagnosed (Figure 7.24). This was more than the number diagnosed in 1998, which was 2,800. By contrast, the numbers of AIDS diagnoses and deaths in HIV-infected individuals declined after the introduction of effective therapies in the mid-1990s,

and in more recent years have remained relatively constant, with 780 reports of AIDS and nearly 4,000 deaths so far reported for 2002.

Sex between men and women overtook sex between men as the most common route of HIV transmission in 1999. The 3,300 new HIV infections diagnosed in 2002 that were heterosexually acquired represent more than three times the number in 1996, when less than 900 such infections were diagnosed annually. Two thirds (2,100) of these heterosexually acquired HIV infections diagnosed in 2002 were in women, and three quarters of the total in both men and women (2,500) were attributed to infection in Africa.

There have also been recent rises in the incidence of other sexually transmitted infections, especially among young people. Between 1995 and 2000 the number of cases of other sexually transmitted diseases among people aged 19 and under more than doubled. In 2002 genital chlamydia was the most common sexually transmitted infection diagnosed in genito-urinary medicine clinics in England and Wales, with a total of over 82,000 cases. Diagnosis of uncomplicated gonorrhoea was the second most common infection with almost 25,000 cases, representing a rise of 13 per cent among males and a 15 per cent rise among females between 2001 and 2002. Although the number of cases of primary and secondary syphilis diagnosed was much lower in 2002 at just over 1,200, between 2001 and 2002 this disease showed the largest relative increase, rising by 72 per cent in males and by 36 per cent in females.

Chapter 8 **Social Protection**

Carers and caring

- At the time of the 2001 Census there were over 440,000 residents who had been living, or intended to live, for six months or more in communal medical and care establishments in Great Britain. Eighty per cent of these people were over state pension age and most of these lived in either a residential care home or nursing home. (Table 8.1)

- In April 2001 there were 5.9 million informal carers in the United Kingdom, representing 10 per cent of the population. The majority of these carers were female (3.4 million compared with 2.5 million males). (Table 8.3)

Sick and disabled

- In 2001/02, 39 per cent of expenditure on hospital and community health services in England was spent on people aged 65 and over, although they only comprised 16 per cent of the population. (Page 123)

Older people

- In 2001/02, 61 per cent of male employees and 53 per cent of female employees contributed to either an occupational, personal, stakeholder or a combination of these pensions. (Table 8.13)

Families and children

- In autumn 2002, a third of children under 15 in the United Kingdom whose mother was in employment had been looked after by a grandparent at some point in the previous week. (Table 8.15)

- At March 2002 nearly 60,000 children were being looked after by local authorities in England. The most common reason for a child to be taken into care in England was abuse or neglect (62 per cent). (Table 8.16)

Table 8.1

Residents[1] in communal medical and care establishments[2]: by age[3], 2001

Great Britain   Thousands

	Under state pension age	Over state pension age[4]	All residents[4]
NHS			
Psychiatric hospital/home	9	5	14
Other hospital/home	14	10	24
Local authority			
Residential care home	5	36	42
Children's home	2	-	3
Other medical and care home	1	1	1
Housing association			
Home or hostel	4	7	10
Other[5]			
Residential care home	34	150	183
Nursing home	11	136	147
Psychiatric hospital/home	3	4	7
Children's home	2	-	2
Other medical and care home	3	5	8
Total	87	355	442

1 Any person who had been living, or intended to live, in the establishment for six months or more, excluding the owner, staff or their relatives.
2 A communal establishment is an establishment providing residential accommodation which is supervised, either full- or part-time.
3 State pension age is 60 for women and 65 for men.
4 Total includes 2,000 people who reported that they lived in a nursing home and that it was managed by a local authority. Local authorities do not run nursing homes.
5 Includes charities, voluntary organisations and private companies.

Source: Census 2001, Office for National Statistics; Census 2001, General Register Office for Scotland

Figure 8.2

Number of contact hours of home help and home care: by sector

England

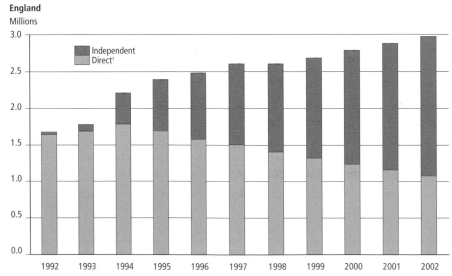

1 Directly provided by local authorities.
Source: Department of Health

Social protection describes the help given to those who are in need or are at risk of hardship through, for example, illness, low income, family circumstances or age. Central government, local authorities and private bodies (such as voluntary organisations) can provide help and support. The type of help provided can be direct cash payments such as social security benefits or pensions; payments in kind such as free prescriptions or bus passes; or the provision of services such as through the National Health Service (NHS). Unpaid care, such as that provided by informal carers, also plays a part in helping people in need.

Carers and caring

At the time of the 2001 Census there were over 440,000 residents who had been living, or intended to live, for six months or more in communal medical and care establishments in Great Britain (Table 8.1). Eighty per cent of these people were over state pension age and the majority of these lived in either a residential care home or nursing home. The independent sector provided the majority of places, although funding would in many cases have been provided by the public sector.

Local authority home care services assist people to continue living in their own home, and to function as independently as possible. During a survey week in September 2002, local authorities in England provided or purchased nearly 3 million hours of home care services for nearly 370,000 households (Figure 8.2). Between 1992 and 2002 the number of contact hours increased by 77 per cent.

As with the provision of residential care home places, the independent sector now provides much of the care, although the funding for this care may be provided by the public sector. In 2002 around 64 per cent of all contact hours were provided by the independent sector (which includes the private and voluntary sectors) compared with 2 per cent in 1992.

The number of contact hours provided by the independent sector increased by 22 per cent between 2000 and 2002, while the number of hours provided directly by local authorities fell by 13 per cent.

The type of help provided is changing, with more hours of help being provided to fewer households. Between September 2000 and September 2002 there was an increase of 7 per cent in the number of contact hours provided and a fall of nearly 8 per cent in the number of households receiving that care. In September 2000, 29 per cent of households receiving home care received ten or more visits and 17 per cent received ten or more hours of help. These figures increased each year so that in 2002, 35 per cent of visited households received ten or more visits and 21 per cent received ten or more hours of help.

Informal carers are people who provide unpaid care for family members, friends, neighbours or others who are sick, disabled or elderly. In April 2001 there were 5.9 million informal carers in the United Kingdom (Table 8.3). The majority of these carers were female (3.4 million compared with 2.5 million males). Around a quarter of both male and female carers were aged 45 to 54 with around a fifth of carers falling in each of the adjacent age groups (35 to 44 and 55 to 64).

Two thirds of all carers were caring for less than 20 hours per week and a fifth were caring for 50 hours or more. Women were slightly more likely than men to be caring for 50 hours or more while men were slightly more likely than

Table 8.3

Informal carers[1] who live in households: by age and sex, 2001

United Kingdom

	All providing care[1] (thousands)		Percentage providing 50 or more hours a week	
	Males	Females	Males	Females
5–15	53	61	7	8
16–24	125	165	8	13
25–34	230	376	15	23
35–44	422	665	17	21
45–54	613	896	15	17
55–64	519	697	19	23
65–74	319	370	31	34
75–84	155	149	44	44
85 and over	24	20	54	47
Total	2,460	3,399	20	22

1 Those who provide unpaid care (looking after, giving help or support) to family members, neighbours or relatives.

Source: Census 2001, Office for National Statistics; Census 2001, General Register Office for Scotland; Census 2001, Northern Ireland Statistics and Research Agency

women to be caring for less than 20 hours. However for those aged 85 and over, male carers were more likely than female carers to be caring for 50 hours or more (54 per cent compared with 47 per cent).

In 2001 there were 179,000 male carers and 169,000 female carers aged 75 and over – representing 12 per cent of men within this age group and 7 per cent of women. Older men are more likely than older women to be married and therefore a larger proportion of men are able to provide care to their spouses, as well as receive care (see the lead article on page 1). Older women are more likely than older men to be living alone and are therefore more likely to receive care from personal social services (see page 125). In Great Britain, although there was little difference between the proportions of men and women receiving home help in most age groups,

Figure **8.4**

Types of help given to main person cared for: by sex of carer[1], 2000/01

Great Britain
Percentage of carers

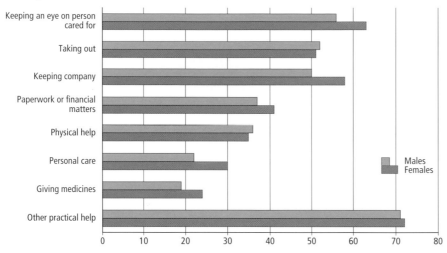

1 See Appendix, Part 8: Informal carers.

Source: General Household Survey, Office for National Statistics

Table **8.5**

NHS in-patient activity for sick and disabled people[1]

United Kingdom

	1981	1991/92	1999/2000	2000/01	2001/02
Acute[2]					
Finished consultant episodes[3] (thousands)	5,693	6,729	7,999	8,076	8,204
In-patient episodes per available bed (numbers)	31.1	45.9	63.5	63.7	64.4
Mean duration of stay (days)	8.4	6.0	5.6	5.1	4.9
Mentally ill					
Finished consultant episodes[3] (thousands)	244	281	271	265	257
In-patient episodes per available bed (numbers)	2.2	4.0	6.5	6.4	6.5
Mean duration of stay (days)	..	114.8	60.6	58.4	54.6
People with learning disabilities					
Finished consultant episodes[3] (thousands)	34	62	42	43	40
In-patient episodes per available bed (numbers)	0.6	2.2	4.8	5.3	5.6
Mean duration of stay (days)	..	544.1	104.8	90.4	117.8

1 Excludes NHS beds and activity in joint-user and contractual hospitals, except in Scotland.
2 Wards for patients, excluding elderly, maternity and neonate cots in maternity units.
3 All data for Wales and Scotland, and for Northern Ireland except acute data after 1986, are for deaths, discharges and transfers between specialities. See Appendix, Part 8: In-patient activity.

Source: Department of Health; National Assembly for Wales; National Health Service in Scotland; Department of Health, Social Services and Public Safety, Northern Ireland

a greater of proportion of women than men aged 85 and over received private or local authority home help in 2001/02.

The General Household Survey found that in 2000/01 the majority of the people being cared for by informal carers were female. This gender difference was only evident when the person being cared for lived in a different household from the carer – three quarters of people being cared for who lived in a different household from the carer were women. The majority of carers who provided care to someone who lived elsewhere were women and two thirds were providing care to a parent or parent-in-law.

In 2000/01 the most common type of help given by informal carers was keeping an eye on the cared-for person, followed by keeping them company and taking them out (Figure 8.4). Women were more likely than men to provide most types of help, especially personal care, keeping an eye on the cared for person and keeping them company. Roughly equal proportions of men and women carers provided physical help or took the cared-for person out.

Sick and disabled people

The NHS offers care and help to sick and disabled people. In the United Kingdom the number of acute finished consultant episodes rose by 44 per cent between 1981 and 2001/02 to reach 8.2 million (Table 8.5). The average length of stay for acute patients was just under 5 days in 2001/02, which is around the same as in 2000/01, but three and a half days shorter than in 1981.

In 2001/02 there were 257,000 finished episodes for the mentally ill, which is 5 per cent higher than in 1981 but 9 per cent lower than in 1991/92. The mean duration of stay for the mentally ill was nearly 55 days in 2001/02, which is half the number in 1991/92. Despite the overall fall, the average stay increased between 1997/98 and 1998/99 to around 75 days before declining further. For people with learning disabilities there were 40,000 episodes in 2001/02 and the average length of stay was nearly 118 days, up from just over 90 days in 2000/01.

In 2001/02 there were 12 million finished episodes in NHS hospitals in England, over 6 million of which involved an operation. The categories of bones and joints, upper and lower digestive tracts, pregnancy and childbirth, urinary, and eye accounted for nearly half of the main operations within these finished episodes (Table 8.6). The average length of stay for all finished episodes involving operations was 5.8 days. For finished episodes involving operations on the upper digestive tract, the average length of stay was 12.9 days, compared with 1.8 days for eye operations.

Females accounted for 56 per cent of all the finished episodes involving operations, but there was variation in types of operation between the sexes. Within the urinary category, 69 per cent of the 370,000 bladder procedures were undertaken on males. The majority of eye operations (60 per cent) involved the removal of cataracts and replacement of the lens, and 63 per cent of these operations were for women. Women also had 68 per cent of the 70,000 hip replacements. This is largely an age effect since they are more likely than men to live long enough to develop these health problems. Episodes which involved hip replacements or cataract operations

were for patients whose average ages were 73 and 75, respectively.

Older people receive a large proportion of health service expenditure. In 2001/02, nearly £32 billion was spent on hospital and community health services in England and 39 per cent of this was spent on people aged 65 and over, although they only comprised 16 per cent of the population. People aged 16 to 44 accounted for 26 per cent and those aged 45 to 64 accounted for a further 19 per cent. Total spending on children aged under 16 (including births) was 16 per cent of the total.

In terms of spending per head of population, those aged 85 and over account for the largest proportion of hospital and community health service expenditure in England. In 2001/02 spending on all age groups was £646 per person, but for those aged 85 and

over the spending was more than five times this amount at £3,315 per person (Figure 8.7). Expenditure per head on

Table **8.6**

Selected operations[1] in NHS hospitals, 2001/02

England

	Mean age	Length of stay (days)	Males (percentages)	Females (percentages)	Finished episodes (=100%) (thousands)
Bones and joints[2]	51	8.2	48	52	543.5
Upper digestive tract	58	12.9	49	51	538.3
Pregnancy and childbirth	29	3.0	.	100	532.2
Urinary	64	6.4	70	30	517.2
Lower digestive tract	54	7.5	49	51	462.4
Eye	68	1.8	41	59	412.2
All finished episodes	50	5.8	44	56	6,443.8

1 The main recorded procedure performed during each episode. See Appendix, Part 8: In-patient activity.
2 Excludes skull and spine.

Source: Department of Health

Figure **8.7**

Hospital and community health service expenditure: by age of recipient, 2001/02

England

£ per head of population

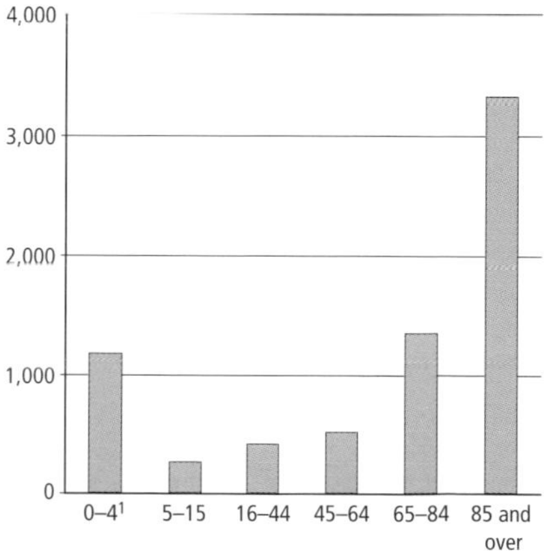

1 Includes birth.

Source: Department of Health

Figure **8.8**

Consultations with an NHS GP[1]: by sex and age, 2001/02

Great Britain
Percentages

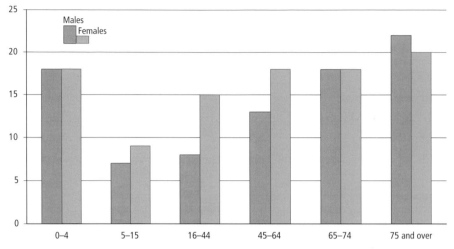

1 Percentage of people who had consulted an NHS GP in the 14 days before the interview.
Source: General Household Survey, Office for National Statistics

Figure **8.9**

Satisfaction with NHS GPs and dentists[1]

Great Britain
Percentages

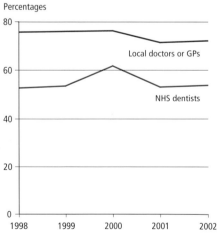

1 Respondents who said that they were 'very satisfied' or 'quite satisfied' when asked 'From your own experience, or from what you have heard, please say how satisfied or dissatisfied you are with the way in which each of these parts of the National Health Service runs nowadays'. Those who did not answer are excluded.

Source: British Social Attitudes Survey, National Centre for Social Research

the 5 to 15 age group was the lowest at £259, less than a tenth of the figure for those aged 85 and over. Spending on the under 5s (including births) was £1,172 per head, around twice the overall average.

People can consult their general medical practitioner (GP) for a number of services including vaccinations and general health advice, as well as the dispensing of prescriptions and the diagnosis of illness. In 2001/02, around 13 per cent of people in Great Britain had consulted their NHS GP in the 14 days before the interview. Females were more likely than males to consult their GPs and this was most prevalent in the 16–44 age group (15 per cent of females compared with 8 per cent for males) (Figure 8.8). Women of this age are more likely to be planning families or using health services associated with

pregnancy and childbirth. In Northern Ireland 14 per cent of people had consulted their GP in the previous two weeks, 17 per cent of females and 12 per cent of males.

The British Social Attitudes survey has found that levels of dissatisfaction with the health service in Great Britain are influenced by the political environment and expenditure on the NHS. Dissatisfaction with the NHS as a whole rose rapidly in the 1980s, fell in the 1990s and then rose sharply in 1996. After the change of government in 1997 dissatisfaction fell, but has since risen again.

In 2002, 72 per cent of people were very or quite satisfied with their local NHS doctors or GPs (Figure 8.9). Levels of satisfaction declined in the mid-1990s, but remained stable at around 76 per cent between 1998 and 2000 before falling to 71 per cent in 2001. Satisfaction with NHS dentists declined throughout the mid 1990s, before stabilising at 53 per cent in the late 1990s. In 2000 satisfaction with NHS dental services increased to 62 per cent before returning to the earlier level of around 53 per cent in 2001 and 2002. The reasons for the boost in 2000 are not clear, although it could be due to the higher profile that dentistry received during 2000, culminating in the publication of a national strategy by the Government in the autumn.

The proportions of people who were satisfied with in-patient and out-patient hospital services remained steady between 1996 and 1998. Levels of satisfaction rose in 1999 and 2000 before falling again in 2001. Satisfaction remained low in 2002, with just over 50 per cent of people saying that they were very or quite satisfied with being in hospital as an in-patient or attending hospital as an out-patient.

In 2002, people who had used a hospital service in the previous year were more likely to say that they were satisfied with the service than those who had not. The effect was particularly evident for in-patient services, with 78 per cent of those who had been in-patients saying that they were very or quite satisfied, compared with 46 per cent of those who had not been an in-patient. There was a similar but smaller relationship for out-patient services.

Levels of satisfaction with GPs remain relatively high compared with other services, and use of GP services has less of an effect on feelings of satisfaction. Among those who had visited their GP in the previous 12 months, 75 per cent said that they were very or quite satisfied, compared with 65 per cent of those who had not used GP services.

There are a number of cash benefits available to sick and disabled people. Disability living allowance (DLA) is a benefit for people who are disabled, have personal care needs, mobility needs or both and who claim before their 65th birthday. Attendance Allowance (AA) is paid to people who become disabled after age 65 and are so severely disabled (physically or mentally) that they need someone to help with their personal care needs. In February 2003, 2.5 million people were receiving DLA and 1.3 million people were receiving AA. The number of people receiving DLA increased by 25 per cent between 1998 and 2003, while there was a 10 per cent increase in AA recipients. These increases are due to changes in conditions for benefit entitlement, demographic changes and increased take-up.

The most common condition for which DLA was being received in February 2003 was arthritis (Table 8.10). Other common conditions included 'other mental health causes' such as psychosis and dementia, learning difficulties and back ailments. The most common condition for which AA was being received was arthritis (388,000) followed by frailty (188,000), mental health causes (123,000) and heart disease (122,000).

Older people

The number of people aged 65 and over in the United Kingdom rose by 27 per cent between 1971 and 2002 (see Chapter 1, Table 1.3). Although older people occupy the majority of places in residential nursing or care homes (see Table 8.1), most people over the state pension age live in households. In 2001 nearly all people (99 per cent) aged 65 to 69 in England and Wales lived in households. However the proportion of people living in households decreases as age increases – 53 per cent of those aged 100 and over lived in households.

In 2001/02, the General Household Survey found that the use of personal social services, such as home help, among older people who live in households, broadly increased as age increased (Table 8.11 – see overleaf). For example, in Great Britain, 2 per cent of those aged 65 to 69 had used the services of a district nurse or health visitor in the month before the interview, compared with 10 per cent of those aged 80 to 84 and 19 per cent of those aged 85 and over. Elderly people who live alone are more likely than elderly people in other kinds of households to utilise personal social services such as home help and meals-on-wheels.

Table **8.10**

Recipients of disability living allowance (DLA): by main disabling condition, 2003[1,2]

Great Britain

	Thousands
Arthritis	500.9
Other mental health causes[3]	334.3
Learning difficulties	239.2
Back ailments	216.5
Muscle/bone/joint disease	196.8
Heart disease	155.3
Stroke related	98.7
Chest disease	85.7
Blindness	60.4
Malignant disease	59.2
Epilepsy	57.1
Diabetes mellitus	46.8
Deafness	29.8
Parkinson's disease	13.6
Skin diseases	13.5
Renal disorders	11.5
AIDS	7.1
Other	342.6
All conditions	2,468.9

1 At 28 February.
2 Where more than one disability is present, only the main disabling condition is recorded.
3 Includes psychosis and dementia.

Source: Department for Work and Pensions

Table **8.11**

Use of personal social services[1] by people aged 65 and over and living in households: by age, 2001/02

Great Britain

Percentages

	65–69	70–74	75–79	80–84	85 and over	All aged 65 and over
Private home help	5	6	10	17	28	10
District nurse/health visitor	2	3	5	10	19	6
Local authority home help	1	2	3	7	18	4
Day centre	1	2	2	5	9	3
Lunch club	1	3	4	5	7	3
Meals-on-wheels	0	0	1	4	7	2
Social worker	0	1	2	1	5	1
Voluntary organisation	1	1	1	2	4	1

1 Those that had used each service in the month prior to the interview.

Source: General Household Survey, Office for National Statistics

Table **8.12**

Receipt of selected social security benefits for pensioners[1]: by family type[2], 2001/02

Great Britain

Percentages

	Couple	Single	
		Males	Females
Retirement pension	98	98	96
Incapacity or disablement benefits[3]	25	20	19
Council tax benefit	17	31	38
Housing benefit	10	25	27
Working families tax credit or income support	6	15	24
Any benefit or tax credit[4]	100	99	99

1 Aged 60 and over for females and 65 and over for males; for couples, where the head is over pension age.
2 See Appendix, Part 8: Benefit units.
3 Incapacity benefit, disability living allowance (care and mobility components), severe disablement allowance, industrial injuries disability benefit, war disablement pension, attendance allowance and disabled persons tax credit.
4 Components do not add to the total as each benefit unit may receive more than one benefit.

Source: Family Resources Survey, Department for Work and Pensions

Older people form the largest category of expenditure from both central government and local authorities (see pages 131 and 132). Much of government expenditure on social protection for older people is on the provision of the state retirement pension. In 2001/02 nearly all people over pension age (women aged 60 and over and men aged 65 and over) received the state retirement pension (Table 8.12). In addition, many older people also received other social security benefits such as council tax benefit or housing benefit, particularly if they were single. Female pensioners living alone are more likely than their male counterparts to be receiving council tax benefit and working family tax credit or income support.

There is an increasing emphasis on people making their own provision for retirement, through either an occupational or personal (private) or stakeholder pension. Occupational pensions are schemes set up and provided through people's employers. All employers with five or more employees are required to provide their employees with access to a stakeholder pension scheme if they do not provide access to an occupational scheme or a personal pension, with an employer contribution of at least 3 per cent. Personal pension, schemes are offered by financial service companies into which people (and sometimes their employers) make contributions to provide a pension on retirement.

In 2001/02, 61 per cent of male employees and 53 per cent of female employees contributed to either an occupational, personal, stakeholder or a combination of these pensions (Table 8.13). Among the age group 16 to 34 female employees are as likely as their male counterparts to be contributing to a pension scheme, but for all older age groups male employees are more likely than female employees to contribute to such schemes.

Families and children

Child benefit is paid for all children aged under 16 (or under 19 and studying up to A level, NVQ level 3 or equivalent). It is a universal payment, not affected by income or savings or national insurance contributions, which is received by nearly all families with dependent children.

In 2001/02 child benefit was received by 97 per cent of families in Great Britain with dependent children where the head of the household was below state pension age (Table 8.14). Single parent families were more likely than couple families to be receiving some other benefits such as working families tax credit or income support, council tax benefit or housing benefit. This reflects the economic activity of lone-parent families – lone mothers, who form the majority of lone-parent families, are less likely to be working than mothers with a partner, particularly if their youngest child is below 5 years of age (see Table 4.5).

A number of changes in society have led to an increased requirement for day care and childminding options for parents with children. Changes in the labour market mean that there are more women in the workplace (see Chapter 4) – in particular more women with dependent children are working.

Demographic changes mean that the proportion of the younger generation who have an elderly parent alive has increased, suggesting that grandparents may be available to help with care of

Table **8.13**

Pension provision: by selected employment status[1] and sex, 2001/02

Great Britain
Percentages

	Males	Females
Employees		
Occupational pension only	46	44
Personal or stakeholder pension only	12	7
Any of these pensions	61	53
No pension scheme	39	47
Self-employed		
Occupational pension only	1	2
Personal or stakeholder pension only	46	25
Any of these pensions	47	29
No pension scheme	53	71

1 Includes employees and self-employed people, but not 'others'. See Appendix, Part 8: Pension provision.

Source: Family Resources Survey, Department for Work and Pensions

Table **8.14**

Receipt of selected social security benefits for families below pension age[1]: by family type[2], 2001/02

Great Britain
Percentages

	Single person with dependent children	Couple with dependent children
Child benefit	97	97
Working families tax credit or income support	76	15
Council tax benefit	53	8
Incapacity or disablement benefits[3]	8	8
Housing benefit	50	7
Jobseekers' allowance	0	2
Any benefit or tax credit	98	98

1 A single adult or couple living as married and any dependent children, where the head of the household is below pension age (60 and over for females and 65 and over for males).
2 See Appendix, Part 8: Benefit units.
3 Incapacity benefit, disability living allowance (care and mobility components), severe disablement allowance, industrial injuries disability benefit, war disablement pension, attendance allowance and disabled persons tax credit.

Source: Family Resources Survey, Department for Work and Pensions

Table **8.15**

Informal childcare arrangements[1] for children whose mothers are in employment[2], autumn 2002[3]

United Kingdom

	Percentages[4]
Child's grandparents	34
Friends or neighbours	7
Childminder	7
Child's brother or sister	6
Non-resident parent or ex-partner	5
Nanny/au pair[5]	1
Other relatives	8
Other non-relatives	2
None of these/does not require minding	46

1 Respondents with children under 15 years of age were asked to identify all those who at any time, on any day during the reference week looked after the child in question, other than the resident parent/guardian.
2 Estimates have not been adjusted for cases where the mother's labour market status is not known.
3 These estimates are not seasonally adjusted and have not been adjusted to take account of the Census 2001 results. See Appendix, Part 4: LFS reweighting.
4 Figures do not sum to 100 per cent because respondents could indicate more than one type of carer.
5 Includes live-in and day nannies.

Source: Labour Force Survey, Office for National Statistics

Table **8.16**

Children looked after by local authorities[1]: by type of accommodation[2]

England

Thousands

	1992	1997	2001	2002
Foster placements	32.4	33.5	38.3	39.2
Placement with parents	6.4	5.2	6.9	6.7
Children's homes[3]	..	6.6	6.8	6.8
Placed for adoption	2.8	2.4	3.4	3.6
Living independently or in residential employment	2.1	1.2	1.2	1.1
Residential schools	..	0.8	1.1	1.1
Other accommodation	2.1	1.6	1.2	1.1
All looked after children	55.5	51.2	58.9	59.7

1 Excludes children looked after under an agreed series of short-term placements.
2 At 31 March.
3 Includes local authority, voluntary and private children's homes and secure units.

Source: Department of Health

their grandchildren. In autumn 2002 the Labour Force Survey found that 34 per cent of children under 15 whose mother was in employment had been looked after by a grandparent at some point in the previous week (Table 8.15).

In cases where parents are unable to provide proper care for children, local authorities can take them into care. These children are usually described as being 'looked after'. As at March 2002 there were 59,700 children being looked after by local authorities in England. The majority of these children, 39,200, were cared for in foster homes (Table 8.16). Some children who are being looked after by a local authority go on to be adopted. In 2002 around 3,600 children were placed for adoption, compared with 2,400 in 1997.

The most common reason in 2002 for a child to be taken into care in England was abuse or neglect (62 per cent). Among other reasons were family dysfunction (10 per cent), absent parenting (7 per cent), family in acute stress (7 per cent) and parent's illness or disability (6 per cent). Most of these children are the subject of care orders (64 per cent) or voluntary agreements (32 per cent).

The numbers of looked-after children in England who gained at least one GCSE or GNVQ has increased from 49 per cent in 2000 to 53 per cent in 2002, although it was below the average for all children (95 per cent). Just after leaving school 56 per cent of looked-after children were in full-time education, compared with 72 per cent of all children. A larger proportion of looked-after children were unemployed than all children (24 per cent compared with 6 per cent), but slightly larger proportions were in full-time training (8 per cent compared with 7 per cent for all children).

Not all children who are referred to local authority social services go on to be looked-after. Children who have more serious problems may be placed on a local authority child protection register. Some of these are taken into care, but not all. Likewise not all children in care are on child protection registers. Registration on a child protection register is a measure taken where it is considered that a child is at continuing risk of significant harm and is in need of a child protection plan.

As at March 2002, there were around 25,700 children on child protection registers in England, with slightly more boys than girls (Figure 8.17). Neglect was the most common reason for both boys and girls to be placed on the register. The type of abuse suffered by the child was similar for each of the sexes, apart from sexual abuse. Sexual abuse accounted for 13 per cent of girls on the register compared with 8 per cent of boys.

Voluntary organisations and charities also play a role in providing help to children who have problems. ChildLine, which runs a 24-hour free telephone counselling service for children, counselled around 120,000 children in 2002/03. The majority of calls or letters – nearly 80 per cent – were from girls. The main types of concern expressed were bullying (22,000), family relationship problems (16,000) and physical abuse (14,000) (Table 8.18). Bullying was the major concern expressed by both girls and boys, accounting for around 20 per cent of enquiries. However girls and boys varied in the other types of concerns they expressed. A higher proportion of girls than boys were counselled regarding pregnancy or concern for others, while a higher proportion of boys expressed a concern

Figure **8.17**

Children on child protection registers[1]: by sex and category of abuse, 2002

England
Thousands

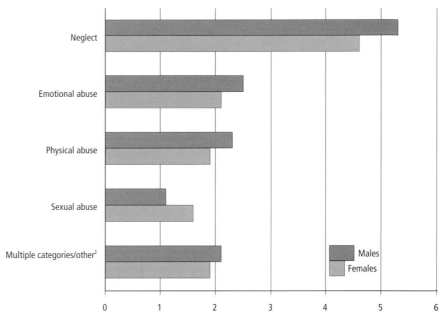

1 As at 31 March.
2 Contains all cases which do not fall into the four main categories.
Source: Department of Health

Table **8.18**

Calls and letters to ChildLine: by type of concern and sex, 2002/03

United Kingdom		Numbers
	Males	Females
Bullying	5,333	16,533
Physical abuse	4,025	9,625
Family relationship[1]	3,081	12,983
Sexual abuse	2,184	6,356
Facts of life	1,974	7,056
Emotional or physical health	1,314	6,030
Concern for others	1,179	8,551
Runaway/homelessness	1,167	2,326
Sexuality	1,042	981
Partner/relationship problems	745	3,657
Other abuse: risk/neglect/emotional	543	1,998
Problems with friends	524	4,389
Smoking/alcohol/drug/solvent abuse	478	1,154
School problem	476	1,458
Pregnancy	317	5,677
In care	217	618
Other[2]	1,568	4,187
Total	26,167	93,579

1 Includes divorce and separation.
2 Includes a range of problems which each add up to less than 1 per cent such as: bereavement, domestic violence, offending, legal, adoption, racism, financial, cultural and religious issues.
Source: ChildLine

Figure **8.19**

Caesarean deliveries in NHS hospitals

England
Percentages

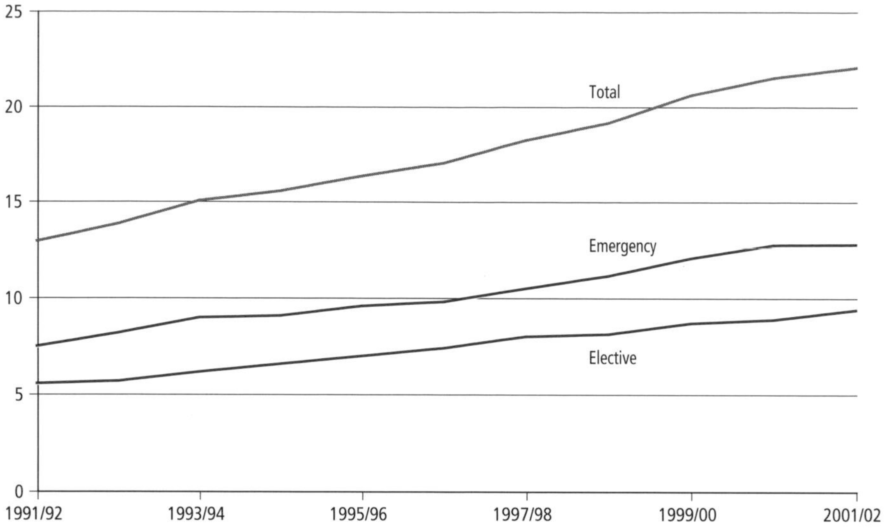

Source: Department of Health

Figure **8.20**

Expenditure on social protection benefits in real terms[1]: by function, 1991/92 and 2001/02

United Kingdom
£ billion at 2001/02 prices

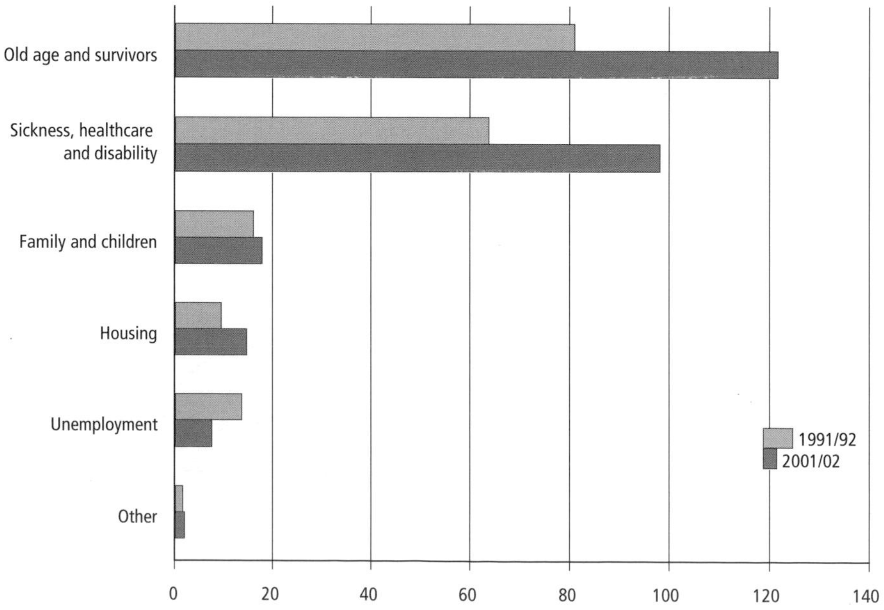

1 *Adjusted to 2001/02 prices using the GDP market prices deflator.*

Source: Office for National Statistics

about physical abuse. The 'facts of life' were a concern for around 8 per cent of both boys and girls who contacted ChildLine. Over 6,000 girls and over 2,000 boys were counselled regarding sexual abuse, which accounted for 7 per cent of girls' enquiries and 8 per cent of boys' enquiries.

An important aspect of social protection provided to families is maternity care. In 2001/02 there were 542,000 deliveries in NHS hospitals in England, a decrease of 17 per cent since 1990/91. Twenty two per cent of deliveries in 2001/02 were by caesarean section, and over half of these were emergency caesareans (Figure 8.19). In the East of England 24 per cent of all deliveries were by caesarean, compared with 20 per cent in both the North East and the East Midlands. Duration of postnatal stay also varies by region. In the North West, 10 per cent of women left hospital on the same day as the birth, compared with 18 per cent of women in the East of England. In recent years the length of time women spend in hospital after ·giving birth has declined, with 81 per cent of women in England leaving hospital within three days in 2001/02 compared with 32 per cent in 1975.

Expenditure

In order for spending on social protection to be compared across the member countries of the European Union (EU), Eurostat has designed a framework for the presentation of information on such expenditure which has been adopted by member states as the European System of integrated Social Protection Statistics (ESSPROS). For this purpose, programmes which are specifically designed to protect people against common sources of hardship are collectively described as expenditure on social protection benefits.

Examples include government expenditure on social security (generally excluding tax credits) and personal social services, sick pay paid by employers, and payments made from occupational and personal pension schemes. Protected persons receive a direct benefit from these programmes, whether in terms of cash payments, goods or services.

In 2001/02 expenditure on social protection in the United Kingdom, using the ESSPROS definitions, was £261 billion. Expenditure on benefits for old age and survivors (such as widows) accounted for nearly half of this expenditure, while spending on benefits for sickness, healthcare and disability accounted for just over a third (Figure 8.20). Between 1991/92 and 2001/02 there was a 50 per cent rise in social protection expenditure on old age and survivors in real terms (after allowing for inflation). This reflects the increase in the number of older people (see Table 1.3).

Expenditure can be expressed in terms of purchasing power parities, to enable direct comparisons between countries. These take account of differences in the general level of goods and services within each country. The differences between countries therefore reflect the differences in the social protection systems, demographic structures, unemployment rates and other social, institutional and economic factors. Measured in this way, the United Kingdom's spending on social protection in 2000 was close to the EU average at £3,680 per person (Figure 8.21). Countries such as Luxembourg, Denmark, Austria and Sweden spent considerably more than this, while countries such as Portugal, Spain, Greece, and Ireland spent the least.

In 2002/03 social security benefit expenditure in Great Britain was £110 billion (Figure 8.22). In the chart, benefit

expenditure is classified according to the main reason a benefit is paid. For example, a disability benefit paid to an elderly person is allocated to the sick and disabled rather than to the elderly recipient group. Principally, benefits for the elderly comprise the state retirement pension and income-related benefits such as income support, housing benefit and council tax benefit paid to people over 60. Benefits for sick and disabled people include statutory sick pay, severe disablement allowance, incapacity benefit and disability living allowance. In 2002/03 over half of social security expenditure in Great Britain, some £57 billion, was for the elderly while over a quarter was for the sick and disabled. Expenditure on families was nearly £18

Figure **8.21**

Expenditure[1] on social protection benefits per head: EU comparison, 2000
£ thousand per head

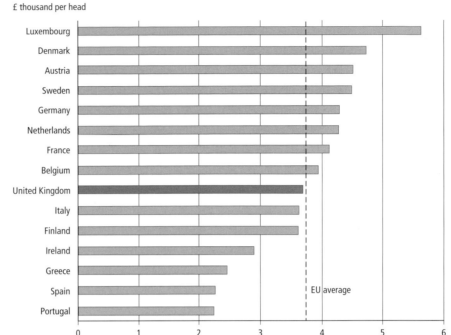

1 Before deduction of tax, where applicable. Tax credits are generally excluded. Figures are purchasing power parities per inhabitant.
Source: Eurostat

Figure **8.22**

Social security benefit expenditure: by recipient group[1], 2002/03
Great Britain
Percentages

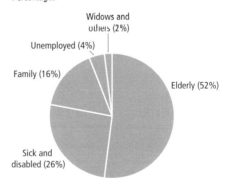

Total expenditure: £109.9 billion

1 See Appendix, Part 8: Benefits to groups of recipients.
Source: Department for Work and Pensions

Figure **8.23**

Local authority personal social services expenditure[1]: by recipient group, 2001/02

England
Percentages

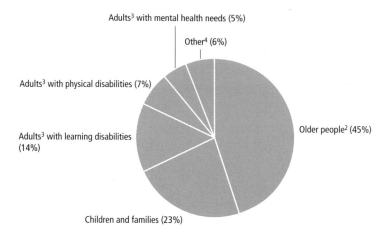

Adults[3] with mental health needs (5%)

Other[4] (6%)

Adults[3] with physical disabilities (7%)

Adults[3] with learning disabilities (14%)

Older people[2] (45%)

Children and families (23%)

Total expenditure: £13.6 billion

1 All figures include overhead costs.
2 Aged 65 and over.
3 Aged 18–64.
4 Includes service strategy and asylum seekers.

Source: Department of Health

billion, around £10 billion of which was for lone parents.

Local authorities offer a range of social protection services such as the provision of home help (see Figure 8.2) and the running of children's homes (see Figure 8.16), day centres and residential homes (see Figure 8.1). Spending on personal social services by local authorities in England was £13.6 billion in 2001/02 (Figure 8.23). People aged 65 or over accounted for just under half of this expenditure (£6.2 billion) and families and children accounted for almost a quarter (£3.1 billion).

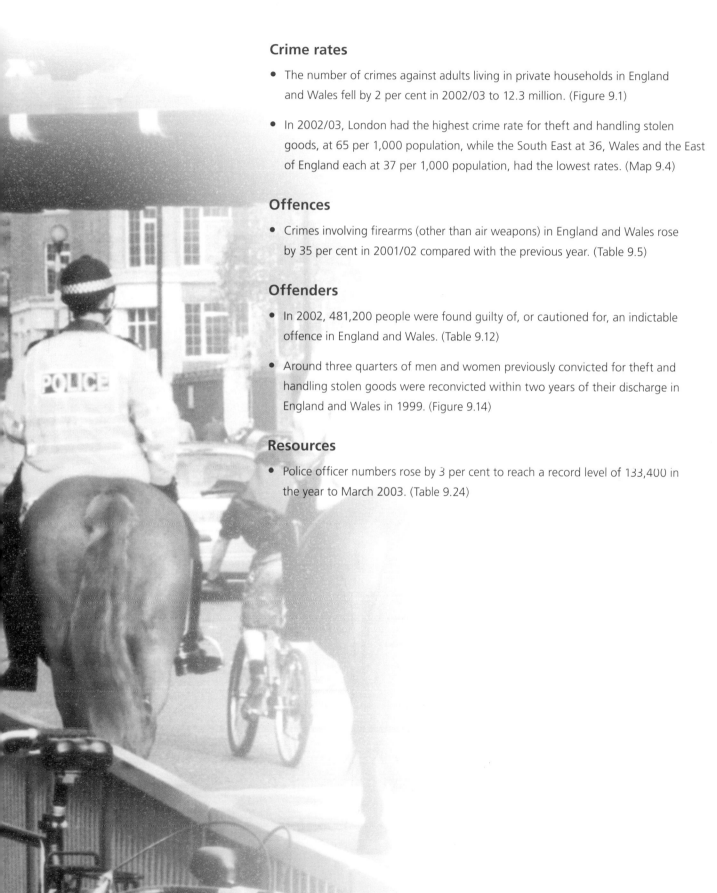

Chapter 9 **Crime and Justice**

Crime rates

- The number of crimes against adults living in private households in England and Wales fell by 2 per cent in 2002/03 to 12.3 million. (Figure 9.1)

- In 2002/03, London had the highest crime rate for theft and handling stolen goods, at 65 per 1,000 population, while the South East at 36, Wales and the East of England each at 37 per 1,000 population, had the lowest rates. (Map 9.4)

Offences

- Crimes involving firearms (other than air weapons) in England and Wales rose by 35 per cent in 2001/02 compared with the previous year. (Table 9.5)

Offenders

- In 2002, 481,200 people were found guilty of, or cautioned for, an indictable offence in England and Wales. (Table 9.12)

- Around three quarters of men and women previously convicted for theft and handling stolen goods were reconvicted within two years of their discharge in England and Wales in 1999. (Figure 9.14)

Resources

- Police officer numbers rose by 3 per cent to reach a record level of 133,400 in the year to March 2003. (Table 9.24)

Figure **9.1**

British Crime Survey offences[1]

England & Wales
Millions

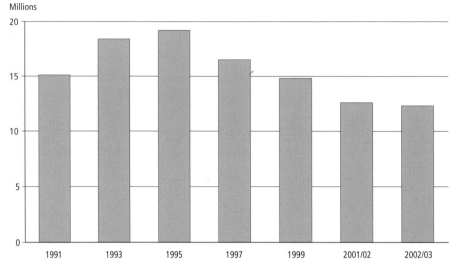

1 All incidents measured by the survey, whether or not they were recorded by the police.

Source: British Crime Survey, Home Office

Table **9.2**

Recorded crime: by type of offence[1], 2002/03

Percentages

	England & Wales	Scotland[2]	Northern Ireland
Theft and handling stolen goods	40	40	29
Theft of vehicles	5	5	6
Theft from vehicles	11	9	5
Criminal damage	19	22	26
Burglary	15	10	13
Violence against the person	14	5	20
Fraud and forgery	6	5	6
Drug offences	2	9	1
Robbery	2	1	2
Sexual offences	1	1	1
Other offences[3]	1	7	2
All notifiable offences (=100%) (thousands)	5,899	427	142

1 See Appendix, Part 9: Types of offences in England, Wales and Northern Ireland, and Offences and crimes.
2 Figures for Scotland refer to 2002.
3 In Northern Ireland includes 'offences against the state'. In Scotland excludes 'offending while on bail'.

Source: Home Office; Scottish Executive; Police Service of Northern Ireland

Crime, in some form, affects many people during the course of their lives. Dealing with crime, and the problems associated with crime, is an ever present concern for both society and government.

Crime rates

The number of crimes against adults living in private households in England and Wales fell by 2 per cent in 2002/03, according to the latest survey evidence from the British Crime Survey (BCS). Crimes recorded by the police, after taking into account recording changes, showed an estimated 3 per cent fall in 2002/03 on the previous year. The box on page 135 gives more details of these two measures of crime.

The BCS estimated that 12.3 million crimes against adults occurred in England and Wales, based on interviews taking place in 2002/03, and covering the 12 months prior to interview (Figure 9.1). BCS crimes rose steadily through the 1980s and into the 1990s, peaking in 1995. They then fell progressively so that by 2002/03 they were only slightly above the level in 1983.

There was a 44 per cent fall in burglary measured by the BCS between 1995 and 2002/03. The BCS estimate for the number of violent incidents experienced by adults in England and Wales (2.8 million) in 2002/03 is unchanged from 2001/02. Vehicle-related thefts fell by 5 per cent. The most common offences against adults living in private households, as measured by the BCS, involved some type of theft (57 per cent). Nineteen per cent of BCS crimes were vehicle-related thefts and 8 per cent were burglaries.

Changes in the methods and rules for recording crime were fully introduced across all police forces in England and

Wales from April 2002. After adjusting for the effects of these recording changes, it is estimated that there was a 2 per cent increase in violent crimes, and a 9 per cent fall in vehicle-related thefts in 2002/03. In the previous year, a substantial increase in firearms offences was recorded (see Figure 9.5).

Of crimes recorded by the police in England and Wales in 2002/03, four fifths were offences against property. These comprised theft and handling stolen goods, which accounted for 40 per cent of all recorded crime, as well as criminal damage, burglary and fraud and forgery (Table 9.2). Theft and handling stolen goods includes thefts of, or from, vehicles. Together they accounted for 17 per cent of all recorded crime in England and Wales.

Criminal damage accounted for a quarter of recorded crime in Northern Ireland while violence against the person accounted for a fifth. These proportions were greater than in England and Wales and in Scotland. The proportion of drug offences in Scotland, at 9 per cent, were relatively high compared with England and Wales and Northern Ireland, at 2 and 1 per cent respectively.

Crime in Scotland increased by 1 per cent in 2002, with a total of 427,000 crimes recorded by the police. In Scotland the term 'crime' is used for the more serious criminal acts (roughly equivalent to 'indictable' and 'triable-either-way' offences in England and Wales). Less serious crimes are termed 'offences'. More details on these differences can be found in the Appendix, Part 9: Offences and crimes.

Recorded crime in Northern Ireland increased by around 2 per cent between 2001/02 and 2002/03. In Northern Ireland the definitions used

are broadly comparable with those in England and Wales.

Just over 9.5 million BCS crimes, around three quarters of the total, are comparable with those recorded by police statistics, with an estimated 43 per cent of these crimes being reported to the police (Table 9.3). Of those reported, an estimated 68 per cent were recorded by the police. The proportion of crimes reported to the police varies according to the type of offence. Reasons for not reporting crimes to the police commonly include the perception on the part of the victim that the incident was too trivial, that the police could not do anything, or that the matter was dealt with privately. Higher proportions (97 per cent in 2002/03) of thefts of vehicles than thefts from vehicles or attempted vehicle theft – are reported to the police as a formal record of the incident is generally needed for insurance purposes. Lower proportions (around a third) of incidents of vandalism and theft from the person are reported. The proportion of crimes reported to the police has been stable since the mid-1990s (at around 45 per cent), considerably higher than the reporting rate in the early 1980s (36 per cent in 1981).

The police may choose not to record a reported crime for a number of reasons. They may consider that the report is mistaken, too trivial or that there is insufficient evidence. Alternatively, the victim may not wish the police to proceed. Recording rates also vary according to the type of offence, with around a fifth of vandalism and comparable violent crimes recorded by the police compared with nearly half of household burglaries.

Sixteen per cent of common assaults were recorded by the police in 2002/03.

Two measures of crime

There are two main measures of the way crime is recorded: the British Crime Survey (BCS) estimates, and administrative data collected by the police. Crime data collected by the police is a by-product of the administrative procedure of completing a record for crimes which they investigate. BCS data are collated by interviewing members of households. The BCS measures all 'incidents' irrespective of whether they were reported to, or recorded by, the police.

Police recorded crime and BCS measured crime have different coverage. Unlike crime data recorded by the police, the BCS is restricted to crimes against adults (aged 16 or over) living in private households and their property, and does not include some types of crime (for example, fraud, murder and so-called victimless crimes).

Table 9.3

Crimes committed within the last 12 months: by outcome, 2002/03

England & Wales		Percentages
	BCS crimes reported to the police	BCS crimes recorded by the police
Vandalism	31	22
Comparable property crime[1]	50	38
Burglary	65	46
Vehicle thefts	50	42
Theft from the person	33	19
Violence[2]	41	21
All comparable crime	43	29

1 Comprises all acquisitive crime: all burglary, vehicle thefts, bicycle theft and theft from the person.
2 Does not include snatch theft.

Source: British Crime Survey, Home Office

Map **9.4**

Theft[1]: by region, 2002/03

Rates per 1,000 population

- 60 and over
- 50–59
- 40–49
- Under 40

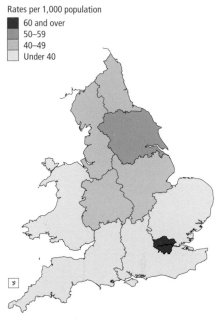

1 Theft and handling stolen goods.
Source: Home Office

Recording of such assaults has been particularly affected by changes introduced in the National Crime Recording Standard (NCRS). The overall recording rate of comparable crime rose by 6 percentage points between 2001/02 and 2002/03, further evidence of the impact of the NCRS.

There is considerable variation in patterns of crime across England and Wales, both geographically and by type of area. Many of these differences may result from the variation in the socio-economic status of these populations (Map 9.4). London in 2002/03 had the highest rates for theft and handling stolen goods, at 65 per 1,000 population, while the South East at 36, and the East of England and Wales at 37 per 1,000 population, had the lowest rates. The average rate for this crime was 45 per 1,000 population. London also had the highest rates for violence against the person. Yorkshire and the Humber had the highest rates for burglary and theft of, and from, vehicles.

Two thirds of all recorded robberies in 2002/03 took place in just five police force areas: the Metropolitan Police, Greater Manchester, West Midlands, West Yorkshire and Avon and Somerset. These five police areas include large cities and highly populated areas. The Metropolitan Police alone recorded 39 per cent of all robberies in England and Wales.

Offences

The incidence of violent crime is still comparatively rare. However, crimes involving firearms rose by 35 per cent in 2001/02 and have doubled since 1997/98 (Table 9.5). Robbery accounted for over half of recorded crimes involving firearms in 2001/02, and violence against the person accounted for a third of such crimes. Comparatively few firearms were used in burglary or criminal damage.

In 2001/02, firearms identified as handguns were used in 59 per cent of firearm offences (excluding those involving air weapons), imitation weapons in 12 per cent and shotguns in 7 per cent. The number of offences involving imitation weapons was 55 per cent higher than in the previous year. In 76 per cent of non-air weapon firearm offences, the weapon was not fired.

Fraud and forgery offences accounted for 6 per cent of all recorded crime offences in 2002/03. The development of new technologies has expanded the capability of criminals to carry out different types of fraud, particularly credit card fraud. New fraudulent practices include skimming, a process where the genuine data on a card's magnetic strip is electronically copied onto another card, without the legitimate cardholder's knowledge. Credit card fraud on phone, mail order, fax or Internet transactions involves using fraudulently obtained card details, usually from discarded receipts, and copied without the cardholder's consent. Industry estimates put the total value of all card fraud at £425 million in 2002.

Table **9.5**

Crimes involving firearms[1]: by offence group

England & Wales

Numbers

	1997/98	1998/99	1999/00	2000/01	2001/02
Robbery	2,836	2,890	3,831	3,965	5,323
Violence against the person	1,463	1,746	2,264	2,517	3,444
Burglary	284	238	309	346	459
Criminal damage	98	104	135	240	369
Other	222	231	304	294	379
All crimes	4,903	5,209	6,843	7,362	9,974

1 Firearms other than air weapons.
Source: Home Office

Recorded crime statistics show all cheque and credit card fraud fell by 18 per cent between 1999/2000 and 2002/03. Private sector data indicate that the value of plastic card fraud has risen by around a third and payment fraud by two thirds between 2000 and 2001. Despite this rise, figures on the number of defendants found guilty of fraud-related offences has fallen over the past three years. Nearly 15,600 defendants were found guilty of indictable fraud offences in England and Wales in 2002, a fall of 13 per cent compared with the peak in 1999 (Table 9.6). Obtaining property by deception was the most common offence, committed by 60 per cent of offenders found guilty of indictable fraud in 2002. Numbers found guilty of this offence have fallen by 19 per cent since 1999. Dishonest representation for obtaining benefit is nearly three times as high as it was in 1999, and is now the second most commonly committed fraud offence.

Drug offences can cover a range of activities, including unlawful production, supply, and most commonly, possession of illegal substances. In 2001, the total number of drug seizures in the United Kingdom rose by 5 per cent to 131,000, following two years of decline (Table 9.7). Seizures are now 21,000 lower than in the last peak in 1998. HM Customs and the National Crime Squad generally seized larger amounts while local police forces made a greater number of smaller seizures.

In terms of the quantity of drugs seized, while the amount of cocaine seized fell by 28 per cent in 2001 to just under 3 tonnes, the amounts of the other main Class A drugs recovered all rose. Cannabis accounted for 71 per cent of

the total number of seizures. Nearly 56 kilograms of crack were recovered, more than double the amount in 2000. Just under 4 tonnes of heroin were seized, 16 per cent more than in the previous year. The number of

doses/tablets of ecstasy rose 17 per cent in 2001 to 7.7 million. The amount of methadone recovered was at its highest level since 1997. Fewer than 10,000 LSD doses were seized, all by local police forces.

Table 9.6

Defendants found guilty of indictable fraud offences

England & Wales   Numbers

	1998	1999	2000	2001	2002
Obtaining property by deception	11,440	11,480	10,540	9,440	9,350
Dishonest representation for obtaining benefit	240	710	1,350	1,950	1,990
Making off without payment	1,250	1,440	1,410	1,320	1,300
Obtaining services by deception	980	1,030	880	880	830
False accounting	1,690	1,620	1,160	870	750
Conspiracy to defraud	470	420	430	450	410
Other offences	1,130	1,100	1,100	1,000	940
All offences	17,200	17,800	16,870	15,910	15,570

Source: Home Office

Table 9.7

Seizures[1] of selected drugs

United Kingdom   Numbers

	1991	1995	1998	1999	2000	2001
Cannabis	59,420	90,935	114,691	98,450	91,695	93,482
Heroin	2,640	6,479	15,192	15,519	16,457	18,168
Ecstasy-type	1,735	5,521	4,850	6,637	9,784	10,411
Cocaine	1,446	2,270	5,209	5,858	6,005	6,984
Amphetamines	6,821	15,462	18,630	13,393	7,073	6,799
Crack	583	1,445	2,488	2,507	2,765	3,688
Methadone	427	942	1,584	1,215	1,171	1,072
LSD	1,636	1,158	623	480	297	168
All seizures	69,807	114,339	151,749	134,101	125,079	130,894

1 Seizures by the police and HM Customs. A seizure can include more than one type of drug. See Appendix, Part 9: Drug seizures.

Source: Home Office

Table **9.8**

Levels of disorder[1]

England & Wales   Percentages

	1994	1996	1998	2000	2001/02	2002/03
Vandalism	29	24	26	32	34	35
Teenagers hanging around	26	24	27	32	32	33
Rubbish or litter lying around	26	26	28	30	32	33
People using or dealing drugs	22	21	25	33	31	32
People being drunk or rowdy	..	..	..	..	22	23
Noisy neighbours	8	8	8	9	10	10
Racial attacks	5	5	5	8	9	8

1 Trends in disorder perceived to be a 'very' or 'fairly' big problem.

Source: British Crime Survey, Home Office

Table **9.9**

Reasons for improving home security[1], 2001/02

England & Wales

	Percentages
Done as part of general improvements to the house	24
Own home was burgled	16
General increase in burglaries in local area	14
Decision taken by landlord/person responsible for accommodation	8
Home was going to be left empty	7
Neighbours' home was burgled	6
To reduce insurance premiums	6
Advice in leaflets etc	5
Friends/relatives home was burgled	5
Advice from police/crime prevention officer	4
Contacted by businesses selling security devices	1
Other	16

1 Based on those who had made improvements to their home security in the year preceding the interview. Percentages do not sum to 100 as respondents could give more than one reason.

Source: British Crime Survey, Home Office

Victims

Any form of civil disorder can have an impact on the quality of people's lives. The percentage of people perceiving disorder to be a 'very' or 'fairly' big problem in their local area increased slightly between 2001/02 and 2002/03, according to the BCS. Proportions considering racial attacks and racial harassment a problem in their local area declined slightly (Table 9.8).

Over a longer period, between 1996 and 2002/03, of the categories shown, vandalism and people using or dealing drugs showed the biggest increases, of 11 percentage points. The proportion mentioning noisy neighbours as a problem remained more constant. In 2001/02, 30 per cent of men aged 16 to 24 reported high levels of disorder in their local area compared with only 7 per cent of men aged 75 and above. The corresponding figures for women were 34 and 8 per cent respectively.

Issues relating to crime prevention have been prominent in initiatives to combat crime. Neighbourhood watch schemes were established in 1982, to encourage members of the public to assist in crime surveillance. There were 160,000 schemes in operation, covering over a quarter of households in the United Kingdom in 2003.

The proportions of households with burglar alarms increased from 18 per cent to 27 per cent between 1994 and 2001/02. Other types of security used were light sensors and window locks. A quarter of householders who had improved their home security said that they had done so as part of overall improvements to their house (Table 9.9). Smaller proportions said they had improved security as a result of their own, or a friend's or neighbour's house being burgled.

Levels of concern about crime are higher among people in neighbourhoods where there is a low sense of community. Older people worry more about crime than younger people and women worry more than men.

Despite being more likely to be the victim of crime, men are less worried than women about most types of crime (Table 9.10). Women are twice as likely as men to be 'very worried' about being mugged, three times more likely to be 'very worried' about being physically attacked and nearly five times more likely to be 'very worried' about being raped. Roughly equal proportions of men and women are worried about theft of, or from, a car. Households in the lowest income groups tend to worry about all types of crime more than households in the higher income groups. The risk of becoming a victim of any form of crime is still historically low at 27 per cent, around the same level as 1981, and one third lower than the risk in 1995 (40 per cent).

Violent crimes comprise around a quarter of the total number of incidents experienced by individuals or households. They can involve actual violence, the threat of violence or simple harassment. Half of all violent crime reported to the BCS did not result in any injury to the victim. The risk of becoming a victim of violent crime for those interviewed by the BCS in 2002/03 was 4 per cent. Men aged 16 to 24 are the most at risk age group. Fifteen per cent of men and 7 per cent women of this age reported that some sort of violence had been used against them. Older men and women are much less likely than younger people to be a victim of violent crime – with less than 1 per cent of those aged 65 and over reporting they had been victim of some sort of violence over the period in question (Table 9.11). Violence has fallen

Table 9.10

Concern about crime[1]: by sex and age, 2002/03

England & Wales
Percentages

	Theft from a car[2]	Theft of a car[2]	Burglary	Mugging	Physical attack	Rape	Insulted or pestered
Men							
16–29	18	20	11	10	9	9	5
30–59	14	15	13	8	7	5	5
60 and over	9	12	11	10	6	2	4
All aged 16 and over	14	15	12	9	7	5	5
Women							
16–29	17	21	18	21	28	30	14
30–59	13	17	17	18	22	24	12
60 and over	11	16	17	20	18	17	9
All aged 16 and over	13	17	17	19	22	23	12

1 Percentages of people who were 'very worried' about each type of crime.
2 Based on respondents residing in households owning, or with regular use of, a vehicle.

Source: British Crime Survey, Home Office

Table 9.11

Victims of violent crime[1]: by sex and age, 2002/03

England & Wales
Percentages

	Domestic	Mugging	Stranger	Acquaintance[2]	All violence
Males					
16–24	0.9	3.2	7.1	5.6	15.1
25–44	0.5	1.1	2.7	1.5	5.5
45–64	0.2	0.4	1.3	0.8	2.7
65–74	0.0	0.2	0.6	0.4	1.3
75 and over	0.0	0.1	0.1	0.2	0.4
All aged 16 and over	0.4	1.0	2.5	1.7	5.3
Females					
16–24	1.9	1.3	1.5	2.8	6.9
25–44	1.1	0.6	0.7	1.2	3.4
45–64	0.4	0.5	0.4	0.8	2.0
65–74	0.0	0.4	0.2	-	0.7
75 and over	0.0	0.5	0.1	0.1	0.6
All aged 16 and over	0.7	0.6	0.6	1.1	2.9

1 Percentage victimised once or more.
2 Assaults in which the victim knew one or more of the offenders at least by sight.

Source: British Crime Survey, Home Office

by 19 per cent since 1999 and by 24 per cent since 1997, due mainly to reductions in domestic and acquaintance violence. Figures on domestic violence are always difficult to quantify. However, the 1996 BCS included a self-completion module on domestic violence. An estimated that 23 per cent of women and 15 per cent of men aged 16 to 59 said a current or former partner had physically assaulted them at some time in their lives. These figures increased to 26 per cent and 17 per cent respectively when frightening threats were included.

Offenders

In 2002, over 481,000 people were found guilty of, or cautioned for, an indictable offence in England and Wales of which just over four fifths were men (Table 9.12). Young people offended the most, peaking at age 19 for males and age 15 for females. Theft was the most common offence committed by both male and female offenders. Over half of all female offenders were found guilty or cautioned for theft-related offences compared with around a third of all male offenders.

In England and Wales a formal caution may be given by a senior police officer when an offender has admitted his or her guilt, there is sufficient evidence for a conviction and it is not in the public interest to institute criminal proceedings. Cautions are more severe than a reprimand – in order for a caution to be given, there must be sufficient evidence gathered by the police of the likelihood of a successful prosecution; details of cautions given remain on an individual's record. In 2002, 143,000 cautions for indictable offences in England and Wales were given – 60,000 fewer than in 1995 but 39,000 more than in 1981 (Table 9.13). The two offence categories receiving the highest number of cautions were theft and handling stolen goods and drug offences.

From June 2000 the *Crime and Disorder Act 1998* came into force nationally and removed the use of cautions for persons under 18 and replaced them with reprimands and final warnings. The cautioning rate for indictable offences, that is the number of offenders cautioned as a percentage of those found guilty or cautioned (excluding motoring offences), is higher for juvenile offenders than for adult offenders. The

Table **9.12**

Offenders found guilty of, or cautioned for, indictable offences[1]: by sex, type of offence and age, 2002

England & Wales

Rates per 10,000 population

	10–15	16–24	25–34	35 and over	All aged 10 and over (thousands)
Males					
Theft and handling stolen goods	86	183	104	17	131.5
Drug offences	18	159	62	9	84.1
Violence against the person	31	77	32	9	51.8
Burglary	29	49	21	2	30.4
Criminal damage	13	18	7	2	12.5
Robbery	6	14	4	0	7.2
Sexual offences	3	4	3	2	5.0
Other indictable offences	11	102	59	12	69.0
All indictable offences	196	606	292	53	391.5
Females					
Theft and handling stolen goods	51	67	32	6	50.1
Drug offences	2	15	9	1	9.8
Violence against the person	11	12	5	1	9.5
Burglary	3	3	1	0	2.1
Criminal damage	2	2	1	0	1.6
Robbery	1	1	0	0	0.9
Sexual offences	0	0	0	0	0.1
Other indictable offences	3	20	13	2	14.4
All indictable offences	74	119	61	12	88.6

1 See Appendix, Part 9: Types of offences in England and Wales.
Source: Home Office

cautioning rate is higher for females than for males at all age groups.

A relatively small number of offenders are responsible for a disproportionately high number of offences. Often, offending patterns of behaviour are established at an early age. Those offenders who have the most court appearances are most likely to have more court appearances. Those with fewer court appearances are most likely to offend once or twice.

Around three quarters of men and women previously convicted for theft and handling stolen goods, and a similar proportion of men convicted for burglary, were reconvicted within two years of their discharge in England and Wales in 1999 (Figure 9.14). For robbery and violence against other people, around half of men were reconvicted in the same period, while the equivalent proportions for women were slightly lower. However, less than a sixth of men convicted for sexual offences were reconvicted within two years of their discharge. Around nine out of ten young male offenders convicted of theft of, or from, a vehicle or from a shop, were reconvicted within two years. Reconviction rates for those with a first conviction are much lower than for those who had previous convictions. The rate for all first time offenders was 17 per cent compared with 40 per cent for those with one or two previous convictions and 78 per cent for those with 11 or more previous convictions.

Police and courts action

Under the *Police and Criminal Evidence Act,* implemented in January 1986, the police have certain powers covering stop and searches of people or vehicles, road checks, detention and intimate searches of people. In 2001/02 the police stopped and searched 741,000 people or vehicles

Table **9.13**

Offenders cautioned for indictable offences[1]: by type of offence

England & Wales
Thousands

	1981	1991	1995	1998	2001	2002
Theft and handling stolen goods	79.2	108.5	104.9	83.6	63.5	54.2
Drug offences	0.3	21.2	48.2	58.7	39.4	44.9
Violence against the person	5.6	19.4	20.4	23.5	19.5	23.6
Burglary[2]	11.2	13.3	10.5	8.4	6.4	5.8
Fraud and forgery	1.4	5.6	7.9	7.4	5.8	5.3
Criminal damage	2.1	3.8	3.8	2.7	3.4	3.1
Sexual offences	2.8	3.3	2.3	1.7	1.2	1.1
Robbery	0.1	0.6	0.6	0.6	0.5	0.4
Other	1.3	4.1	4.0	5.0	4.2	4.4
All offenders cautioned	103.9	179.9	202.6	191.7	143.9	142.9

1 Excludes motoring offences.
2 See Appendix, Part 9: Offenders cautioned for burglary.

Source: Home Office

Figure **9.14**

Prisoners reconvicted within two years of discharge in 1999: by original offence

England & Wales
Percentages

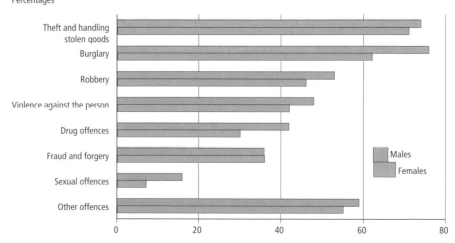

1 Includes criminal damage, motoring offences and other indictable and summary offences.
Source: Home Office

Table 9.15

Reasons for stop and searches made by police

England & Wales | | | | | | Thousands

	1987	1991	1995	1998/99	2000/01	2001/02
Stolen property	49	114	253	436	296	292
Drugs	38	110	232	362	237	267
Going equipped[1]	14	51	126	151	89	82
Offensive weapons	8	16	39	56	47	54
Firearms	1	2	5	7	8	9
Other	8	11	34	69	37	37
All	118	304	690	1,081	714	741

1 Persons found in possession of an article capable of being used in connection with a crime.

Source: Home Office

Table 9.16

Detection rates for recorded crime[1]: by type of offence, 2002/03

			Percentages
	England & Wales[2]	Scotland[3]	Northern Ireland
Drug offences	93	99	68
Violence against the person	54	81	51
Sexual offences	43	77	47
Rape	36	77	47
Fraud and forgery	26	82	28
Robbery	18	38	13
Theft and handling stolen goods	16	34	14
Theft of vehicles	15	35	11
Theft from vehicles	6	18	3
Burglary	12	26	10
Criminal damage	13	22	13
Other crimes[4]	69	99	40
All recorded crime	24	46	23

1 See Appendix, Part 9: Types of offences in England and Wales; Types of offences in Northern Ireland, and Offences and crimes.
2 Detection rates may be influenced by the National Crime Recording Standard recording changes.
3 Figures for Scotland are for 2002.
4 The Northern Ireland figure includes offences against the state.

Source: Home Office; Scottish Executive; Police Service of Northern Ireland

in England and Wales, 4 per cent more than in 2000/01 (Table 9.15). Suspicion of possession of stolen property and possession of drugs are the two biggest reasons why individuals are stopped and searched. The number of stop and searches by the Metropolitan Police Force rose by 18 per cent in 2001/02, increasing its share of the national total by 3 percentage points to 27 per cent.

Under recorded crime counting rules, a crime is 'detected' if a suspect has been identified and interviewed and there is sufficient evidence to bring a charge. There does not have to be a prosecution: for example, the offender may accept a caution or ask for the crime to be taken into consideration by the court, or the victim may not wish to give evidence.

Detection rates, still known as clear-up rates in Scotland, vary according to the type of offence. Drug offences were the most likely type of crime to be detected in 2002/03 and theft from vehicles was the least likely (Table 9.16). Less than a fifth of robberies were detected in England and Wales and in Northern Ireland, compared with nearly two fifths cleared up in Scotland in 2002. In England and Wales, there were 1.4 million detected crimes in 2002/03, 8 per cent higher than in the previous year. The overall detection rate was 23.5 per cent, under counting rules introduced in 1998/99, similar to the rate in 2001/02 (23.4 per cent). The introduction of the NCRS may also have had an effect on the detection rate, but the effect of this is difficult to quantify. In 2002/03 13 per cent of the total of recorded offences resulted in a charge or summons. Scotland had a clear-up rate of 46 per cent in 2002 and Northern Ireland had a comparable rate of 23 per cent in 2002/03. Often, there may be a time lapse between an offence being committed and the police clearing it up.

When an offender has been charged, or summonsed and then found guilty, the court will impose a sentence. Sentences in England, Wales and Northern Ireland can include immediate custody, a community sentence, a fine or, if the court considers that no punishment is necessary, a discharge. In 2002, 337,000 people were sentenced for indictable offences in England and Wales (Table 9.17). The form of sentence varied according to the type of offence committed. In 2002 those sentenced for drug offences were the most likely to be fined, with 44 per cent receiving this form of sentence. Forty six per cent of male offenders received a fine when being sentenced for drug offences compared with 26 per cent of female offenders.

In the BCS adults were asked their views on sentencing handed down by the courts. The proportion who thought such sentencing was much too lenient fell from just over a half in 1996 to just over a third in 2001/02. Those thinking sentencing by the courts was about right has changed relatively little, at around one in five of those surveyed.

Offenders sentenced for robbery were the most likely to be sentenced to immediate custody, while those sentenced for fraud and forgery and criminal damage were the most likely to receive a community sentence. In 2001, approximately 11 per cent of those sentenced by Scottish courts received either a probation or community service order, and 14 per cent received a custodial sentence.

Custodial sentences are normally given by courts for the most serious, dangerous and persistent offenders. A

defendant may choose in court to either plead guilty or go on to contest the case by pleading not guilty. Appeals against decisions made at magistrates' courts are heard in the Crown Court, while those against Crown Court decisions are made at the Court of Appeal. In 2002, over 1,900 appeals against conviction and around 5,800 appeals against sentence were started in England and Wales by the Court of Appeal (Criminal Division).

Just over 1.3 million defendant cases were prosecuted in magistrates' courts by the Crown Prosecution Service in the year ending June 2002, 1 per cent more than in the previous year. The Crown Prosecution Service is the government agency that handles the bulk of prosecutions in England and Wales: other prosecuting authorities in magistrates' courts include HM Customs and Excise, the DVLA, and the Environment Agency.

Table **9.17**

Offenders sentenced for indictable offences[1]: by type of offence and type of sentence[2], 2002

England & Wales
Percentages

	Discharge	Fine	Community sentence	Fully suspended sentence	Immediate custody	Other	All sentenced (=100%) (thousands)
Theft and handling stolen goods	20	19	37	-	22	2	126.7
Drug offences	19	44	18	-	17	1	49.0
Violence against the person	10	11	44	1	31	3	37.8
Burglary	3	2	42	-	51	1	26.4
Fraud and forgery	16	15	45	2	21	2	18.1
Criminal damage	21	16	45	-	11	7	10.8
Motoring	5	40	27	1	26	-	8.5
Robbery	-	-	22	-	76	1	7.7
Sexual offences	5	6	28	1	59	2	4.4
Other offences	10	43	19	1	17	11	47.4
All indictable offences	15	23	33	1	25	3	336.7

1 See Appendix, Part 9: Types of offences in England and Wales.
2 See Appendix, Part 9: Sentences and orders.

Source: Home Office

Figure **9.18**

Outcome of cases at the magistrates' courts, 2001–02

England & Wales
Percentages

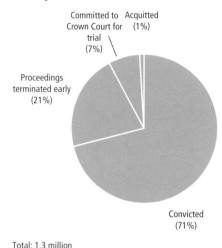

Committed to Crown Court for trial (7%)

Acquitted (1%)

Proceedings terminated early (21%)

Convicted (71%)

Total: 1.3 million

Source: Crown Prosecution Service

Prosecutions for indictable and less serious summary non-motoring offences increased by 2 per cent, while prosecutions for summary motoring offences fell by 1 per cent. The number of defendants committed for trial at the Crown Court increased by 4 per cent over the previous year. Nearly three quarters of defendants prosecuted by the Crown Prosecution Service were convicted; 1 per cent were acquitted and around a fifth of cases were terminated early (Figure 9.18).

The Crown Prosecution Service prosecuted 103,600 defendants at the Crown Court in the year ending June 2002; 18 per cent of defendants were committed for sentence (after having been found guilty at magistrates' courts). Over 80 per cent of defendents were committed. Changes in the handling of offences meant that more serious (indictable only) offences are tried at the Crown rather than magistrates' courts.

Prisons and probation

Prisons are the usual and eventual destination for offenders receiving custodial sentences. Offenders initially given non-custodial sentences who break the terms of their sentence are then liable to receive custodial sentences. Sentenced prisoners are classified into different risk-level groups for security purposes. Women prisoners are held in separate prisons or in separate accommodation in mixed prisons. Young offenders receiving custodial sentences have traditionally been separated from adult offenders, enabling them to receive additional educational and rehabilitative treatment.

In England and Wales, after a stable period, there has been a recent increase in the prison population, to almost 73,000 in early 2003, an increase of over 25,000 since 1990 (Figure 9.19). Remand prisoners comprise around a sixth of the total prison population. The average annual prison population in Scotland is over 6,000 and the average prison population in Northern Ireland (based on monthly counts) is under 1,000.

Eligible prisoners who pass a risk assessment may be released overnight on temporary licence for precisely defined activities which cannot be undertaken in the prison. Around 287,000 licences were issued in 2002, 58 per cent more than in 1996 (Figure 9.20). Around 60 per cent of these licences (177,000) were connected with prisoners obtaining additional facilities, such as reparation, training and education and 'working out' schemes, allowing prisoners experience of regular employment in the community. Just over 50,000 licences were for local visits. Fewer licences were granted for compassionate grounds (including

Figure **9.19**

Prison population

England & Wales
Thousands

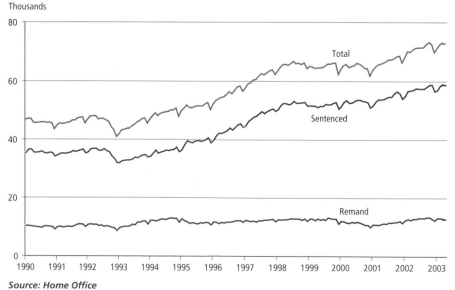

Source: Home Office

medical visits). In 2002/03, 3,180 prisoners were released on parole and over 55,000 were eligible for home detention curfew in England and Wales in 2002.

White males made up 84 per cent of the male prison population of British nationals in England and Wales in 2002 (Table 9.21). Black British nationals accounted for 11 per cent of the sentenced population in prison, 13 per cent of the remand population and 21 per cent of fine defaulters. The ethnic grouping of the female British prison population follows roughly similar proportions.

Within the sentenced British female prison population, there are considerable differences in offence types between White females and those from ethnic minorities. The proportion of Black British females sentenced for drug offences (45 per cent) was almost twice the proportion of White British females (25 per cent).

Civil justice

While this chapter has so far looked at cases where a charge has been made as part of the official legal system, for example by the Crown Prosecution Service in England and Wales, a case may also be brought under civil law by others, including an individual or a company. The majority of these cases are handled by the county courts and the High Court in England, Wales and Northern Ireland and by the sheriff court and Court of Session in Scotland. The High Court and Court of Session deal with the more substantial and complex cases. Civil cases may include breach of contract, claims for debt, negligence and recovery of land. Smaller cases, such as claims for unfair dismissal and disputes over social security benefits, are held by tribunals.

Figure 9.20

Number of releases on temporary licence: by type of licence

England & Wales
Thousands

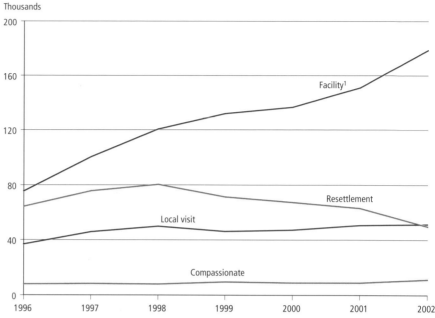

1 Available for prisoners who have served at least a quarter of their sentence. Release can be granted to participate in employment or community work, further education and job or housing interviews.

Source: Home Office

Table 9.21

Prison population of British nationals: by ethnic group

England & Wales   Percentages

	1996	1997	1998	1999	2000	2001	2002
Males							
White	86	86	86	86	86	85	84
Black	11	10	10	10	10	11	11
Asian	2	2	2	2	2	2	3
Chinese and other	1	2	2	2	2	2	2
Total male population (=100%) (thousands)	48.7	54.3	57.8	56.4	56.2	55.7	59.1
Females							
White	84	84	85	85	85	86	84
Black	13	13	12	12	12	12	11
Asian	1	1	1	1	1	1	1
Chinese and other	2	2	3	2	2	2	3
Total female population (=100%) (thousands)	2.0	2.3	2.6	2.7	2.8	3.0	3.5

Source: Home Office

Figure **9.22**

Writs and summonses issued[1]

England & Wales
Millions

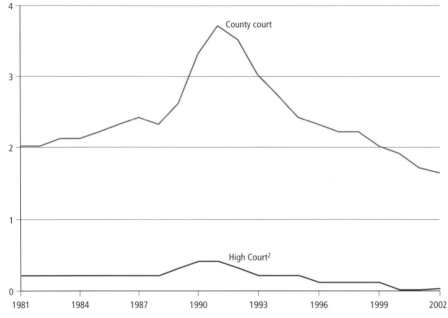

1 See Appendix, Part 9: Civil courts.
2 Queen's Bench Division.

Source: Court Service

explained, in part, by the increase in lending as a consequence of financial deregulation. In 2002 claims connected with debt recovery still accounted for over half the total number of 1.6 million claims issued. After debt recovery, the second and third most common types of claims related to recovery of land and personal injury.

In England and Wales, the Legal Services Commission operates the Community Legal Service (CLS), which funds civil legal, and advice services and civil representation. The Commission was launched in April 2000, replacing the Legal Aid Board. The type of practical help offered by the CLS includes legal help, help at court, mediation and representation on tribunals. Immigration, housing and welfare benefits make up about two thirds of the new (non-family) matters handled by the CLS where legal help is offered.

Civil representation certificates are issued where court proceedings are in prospect. Housing was the area where most certificates were issued in 2002/03, followed by clinical negligence and immigration and nationality (Table 9.23). Over three quarters of the cases where investigative help rather than full representation was authorised were made up of clinical negligence, where extensive research is often necessary to establish whether there is a case to answer.

Resources

A large share of expenditure on the criminal justice system has been traditionally spent on the police force. Police officer numbers reached record levels with over 133,000 officers at 31 March 2003 (Table 9.24). This was an increase of 3 per cent compared with a

Most tribunals deal with cases that involve the rights of private citizens against decisions of the State in areas such as social security, income tax and mental health. Some tribunals deal with other disputes, such as employment. In all, there are some 80 tribunals in England and Wales, together dealing with over 1 million cases a year.

Following the issuing of a claim, many cases are settled without the need for a court hearing. The total number of claims issued in county courts in England and Wales rose sharply from 2.3 million in 1988 to peak at 3.7 million in 1991 (Figure 9.22). This rise may be

year earlier. The Metropolitan Police service is the largest force, accounting for 21 per cent of all officers. The government sets employment targets for the recruitment, retention and progression of minority ethnic officers in England and Wales. The targets are intended to ensure that by 2009, forces will reflect their minority ethnic population. At 31 March 2003 there were nearly 3,900 officers from minority ethnic backgrounds (up from 3,400 a year previously) representing 2.9 per cent of the police service. West Midlands and the Metropolitan Police have the largest proportion of minority ethnic officers (5.6 per cent) followed by Bedfordshire and Leicestershire (4.5 per cent).

Over 25,000 police officers in England and Wales were female, representing 19 per cent of the total, a 1 percentage point increase on the previous year. The proportion of women in more senior ranks remains low: 21 per cent of constables were females compared with 6 per cent of Chief Superintendents. Scotland had 15,500 police officers at 30 June 2003, and Northern Ireland had 8,700 police officers at 31 March 2003. Police resources across the United Kingdom are augmented by a range of other civilian staff, special constables and traffic wardens. The National Crime Squad, National Criminal Intelligence Service and central services had 1,940 officers on secondment.

Table 9.23

Certificates issued on civil non-family proceedings, 2002/03

England & Wales | | | Numbers

	Investigative help	Full representation	Total certificates issued[1]
Housing	360	12,216	12,576
Clinical negligence	4,862	1,444	6,307
Immigration and nationality	50	2,865	2,915
Actions against the police etc[2]	160	848	1,008
Personal injury	114	839	980
Public law	91	809	900
Consumer	150	630	780
Education	153	509	662
Debt	45	497	542
Community care	22	411	433
Mental health	11	152	163
Employment	10	127	137
Welfare benefits	2	85	87
Miscellaneous	250	1,591	1,841
Total	6,280	23,023	29,331

1 Includes 28 certificates issued for support funding.
2 Includes actions against the police and other arresting authorities.

Source: Legal Services Commission

Table 9.24

Police officer strength[1]: by rank, sex and ethnic group, at 31 March 2003

England & Wales | | | Numbers

	Males	Females	All ethnic minorities
ACPO[2] ranks	179	16	3
Chief Superintendent	432	28	5
Superintendent	728	70	19
Chief Inspector	1,521	141	26
Inspector	5,743	539	118
Sergeant	16,582	2,150	400
Constable	82,186	22,194	3,297
All ranks	107,371	25,139	3,868

1 Full-time equivalents employed in the 43 police force areas in England and Wales. With officers on secondment, the total police force strength was 133,366.
2 Police officers who hold the rank of Chief Constable, Deputy Chief Constable or Assistant Chief Constable, or their equivalent.

Source: Home Office

Chapter 10 **Housing**

Housing stock and housebuilding

- By 2002 there were 25.0 million dwellings and 24.3 million households in Great Britain, compared with 19.2 million and 18.8 million, respectively, in 1972. (Page 150)

Tenure and accommodation

- Between 1981 and 2002 the number of owner-occupied dwellings in Great Britain increased by almost 43 per cent to reach 17.4 million. (Figure 10.5)

- In 2001 around half of people in England and Wales of Bangladeshi, Black African or Other Black ethnic origin lived in accommodation in the social rented sector. Those from the Indian group were the most likely to be owner occupiers at 80 per cent. (Table 10.10)

Homelessness

- In 2002/03 more than a third of acceptances of homelessness in England arose because parents, relatives or friends (mostly parents) were no longer willing or able to provide accommodation. (Page 158)

Housing condition and satisfaction with area

- In 2001 there were 7 million dwellings in England which failed to meet the decent home standard, representing a third of the total number of dwellings. (Page 159)

Housing mobility

- During 2002, 1.6 million property transactions took place in England and Wales, of which just over 1.4 million were residential transactions. (Figure 10.18)

Figure **10.1**

Dwellings[1]

Great Britain
Millions

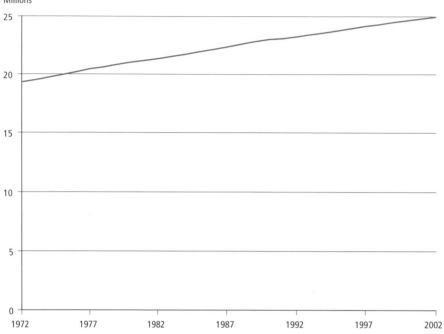

1 See Appendix, Part 10: Dwelling stock.

Source: Office of the Deputy Prime Minister

Table **10.2**

Type of accommodation: by construction date, 2002/03

England   Percentages

	Before 1919	1919– 1944	1945– 1964	1965– 1984	1985 or later	All
House or bungalow						
Detached	13	12	18	30	26	100
Semi-detached	12	29	32	19	9	100
Terraced	36	20	16	19	9	100
Flat or maisonette						
Purpose-built	5	9	24	41	22	100
Conversion	71	15	7	3	4	100
All dwellings[1]	20	20	22	24	14	100

1 Includes other types of accommodation, such as mobile homes.

Source: Survey of English Housing, Office of the Deputy Prime Minister

Over the last 20 years a growing population and the trend towards smaller households has contributed to a higher demand for housing in the United Kingdom. During the same period there has been a substantial increase in the number of owner-occupied homes. While falls in interest rates over the past two years have benefited many home owners with mortgages, they have also contributed to large increases in house prices and a fall in the number of first time buyers.

Housing stock and housebuilding

By 2002 there were 25.0 million dwellings and 24.3 million households in Great Britain, representing increases of around 30 per cent in both since 1972, when there were 19.2 million dwellings and 18.8 million households (Figure 10.1). The 2001 Census showed that 96 per cent of available household spaces in England were occupied, with 3.2 per cent of the stock vacant and the remaining 0.6 per cent used as second homes or holiday accommodation. The proportion of second and holiday homes was twice this average in Wales (1.2 per cent) and in Scotland (1.3 per cent).

To minimise greenfield development (that is, building on land that has not previously been developed) and to encourage urban regeneration, the Government wishes to see unoccupied homes brought back into use. Some dwellings are vacant for short periods pending sale or re-letting, but others may be vacant for longer while awaiting demolition or renovation. The 2001 Census showed that the northern regions of England had higher than average levels of vacant stock. The North West had 125,000 vacant properties (4.2 per cent), nearly a fifth of all the vacant properties in England.

In contrast only 2.5 per cent of household spaces were vacant in London.

Sixty per cent of England's housing stock was built after 1944, though this varies by region ranging from 37 per cent in London to 71 per cent in the East of England. Between the two world wars there was a shift in the type of home that was being built, from terraced to semi-detached housing (Table 10.2). From the mid-1960s there was a further switch from semi-detached to detached housing. Over half of the current stock of detached housing was built after 1964 compared with just over a quarter of semi-detached housing. The majority of the current stock of purpose-built flats was built post-Second World War. Only 5 per cent of this type of dwelling was built before 1919.

The damage caused to the nation's housing stock during the Second World War made the provision of new housing a post-war government priority. In the early post-war years local authorities undertook the majority of housing construction. Private enterprise housebuilding increased dramatically during the mid-1950s, and has been the dominant sector for new housebuilding since 1959. The peak for housebuilding completions in the United Kingdom was in 1968 when 426,000 dwellings were completed, 53 per cent by private enterprises and 47 per cent by the social sector, primarily local authorities (Figure 10.3). In 2002/03 there were 184,000 completions, of which 89 per cent were by the private enterprise sector. Registered social landlords (predominately housing associations) now dominate building in the social sector, accounting for 98 per cent of completions in this sector in 2002/03.

The Government's national target is that, by 2008, 60 per cent of additional housing in England should be provided on brownfield land (previously developed land) or by re-using existing buildings. In 2002, 64 per cent of new housing was built on brownfield land. Proportions varied between regions. London had the highest (90 per cent), while in the North East, South West and East Midlands less than 50 per cent of additional homes were built on brownfield sites.

Over the past 30 years there has been a marked change in the number of bedrooms in newly built dwellings. In 2002/03, 34 per cent of newly built homes in England had four or more bedrooms, compared with only 7 per cent in 1971 (Table 10.4). The percentage of new dwellings constructed with one bedroom grew from 15 per cent in 1971 to 23 per cent in 1981, reflecting the demand caused

Figure **10.3**

Housebuilding completions[1]: by sector

United Kingdom
Thousands

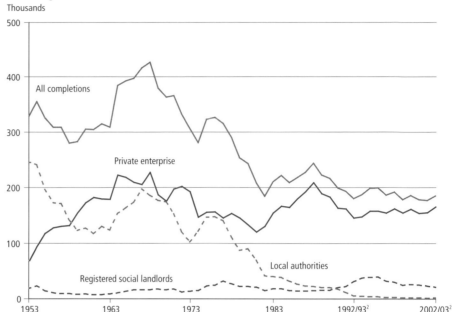

1 See Appendix, Part 10: Dwelling stock and dwellings completed.
2 From 1990/91 data are for financial years.

Source: Office of the Deputy Prime Minister; National Assembly for Wales; Scottish Executive; Department of the Environment, Northern Ireland

Table **10.4**

Housebuilding completions: by number of bedrooms

England				Percentages
	1971	1981	1991/92	2002/03
1 bedroom	15	23	19	6
2 bedrooms	23	25	32	29
3 bedrooms	54	38	29	30
4 or more bedrooms	7	14	20	34
All houses and flats (=100%) (thousands)	295	171	155	138

Source: Office of the Deputy Prime Minister

Figure **10.5**

Stock of dwellings[1]: by tenure

Great Britain[2]
Millions

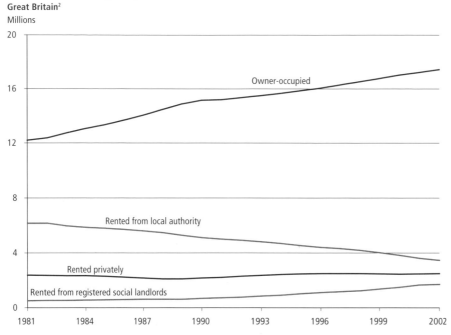

1 See Appendix, Part 10: Dwelling stock.
2 Data for England and Wales are at 31 March, and for Scotland they are at 31 December the previous year, except for 1991 where census figures are used.

Source: Office of the Deputy Prime Minister

Table **10.6**

Tenure: by type of accommodation[1], 2001

England & Wales   Percentages

	House or bungalow			Flat or maisonette		All dwellings[2] (=100%) (millions)
	Detached	Semi-detached	Terraced	Purpose-built	Other	
Owner-occupied						
Owned outright	35	35	22	6	2	6.4
Owned with mortgage	27	36	29	5	3	8.4
Shared ownership	6	34	33	21	5	0.1
Rented from social sector						
Council	4	31	26	37	3	2.9
Other	3	23	26	40	8	1.3
Rented privately						
Private landlord or letting agency	9	17	28	20	25	1.9
Employer of a household member	22	31	20	11	16	0.1
Relative or friend of a household member	14	26	34	13	13	0.1
Other	18	23	19	19	20	0.1
Lives rent free	19	28	20	23	10	0.4
All tenures	23	32	26	13	5	21.6

1 All household spaces in unshared dwellings.
2 Includes caravans or other mobile or temporary structures.

Source: Census 2001, Office for National Statistics

by the growth in the number of single person households. The proportion fell again from 1991/92 and by 2002/03, only 6 per cent of new dwellings had one bedroom.

The rise in the number of bedrooms in dwellings may reflect an increased expectation that each child should have a separate bedroom. It may also reflect householders' aspirations to purchase homes with an extra room to use as a spare bedroom, a storage room or a home-office. The number of bedrooms in a completed dwelling varies by tenure. Of the houses and flats completed by registered social landlords (RSLs) in 2002/03, around 9 per cent had four or more bedrooms compared with 36 per cent of those completed by private enterprises.

Tenure and accommodation

The increase in owner-occupation has been a notable feature of the past century. At the start of the 20th century, almost all dwellings in England, 89 per cent, were privately rented and only a small proportion, 10 per cent, were owner-occupied. The 1950s saw a period of growth in prosperity alongside initiatives to improve housebuilding; this was accompanied by deregulation in both planning and the building industry. Thus, owner-occupation increased from 29 per cent in 1951 to 45 per cent in 1964. Between 1981 and 2002 the number of owner-occupied dwellings in Great Britain increased by almost 43 per cent to reach 17.4 million, more than double the number of rented dwellings (Figure 10.5). During the same period the number of private rented dwellings increased by 5 per cent to 2.5 million and the number of dwellings rented in the social sector decreased by 23 per cent to 5.1 million.

The growth in owner occupation since the early 1980s has in part been due to a number of schemes that aim to increase low-cost home ownership, such as the right to buy scheme. Owner occupation is lower in Scotland (64 per cent) than in either England or Wales (70 and 73 per cent, respectively). The only sector where there has been a decline in stock since 1981 is in dwellings rented from local authorities. This reflects large scale stock transfers to registered social landlords whose stock rose by 256 per cent during this period.

The Census provided a comprehensive picture of the type of tenure and accommodation. In April 2001, 81 per cent of households in England and Wales lived in a house or bungalow, with semi-detached and terraced being the most common type of dwelling (Table 10.6). The type of accommodation varies by tenure. Owner occupiers are far more likely to live in houses than renters in either the social or private sectors. The proportion of those in shared ownership properties (part-rent part-buy) who lived in a house or bungalow was lower than for those who owned outright or with a mortgage. In contrast social sector renters were far more likely than owners to live in purpose-built flats. Those living in shared ownership properties were also more likely than other owner occupiers to live in a flat, although less likely to do so than social renters.

Tenure varies markedly according to the type of household. In 2001 lone parents with dependent children were far more likely than any other type of household to rent their property (Table 10.7). While only 34 per cent of lone parent with dependent children households lived in owner-occupied property, 46 per cent lived in accommodation rented from the social sector and 19 per cent

Table **10.7**

Tenure: by household composition, 2001

England & Wales   Percentages

	Owned[1]	Rented from council	Other social rented[2]	Rented privately or living rent free[3]	All households
One person					
Under pensionable age	56	15	8	21	100
Over pensionable age	58	21	10	10	100
One family					
All pensioners	81	10	4	4	100
Couple households					
No children	81	6	2	11	100
Dependent children	80	9	4	7	100
Non-dependent children only	85	8	3	4	100
Lone parent					
Dependent children	34	31	15	19	100
Non-dependent children only	66	21	6	7	100
Other households[4]	57	12	5	26	100
All households	69	13	6	12	100

1 Either owned outright, owned with a mortgage or loan, or paying rent and part-mortgage (shared ownership).
2 Includes rented from registered social landlord, housing association, housing co-operative and charitable trust.
3 See Appendix, Part 10: Private rented and living rent free.
4 Comprising two or more unrelated adults or two or more families.

Source: Census 2001, Office for National Statistics

Figure **10.8**

Owner-occupied dwellings: EU comparison, 2000

Percentages

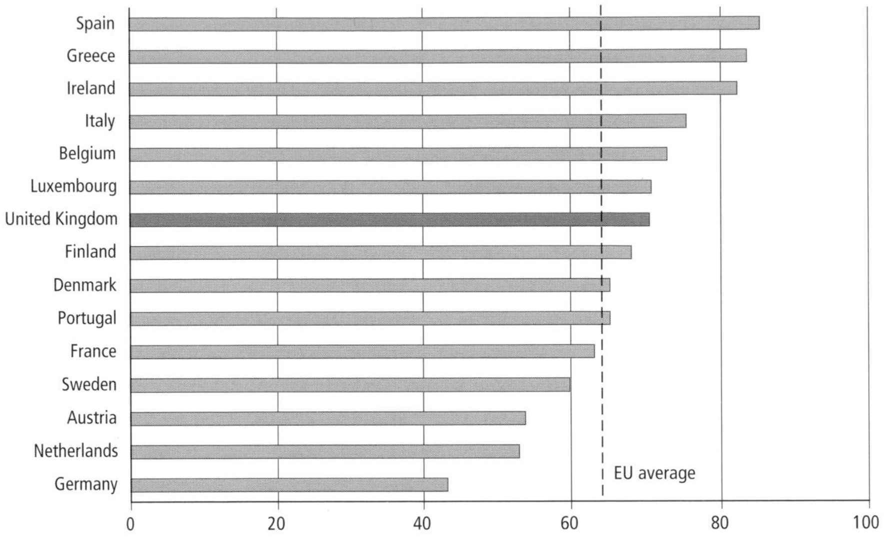

Spain
Greece
Ireland
Italy
Belgium
Luxembourg
United Kingdom
Finland
Denmark
Portugal
France
Sweden
Austria
Netherlands
Germany

EU average

Source: Eurostat

Table **10.9**

Tenure: by economic activity status of household reference person[1], 2001

England & Wales   Percentages

	Owner occupied	Rented from council	Other social rented	Rented privately or living rent free[2]	All
Economically active					
Employee	76	8	4	12	100
Self-employed	83	4	2	10	100
Unemployed	30	33	14	23	100
Full-time student	22	12	8	59	100
All economically active	75	9	4	12	100
Economically inactive					
Retired	75	14	6	5	100
Student	20	15	11	55	100
Looking after home/family	21	38	18	22	100
Permanently sick or disabled	33	36	16	15	100
Other	35	31	13	20	100
All economically inactive	57	22	9	12	100
All tenures	70	12	6	12	100

1 Households with a household reference person aged 16-74 years. See Appendix, Part 10: Household reference person.
2 See Appendix, Part 10: Private rented and living rent free.

Source: Census 2001, Office for National Statistics

rented privately. In contrast, 80 per cent of households comprising a couple with dependent children owned their own property and only 13 per cent rented from the social sector. Similarly, 81 per cent of pensioner households were owner occupiers, compared with only 58 per cent of lone pensioner households.

Owner occupation in the United Kingdom, at 71 per cent, is just above the average for all EU countries (Figure 10.8). In 2000 the highest rates of owner occupation in the EU were in Spain, Greece and Ireland, at over 80 per cent. Germany had the lowest level of owner occupation at just over 40 per cent. In all EU countries owner occupiers were more likely to live in a house than a flat. On average, 80 per cent of those living in a house in the EU were owner occupiers compared with only 38 per cent of those living in a flat.

Tenure is also linked to economic activity status. At the time of the 2001 Census, over three quarters of employed, self-employed and retired heads of household were owner occupiers (Table 10.9). In contrast, less than a third of unemployed heads of household and just over a fifth of full-time students who were also in paid employment owned their own home, either outright or with a mortgage. Renting from a council was the most common form of tenure among those who were looking after a home or family, or those who were permanently sick or disabled. In contrast, less than a tenth of employed or self-employed heads of household rented from a council.

Tenure patterns also vary markedly by ethnic group. In 2001 around half of people of Bangladeshi, Black African or Other Black ethnic origin lived in accommodation in the social rented sector (Table 10.10). These were around six times the proportion of people from the Indian group, which had the lowest proportion. In contrast, those from the Indian group were the most likely to be owner occupiers, with four in five owning either outright or with a mortgage. Around 70 per cent of those of White British or Pakistani origin were also owner occupiers. Owner occupation was lowest among those of Black African origin at 25 per cent. Overall 69 per cent of the population in England and Wales lived in owner-occupied properties. Around a quarter of those of White British and Irish and Indian and Pakistani origin owned their home outright as did a fifth of those of Chinese origin.

The type of home in which people live is often a reflection of the size and type of their household. In 2001 married couples

Table 10.10

Tenure: by ethnic group, 2001

England & Wales   Percentages

	Owned outright	Owned with a mortgage or loan	Rented from council	Other social rented[1]	Rented privately[2]	Other[3]	All tenures (=100%) (millions)
White							
British	25	46	12	5	8	4	45.5
Irish	26	37	14	7	11	5	0.6
Other White	19	32	8	5	28	8	1.3
Mixed							
White and Black Caribbean	7	34	28	16	10	5	0.2
White and Black African	7	32	22	14	18	7	0.1
White and Asian	15	47	12	7	14	6	0.2
Other mixed	12	40	15	9	16	6	0.2
Asian or Asian British							
Indian	27	52	5	3	10	3	1.0
Pakistani	27	43	9	6	12	4	0.7
Bangladeshi	9	29	33	15	10	4	0.3
Other Asian	16	43	9	7	19	7	0.2
Black or Black British							
Black Caribbean	12	36	25	15	7	5	0.6
Black African	5	20	33	17	18	7	0.5
Other Black	7	28	30	20	9	5	0.1
Chinese or other							
Chinese	21	37	8	4	18	12	0.2
Other	11	28	12	8	30	11	0.2
All people	24	45	12	5	9	4	52.0

1 Includes rented from registered social landlord, housing association, housing co-operative and charitable trust.
2 See Appendix, Part 10: Private renting and living rent free.
3 Includes living rent free, living in a communal establishment and shared ownership.

Source: Census 2001, Office for National Statistics

Table **10.11**

Accommodation type: by household composition, 2001

England & Wales

Percentages

	House or bungalow			Flat, maisonette or apartment				
	Detached	Semi-detached	Terraced (including end terrace)	In a purpose built block of flats	Part of a converted or shared house	In a commercial building	Other[1]	All occupied household spaces
One person								
Under pensionable age	10	20	26	28	12	2	1	100
Over pensionable age	18	30	22	25	4	_	1	100
One family								
All pensioners	35	36	19	8	1	_	1	100
Married couple								
No children	35	34	22	5	2	1	_	100
Dependent children	32	38	25	3	1	1	_	100
Non-dependent children only	32	40	24	2	1	1	_	100
Cohabiting couple								
No children	15	27	31	16	10	2	_	100
Dependent children	15	37	36	8	2	1	_	100
Non-dependent children only	21	38	32	6	2	1	_	100
Lone parent								
Dependent children	10	34	37	15	3	1	_	100
Non-dependent children only	17	38	32	10	2	1	_	100
Other households[2]	18	28	31	13	7	2	_	100
All households	23	32	26	13	4	1	_	100

1 Includes caravans or other mobile or temporary structures.
2 Comprising two or more unrelated adults or two or more families.

Source: Census 2001, Office for National Statistics

with children, were the most likely to live in a house (Table 10.11). A lower proportion of lone parent families with children did so. One person households were the least likely to live in a house with those under pensionable age being by far the least likely. Over four out of ten of one person households below pension age lived in a flat, maisonette or apartment. This type of accommodation was almost four times as common for lone parents with dependent children (19 per cent) than for married couples with dependent children (5 per cent).

There are also wide variations in the type of accommodation different ethnic groups live in. These differences are closely linked to type of tenure (see Table 10.10), location and household size, with those living in inner cities being more likely than others to live in flats or maisonettes. In 2001 those of Pakistani ethnic origin were the most likely to live in a house or bungalow with 90 per cent of this group doing so (Table 10.12). Similar proportions of those of White British and Indian descent also lived in a house or bungalow. The proportion of White Irish and Other Whites who lived in a house or bungalow was lower at 74 per cent and 64 per cent, respectively. Those of Black African ethnic origin were by far the least likely to live in a house or bungalow at only 42 per cent, and the most likely to live in a flat or maisonette (55 per cent). Those of Chinese ethnic origin were the most likely to be living in a communal establishment, with 9 per cent doing so. Most were living in educational establishments.

Homelessness

Local housing authorities have a statutory obligation to ensure that suitable accommodation is available for applicants who are eligible for assistance, have become homeless through no fault of their own, and who fall within a priority need group (this is the 'main homeless duty'). Among the priority need groups are families with children, and households that include someone who is vulnerable, for example because of pregnancy, domestic violence, old age, or physical or mental disability. Priority need categories were extended in July 2002 to include other vulnerable groups such as applicants aged 16 or 17, and care leavers aged 18 to 20. During 2002/03, over 278,000 decisions on applications for housing from households eligible under the homelessness provisions of the *Housing Act 1996* were made in England. This was an increase of 9 per cent on the previous year.

Almost half (129,000), of the applications made in 2002/03 were accepted as homeless and in priority need. This represented 10 per cent more than the previous year. The presence of dependent children in the household was the primary reason for priority need

Table **10.12**

Accommodation type[1]: by ethnic group, 2001

England & Wales   Percentages

	House or bungalow	Flat, maisonette or apartment	Communal establishments[2]	All people[3] (=100%) (millions)
White				
British	87	11	2	45.5
Irish	74	23	3	0.6
Other White	64	31	4	1.3
Mixed				
White and Black Caribbean	75	23	2	0.2
White and Black African	63	34	3	0.1
White and Asian	78	19	2	0.2
Other mixed	71	27	3	0.2
Asian or Asian British				
Indian	85	13	1	1.0
Pakistani	90	10	1	0.7
Bangladeshi	61	38	1	0.3
Other Asian	73	24	3	0.2
Black or Black British				
Black Caribbean	63	35	2	0.6
Black African	42	55	3	0.5
Other Black	58	40	2	0.1
Chinese or other ethnic group				
Chinese	65	27	9	0.2
Other ethnic group	59	34	6	0.2
All people	85	13	2	52.0

1 Excluding people living in shared accommodation.
2 Includes medical, care, educational and other establishments.
3 Includes caravans or other mobile or temporary structures.

Source: Census 2001, Office for National Statistics

Figure **10.13**

Homeless households in priority need accepted by local authorities: by need category[1], 2002/03[2]

England
Percentages

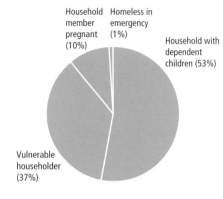

Household member pregnant (10%)

Homeless in emergency (1%)

Household with dependent children (53%)

Vulnerable householder (37%)

Total: 129.3 thousand

1 Where a household qualifies under two or more categories, only the main one is recorded.
2 Priority need categories were extended in July 2002 to include other vulnerable client groups such as care leavers aged 18–20.

Source: Office of the Deputy Prime Minister

acceptance in over half of the cases and since 1997 this has ranged between 50 and 60 per cent of all acceptances (Figure 10.13). A further 10 per cent of acceptances in 2002/03 were households that included a pregnant women. Other acceptances included applicants who were vulnerable because of mental illness (9 per cent), domestic violence (5 per cent), physical disability (5 per cent) or old age (3 per cent).

Homelessness often results from changes in personal circumstances. In 2002/03 more than a third of acceptances in England arose because parents, relatives or friends (mostly parents) were no longer willing or able to provide accommodation. This proportion has gradually risen since 1997, when it represented 27 per cent of acceptances. Just over a fifth of acceptances in 2002/03 were because

of the breakdown of a relationship with a partner; two thirds of these involved violence. At less than 2 per cent, the proportion of acceptances resulting from mortgage arrears was much less than at its peak level (12 per cent during 1991) and has been at or below 5 per cent since September 1998.

Most households that are accepted as owed a main homeless duty are provided with temporary accommodation. The number of households in temporary accommodation rose during the 1980s but fell again during the early to mid 1990s. Since then there has been a steady increase in the numbers and in December 2002 the number in temporary accommodation was almost 85,000, an increase of 8 per cent on the previous year. Most of these households were living in self-contained properties leased in the private sector (31 per cent), or in local authority or housing association stock let on a temporary basis (32 per cent). Fifteen per cent were living in B&B hotels and 11 per cent were in hostels or women's refuges (Figure 10.14).

Housing condition and satisfaction with area

One of the Government's key housing policy aims is to provide everyone with the opportunity to live in a decent home. The Sustainable Communities Plan, launched in February 2003, places decent homes within the broader framework of raising the quality of life for all communities in England.

To be considered 'decent' a dwelling must meet the statutory minimum standard for housing (that is be fit); be in a reasonable state of repair; have reasonably modern facilities and services; and provide a reasonable degree of

Figure **10.14**

Homeless households[1] in temporary accommodation[2]

England
Thousands

```
30 ┤
   │
   │        Private sector leased        Local authority/
   │                                     housing association
20 ┤
   │
   │
   │                                     Hostels
10 ┤
   │
   │                                              Other[3]
   │        Bed and breakfast
 0 ┼────┬────┬────┬────┬────┬────┬
  1991 1993 1995 1997 1999 2001 2002
```

1 Excludes 'homeless at home' cases (see Appendix, Part 10: Homeless at home).
2 Data are as at 31 December, and include households awaiting the outcome of homeless enquiries.
3 Includes mobile homes such as caravans and portacabins, or being accommodated directly with a private sector landlord.

Source: Office of the Deputy Prime Minister

thermal comfort. According to the English House Condition Survey, there were 7 million non-decent dwellings in 2001, a third of the total number of dwellings in England. This was a fall of a quarter since the previous survey was undertaken in 1996, when 9.4 million dwellings (46 per cent) were non-decent. The most common reason for a dwelling to be deemed non-decent in 2001 was the failure to meet the thermal comfort criterion (5.6 million dwellings).

There were 6.7 million households living in non-decent homes in 2001, compared with 8.9 million in 1996, a fall of 25 per cent over the five years. In 2001, nearly two thirds of non-decent homes were owner occupied (Figure 10.15). People living alone, sharing with unrelated others or lone parents comprised around half of households living in non-decent homes. These households were more likely than average to live in non-decent homes. The reduction in non-decent homes since 1996 has been generally consistent across all sections of the population, suggesting little change in the position of different groups to one another.

Other important indicators of housing standards are overcrowding and under-occupancy. The bedroom standard measures the number of bedrooms actually available to a household against the number of bedrooms required, given the household's size and composition (see Appendix, Part 10: Bedroom standard). In 2002/03, 2 per cent of households in England were below the bedroom standard and hence defined as overcrowded (Table 10.16). In contrast 36 per cent of households had two or more bedrooms above the standard and could therefore be said to be under-occupying. Under-occupation was

most common in the owner-occupied sector, where 57 per cent of households that owned their property outright and 37 per cent of those buying with a mortgage were two or more bedrooms above the bedroom standard.

Environmental problems tend to be concentrated in city and other urban centres. The English House Condition Survey estimated that in 2001, 2.5 million dwellings were affected by substantial problems associated with heavy traffic and parking, 1.0 million by poorly maintained/neglected buildings, private gardens and public spaces and 0.5 million by vandalism, graffiti and boarded up buildings. Some dwellings are affected by more than one of these problems.

Around one in nine (2.4 million) of all dwellings in England are located in poor neighbourhoods, characterised by concentrations of housing and

Figure **10.15**

Households whose accommodation does not meet the decent homes standard: by tenure, 2001

England
Percentages

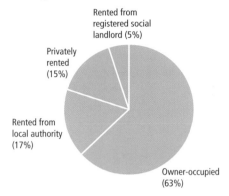

Total: 6.7 million

Source: English House Condition Survey, Office of the Deputy Prime Minister

Table **10.16**

Overcrowding and under-occupation[1]: by tenure, 2002/03

England   Percentages

	Overcrowded[2]	Under-occupied[3]
Owner-occupied		
Owned outright	1	57
Owned with mortgage	2	37
Rented from social sector		
Local authority	6	15
Registered social landlord	4	9
Rented privately[4]		
Unfurnished	3	19
Furnished	7	11
All tenures	2	36

1 See Appendix, Part 10: Bedroom standard.
2 One or more below bedroom standard.
3 Two or more above bedroom standard.
4 Includes rent-free accommodation.

Source: Survey of English Housing, Office of the Deputy Prime Minister

Table **10.17**

Residents' views of problems in their neighbourhood: by whether living in a poor or other neighbourhood[1], 2001

England

Percentages

	Poor neighbourhood	Other neighbourhood	All
Litter and rubbish in the streets	57	34	36
Problems with street parking	48	37	38
Fear of being burgled	47	33	34
Problems with dogs/dog mess	41	32	33
General level of crime	40	23	25
Vandalism and hooliganism	36	21	22
Heavy traffic	35	26	27
Troublesome teenagers/children	34	19	21
Poor state of open spaces/gardens	29	14	15
Presence of drug dealers/users	28	11	13
Pollution (including air quality and traffic fumes)	23	15	16
Graffiti	21	11	12
Problems with neighbours	20	11	12
Racial harassment	6	2	3

1 See Appendix, Part 10: Poor neighbourhoods.

Source: English House Condition Survey, Office of the Deputy Prime Minister

Figure **10.18**

Property transactions[1]

England & Wales
Millions

1 See Appendix, Part 10: Property transactions.

Source: Inland Revenue

environmental problems associated with misuse and neglect of the area (see Appendix, Part 10: Poor neighbourhoods). Over half of dwellings in poor neighbourhoods are non-decent.

Residents of poor neighbourhoods are much more likely than those living elsewhere to view their neighbourhood as having a wide range of problems. Almost six in ten residents living in poor neighbourhoods indicated some level of problem with litter and rubbish and almost half cited problems with street parking and the fear of being burgled (Table 10.17). Around a third of those living in other neighbourhoods considered that there were problems with street parking, litter and rubbish in the streets, that they had a fear of being burgled and that there were problems with dogs or dog mess in their area.

Housing mobility

The mobility of owner occupiers is linked to the housing market. Over the past half century, the housing market and the economy have mirrored one another closely with booms and slumps in one tending to contribute to the other. The number of property transactions that took place rose markedly during the 1980s, mainly as a result of existing owner-occupiers moving home (Figure 10.18). Market activity by first-time buyers and public sector tenants (right to buy purchases) were also factors, but contributed to a lesser extent. The boom was further amplified by the demographic impact of the coming of age of baby boomers and by the liberalisation of the credit market in the early 1980s when more new households opted for ownership rather than renting. In 1989, the 'bubble burst', when interest rates rose and the economic recession set in. The number of transactions fell during this period but has since increased. During 2002, 1.6 million property transactions took place in England and Wales, of which just over 1.4 million were residential transactions.

In most of the housing moves that occurred during 2002/03 in England, households remained within the same sector (Table 10.19). The most common type of move was from one owned property to another (613,000 moves), accounting for just over three fifths of the households currently in owner-occupied accommodation who had been resident for less than one year. Moves from one privately rented property to another (433,000) accounted for three fifths of moves within this sector. About half of the total number of moves made during 2002/03 were either within, to or from the private rented sector, illustrating how important this sector is in facilitating mobility within the housing market.

People have different reasons for moving, but for most continuing households, the main reasons were the desire for a larger or better home (25 per cent) or for work (12 per cent). For new heads of household, to live independently was the most common reason for having moved (41 per cent), followed by personal reasons, such as marriage or cohabitation (20 per cent).

As illustrated in Figure 10.5, over recent decades there has been an increase in the proportion of owner-occupied dwellings. This increase has in part been due to a number of schemes that aim to increase low-cost home ownership. Since the early 1980s, public tenants with secure tenancies of at least two years' standing have been entitled to purchase their own home. This scheme was particularly popular during the

1980s with peaks of almost 200,000 sales in 1982 in Great Britain and again in 1989, following more buoyant conditions in the housing market and changes in the legislation that enabled more tenants to buy. In 2002 there were 78,000 sales of right to buy properties, an increase of 18 per cent on the previous year and accounting for much of the increase in the total number of sales and transfers between 2001 and 2002. Other low cost ownership schemes involve, for example, buying part of a house and renting the remainder from a registered social landlord. Since the late 1990s large scale voluntary transfers have

Table **10.19**

Households resident under one year: current tenure by previous tenure, 2002/03

England | | | | | | | Percentages

	Previous tenure						
	New household	Owned outright	Owned with a mortgage	Rented from local authority	Rented from registered social landlord	Rented privately[1]	All tenures
Current tenure							
Owner-occupied							
Owned outright	5	62	27	–	0	5	100
Owned with a mortgage	16	5	54	2	2	22	100
Rented from social sector							
Local authority	20	4	5	44	6	21	100
Registered social landlord	18	5	5	22	28	23	100
Rented privately							
Unfurnished	17	4	19	4	3	52	100
Furnished	24	4	7	1	3	61	100
All tenures	17	9	28	8	4	33	100

1 The split between privately rented unfurnished and privately rented furnished is not available for previous tenure.

Source: Survey of English Housing, Office of the Deputy Prime Minister

Figure **10.20**

Sales and transfers of local authority dwellings[1]

Great Britain
Thousands

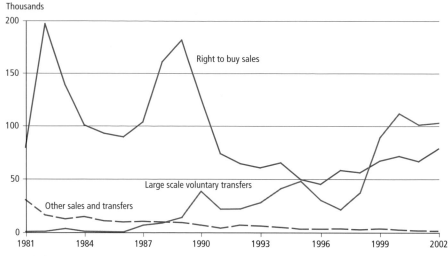

1 Excludes new town and Scottish Homes sales and transfers. See Appendix, Part 10: Sales and transfers of local authority dwellings.

Source: Office of the Deputy Prime Minister; National Assembly for Wales; Scottish Executive

Figure **10.21**

Average property prices

United Kingdom
£ thousand

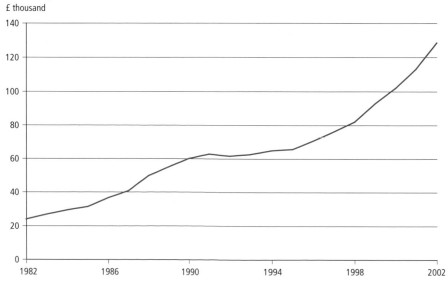

Source: Office of the Deputy Prime Minister

been the main contributors to the transfer of ownership from local authorities to other owners, mainly housing associations (Figure 10.20). In 2002 a further 102,000 dwellings were transferred from local authorities, bringing the total number that had been transferred since 1981 to 725,000.

Housing costs and expenditure

The average price of dwellings bought and sold in the United Kingdom in 2002 was £128,000 (Figure 10.21). There are marked variations in house price according to the type of accommodation purchased and where it is located. Buyers in London in 2002 paid almost three times more for a detached house than those living in Northern Ireland: £356,000 and £130,000, respectively. Similarly a terraced house was almost four times more expensive to buy in London compared with the North East: £217,000 and £55,000, respectively.

A feature of home ownership in the United Kingdom is the relatively large number of homes purchased with a mortgage. Approximately three quarters of house purchases are financed with a mortgage loan facility. In 2002, 76 per cent of loans for home purchase were obtained through banks and 17 per cent through building societies, with 7 per cent through other lenders.

Those buying a home can choose from a variety of different types of mortgage, the most common being repayment and interest-only. With repayment mortgages, the debt and the interest are both repaid during the life of the mortgage (usually 25 years). Around 81 per cent of all new mortgages were standard repayment mortgages in 2002. Interest-only mortgages, which include endowment policies, ISAs (individual savings accounts) and personal pensions, account for the bulk of other mortgages. Since the late 1980s there has been a decrease in the popularity of endowment mortgages because of the possibility that investments may not grow fast enough to repay the capital borrowed. In 1988, 83 per cent of new mortgages for house purchase were endowment mortgages but by 2002 this had fallen to 5 per cent. The proportion of fixed (as opposed to variable) rate mortgages is markedly lower in the United Kingdom than in many other countries. Research published by the Council of Mortgage Lenders in July 2002 suggested that flexible mortgages are accounting for a rapidly growing share of the mortgage market. Flexible mortgages allow people to pay off some of the loan early through overpayments and lump sum investments; and to borrow funds back by withdrawing lump sums.

Affordability is a concern to both first-time buyers and moving owner-occupiers. Although recent UK base interest rates have been at low levels compared with previously, repaying mortgages still often consumes a substantial proportion of people's income. In 1972, first-time buyers spent on average, 15 per cent of their household income on mortgage repayments and owner occupiers who moved and bought a new home, 14 per cent. The proportion of income paid as a mortgage in recent years is higher: in 2002 first-time buyers spent 18 per cent of their income on mortgage repayments and moving owner-occupiers, 17 per cent. These were not as high as during the last property boom when the proportion paid by first-time buyers in 1990 was 28 per cent and 26 per cent for moving owner-occupiers (Figure 10.22).

Figure **10.22**

New mortgages: average mortgage repayment[1] as a percentage of average household income

United Kingdom
Percentages

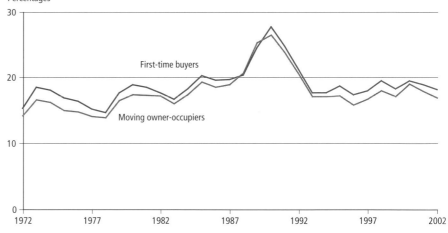

1 Repayments are calculated on the basis of the average advance, after tax relief. Based on a repayment mortgage.

Source: Office of the Deputy Prime Minister

The warning given with every mortgage is that 'your home is at risk if you do not keep up repayments on a mortgage or other loan secured on it' and the same is true of rented property. When people fall behind with rent or mortgage repayments and are unable to reach an alternative payment arrangement with their landlord or mortgage lender, a county court possession summons may be issued, with the view to obtaining a court order. Not all orders will result in repossession; it is not uncommon for courts to make suspended orders which provide for arrears to be paid off within a reasonable period. If the court decides not to adjourn the proceedings or suspend a possession order, the warrant will be executed and the home repossessed by the landlord or mortgage lender. As base interest rates and

Figure **10.23**

Mortgage loans in arrears and repossessions[1]

United Kingdom
Thousands

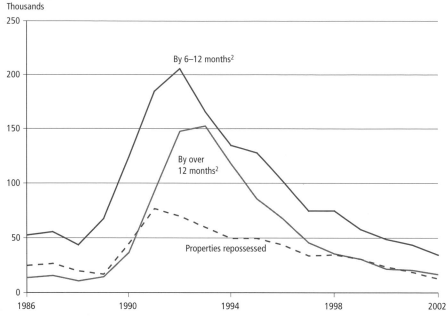

1 Estimates cover only members of the Council of Mortgage Lenders; these account for 98 per cent of all mortgages outstanding.
2 Length of time mortgage loans have been in arrears at end of period.

Source: Council of Mortgage Lenders

Figure **10.24**

Median rent before housing benefit: by region, 2002/03

England
£ per week

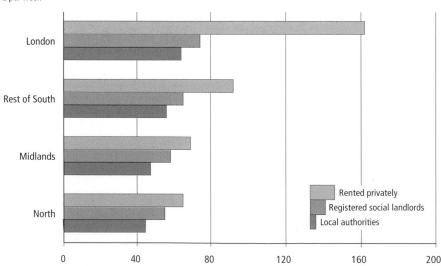

Source: Survey of English Housing, Office of the Deputy Prime Minister

mortgage interest rates rose during the late 1980s and early 1990s, repayments became increasingly difficult for some people, particularly those who had borrowed a high proportion of the value of their properties. Consequently arrears and repossessions increased during this time. However, largely owing to lower interest rates, arrears and repossessions have fallen over the last decade. At its peak in 1992, the number of loans in arrears by 6 to 12 months in the United Kingdom was 205,000. By 2002 this had fallen to 34,000 and the number of homes repossessed was 12,000 (Figure 10.23). According to the Survey of English Housing, many people in England in 2001/02 cited more than one reason for their arrears but for the vast majority, the loss of income was the main contributor.

Regardless of whether the home is owned or rented, housing constitutes a significant proportion of a household's budget. These costs include, for example, structural insurance, council tax payments and repairs and maintenance, as well as mortgage interest payments or rent (net of housing benefit).

In 2002/03 the median weekly rent (before housing benefit) for those living in private accommodation in England was £121. Like house prices, rents vary according to location. Private rents, which are typically higher than social sector rents, ranged from £65 a week in the North to £162 a week in London (Figure 10.24). The cost of renting from the local authority ranged from £45 in the North to £64 in London.

Chapter 11 **Environment**

Pollution

- Road transport and power stations are the most important single sources of air pollution in the United Kingdom. In 2001 road transport accounted for 62 per cent of carbon monoxide emissions, while power stations produced 66 per cent of sulphur dioxide emissions. (Page 167)

Climate change

- Overall, UK emissions of carbon dioxide fell by 15 per cent between 1971 and 2001. (Figure 11.7)

Waste management

- In 2001/02, 77 per cent of municipal waste in England was disposed to landfill, 13 per cent was recycled or composted, and 9 per cent was incinerated with energy recovery. (Table 11.9)

Use of resources

- UK domestic energy consumption increased by almost a third between 1971 and 2001, to 48.5 million tonnes. However, in terms of energy use per household the increase was only 5 per cent, from 1,870 to 1,960 kilogrammes of oil equivalent. (Table 11.14)

Countryside, farming and wildlife

- North sea stocks of cod have declined steadily since the early 1980s, and were 80 per cent lower in 2002 than in 1982. (Figure 11.17)

Environmental concerns and behaviour

- The volume of noise complaints to Environmental Health Officers in England and Wales more than doubled between 1990/91 and 2001/02. (Table 11.22)

Figure **11.1**

Emissions of selected air pollutants

United Kingdom
Million tonnes

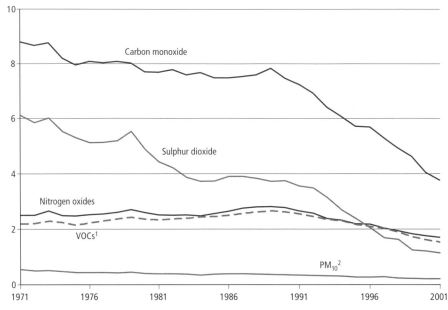

1 Volatile organic compounds.
2 Particulate matter that is less than 10 microns.

Source: Department for Environment, Food and Rural Affairs' National Air Quality Information Archive

Figure **11.2**

Days with moderate or higher air pollution

United Kingdom
Average number of days per site

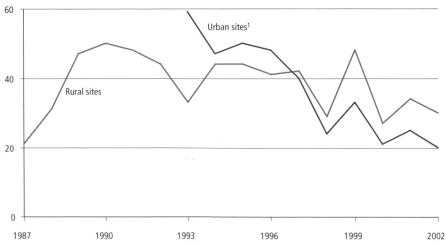

1 Data for urban sites not available before 1993.

Source: Department for Environment, Food and Rural Affairs; NETCEN

The condition of the environment impacts on and is impacted by society locally, nationally and internationally. Phenomena such as industrial pollution and climate change have had, or are likely to have, profound implications both for individuals and the United Kingdom as a whole.

Pollution

Many of the activities we undertake each day produce pollutants which can harm the environment as well as affect human health. However, emissions of the major air pollutants in the United Kingdom have been falling since the 1970s, and generally the rate of decline accelerated in the 1990s (Figure 11.1). Carbon monoxide (CO) reduces the capacity of the blood to carry and deliver oxygen. Emissions of CO fell by 16 per cent between 1970 and 1990, followed by a 50 per cent reduction between 1990 and 2001, mainly as a result of the introduction of catalytic converters in petrol cars.

Sulphur dioxide (SO_2) is an acid gas which can affect both human health and vegetation. It affects the lining of the nose, throat and lungs, particularly among those with asthma and chronic lung disease. SO_2 emissions fell by 68 per cent between 1991 and 2001, largely as a result of a reduction in coal use by power stations and the introduction of the desulphurisation of flue gas at two power stations. Nitrogen oxides (NOx) are also acid gases and can have similar effects. Emissions fell by 36 per cent between 1991 and 2001.

Particulate matter that is less than 10 microns in diameter, known as PM_{10}, is generated primarily by combustion processes, as well as from processes such as stone abrasion during construction, mining and quarrying.

Particulate matter is responsible for causing premature deaths among those with pre-existing heart and lung conditions. Emissions fell by 42 per cent between 1991 and 2001.

Road transport and power stations are the most important single sources of air pollutants in the United Kingdom. In 2001 road transport accounted for 62 per cent of CO emissions, and for 46 per cent of NOx emissions. Although the level of road traffic has continued to grow over the last decade (see Chapter 12), changes in vehicle technology have reduced the impact of emissions from this sector. In 1991 road transport accounted for 73 per cent of CO emissions and for 48 per cent of NOx emissions. Power stations produced 66 per cent of SO_2 and 23 per cent of NOx emissions in 2001, compared with 72 per cent and 26 per cent, respectively, in 1991.

One result of the reduction in emissions of air pollutants has been a fall in the average number of days with moderate or higher pollution at urban sites over the last decade (Figure 11.2). In 1993 air pollution monitoring sites in urban areas recorded an average of 59 days per site when air pollution was moderate or higher, but by 2002 this figure had fallen to 20 days. Ozone and PM_{10} are now the major causes of pollution at urban sites. SO_2 used to make a significant contribution, but has now fallen to relatively very low levels. There is no clear trend in pollution at rural sites and it is much more variable, largely due to fluctuations in levels of ozone, the main cause of pollution in such areas. The production of ozone is strongly influenced by the weather – it is created on sunny summer days. The impact of warm weather can been seen in the chart, when the hot summer of 1999 resulted in an increase in the numbers of days with average or higher pollution in both rural and urban areas.

Pollution can also affect the fresh water of the United Kingdom. River water quality is important because rivers are a major source of drinking water and are used by industry, and also because rivers support a wide variety of wildlife and are used extensively for recreation. The numbers, and sources, of serious water pollution incidents vary across the constituent parts of the United Kingdom, although this may in part reflect the different monitoring regimes in England and Wales (where a common regime operates), Scotland and Northern Ireland (Table 11.3). In England the most common identified source in 2002 was the sewage and water industry, which accounted for 20 per cent of serious incidents. In Wales and Northern Ireland the most common source was agriculture, accounting for 24 and 35 per cent of such incidents, respectively, while in Scotland, industry was the most common source, accounting for 29 per cent of incidents.

The total number of serious water pollution incidents each year in the United Kingdom fell through much of the 1990s, in response to tighter pollution controls. This fall appears to have levelled off somewhat, with an average of 1,540 such incidents occurring in each of the years 2000, 2001 and 2002, compared with nearly 2,100 in 1998.

Rivers and canals in the United Kingdom are generally in a favourable condition, and both chemical and biological quality have improved in recent years. In particular, the chemical quality of rivers in England improved markedly between 1990 and 2002, with 93 per cent of river length classified as being in good or fair condition by the later date

Table 11.3

Water pollution incidents[1]: by source, 2002[2]

United Kingdom				Numbers
	England	Wales	Scotland	Northern Ireland
Agriculture	127	23	38	100
Industrial	94	11	55	90
Sewage and water industry	153	15	46	37
Transport	35	1	..	9
Domestic	38	5	..	19
Other[3]	323	41	48	27
Total	770	96	187	282

1 Serious incidents only. See Appendix, Part 11: Water pollution incidents.
2 Figures for Scotland relate to the financial year 2001/02.
3 Figure for Scotland includes transport and domestic.

Source: Environment Agency; Scottish Environment Protection Agency; Environment and Heritage Service (Northern Ireland)

Table **11.4**

Chemical quality[1] of rivers and canals: by country

United Kingdom

Percentage of total river length

	England	Wales	Scotland[2]	Northern Ireland
1990[3]				
Good	43	86	..	44
Fair	40	11	..	51
1995				
Good	55	93	..	45
Fair	35	5	..	43
2000				
Good	64	93	87	59
Fair	29	5	10	37
2002				
Good	65	92	86	55
Fair	28	6	10	42

1 See Appendix, Part 11: Rivers and canals.
2 Data for Scotland are collected on a different basis to the rest of the UK. 'Good' includes unclassified waters which are assumed to be of good condition.
3 Northern Ireland figures are for 1991.

Source: Environment Agency; Scottish Environment Protection Agency; Environment and Heritage Service, Northern Ireland

(Table 11.4). This was, however, still the lowest such percentage for any of the constituent parts of the United Kingdom: Wales had the highest proportion of rivers in good or fair condition in 2002, at 98 per cent.

Improvements in water quality since 1990 are thought to be largely attributable to the investment programme of the water industry and pollution control measures. However, the chemical quality of rivers and canals is not only affected by human activity. Lower than average rainfall and low river flows can also have an adverse effect on river water quality by reducing the dilution of pollutants.

Pollution from the land can also impact on the seas around the United Kingdom. The microbiological quality of bathing

waters can be affected by sewage effluent, storm water overflows and river-borne pollutants which could affect human health. The EC's bathing water directive gives mandatory values for a number of physical, chemical and microbiological parameters at bathing waters, among which total and faecal coliforms are considered to be the most important (coliforms are bacteria which inhabit the intestines of humans and other vertebrates).

In recent years, there has been an increase in the number of UK bathing waters complying with the bathing water directive coliform standards during the bathing season (Table 11.5). In England this amounted to an increase of 9 percentage points between 1998 and 2002, to 99 per cent compliance. Wales achieved 100 per cent compliance

in 2002 and Northern Ireland 94 per cent. Scotland's beaches showed the biggest improvement among the United Kingdom's constituent countries over the period, moving from 52 per cent to 91 per cent compliance.

Climate change

Both global and local (central England) average temperatures rose during the 20th century (Figure 11.6). Global temperatures rose consistently during the first half of the century and, after stabilising for a period, rose steeply again from 1975. The years 1998, 2001 and 2002 were the three hottest years on record globally. Temperatures in central England also rose in the first half of the century and, after a period of little change, followed the global pattern and rose steeply from the early 1980s. The year 2002 was the fourth warmest on record in central England, with an average temperature of 10.5 degrees centigrade. Only 1949, 1990 and 1999 were warmer – all had an average temperature of 10.6 degrees centigrade.

The role of the Intergovernmental Panel on Climate Change (IPCC) is to assess evidence relevant to understanding the scientific basis for human induced climate change and its potential impacts. The IPCC believes that most of the warming over the last 50 years is attributable to human activities – chief among these is the emission of greenhouse gases, such as carbon dioxide (CO_2), methane (CH_4) and nitrous oxide, largely from the use of fossil fuels.

The IPCC reported in 2001 that, unless actions to control emissions are taken, global temperatures will rise by between 1.4 and 5.8 degrees centigrade by the end of the century. This increase would be much larger than any experienced over the last 10,000 years, and would be likely to have a major impact on the global environment. It is predicted that mean sea levels would rise by 9 to 88 centimetres, increasing the risk of flooding in low lying areas and the pressure on flood defences. An increased frequency of extreme weather events is another possible effect.

The European Union (EU) as a unit is committed under the Kyoto Protocol to reducing emissions of six greenhouse gases by 8 per cent below the 1990 level over the 'commitment period' of 2008 to 2012. The United Kingdom has a legally binding target to reduce emissions by 12.5 per cent relative to 1990 over the same period. The Government intends to move beyond that target towards a 20 per cent reduction by 2010, and has also announced a longer term aim to reduce CO_2 emissions by 60 per cent by 2050. Provisional estimates for 2002 suggest that emissions of greenhouse gases fell by around 15 per cent between 1990 and 2002. This reduction has not been continuous, however, and emissions rose between 1999 and 2001 before falling back again.

In 2001 CO_2 accounted for 85 per cent of greenhouse gas emissions. Most CO_2 emissions are caused by energy consumption. In terms of end users, the industrial and domestic sectors are the most important causes of emissions, closely followed by the transport sector (Figure 11.7 – see overleaf). Emissions of CO_2 fell by 15 per cent between 1971 and 2001, though there are some important variations within this overall trend. Emissions from industry fell steeply in the late 1970s and early 1980s, declined more steadily from that

Table **11.5**

Bathing water – compliance with EC bathing water directive coliform standards[1]: by Environment Agency region

Percentages

	1998	2000	2002
United Kingdom	89	94	98
England	90	95	99
North East	84	91	98
North West	62	82	97
Midlands	.	.	.
Anglian	100	100	100
Thames	100	100	100
Southern	97	97	99
South West	91	96	98
Wales	94	99	100
Scotland	52	84	91
Northern Ireland	94	100	94

1 During the bathing season. See Appendix, Part 11: Bathing waters.

Source: Department for Environment, Food and Rural Affairs

Figure **11.6**

Difference in average surface temperature: comparison with 1961–1990 average

Global and Central England

Degrees C

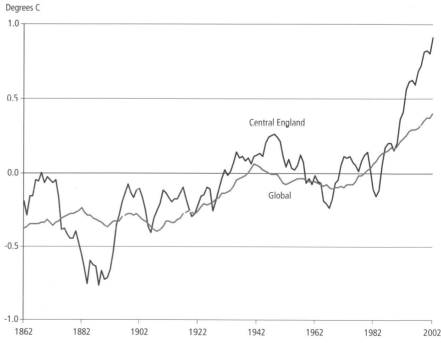

Source: Hadley Centre for Climate Prediction and Research

Figure **11.7**

Emissions of carbon dioxide: by end user

United Kingdom
Million tonnes of carbon equivalent

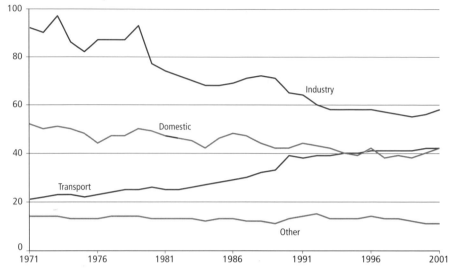

Source: National Environmental Technology Centre

Table **11.8**

Electricity generated from renewable sources

United Kingdom   GWh

	1991	1996	2001	2002
Wind and wave	9	488	965	1,256
Solar photo-voltaics	-	-	2	3
Hydro	4,624	3,393	4,055	4,788
Landfill gas	208	708	2,507	2,679
Sewage sludge digestion	328	410	363	397
Municipal solid waste combustion[1]	151	490	929	958
Other biofuels[2]	1	197	777	870
Wastes[3]	88	417	479	494
Total	5,409	6,102	10,077	11,444

1 *Biodegradable part only.*
2 *Includes electricity from farm waste digestion, poultry litter combustion, meat and bone combustion, straw and short rotation coppice.*
3 *Non-biodegradable part of municipal solid waste plus tyres.*

Source: Department of Trade and Industry

point, and then levelled off from 1997. The overall result has been a 37 per cent reduction between 1971 and 2001. Domestic emissions fell more steadily over the same period, and were 20 per cent lower by the latter date. Conversely, CO_2 emissions from transport increased by 98 per cent between 1971 and 2001, although they have remained relatively stable since 1996.

The use of renewable sources of electricity will be vital in reducing CO_2 emissions in the future. The amount of electricity produced from such sources in the United Kingdom more than doubled between 1991 and 2002 (Table 11.8). Proportionately, the biggest increases in production came from wind and wave power. Very little energy was generated from wind in 1991, but it accounted for more than a tenth of the electricity generated from renewable sources by 2002. Generation from landfill gas increased the most in absolute terms over the period, and accounted for nearly a quarter of electricity generation from renewables in 2002. See Table 11.13 for more on electricity generation.

While generation from all renewables and waste in the United Kingdom accounted for only 3.0 per cent of UK electricity generation in 2002, this was an increase from 2.6 per cent in 2001 and 1.7 per cent in 1996. This compares with an EU average of 15 per cent in 2000. The UK figure reflects the absence of both high mountains, which would facilitate large scale hydro generation, and extensive forests that would prompt biomass generation, as well as the abundant indigenous coal and gas resources (see Figure 11.12). The Government has set a target to generate 10 per cent of the UK electricity from renewable sources by 2010.

Waste management

The collection and disposal of domestic waste and litter and rubbish from public areas (as well as some commercial waste) is the responsibility of local authorities throughout the United Kingdom. Around 90 per cent of such 'municipal waste' is generated by households, and much of this has traditionally been disposed to landfill, a method which makes little use of the waste and produces greenhouse gases (mainly CO_2 and methane).

In 2001/02, 77 per cent of municipal waste in England was disposed to landfill, while 14 per cent was recycled or composted (Table 11.9). The proportion recycled has grown since 1996/97, as the proportion disposed in landfill sites has fallen. However, the absolute volume of waste disposed in landfill sites has increased over the period, as the overall amount of municipal waste continues to grow year on year. Between 1996/97 and 2001/02 the amount of household waste produced in England increased by 17 per cent, partly because of the rise in the number of households (see Chapter 2: Households and families). Other reasons may include higher living standards and changes in consumer behaviour.

The Government has set a target to recycle 25 per cent of household waste by 2005. In 2001/02, 12 per cent was recycled, compared with 7 per cent in 1996/97. The amount of household waste recycled varies considerably across the country, and in 2001/02 the South East and East had the highest rates, at 18 and 17 per cent, respectively.

Between 1996/97 and 2001/02, the overall amount of waste collected for recycling in England nearly doubled, to 3.2 million tonnes (Table 11.10). Paper and card, and compost constitute a large proportion of this waste, accounting for

31 and 30 per cent, respectively, of the total amount by weight in 2001/02. While the amount of paper and card collected has grown steadily in recent years, the amount of compost has increased more rapidly, more than tripling between 1996/97 and 2001/02.

Table 11.9

Management of municipal waste: by method

England				Thousand tonnes
	1996/97	1998/99	2000/01	2001/02
Landfill	20,631	21,534	22,039	22,317
Incineration with energy from waste	1,446	2,117	2,391	2,459
Recycled/composted[1]	1,750	2,525	3,446	3,907
Other[2]	761	160	182	140
Total	24,588	26,337	28,057	28,823

1 Includes household and non-household sources collected for recycling or for centralised composting; home composting estimates are not included in this total.
2 Includes incineration without energy from waste and refuse derived fuel manufacture. Excludes any processing prior to landfilling and materials sent to materials reclamation facilities (MRFs).

Source: Department for Environment, Food and Rural Affairs

Table 11.10

Materials collected from households for recycling[1]

England				Thousand tonnes
	1996/97	1998/99	2000/01	2001/02
Paper & card	600	811	934	973
Glass	311	349	397	429
Compost[2]	279	455	798	941
Scrap metal & white goods	199	253	310	370
Textiles	32	40	45	43
Cans[3]	18	26	26	26
Plastics	6	8	13	8
Co-mingled	77	136	206	221
Other[4]	155	53	83	165
Total	1,678	2,130	2,812	3,180

1 Includes data from different types of recycling scheme collecting waste from household sources, including private/voluntary schemes such as kerbside and 'bring' systems.
2 Includes organic materials (kitchen and garden waste) collected for centralised composting. Home composting is not included.
3 Includes ferrous and aluminium cans.
4 Includes oils, batteries, aluminium foil, books and shoes.

Source: Department for Environment, Food and Rural Affairs

Kerbside collection by local authorities is one way in which households can recycle their waste, accounting for 30 per cent of waste collected for recycling in 2001/02. Those in non-metropolitan districts recycled more on average than those in metropolitan districts, 190 kilograms per

Figure **11.11**

Winter and summer rainfall[1,2]

England & Wales
Millimetres

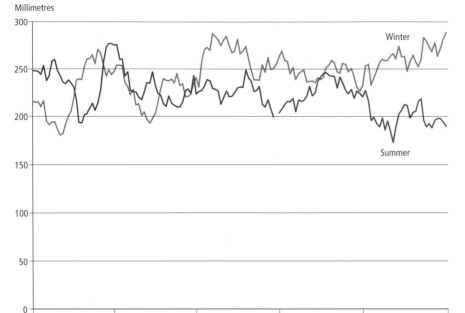

1 Figures are ten-year rolling averages ending in year shown.
2 Winter is December to February, summer is June to August.

Source: Climate Research Unit, University of East Anglia; Hadley Centre; CEH-Wallingford

household per year compared with 77 kilograms, while households in London recycled 101 kilograms per year. Most waste recycled is collected through civic amenity and 'bring' sites, which accounted for 69 per cent of the total in 2001/02.

Use of resources

If predicted changes in precipitation patterns due to climate change occur, water resources could become a major issue in many parts of the world over the next century. According to the United Nations (UN), about one third of the world's population already live in countries suffering from moderate to high water stress (when the demand for water exceeds the available amount during a certain period or when poor quality restricts its use).

Although in a global context the United Kingdom does not suffer from a lack of rain, precipitation varies greatly from region to region. The mountains of western Scotland receive almost ten times the precipitation of the driest parts of south-eastern England, while London is, on average, drier than Paris or Rome. Rainfall across the United Kingdom is usually well distributed through the year, but there has been a recent tendency towards wetter winters and drier summers in England and Wales (Figure 11.11). This has been particularly evident since the 1960s, and over the last ten years winter rainfall has, on average, exceeded summer rainfall by almost 100 millimetres, the greatest margin in a record stretching back to 1766. In contrast, summer rainfall was greater than winter rainfall for extended periods during the 19th century.

The recent trends in rainfall patterns for England and Wales appear to coincide with climate change predictions that winters in the United Kingdom will become wetter and summers drier. In the south and east these changes could amount to as much as a 50 per cent reduction in summer precipitation from the 1961–1990 average by 2080. However, there is considerable uncertainty about future rainfall patterns and given the natural variability of the UK climate any short-term trends should be treated with caution.

The production of energy is another important resource issue, with most production in the United Kingdom coming from fossil fuels. In 2002 overall UK primary fuel production was 2 per cent lower than in the previous year, and 91 per cent of this was accounted for by fossil fuels. The dominant position of coal 30 years ago has been eroded, initially by petroleum and latterly also by natural gas (Figure 11.12). Coal now accounts for just 7 per cent of primary fuels produced, while petroleum accounts for 47 per cent and natural gas for 38 per cent. Production of petroleum increased sharply between 1976 and 1985 as oilfields were discovered and brought into production. The increase in the production of natural gas from the end of the 1980s can be largely attributed to electricity suppliers switching from coal to gas, a cheaper source of fuel.

Although the amounts extracted each year have grown over the last decade, new discoveries mean that UK proven and probable reserves of oil and gas are not much lower than the levels of ten years ago. In 1991, 1.2 billion tonnes of oil remained in proven and probable reserves. By 2002 this figure was 0.9 billion tonnes, even though 1.3 billion tonnes had been recovered over the period.

Electricity generation accounts for a large proportion of the fuel used in the United

Kingdom. In 2002, four fifths of the total demand for coal was for electricity generation, while for natural gas this proportion was just under a third. The United Kingdom generates a similar proportion of its electricity from natural gas to Ireland and Italy: 37 per cent of the total in 2001 compared with an EU average of 17 per cent (Table 11.13). However this was substantially lower than the Netherlands. Production of primary electricity in the United Kingdom (that is, electricity generated from nuclear, hydro and wind sources) remains at low levels compared with most of the rest of the EU, accounting for 25 per cent of UK electricity generation in 2001. This compares with an EU average of 48 per cent.

Figure **11.12**

Production of primary fuels

United Kingdom
Million tonnes of oil equivalent

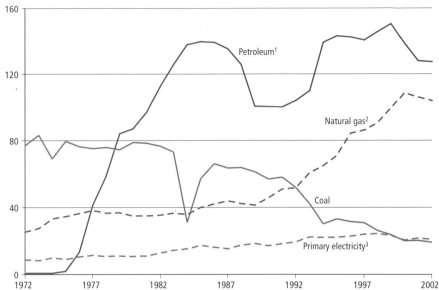

1 Includes crude oil, natural gas liquids and feedstocks.
2 Includes colliery methane.
3 Nuclear, natural flow hydro-electricity and, from 1988, generation at wind stations.

Source: Department of Trade and Industry

Table **11.13**

Electricity generation: by fuel used, EU comparison, 2001

Percentages and thousand gigawatt hours

	Nuclear	Coal and lignite	Petroleum products	Natural and derived gases	Hydro and wind[1]	Biomass and geothermal	Other fuels	All fuels (=100%) (thousand GWh)
Germany	29	50	1	11	6	1	1	582
France[2]	77	..	..	..	14	1	8	549
United Kingdom	23	34	2	37	2	1	-	386
Italy	0	11	27	36	20	3	3	279
Spain	27	30	10	10	21	1	1	238
Sweden	45	1	2	1	49	2	-	162
Netherlands	4	25	3	62	1	4	-	94
Belgium	58	12	2	23	2	1	1	80
Finland	31	23	1	16	18	11	-	74
Austria	0	11	3	15	68	3	-	64
Greece	0	66	16	11	6	0	-	54
Portugal	0	29	20	16	31	4	-	47
Denmark	0	47	11	25	11	6	0	38
Ireland	0	37	21	37	5	-	0	25
Luxembourg	0	0	0	22	73	5	-	1
EU total	33	25	6	17	15	2	2	2,671

1 Includes pumped storage.
2 Breakdown of electricity produced from fossil fuels not reported. 'Other' therefore contains production from coal, natural gas and oil fired power stations.

Source: Eurostat

Table **11.14**

Domestic energy consumption per household: by final use

United Kingdom   Kilograms of oil equivalent

	1971	1981	1991	2001
Space heating	1,090	1,150	1,190	1,210
Water	520	480	460	450
Cooking	110	90	70	50
Lighting and appliances	150	210	240	250
Total	1,870	1,920	1,950	1,960

Source: Building Research Establishment

Table **11.15**

Land by agricultural and other uses, 2002

United Kingdom   Percentages

	England	Wales	Scotland	Northern Ireland	United Kingdom
Agricultural land					
Crops and bare fallow	30	3	7	4	19
Grasses and rough grazing	36	73	67	77	51
Other[1]	5	1	2	1	4
Forest and woodland[2]	8	13	17	6	11
Urban land not otherwise specified[3]	21	10	8	12	16
Total land[4,5] (=100%) (thousand hectares)	12,972	2,064	7,710	1,348	24,093
Inland water[4] (thousand hectares)	76	13	169	64	325

1 Set aside and other land on agricultural holdings, eg farm roads, yards, buildings, gardens, ponds. Excludes woodland on agricultural holdings which is in 'Forests and woodland'.
2 See Appendix, Part II: Forest and woodland.
3 Figures are derived by subtracting land used for agricultural and forestry purposes from the land area. Figures include: land used for urban and other purposes, eg transport and recreation; non-agricultural, semi-natural environments such as sand dunes, grouse moors, non-agricultural grasslands; and inland waters.
4 As at January 2001.
5 Because data come from a number of sources the components do not always add to total.

Source: Department for Environment, Food and Rural Affairs

Domestic energy consumption increased by 36 per cent between 1971 and 2001, from 35.6 to 48.5 million tonnes of oil equivalent. However, in terms of energy use per household the increase was only 5 per cent, from 1,870 to 1,960 kilograms of oil equivalent per household (Table 11.14). Growth in the number of households over the period, in the proportion of households with central heating, and in the ownership of household electrical appliances, have to an extent been offset by improvements in energy efficiency.

In 2001, 85 per cent of energy used in households was for space or water heating. In 1971, 34 per cent of homes in Great Britain were centrally heated – by 2001, this had increased to 90 per cent. The increase in the use of energy for space heating has, however, been somewhat offset by increased levels of home insulation and double glazing. In 1987 just 3 per cent of households which could potentially do so had full insulation, compared with 14 per cent by 2001. Forty seven per cent of households which could potentially do so had four fifths or more of their windows doubled glazed in 2001, nearly three times the proportion in 1987.

Household energy use per person in the United Kingdom in 2000, at 0.72 tonnes of oil equivalent, was broadly similar to other EU countries such as France (0.64 tonnes), the Netherlands (0.65) and Germany (0.75). Within the EU, northern countries generally have higher levels of energy use per household than southern countries, reflecting the fact that much household energy is used for heating. Internationally, G8 countries such as Canada and the USA used considerably more energy, at 1.00 and 0.96 tonnes of oil equivalent per person, respectively, in 2000.

Countryside, farming and wildlife

Three quarters of UK land is still used for agriculture (Table 11.15). Northern Ireland has the largest proportion of agricultural land, at 82 per cent, while England has the smallest, at 71 per cent. There is also considerable variability in the use to which agricultural land is put – 30 per cent of the total area of England is covered by crops and bare fallow, compared with only 3 per cent of Wales, 7 per cent of Scotland and 4 per cent of Northern Ireland.

Over the past ten years, concerns about the possible impact the use of pesticides, BSE in cattle, and the development of genetically modified (GM) crops may have on people's health and the environment have led to an increased interest in organic farming. A dramatic increase in the area of land under organic production occurred from 1998, and by December 2002, 725,000 hectares of land in the United Kingdom were under organic production (Figure 11.16). As at March 2003, Scotland had the largest proportion of organic land, at 8 per cent of its total area. Wales had 4 per cent, England 3 per cent, and Northern Ireland less than 1 per cent

Most land that is organically farmed (or is in the process of being converted to organic farming) in the United Kingdom is used for permanent or temporary pasture – 88 per cent in March 2003. In contrast, 67 per cent of all agricultural land in 2002 was grassland or used for rough grazing. Just 8 per cent of organic land was used for growing cereals and other crops in March 2003, and 2 per cent for fruit and vegetables.

Fish have traditionally formed an important food resource for many people in the United Kingdom. They are also vital elements of ocean ecosystems.

While there is emerging evidence that some species, notably cod and hake, are declining in numbers in the seas around the United Kingdom, stocks of other species, such as herring, have been increasing in recent years (Figure 11.17). After declining to very low levels in the 1970s, stocks of herring have recovered strongly, while haddock stocks have fluctuated dramatically since the 1960s, and continue to do so: they quadrupled between 2000 and 2002.

Stocks of cod in the North Sea and elsewhere are causing particular concern to the Government and other interested parties. After increasing in the 1960s, and fluctuating somewhat in the 1970s, North Sea stocks have declined steadily since the early 1980s, and were 80 per cent lower in 2002 than in 1982. There was, however, a small increase between 2001 and 2002. This depletion in numbers is thought to have occurred through a combination of overfishing,

Figure 11.16

Land under organic crop production[1]

United Kingdom
Thousand hectares

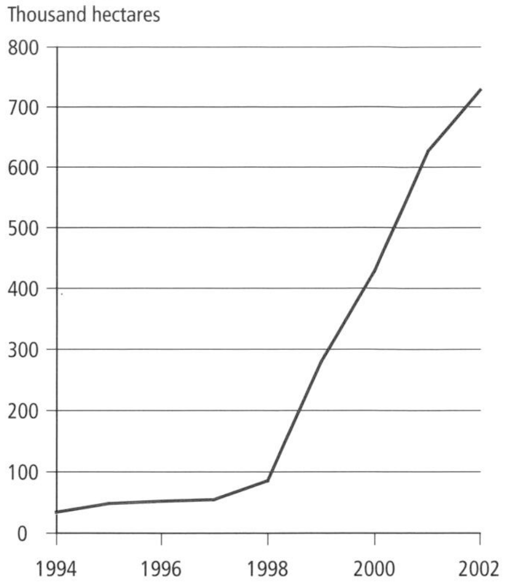

1 As at December each year.

Source: Department for Environment, Food and Rural Affairs

Figure 11.17

North Sea fish stocks[1]

Indices (1963=100)

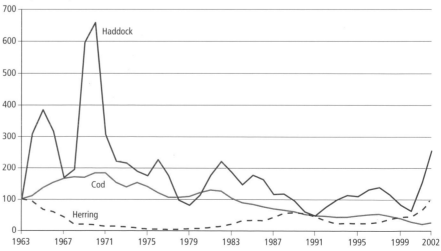

1 Spawning stock biomass.

Source: Centre for Environment, Fisheries and Aquaculture Science; International Council for the Exploration of the Sea

Figure **11.18**

Woodland cover, 1980 and 2002

Percentages

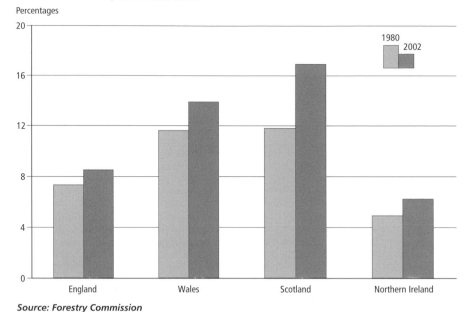

Source: Forestry Commission

Prehistoric and historic clearance of woodland brought the proportion of wooded land in the United Kingdom down to just 5 per cent at the beginning of the 20th century. This rose to 6 per cent by 1947 and 9 per cent by 1980, with much of the increase being driven by the commercial planting of conifers. However, in response to additional incentives for planting native trees and for planting on former agricultural land, the planting of broadleaved trees has outstripped that of conifers since 1993/94. In 2002, 8,300 hectares of broadleaved trees were planted, compared with 3,400 hectares of conifers.

A significant proportion of England's total area is urban land – 11 per cent when last estimated in 1991. In an attempt to minimise the effect of new housebuilding on the countryside, the Government has a target for the proportion of additional housing built on previously developed land (or provided through conversion) to be at least 60 per cent by 2008. In 2002, 31 per cent of land changing to residential use in England was previously used for agriculture, compared with 55 per cent which was previously-developed land (Table 11.19). In 1991 these figures were 38 and 45 per cent, respectively. These changes reflect the increase in the proportion of new housing built on previously developed land, from 50 per cent (excluding conversions) in 1991 to 60 per cent in 2001.

Bird populations are good indicators of the condition of the UK's wildlife. Following an increase in the 1970s, the overall population of wild birds has remained relatively stable over the last 20 years (Figure 11.20). The population increased by 13 per cent between 1970 and 2002, although there was a slight decrease between 2000 and 2002.

small numbers of fish surviving to a size where they are taken commercially, and possible environmental factors. Measures have been put in place that aim to halt and ultimately reverse the decline in cod stocks. These have included restrictions on cod fishing during the key spring spawning periods, cuts in the numbers that can be caught, and a limit to the number of days each month fishermen can spend at sea catching cod.

Woodland constitutes another ecologically natural resource which is also economically important. The proportion of land covered by forest in the United Kingdom has been increasing in recent decades after centuries of

decline. The biggest proportional increase over the last 20 years has occurred in Scotland, already the most heavily forested country (Figure 11.18). Between 1980 and 2002, the proportion of land covered by forest in Scotland grew from 12 to 17 per cent. In Wales it increased from 12 to 14 per cent, and in England from 7 to 9 per cent. In Northern Ireland, the least forested part of the United Kingdom, the area of land covered by woodland grew from 5 to 6 per cent over the same period.

In total around 12 per cent of the total area of the United Kingdom is covered by woodland, well below the EU average, at 37 per cent in 2000.

Species which have increased the most include scarce breeding birds with mainly southern distributions such as the Dartford warbler, which may be benefiting from climate change.

However, populations of a number of species have been declining for many years. The population of farmland species (for example turtledove, skylark and corn bunting) has declined markedly and numbers fell by 42 per cent between 1970 and 2002, largely due to the intensification of agriculture. A number of schemes, such as funding from the Department for Environment, Food and Rural Affairs (Defra) to restore farmland habitats, are now in operation in an attempt to reverse this decline. The population of woodland birds has been less badly affected, and was 15 per cent lower in 2002 than in 1970.

Environmental concerns and behaviour

The use of green spaces is one way in which people can use and enjoy their local environment. Defra's 2001 Survey of Public Attitudes to Quality of Life and to the Environment found that just under half of adults aged 18 or over visited local green spaces or countryside, without using a car or other transport, at least once a month (Table 11.21 – see overleaf). A further quarter did at least occasionally – however, one in ten never did so, while a further one in six said that they had no access without a car or other transport. People aged over 45 were the most likely to visit green spaces on 'most days', while those aged over 65 were also the most likely never to do so.

Noise is an environmental issue which affects many people. It is often a local problem, being caused directly by neighbours – more than two thirds of

Table **11.19**

Land changing to residential use: by previous use[1]

England
Percentages

	1991	1996	2001	2002
Agriculture	38	40	32	31
Urban land not previously developed	12	9	10	9
Other land not previously developed	6	6	4	4
Residential	18	15	17	16
Vacant land previously developed	18	21	24	25
Other land previously developed	9	9	14	15
All land changing to residential use (hectares) (=100%)[2]	5,720	6,175	5,305	..

1 Information relates to map changes recorded by Ordnance Survey as at the end of 2002, where the year of change has been estimated by surveyors from available information. Excludes conversions of existing buildings. Percentages for the most recent years may be revised as new data are added.
2 These figures are subject to upward revision for the most recent years due to the lag between the change occurring and it being recorded.

Source: Office of the Deputy Prime Minister

Figure **11.20**

Population of wild birds[1]

United Kingdom
Indices (1970=100)

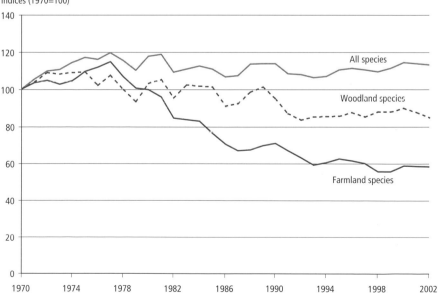

1 It was not possible to complete the Breeding Birds Survey in 2001 because of restrictions imposed during the outbreak of foot-and-mouth disease. Estimates for that year are based on the average for 2000 and 2002 for individual species.

Source: British Trust for Ornithology; Royal Society for the Protection of Birds; Department for Environment, Food and Rural Affairs

Table **11.21**

Frequency of visits to local green spaces or countryside[1], without using a car or other transport: by age, 2001

England   Percentages

	18–24	25–44	45–64	65 and over	All aged 18 and over
Most days	7	13	19	19	16
At least once a week	19	21	19	15	19
At least once a month	16	16	13	9	14
Occasionally	25	27	24	19	24
Not at all	11	8	12	18	11
No access	23	14	13	20	16
Total	100	100	100	100	100

1 Respondents were asked 'During the last 12 months, how often have you used local green spaces/countryside without using a car or other transport (except for passing through them or for work)?'

Source: Department for Environment, Food and Rural Affairs

Table **11.22**

Noise complaints received by Environmental Health Officers[1]: by source

England & Wales   Rates per million population

	1990/91	2000/01	2001/02
Domestic premises	2,264	5,001	5,540
Industrial/commercial premises	913	1,381	1,273
Vehicles, machinery & equipment in streets[2]	..	365	372
Road works, construction and demolition[2]	252	325	347
Road traffic	46	44	37
Aircraft	34	26	101
Other	135	..	..
Total[3]	3,644	7,142	7,670

1 Figures relate to those authorities making returns.
2 From 2000/01 complaints about road works and 'noise in the street' are included with 'vehicles, machinery and equipment in streets'.
3 Data for 1990/91 include noise in streets controlled by the Control and Pollution Act 1974.

Source: The Chartered Institute of Environmental Health

noise complaints received by Environmental Health Officers (EHOs) had domestic premises as their source in 2001/02 (Table 11.22). The volume of noise complaints to EHOs has more than doubled over the last decade, which may reflect an increase in the incidence of nuisance noise and/or an increased tendency to complain among the public.

Local councils also monitor the number and source of noise complaints made in their area. The National Noise Survey 2002 found that among responding councils in England, Wales and Northern Ireland, dogs and amplified music were the most common sources of neighbour noise complaints. Noise from pubs or clubs was the most common reason for complaints about ambient noise.

Chapter 12 **Transport**

Overview

- The total distance travelled by British residents within Great Britain more than tripled between 1952 and 2002, to 746 billion passenger kilometres. The rate of increase slowed after 1989, and between 1992 and 2002 passenger kilometres grew by 10 per cent (Figure 12.1)

- The distance walked by British residents on the public highway has fallen since the 1980s, from 392 kilometres a year on average in 1985–86 to 305 kilometres in 1999–2001. (Figure 12.4)

Access to transport

- In 2001 more than two thirds of one person pensioner households and just under half of lone parent families with dependent children in Great Britain did not have access to a car. (Table 12.10)

The roads

- In 2002 there were 30.6 million licensed vehicles in Great Britain. In 1981 there were 19.3 million, and in 1961 just under 9 million. (Page 187)

The railways

- The number of journeys made on railways in Great Britain grew by over a quarter between 1995/96 and 2002/03, to 2,072 million. (Table 12.18)

Transport safety

- Almost all passenger deaths in transport accidents in Great Britain occur on the roads. In 2002 there were a total of 3,431 deaths of road users in accidents, compared with an annual average figure of 3,578 in 1994–98. (Page 192)

Figure **12.1**

Passenger transport: by mode[1]

Great Britain
Billion passenger kilometres

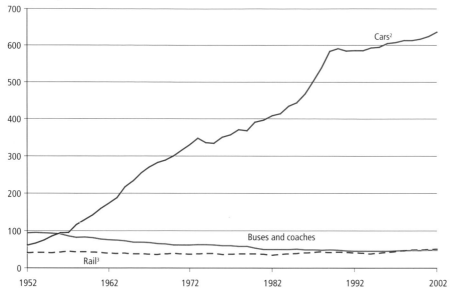

1 Road transport data from 1993 are calculated on a new basis and are not directly comparable
   with earlier years. See Appendix, Part 12: Road traffic.
2 Includes vans and taxis.
3 Financial years. National rail, urban metros and modern trams.

Source: Department for Transport

Table **12.2**

Trips per person per year: by main mode and purpose[1], 1999–2001

Great Britain   Percentages

	Car	Walk	Bus, coach and rail[2]	Other	All modes
Social/entertainment	26	19	18	28	24
Shopping	20	23	24	12	21
Other escort and personal business	22	14	10	10	18
Commuting	17	7	27	26	15
Education	3	11	15	12	7
Escort education	4	8	1	-	5
Business	4	1	2	4	3
Holiday/day trip	3	1	3	7	3
Other, including just walk	-	16	-	-	4
All purposes (=100%) (numbers)	639	263	78	40	1,019

1 See Appendix, Part 12: National Travel Survey.
2 Includes London Underground.

Source: National Travel Survey, Department for Transport

In many respects, recent trends in transport are continuations of longer term patterns. The distance travelled each year, the number of vehicles on the roads, and the volume of international travel all continue to increase. However, there is evidence that some of the major changes that have occurred since the 1970s have slowed in pace, or even reversed, over the last decade. For example, although the average distance each person travels each year within the United Kingdom continues to increase, albeit at a slower rate than previously, the number of trips made has fallen in recent years.

Overview

The total distance travelled by British residents within Great Britain more than tripled between 1952 and 2002 to 746 billion passenger kilometres. Travel by car, van and taxi grew fastest, from 58 billion to 634 billion passenger kilometres (Figure 12.1). Since the early 1960s the car has been the dominant means of transport, accounting for 85 per cent of all passenger kilometres travelled in 2002. The rapid rates of increase that occurred particularly in the 1960s and 1980s were replaced by more gradual growth through the 1990s – the total distance travelled by car rose by 9 per cent between 1992 and 2002.

In contrast, buses and coaches and the railways each accounted for just 6 per cent of all passenger kilometres in 2002. Overall, travel by rail grew from 38 billion to 48 billion passenger kilometres between 1952 and 2002. There was a decline in the number of passenger kilometres for much of this period, with a low point of 31 billion in 1982, but recent years have seen a marked increase with numbers rising by over a third between 1994 and 2002. Travel on buses and coaches amounted to 92 billion passenger kilometres in 1952, and fell steadily to around 43 billion in 1992. After remaining broadly steady for much of the 1990s, numbers rose slowly to 46 billion in 2002.

The National Travel Survey (NTS) found that British residents of all ages travelled on average 11,000 kilometres a year within Great Britain in 1999–2001, 600 more than in 1989–91. There are considerable variations in the distances travelled by people of different age groups. Men aged 40 to 49 travelled the furthest, 19,300 kilometres a year in 1999–2001, whereas women aged 70 and over travelled the shortest overall distance, 4,400 kilometres a year. As the total distance travelled within Great Britain continued to increase over the last decade, so did the average length of trips. In 1989–91 the average length of a trip was 9.6 kilometres. This had increased by 13 per cent, to 10.8 kilometres, by 1999–2001. Males' trips tend on average to be longer than females', 12.6 kilometres compared with 9.1 kilometres in 1999–2001.

In 1999–2001, British residents made just over 1,000 trips a year within Great Britain (Table 12.2). Socialising/entertaining and shopping were the most common reasons for travelling, accounting for 24 and 21 per cent of all trips respectively. Although the average number of trips made per person has declined over the last decade, from just under 1,100 a year in 1989–91, the reasons for travelling have remained relatively stable.

Car access levels can have a major impact on the number of trips people make. In 1999–2001, people who were the main driver of a car (see Appendix, Part 12: National Travel Survey) made on average 1,230 trips a year (Table 12.3). This compared with 1,020 trips made by 'other' drivers, and only 750 trips made

Table 12.3

Trips per person per year: by car access and main mode of transport, 1999–2001

Great Britain   Percentages

	People in households with car				People in households without car	All
	Main driver	Other driver	Non-driver	All		
Car	81	63	54	71	17	63
Walk	15	24	32	21	51	26
Local bus	1	4	7	3	20	6
Rail[1]	1	4	1	2	3	2
Bicycle	1	2	2	1	2	2
Other[2]	1	3	3	2	6	3
All modes (=100%) (numbers)	1,231	1,023	902	1,088	752	1,019

1 Includes London Underground.
2 Includes motorcycles.

Source: National Travel Survey, Department for Transport

by people living in a household without a car. Women who are main or other drivers of household cars make more trips each year than men in the same position – female main drivers made around 1,290 trips each year in 1999–2001, compared with 1,190 trips made by men.

Drivers of cars also travel much further each year than non-drivers. In 1999–2001, main drivers of cars travelled 16,500 kilometres a year on average, and other drivers travelled 12,000 kilometres. Non-drivers living in households with cars travelled on average 7,200 kilometres, while people living in households without a car travelled only 4,400 kilometres.

Although more than 79 per cent of all passenger mileage was travelled by car in 1999–2001, cars provided the means of transport for only 63 per cent of all trips made (see Table 12.2). Most short trips are made on foot, and walking accounted for 80 per cent of all trips under a mile (1.6 kilometres) in 1999–2001. Trips

under a mile in length in turn represented around a quarter of all trips made.

The distance walked by British residents on the public highway has fallen since the 1980s, from 392 kilometres a year on average in 1985–86 to 305 kilometres in 1999–2001 (Figure 12.4 – see overleaf). The biggest reduction has been among the 10 to 19 age group, who, in 1999–2001, walked just three quarters of the distance those of a similar age did in 1985–86. There are concerns that the decline in walking among the under 16s is one of the factors behind increased levels of teenage obesity, and the Government has introduced a number of initiatives attempting to address this problem. Safe Routes to Schools projects, for example, seek to increase the number of pupils walking to school.

There is evidence to suggest that it may be difficult to persuade some people to walk more often. The British Social Attitudes survey found that in 2002 42 per cent of adults aged over 18

Figure **12.4**

Average distance walked[1] per person per year: by age

Great Britain
Kilometres

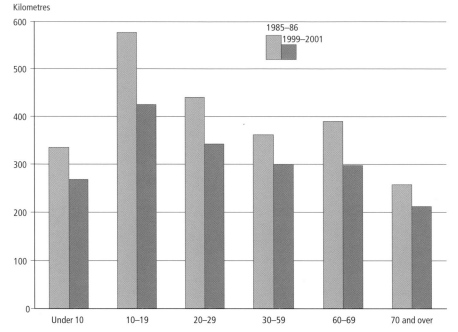

Legend: 1985–86, 1999–2001

1 On the public highway or other unrestricted areas which are paved or tarred. Includes all walks of over 50 yards in distance.

Source: National Travel Survey, Department for Transport

Figure **12.5**

Goods moved by domestic freight transport: by mode

Great Britain
Billion tonne kilometres

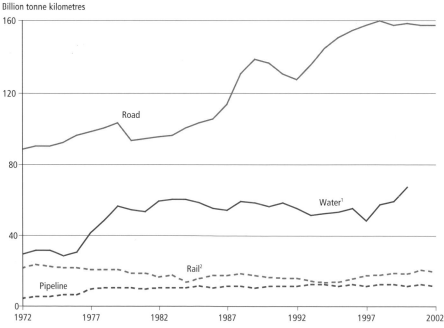

1 2001 and 2002 data not available.
2 From 1991 data are for financial years.

Source: Department for Transport

disagreed with the statement 'many of the journeys I now make by car I could just as easily walk', while 37 per cent agreed. In general, younger people were more likely to agree with the statement than older people.

The volume of goods transported within Great Britain has grown markedly over the last 30 years, although it has remained broadly stable since 2000 (Figure 12.5). Much of this increase can be attributed to the movement of goods by road, which grew from 88 billion tonne kilometres in 1972 to 157 billion in 2002. The volume of freight carried by water also rose over the period, from 29 to 67 billion tonne kilometres in 2000. The volume of goods moved by rail in 2002, 19 billion tonne kilometres, was around 10 per cent lower than in 1972, although it fell to a low of 13 billion in 1994 and 1995.

Increases in both weight of goods carried and length of haul are behind the increases in the volume of goods transported by road. Between 1992 and 2002 the weight of freight rose by 11 per cent to 1,627 million tonnes, and the average length of haul also rose by 11 per cent, to 92 kilometres (although this was 2 kilometres lower than in 2001).

Prices and expenditure

UK transport prices increased substantially during the 1980s and 1990s (Table 12.6). Between 1981 and 1991 there were rises of 63 per cent in the 'All motoring' index of the retail prices index (RPI) and 86 per cent in the 'All fares and other travel index'. These were greater than the increases between 1991 and 2003 (47 per cent and 52 per cent, respectively). However, the increases in motoring costs in the later period outpaced general inflation, which was not the case between 1981 and

1991: the 'All items' RPI increased by just 37 per cent between 1991 and 2003. Prices on public transport rose by even more – bus and coach fares increased by 69 per cent between 1991 and 2003.

Since 2000, the increases in motoring prices have levelled off, and between 2001 and 2003 there was little overall movement in the 'All motoring' index. This was largely due to a fall in the prices paid to purchase vehicles, and by 2003 such prices were only 3 per cent above 1991 levels. Petrol and oil prices fell by 3 per cent between 2001 and 2003; they were 8 per cent lower in 2002 than 2001, but then rose by 7 per cent between 2002 and 2003.

After taking into account the effect of inflation, household expenditure on transport and travel increased by 22 per cent between 1990 and 2002/03 (Table 12.7). If expenditure in 2002/03 is compared with 1991, the increase is larger – 30 per cent – because expenditure on transport and travel fell in real terms between 1990 and 1991 due to the recession at that time. The average amount households spent on transport and travel continued to grow between 2001/02 and 2002/03, at 1 per cent. This contrasts with a 1 per cent fall in overall household expenditure over the same period.

However, the increase in household expenditure on transport and travel over the 1990s was smaller than over the previous decade. For example, household expenditure on motoring rose by 36 per cent between 1980 and 1990, and by 26 per cent between 1990 and 2002/03. Expenditure on motor vehicle insurance and taxation grew the most over the later period, by 69 per cent, increasing by 16 per cent between 2001/02 and 2002/03 alone.

Table 12.6

Passenger transport prices[1]

United Kingdom

Indices (1991=100)

	1981	1986	1991	1996	2002	2003
Motoring costs						
Vehicle tax and insurance	45	66	100	136	198	203
Maintenance[2]	51	71	100	129	169	179
Petrol and oil	64	93	100	137	172	183
Purchase of vehicles	70	81	100	114	106	103
All motoring expenditure	61	81	100	125	145	147
Fares and other travel costs						
Bus and coach fares	51	70	100	132	163	169
Rail fares	50	68	100	130	155	158
Other	74	79	100	115	135	141
All fares and other travel	54	72	100	123	147	152
Retail prices index	54	74	100	115	133	137

1 At January each year based on the retail prices index. See Appendix, Part 6: Retail prices index.
2 Includes spares and accessories, repairs and motoring organisation membership fees.

Source: Office for National Statistics

Table 12.7

Household expenditure on transport in real terms[1]

United Kingdom

£ per week

	1980	1990	1991	2001/02	2002/03
Motoring					
Cars, vans and motorcycle purchase	..	22.84	20.97	25.91	25.57
Repairs, servicing, spares and accessories	..	6.30	5.68	6.84	6.79
Motor vehicle insurance and taxation	..	6.38	6.29	9.27	10.78
Petrol, diesels and other oils	..	11.00	11.25	15.09	14.83
Other motoring costs	..	1.14	1.17	1.98	2.03
All motoring expenditure	34.92	47.65	45.37	59.09	60.00
Fares and other travel costs					
Rail and tube fares	..	1.53	1.28	1.66	1.57
Bus and coach fares	..	1.74	1.66	1.37	1.28
Taxi, air and other travel costs[2]	..	4.48	3.49	4.78	4.86
All fares and other travel costs[3]	7.16	8.72	7.42	8.88	8.81
All transport and travel	42.08	56.37	52.79	67.97	68.81
All expenditure groups	288.02	348.11	344.47	401.43	396.84

1 At 2002/03 prices deflated by the 'All items' retail prices index.
2 Includes combined fares.
3 Includes expenditure on bicycles, boats – purchases and repairs.

Source: Expenditure and Food Survey, Office for National Statistics

Figure **12.8**

Expenditure on transport as a proportion of total household expenditure: EU comparison, 2000

Percentages

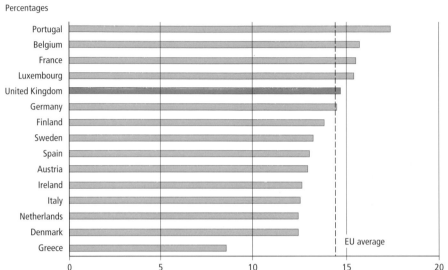

Source: Eurostat; National Statistical Offices

Table **12.9**

Full car driving licence holders: by sex and age

Great Britain   Percentages

	1975–76	1985–86	1989–91	1994–96	1999–2001
Males					
17–20	36	37	52	50	41
21–29	78	73	82	81	81
30–39	85	86	88	88	89
40–49	83	87	89	89	91
50–59	75	81	85	88	88
60–69	58	72	78	82	86
70 and over	32	51	58	63	69
All aged 17 and over	69	74	80	81	82
Number of licence holders (millions)	13.4	15.1	16.7	17.1	17.6
Females					
17–20	20	29	35	38	31
21–29	43	54	64	67	66
30–39	48	62	67	73	77
40–49	37	56	66	74	77
50–59	24	41	49	59	69
60–69	15	24	33	41	57
70 and over	4	11	15	19	25
All aged 17 and over	29	41	49	56	60
Number of licence holders (millions)	6.0	9.2	11.1	12.6	14.0

Source: National Travel Survey, Department for Transport

When household expenditure patterns across the EU are put on a comparable basis, UK households spend a broadly similar proportion of their overall expenditure on transport to the average; 15 per cent compared with the average of 14 per cent in 2000 (Figure 12.8) The country which spent the highest proportion of household expenditure on transport was Portugal, at 17 per cent, while the country that spent the least was Greece, at 9 per cent.

There are considerable variations between countries with regard to how household expenditure on transport is apportioned. In 2000, 35 per cent of household expenditure on transport in the United Kingdom went on the purchase of personal transport equipment, close to the EU average of 34 per cent. However, only 39 per cent of UK household expenditure went toward the operation of that equipment – such as buying fuel and spare parts, and paying for maintenance – compared with an EU average of 49 per cent. Conversely, 26 per cent of UK expenditure was on purchased transport, such as rail and bus fares, compared with an average of 17 per cent.

Access to transport

Just as the ability to drive a car influences the distance and manner in which people travel, it can also affect individuals' ability to find work, access services and conduct their social lives. The ONS Omnibus Survey found that in spring 2001, 11 per cent of people without a household car reported difficulty in visiting their GP, compared with 4 per cent of those with a car. For main food shopping, these figures were 13 per cent and 5 per cent, respectively.

More men than women hold full car driving licences in Great Britain, 82 per cent compared with 60 per cent in

1999–2001 (Table 12.9). However, women have been catching up for a number of years. Between 1975–76 and 1999–2001, while the number of men holding a licence rose by nearly a third to 17.6 million, the number of women holding a licence more than doubled to 14.0 million.

Contrary to the general trend, the proportion of the youngest age groups holding licences has fallen over the last decade – 52 per cent of men aged 17–20 held a licence in 1989–91, compared with 41 per cent in 1999–2001. This may be due to the car driving test becoming more difficult, and/or the introduction of the theory element to the test. Test pass rates were 47 per cent among men and 40 per cent among women in 2002/03, compared with 56 and 46 per cent, respectively, in 1992.

In 2001, one in four households in Great Britain did not have access to a car (Table 12.10). Access is not spread evenly across households of different types. Data from the 2001 Census show that more than two thirds of one person pensioner households in Great Britain did not have access to a car, and just under half of lone parent households with dependent children were in the same position. In contrast, nearly two thirds of couple family households with only non-dependent children had access to two or more cars. Less than one in ten of these households did not have access to a car.

The proportion of households without a car or van also varies geographically across Great Britain. In 2001, the rate of car ownership was higher than 50 per cent in all areas, with the exception of nine inner London boroughs and Glasgow city (Map 12.11 – see overleaf). Households in London and other urban areas were least likely to have a car, whereas households in rural areas, and particularly

Table 12.10

Number of cars per household[1]: by household composition, 2001

Great Britain			Percentages
	No car	One car	Two or more cars
One person			
Under state pension age	39	55	5
Over state pension age	69	30	1
All	53	43	3
One family and no others			
All pensioner	22	63	15
Couple family households[2]	8	41	51
No children	9	46	45
With dependent child(ren)[3]	7	40	53
Non-dependent children only	7	27	65
Lone parent households	43	46	11
With dependent child(ren)[3]	48	47	5
Non-dependent children only	33	43	24
All	15	45	40
Other households			
With dependent child(ren)[3]	22	38	39
All student	44	30	26
All pensioners	44	43	13
Other	25	35	40
All	26	37	37
All households	27	44	29

1 Includes any company car or van if available for private use.
2 Includes both married and cohabiting couple family households.
3 A dependent child is a person in a household under 16 (whether or not in a family) or a person aged 16 to 18 who is a full-time student in a family with parent(s).

Source: Census 2001, Office for National Statistics; Census 2001, General Register Office for Scotland

in the south, were the most likely. The areas where households with cars accounted for more than 85 per cent of all households were mainly found in the south of England.

Not having access to a car increases the use of, and reliance on, public transport. The National Travel Survey found that in 1999–2001, people in households without a car made 20 per cent of their trips by bus, while people in households with one or more cars made only 3 per cent of their trips that way. The July 2002 Omnibus Survey found that certain

groups of people – women, the young, the old and those living in deprived areas – were more likely to be regular users of buses. Among people living in the 20 per cent most deprived wards, 43 per cent said they used local buses at least once a week, whereas among those living in the 20 per cent least deprived wards the proportion was only 16 per cent.

The main reason for not using the bus in 2002 among those who used it once a month or less, or never, was that it was 'easier by car' – seven out of ten of those questioned gave this

Map **12.11**

Households without a car or van, 2001

Percentages

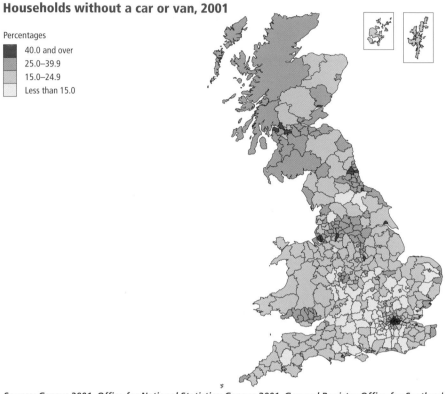

Source: Census 2001, Office for National Statistics; Census 2001, General Register Office for Scotland

Figure **12.12**

Reasons for infrequent bus use, July 2002[1]

Great Britain
Percentages

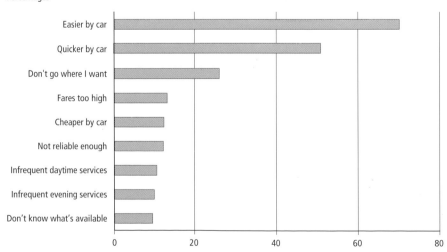

1 Reasons given by people who said they used buses once a month or less, including never.

Source: Omnibus Survey, Office for National Statistics

response (Figure 12.12). Over half said that it was 'quicker by car', while a quarter said buses 'don't go where I want'. By contrast, only 6 per cent said that there was 'no bus stop nearby', and 'infrequent day-time services' and 'infrequent night-time services' were each cited by around 10 per cent of respondents. (See Table 12.17 for more on opinions of buses.)

Travel to work and school

For people in work, the daily commute is probably the most important regular trip they make. Most trips to work are made by car or van, and have a major impact on the volume of traffic on the roads. Among the constituent parts of Great Britain, people in Wales were the most likely to travel to work in a car or van in 2001 at 70 per cent. People in London were the least likely, with only 36 per cent of people living in the capital using the car to get to work; most of the areas in Great Britain in which less than 50 per cent of people travelled to work by car or van were in London (Map 12.13).

The way in which people in different socio-economic groups travel to work also varies. Those in managerial and professional occupations (See Appendix, Part 1: NS-SeC) were both the most likely to drive themselves to work in a car or van (63 per cent did so) and the most likely to travel by train, underground or metro (11 per cent). In contrast, people in routine and semi-routine occupations were the least likely to drive themselves to work (48 per cent) and among the least likely to travel by train, underground or metro (3 per cent – only small employers and own account workers were less likely to use the train). People in routine and semi-routine occupations were the most likely to be driven to work in a car or van by someone else (9 per cent) or to walk (17 per cent).

The ways in which children travel to school have changed over the last ten years. In general, fewer are walking and more are travelling in cars (Table 12.14). For example, in 1989–91, 27 per cent of trips to school taken by 5 to 10 year olds were in a car or van; by 1999–2001 this figure had risen to 39 per cent. The average length of trips to school also increased over the same period – from 2.0 to 2.6 kilometres for children aged 5 to 10, and from 4.5 to 4.8 kilometres for those aged 11–16. Since trips to school usually take place at the same time each morning and evening, they have a major impact on levels of congestion in residential areas. At 8.50 am, the peak time for school traffic, an estimated 17 per cent of all cars on the road in urban areas are taking children to school.

The roads

The number of licensed vehicles on Great Britain's roads has increased dramatically since the middle of the last century. In 1961 there were just under 9 million licensed vehicles. By 1981 there were 19.3 million, and by 2002, 30.6 million. Private cars have accounted for an increasing proportion of this total – 59 per cent in 1961, 77 per cent in 1981, and 84 per cent in 2002. In contrast, the overall length of Great Britain's road network has increased more slowly: between 1962 and 2002 it grew by around a quarter, to 392,000 kilometres.

The increase in the number of motor vehicles, and the greater distances travelled by individuals, has led to large increases in the average daily flow of vehicles. Between 1981 and 1991 average traffic flows rose by 41 per cent. Growth slowed in the 1990s, but daily traffic

Map **12.13**

Travel to work by car or van, 2001

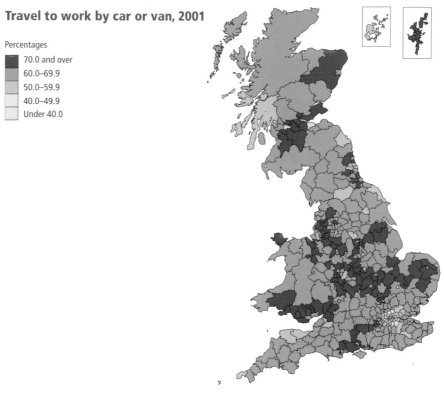

Percentages
- 70.0 and over
- 60.0–69.9
- 50.0–59.9
- 40.0–49.9
- Under 40.0

Source: Census 2001, Office for National Statistics; Census 2001, General Register Office for Scotland

Table **12.14**

Trips to and from school per child per year: by main mode, 1989–91 and 1999–2001

Great Britain   Percentages

	Age 5–10		Age 11–16	
	1989–91	1999–2001	1989–91	1999–2001
Walk	62	54	48	43
Bicycle	1	1	5	2
Car/van	27	39	14	18
Private bus	4	3	10	9
Local bus	4	3	20	23
Rail	-	-	1	2
Other	1	1	3	2
All modes	100	100	100	100
Average length (kilometres)	2.0	2.6	4.5	4.8

Source: National Travel Survey, Department for Transport

Table **12.15**

Average daily flow[1] of motor vehicles: by class of road[2]

Great Britain   Thousands

	1993	1997	2001	2002
Motorways[3]	57.5	65.8	71.5	72.9
Urban major roads	18.9	19.8	20.1	20.1
Trunk	31.8	33.6	36.1	36.0
Principal	17.4	18.2	18.3	18.4
Rural major roads	8.8	9.8	10.3	10.5
Trunk	14.2	15.9	17.1	17.6
Principal	6.5	7.1	7.4	7.5
All major roads	11.2	12.2	12.6	12.8
All minor roads	1.3	1.3	1.4	1.4
All roads	2.9	3.2	3.3	3.4

1 Flow at an average point on each class of road.
2 See Appendix, Part 12: Road traffic.
3 Includes motorways owned by local authorities.

Source: Department for Transport

Figure **12.16**

Bus travel[1]

Great Britain
Indices (1981/82=100)

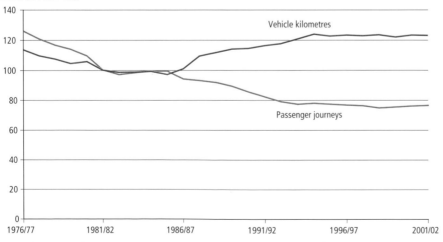

1 Local services only. Includes street-running trams and trolley buses but excludes modern 'supertram' systems.

Source: Department for Transport

flows still increased by 17 per cent in the ten years to 2002 (Table 12.15). On motorways specifically, which account for around a fifth of all road traffic, traffic flows increased by 27 per cent between 1993 and 2002.

One consequence of increased traffic can be lower average speeds, especially in urban areas. The Department for Transport found that average speeds at peak periods in England's large urban areas (not including London) fell by 0.5 miles per hour between 1999/2000 and 2002, to 21.2 miles per hour. Average off-peak speeds, 25.9 miles per hour in 2002, remained almost unchanged over the period.

While buses and coaches accounted for only 1 per cent of motor vehicle traffic in 2002, they remain an important form of public transport. Indeed, buses are the most widely used form of public transport. Over 4.3 billion journeys were made by local bus in Great Britain in 2001/02, more than twice the number of journeys made by rail (see Table 12.18). Travel in London accounts for about a third of all passenger journeys on local buses. After a long period of post-war decline, which continued into the 1990s, local bus use in terms of passenger journeys stabilised towards the end of the decade (Figure 12.16). The distance travelled by buses increased from a low point in the mid-1980s until the mid-1990s, before it too stabilised.

The Government aims to promote bus use in order to reduce traffic congestion and pollution, and has a target to increase bus use in England by 10 per cent from 2000 levels by 2010. One way to meet this target might be to persuade people to swap the car for the bus. However, opinions on the relative merits of buses and cars may act as something of a barrier to such a plan. In 2002 the British

Table **12.17**

Attitudes towards car and bus use, 2002

Great Britain   Percentages

	Agree or strongly agree	Neither agree nor disagree	Disagree or strongly disagree	Other[1]	All
For the sake of the environment, car users should pay higher taxes	14	12	70	4	100
Driving one's car is too convenient to give up for the sake of the environment	38	22	33	8	100
People should be allowed to use their car as much as they like, even if it causes damage to the environment	20	25	48	7	100
I would only travel somewhere by bus if I had no other way of getting there	63	5	29	3	100
Travelling by bus is mainly for people who can't afford anything better	15	13	70	2	100

1 Includes 'can't choose' and not answered.

Source: British Social Attitudes Survey, National Centre for Social Research

Social Attitudes survey found that nearly two thirds of people agreed with the statement, 'I would only travel somewhere by bus if I had no other way of getting there' (Table 12.17). Opinions on the possibility of using cars less were more divided – around a third of people disagreed with the statement, 'driving one's car is too convenient to give up for the sake of the environment', while more than one third agreed with this statement.

The railways

The number of journeys made on Great Britain's railways rose by 13 million between 2001/02 and 2002/03, to 2,072 million (Table 12.18). The number of passenger journeys were around 1,200 million in the early 1980s, but, apart from a period in the early 1990s, have generally increased since then, and grew by over a quarter between 1995/96 and 2002/03.

National rail and London Underground accounted for 47 and 45 per cent, respectively, of all rail journeys in 2002/03. Although the number of

Table **12.18**

Rail journeys[1]: by operator

Great Britain   Millions

	1981	1991/92	1995/96	2000/01	2001/02	2002/03
Main line/underground						
National rail	719	792	761	957	960	976
London Underground	541	751	784	970	953	942
Glasgow Underground	11	14	14	14	14	13
All national rail and underground	1,271	1,557	1,559	1,941	1,927	1,931
Light railways and trams						
Docklands Light Railway	.	8	14	38	41	46
Tyne and Wear Metro	14	41	36	33	33	37
Manchester Metrolink	.	.	13	17	18	19
Croydon Tramlink	.	.	.	15	18	19
South Yorkshire Supertram	.	.	5	11	11	12
West Midlands Metro	.	.	.	5	5	5
Blackpool Corporation Tram	6	5	5	4	5	5
All light railways and trams	20	54	73	124	132	141
All journeys by rail	1,291	1,611	1,632	2,065	2,059	2,072

1 Excludes railways and tramways operated principally as tourist attractions.

Source: Department for Transport

Table **12.19**

Opinion on rail services, 2002

Great Britain | | | | | Percentages

	Agree and strongly agree	Neither agree nor disagree	Disagree and strongly disagree	Other[1]	All
It is easy to find out what time trains run	59	13	21	8	100
Trains generally run often enough	40	15	35	10	100
Trains generally run on time	20	16	57	8	100
Train fares are fairly reasonable	16	11	65	8	100
Trains are a fast way to travel	59	15	18	7	100
It is difficult to find out the cheapest train fares	55	16	19	10	100
Trains have a good safety record	32	23	38	7	100

1 Includes 'can't choose' and not answered.

Source: British Social Attitudes Survey, National Centre for Social Research

Table **12.20**

International travel: by mode[1]

United Kingdom | | | | | | Millions

	1981	1991	1996	2000	2001	2002
Visits abroad by UK residents						
Air	11.4	20.4	27.9	41.4	43.0	44.0
Sea	7.7	10.4	10.7	9.6	9.7	10.0
Channel Tunnel	.	.	3.5	5.8	5.6	5.3
All visits abroad	19.0	30.8	42.1	56.8	58.3	59.4
Visits to the United Kingdom by overseas residents						
Air	6.9	11.6	16.3	17.8	16.1	17.1
Sea	4.6	5.5	6.2	4.3	4.0	4.4
Channel Tunnel	.	.	2.7	3.1	2.8	2.7
All visits to the United Kingdom	11.5	17.1	25.2	25.2	22.8	24.2

1 Mode of travel from, and into, the United Kingdom.

Source: International Passenger Survey, Office for National Statistics

passenger journeys on national rail rose between 2001/02 and 2002/03, the number made on London Underground fell, continuing a reduction in journey numbers in the previous year. Transport for London estimates that between 2002 and 2003 the number of people entering central London fell by around 5 per cent, due to factors such as a fall in overseas tourists and the temporary closure of the Central Line which occurred in the spring of 2003.

Light railways and trams, however, have become increasingly popular in recent years. Several new lines were built during the 1990s, and more are planned over the next decade. Passenger numbers continue to increase, rising by 14 per cent between 2000/01 and 2002/03.

In October 2002, Network Rail, a not-for-profit company took over as the national track authority, replacing Railtrack Plc which had been put into administration a year before. Some rail franchises were brought to an early end from 2001 onwards, replaced by others which offered improved performance.

In 2002, the British Social Attitudes survey found a wide range of views on the railways (Table 12.19). Sixty five per cent of people disagreed or strongly disagreed with the statement 'train fares are fairly reasonable', compared with only 16 per cent who agreed, while 55 per cent agreed that 'it is difficult to find out the cheapest train fares'. However, views on rail services were not entirely negative, with 59 per cent agreeing that 'trains are a fast way to travel' compared with 18 per cent who disagreed.

There is some evidence that opinions about the condition of the rail system may be worse than the reality. The survey found that 57 per cent of people disagreed with the statement that 'trains generally run on time', compared with 20 per cent who agreed. This is in contrast to the Strategic Rail Authorities' public performance measure, which found that 78 per cent of trains arrived on time in 2001/02, rising slightly to 79 per cent in 2002/03.

International travel

UK residents are making more trips abroad each year than ever before, over three times as many in 2002 as in 1981 (Table 12.20). The importance of air travel has grown consistently over the period. In 1981, it accounted for 60 per of all trips taken abroad, but by 2002, this figure had risen to 74 per cent. Conversely, the relative importance of sea travel has declined, from 41 per cent of all trips in 1981 to just 17 per cent in 2002.

The number of foreign visitors to the United Kingdom has also grown over the last two decades. The number of overseas visitors rose by 125 per cent between 1981 and 1998, to a high of 25.7 million. However, in subsequent years numbers fell back slightly, and in 2001 were severely affected by both the outbreak of foot-and-mouth disease and the terrorist attacks of September 11. Although visitor numbers increased in 2002, they did not reach the levels of earlier years.

International travel accounts for almost 90 per cent of all air travel in the United Kingdom in terms of terminal passengers (that is, not counting those in transit). The increase in the number of people travelling by plane over the last two decades is both a continuation, and a quickening, of a long term trend. Between 1952 and 2002, the number of terminal passengers at UK airports rose from 2.8 million to 188.8 million (Figure 12.21). The rate of increase was continuous but steady until the early 1970s, since when it has been much

Figure 12.21

Terminal passengers at civil airports[1]

United Kingdom
Millions

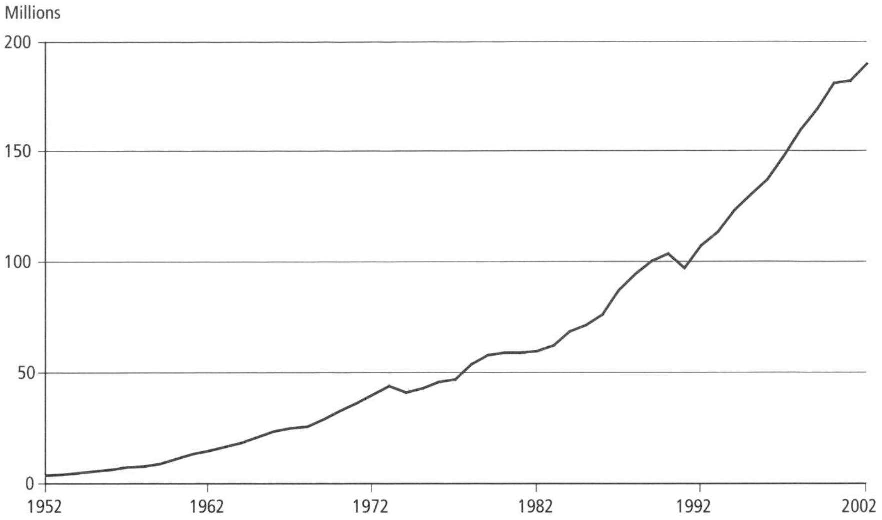

1 Domestic passengers are counted both at airport of departure and arrival.

Source: Department for Transport

steeper, but also more erratic, with the numbers of passengers falling in the recession year of 1974, and in 1991, the year of the Gulf war, before continuing upward. There was also a marked flattening of the upward trend in 2001 (again the result of foot-and-mouth and September 11) but numbers resumed their steep rise in 2002.

The Department for Transport forecasts that demand for air travel is set to continue well into the 21st century. Mid-range estimates suggest that between 2005 and 2020, the number of terminal passengers at UK airports will grow from 229 million to 401 million. The growth in international passengers is forecast to outstrip that in domestic, with growth of nearly 80 per cent, compared with nearly 70 per cent.

Table **12.22**

Passenger death rates[1]: by mode of transport

Great Britain — Rate per billion passenger kilometres

	1993	1997	2001	2002
Motorcycle	106.0	119.0	112.3	111.3
Walk	70.1	57.6	47.7	44.8
Bicycle	46.5	44.9	32.7	29.5
Car	3.2	3.1	2.9	2.8
Van	1.6	1.0	0.9	1.0
Bus or coach	0.7	0.3	0.2	0.4
Rail[2]	0.4	0.5	0.2	0.3
Water[3]	0.0	0.0	0.4	0.0
Air[3]	0.0	0.0	0.0	0.0

1 See Appendix, Part 12: Passenger death rates.
2 Financial years. Includes train accidents and accidents occurring through movement of railway vehicles.
3 Data are for United Kingdom.

Source: Department for Transport

Figure **12.23**

Average number of people killed or seriously injured in road accidents on weekdays: by road user type and time of day[1], 2002

Great Britain
Number per day

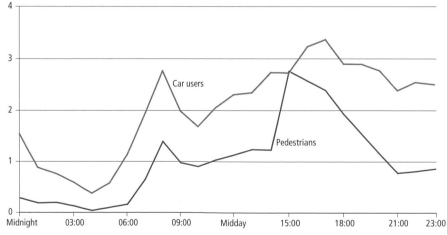

1 For each hour beginning at time shown.

Source: Department for Transport

Transport safety

The safety levels of most major forms of transport are much improved over the levels of the early 1980s, and improvements in most areas have continued since 1993 (Table 12.22). Despite improvements in road safety, other forms of transport, such as rail, air and sea continue to have much lower death rates from accidents. Motorcycling, walking and cycling are by some margin the most dangerous forms of transport. Death rates among motorcyclists were 40 times greater than those among car users in 2002.

Almost all passenger deaths in transport accidents in Great Britain occur on the roads. In 2002 there were a total of 3,431 deaths of road users in accidents, compared with an annual average figure of 3,578 in 1994–98, and 5,846 in 1981. In 2002, 23 per cent of those killed were pedestrians, 4 per cent pedal cyclists, 18 per cent riders or passengers of two-wheeled motor vehicles, and 51 per cent occupants of cars. Occupants of buses, coaches and goods vehicles accounted for the remaining 4 per cent of deaths.

The number of pedestrians killed each year has fallen steadily since the mid-1990s, and the 2002 figure of 775 was 23 per cent lower than the yearly average for the period 1994–98. Conversely, the number of car users killed in 2002 was little changed from the annual average in 1994–98, 1,747 compared with 1,762, although this figure fell to a low of 1,665 in 2000.

A total of 27,800 people were killed or seriously injured on Great Britain's roads on weekdays during 2002, or an average of 107 people each day. The incidence of people being killed or seriously injured in road accidents is not uniform throughout the day, however. Among pedestrians and car users most casualties occur in the morning and evening 'rush hours', with the highest number coming during the extended evening period (Figure 12.23). The first peak occurs in the hour beginning at 08: 00: 719 car users and 362 pedestrians were killed or seriously injured during this hour in 2002. The number of pedestrians killed or seriously injured is highest during the hour starting at 15: 00 (during which many schools finish for the day), and there were 718 casualties during this hour in 2002. The number of car users killed or seriously injured reaches its highest in the hour starting at 17:00 (876 people in 2002), or over three a day on average.

The United Kingdom has a good record for road safety compared with most other EU countries. In 2001 it had the lowest road death rate in the EU, at 6.1 per 100,000 population (Figure 12.24). The highest road death rate in the EU was in Portugal, at 21.0 per 100,000 population (in 2000). The UK rate was also substantially lower than those for other industrialised nations such as Japan (7.9 per 100,000 population), Australia (9.0) and the United States (14.8).

The United Kingdom also has a relatively good record in terms of overall road accidents involving children. In 2001 the UK death rate for children aged 0 to 14, at 1.7 per 100,000 of population, was the fourth lowest in the EU. Sweden had the lowest rate, at 1.1 per 100,000 population, while in France the rate was 2.7 and in Ireland it was 3.2. However, in terms of child pedestrian deaths the UK rate of 0.9 per 100,000 population in 2001 was above that of many EU countries, including the Netherlands (0.4), France (0.5) and Germany (0.6).

Figure 12.24

Road deaths: EU comparison, 2001[1]

Rate per 100,000 population

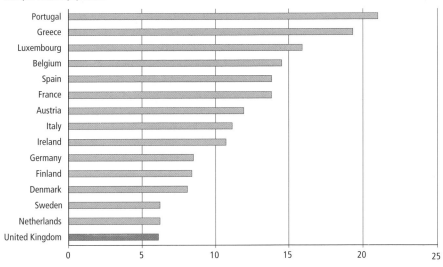

1 Data for Portugal, Greece and Italy are for 2000.

Source: Department for Transport

Chapter 13 Lifestyles and Social Participation

Everyday tasks

- Women spent an average 3 hours 35 minutes a day doing household tasks (cooking and washing up, housework, and washing and ironing), around 1 hour 30 minutes longer than men. (Page 194)

Leisure activities

- In 2002 around 85 per cent of men and women watched television every day. The most popular type of programme across age groups was the news. (Table 13.5)

e-Society and communications

- Three quarters of all adults in the United Kingdom owned or used a mobile phone in May 2003. (Page 203)

- Household Internet access was five times greater in 2003 than in 1998; from 9 per cent of households in the UK accessing the Internet in April to June 1998 to 47 per cent in April to June 2003. (Page 204)

Holidays and tourism

- Nearly 40 million holidays were taken abroad in 2002. The most popular destination continued to be Spain. (Page 206)

Social participation

- Two thirds of people enjoyed living in their neighbourhood and two fifths felt they could trust their neighbours. (Table 13.23)

Figure **13.1**

Time spent on main activities by full-time workers[1], 2000–01

United Kingdom
Hours per day

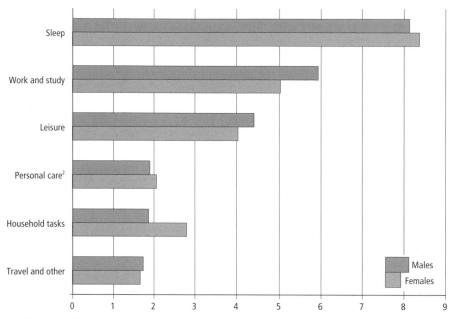

1 Adults aged 16 and over.
2 Eating, washing and dressing.

Source: UK 2000 Time Use Survey, Office for National Statistics

Figure **13.2**

Time spent on household tasks: by age and sex, 2000–01

United Kingdom
Hours per day

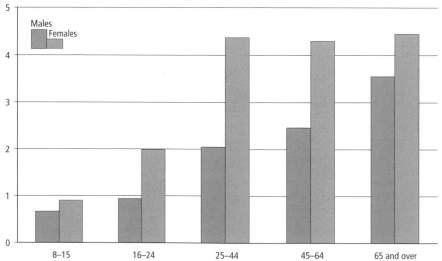

Source: UK 2000 Time Use Survey, Office for National Statistics

The ways in which people spend their time outside work have altered considerably over the past few decades. Changes in working patterns, technological advances and income all influence the time people spend on different activities.

Everyday tasks

Details of what people spend their time doing each day were recorded in the UK 2000 Time Use Survey. Respondents were asked to keep a detailed diary of how they spent their time on one day during the week and on one day at the weekend. The survey found that there were substantial differences between men and women and different age groups in the amount of time spent on various activities. Overall, men spent more time in paid employment than women – an average of 3 hours 48 minutes a day for all men, compared with just over 2 hours a day for all women. Conversely men spent less time than women doing household tasks (cooking and washing up, housework, and washing and ironing) – an average of 2 hours a day compared with 3 hours and 35 minutes for women. The differences between men and women were smaller for those in full-time work, with men spending nearly an hour a day more than women in paid work (including study), and women spending nearly an hour a day more than men on household tasks (Figure 13.1). Men working full time had an average 23 minutes a day more 'leisure time' than women in full-time work.

Women aged 25 and over spent more than 4 hours a day on household tasks, compared with 2 hours a day spent by women aged between 16 and 24, and less than 1 hour a day by girls aged 8 to 15 (Figure 13.2). The amount of time spent by men on household tasks increased more gradually with age. Men aged 25 to 44 spent just over 2 hours a day on household tasks. This rose to just over 3 hours 30 minutes a day for men aged 65 and over. Males aged between 8 and 24 spent less than 1 hour a day on household tasks.

There are traditional patterns and divisions of labour within the household. When people living in couple households were asked who does various household tasks, 82 per cent of women said they usually or always did the laundry, compared with 8 per cent of men (Table 13.3). Three quarters of men agreed that this task was usually or always carried out by their partner or spouse. Eight in ten of men said that they usually or always looked after small repairs to the home, compared with one in ten women. Shopping for groceries was the household task most often done together or done equally by men and women. However, only one in ten men said they usually or always did the grocery shopping by themselves, compared with half of women. Women were more likely than men to look after sick family members (62 per cent usually or always did so, compared with 6 per cent of men), although 46 per cent of men and 35 per cent of women also said that this activity was about equal or done together.

Table 13.3

Division of household tasks[1]: by sex, 2002

Great Britain   Percentages

	Always me	Usually me	About equal or both together	Usually spouse or partner	Always spouse or partner	Done by a third person	Total
Males							
Does the laundry	3	5	16	37	38	2	100
Makes small repairs around the home	36	44	12	3	2	3	100
Looks after sick family members	2	4	46	31	15	2	100
Shops for groceries	3	6	48	28	14	1	100
Does the household cleaning	2	5	32	38	17	5	100
Prepares the meals	3	11	30	37	18	1	100
Females							
Does the laundry	52	29	14	2	1	1	100
Makes small repairs around the home	3	7	21	47	18	4	100
Looks after sick family members	29	33	35	1	1	1	100
Shops for groceries	22	27	44	5	2	1	100
Does the household cleaning	31	33	28	3	1	4	100
Prepares the meals	29	33	29	7	2	1	100

1 Based on people either married or living as married to the question, 'In your household who does the following things?'

Source: British Social Attitudes Survey, National Centre for Social Research

Table **13.4**

Time spent on selected free time activities of full-time workers[1], 2000–01

United Kingdom

Hours and minutes per day

	Males		Females	
	Weekday	Weekend	Weekday	Weekend
TV, video and radio	2:02	2:52	1:39	2:13
Socialising	0:32	1:19	0:44	1:30
Games and hobbies	0:18	0:29	0:09	0:16
Reading	0:15	0:24	0:16	0:27
Sports and exercise	0:11	0:26	0:09	0:15
Attending entertainment and cultural events	0:03	0:15	0:05	0:12

1 Adults aged 16 and over.

Source: UK 2000 Time Use Survey, Office for National Statistics

Table **13.5**

Interest in television programme type[1]: by age, 2002

Great Britain

Percentages

	16–24	25–64	65 and over	All aged 16 and over
News	83	94	97	93
Factual	69	87	84	84
Drama	75	80	87	81
Entertainment	89	76	70	77
Regional	50	72	85	71
Current affairs	57	68	79	68
Educational	45	61	52	57
Sports	51	54	53	53
Arts	30	33	43	35
Children's	41	33	17	31
Religious	11	19	51	24

1 The data refer to those who said they were 'very' or 'fairly' interested in each type of programme.

Source: Independent Television Commission

Leisure activities

All men and women who worked full time spent most of their free time watching television or videos or listening to the radio (Table 13.4). Socialising was the next most common free time activity for both sexes. Men spent more time than women watching television or listening to the radio, and on games and hobbies. They also spent more time on a day at the weekend on sports than did the women. Women spent an hour and a half of their free time on a day at the weekend on socialising. They spent less time on games and hobbies or sports, preferring to read.

The Public's View survey showed that around 85 per cent of men and women watched television every day in 2002. The news was popular with both men and women, and across all adult age groups, with 93 per cent of people surveyed being interested in this type of programme (Table 13.5). For 16 to 24 year olds, entertainment programmes were the next most popular, while the 25 to 64 age group preferred factual programmes. Interest in current affairs, regional, arts and religious programmes increased with age, attracting the highest interest among the 65 and over age group. Drama programmes were popular across all age groups. Apart from the news, men and women were interested in different types of programme. Men were more interested than women in watching factual programmes (89 per cent compared with 79 per cent), current affairs (75 per cent compared with 62 per cent) and sports (74 per cent compared with 34 per cent). Women were more interested in watching drama (88 per cent compared with 73 per cent) and children's programmes (36 per cent and 25 per cent, respectively).

Radio continues to be popular, with over 90 per cent of the total adult population tuning in at least once a week in spring 2002. Overall, men listened to the radio for a greater number of hours than women (Table 13.6). Radio 2 was the most popular station among both men and women, followed by Radio 4 and BBC local radio. Men spent a greater proportion of their listening time than that of women tuned in to Radio Five Live, while women were more likely than men to listen to Radio 4. The BBC attracted just over half the audience share, while commercial radio stations together had just under half. According to RAJAR (Radio Joint Audience Research Limited) 14 per cent of adults in the United Kingdom said they had listened to the radio online between 23 June and 14 September 2003, compared to 10 per cent for the same period two years earlier. Online listening is most popular among the younger age groups, men and higher socio-economic groups. Regular Internet users are more than twice as likely as the average adult to listen online.

Listening to music is another popular leisure activity. In 2002, record companies sold over 225 million albums in the United Kingdom. Even though sales of LPs and cassettes decreased, CD sales continued to increase, with 3 million more CDs sold in 2002 than in the previous year. Fifty seven per cent of people aged 12 to 74 purchased at least one album in 2002, whereas 16 per cent purchased at least one single. Singles were more popular with teenagers than with any other age group. Thirty eight per cent of 12 to 19 year olds bought a single in 2002, compared with 15 to 18 per cent of those aged 20 to 49, and 5 per cent of those aged 60 to 74 (Figure 13.7 –

see overleaf). Album sales were more uniform among people aged between 12 and 49. The Audio Visual Trak Survey also indicated that women spent more on singles and albums in 2002 than they

had done in the preceding three years; for the first time in four years they accounted for a higher proportion of spending on singles than men (by 2 per cent).

Table **13.6**

Share of radio listening: by station, Quarter 1 2003[1]

United Kingdom		Percentages
	Males	Females
BBC		
BBC Radio	19	7
BBC Radio 2	16	15
BBC Radio 3	1	1
BBC Radio 4	10	14
BBC Radio Five Live	7	3
BBC World Service	1	1
BBC local/regional	11	13
All BBC	55	52
Commercial		
Classic FM	4	5
talkSPORT (Talk radio)	2	1
Virgin radio (AM only)	2	1
Digital radio stations[2]	1	1
All national commercial	9	7
All local commercial	35	39
All commercial	44	46
Other listening[3]	2	2
All radio stations (=100%) (hours listened)	570,769	522,762

1 Adults aged 15 and over. Quarter fieldwork carried out between 6 January and 23 March.
2 Only accessed via a DAB digital radio, digital television or digital radio via the Internet.
3 Other listening includes non-subscribers to RAJAR, including student/hospital stations, foreign and pirate stations.
Source: RAJAR/RSL

Figure **13.7**

Music sales: by age[1], 2002

United Kingdom
Percentages

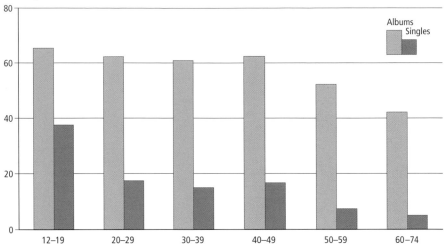

1 Proportion of the population that made at least one album or single purchase during 2002.

Source: British Phonographic Industry/TNS

Figure **13.8**

VHS and DVD video rental shares: by genre, 2002

United Kingdom
Percentages

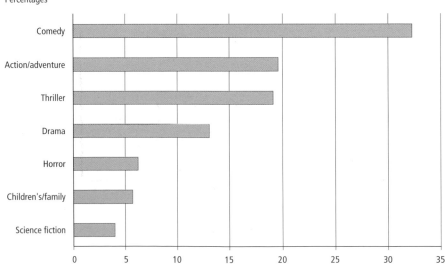

Source: British Video Association

Digital Versatile Disc (DVD), which can play music, video and games, was launched in the United Kingdom in April 1998. Since then, hardware and software sales have increased rapidly. According to the British Video Association, DVD is the fastest selling consumer electronics format of all time, selling faster than VHS cassette recorders and audio CD players did at the same stage of their launch. During 2002, 169 million VHS and DVD videos were sold. Sales of DVDs more than doubled between 2001 and 2002, while sales of VHS cassettes decreased by 15 per cent. Feature films accounted for almost 70 per cent of videos and DVDs sold. *The Lord of the Rings: the Fellowship of the Rings* and *Harry Potter and the Philosopher's Stone* were the top retail titles in the United Kingdom in 2002 for both VHS video and DVD. Comedy, drama and action/adventure were the most popular categories of film, accounting for over half of film sales. Comedy, thriller and action/adventure were the three most popular categories of video rentals, accounting for 71 per cent of rentals (Figure 13.8). Over 174 million videos and DVDs were rented in 2002, approximately eight per household, but 10 million lower than in 2001.

Attendance at many cultural events has remained relatively stable in recent years (Table 13.9). Nearly two thirds of people aged 15 and over said they attended the cinema these days, while fewer than one in ten said they attended the ballet, opera or contemporary dance. Some other cultural events like going to the theatre, art galleries and exhibitions have also been consistently popular. Attendance at museums and galleries increased between 2000/01 and 2002/03.

Young people aged 15 to 24 are the most likely age group to go to the cinema (Figure 13.10). In 2002, 50 per cent of this age group reported that they went to the cinema once a month or more in Great Britain, compared with 17 per cent of those aged 35 and over. There has also been a growth in cinema attendance among children. In 2002, over a third of 7 to 14 year olds went to the cinema at least once a month. Of these, almost a tenth were accompanied by a grandparent, and nearly two thirds had been with a friend their own age. Over half of 15 to 34 year olds and almost three quarters of those aged 35 and over who went to the cinema once a month or more went with their partner or spouse. There were an estimated 176 million cinema admissions in the United Kingdom in 2002, the second highest in the EU after France, with 185 million admissions. Ireland had the highest admissions rate in the EU at 4.2 per head in 2001, compared with 2.6 per head in the United Kingdom and 5.4 per head in the United States.

The National Readership Survey estimated that 43 per cent of women and 57 per cent of men aged 15 and over in Great Britain read a national morning newspaper in 2002–2003 . The *Sun*, *Daily Mirror* and the *Daily Mail* are the most commonly read newspapers, each read by more than 10 per cent of men and women. *The Telegraph* was the most commonly read broadsheet daily newspaper, read by 5 per cent of adults.

The *Daily Mail* and *The Times* are the only daily national newspapers that had a higher readership in 2003 than they did 20 years ago, whereas the *Daily Express'* and *Daily Mirror'*s readership more than halved during the same period.

Table **13.9**

Attendance at cultural events[1]

Great Britain						Percentages
	1986/87	1996/97	1998/99	2000/01	2001/02	2002/03
Cinema	31	54	57	55	57	61
Plays	23	24	22	23	24	24
Art galleries/exhibitions	21	22	21	21	22	24
Classical music	12	12	11	12	12	13
Ballet	6	7	6	6	6	7
Opera	5	7	6	6	6	7
Contemporary dance	4	4	4	4	5	5

1 Percentage of resident population aged 15 and over attending 'these days'. See Appendix, Part 13: Cultural events.

Source: Target Group Index, BMRB International; Cinema Advertising Association

Figure **13.10**

Cinema attendance[1]: by age

Great Britain
Percentages

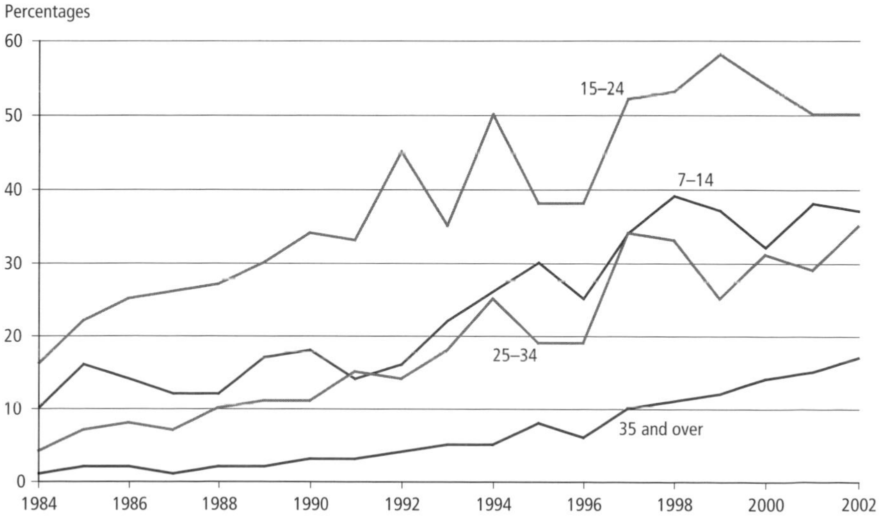

1 Respondents who said that they attend the cinema once a month or more.

Source: Cinema Advertising Association/Cinema and Video Industry Audience Research

Figure **13.11**

Reading preferences: by sex[1], 2001

England
Percentages

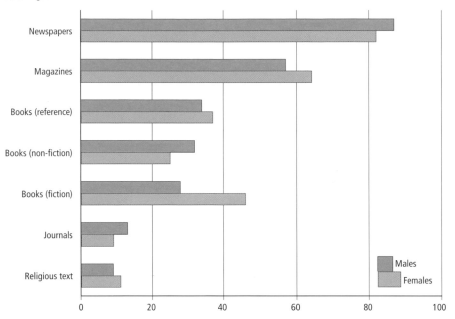

1 Adults aged 16 and over. Respondents were asked what they had read in the last seven days. More
than one response could be given.

Source: National Reading Campaign; Omnibus Survey, Office for National Statistics

Table **13.12**

Reasons for visiting a library: by age and activity, 2000[1]

United Kingdom   Percentages

	16–24	25–44	45–64	65 and over	All adults
Borrow or return book(s)	50	70	77	86	74
Browse	30	30	31	27	30
Seek information	33	22	23	17	23
Read newspaper or magazine	11	11	14	17	14
Study or work	26	8	5	3	8
Borrow or return video(s)	8	15	7	3	8
Borrow or return cassette(s)	3	7	7	5	7
Use photocopier	8	6	6	5	6
Borrow or return CD(s)	8	8	4	1	5
See exhibition or event	1	2	3	3	3
Other reason	16	13	9	6	8

1 Percentages of those who visited a library. Percentages do not add up to 100 per cent as
respondents could give more than one answer.

Source: Policy Studies Institute

In 2001, the National Reading Campaign Survey indicated that over 80 per cent of men and women had read newspapers in the last seven days while 61 per cent said they had read magazines (Figure 13.11). Just under half of women said they had read fiction in the last seven days compared to just over a quarter of men. Around two thirds of men and women had read a book because the subject matter interested them. This was the most common reason for wanting to read a book, followed by wanting to obtain information. Women were more likely to act on the recommendations of a friend (48 per cent compared with 30 per cent of men) and were more likely to read a book to relax (45 per cent compared with 29 per cent).

In Great Britain more than 34 million people (58 per cent of the population) were registered members of their local library and, of these, around 20 per cent borrow at least once a week. Many libraries have collections of CDs, records, audio- and video-cassettes, and DVDs for loan to the public. Reasons for visiting the library vary with age (Table 13.12). In the United Kingdom, 50 per cent of 16 to 24 year olds who visited a library said they used a library to borrow or return books in 2000, compared with 86 per cent of people aged 65 or over. A third of 16 to 24 year olds used the library to seek information and over a quarter went to the library to study. The 25 to 44 age group were the largest borrowers of videos.

e-Society and communications

The impact of technology on everyday life is growing. Ownership of sophisticated media products affects how people behave, communicate, obtain information and interact. Two areas that are having major impacts on our lives are ownership of mobile phones and access to the Internet. Household ownership of mobile phones in the United Kingdom more than quadrupled between 1996/97 and 2002/03 to 70 per cent, while household Internet access also increased from 10 per cent in 1998/99 to 45 per cent in 2002/03 (Figure 13.13) Ownership of other technological goods also continued to increase. By 2002/03, more than four in five households had a CD player and over half of all households had a home computer. In 2002/03, 31 per cent of households had a DVD player. This was the first time this information was recorded on the Expenditure and Food Survey.

According to the Oftel Residential Survey, 75 per cent of all adults in the United Kingdom owned or used a mobile phone in May 2003. Twenty one per cent used their mobile as their main method of telephony, with 8 per cent of homes only having a mobile, and no fixed line phone.

Ownership of mobile phones varied with age (Figure 13.14). Nearly 90 per cent of people between the ages of 15 and 34 owned or used a mobile phone in February 2003. This proportion declined with age; less than a quarter of those aged 75 and over owned or used a mobile phone. However in the two years between 2001 and 2003, the largest increases occurred among the older age groups, with the proportion of people aged 75 and over with a mobile phone nearly doubling.

According to the Young People and ICT Survey carried out in England for the Department for Education and Skills in September and October 2002, 41 per cent of girls and 30 per cent of boys aged 5 to 18, and in full-time education, owned a mobile phone. Again, ownership increased with age: 12 per

Figure **13.13**

Households with selected durable goods[1]
United Kingdom
Percentages

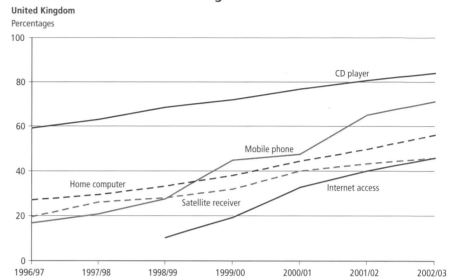

1 Based on weighted data. Data from 1998/99 onwards include children's expenditure.
Source: Family Expenditure Survey and Expenditure and Food Survey, Office for National Statistics

Figure **13.14**

Adult mobile phone ownership or use: by age, 2001 and 2003[1]
United Kingdom
Percentages

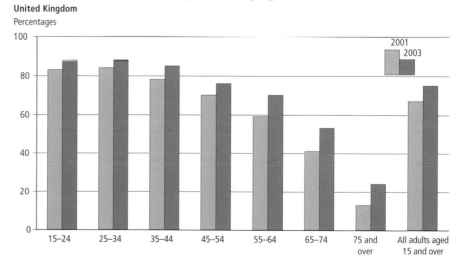

1 At February.
Source: Oftel

Table **13.15**

Households with Internet access: by household type

United Kingdom		Percentages
	1998/99	2002/03
One person		
Over state pension age	1	7
Under state pension age	8	36
Couple without children		
Over state pension age	2	21
Under state pension age	14	55
All other adults without children	16	57
Lone parent	5	35
Couple with children	16	69
All other adults with children	20	52

Source: Family Expenditure Survey and Expenditure and Food Survey, Office for National Statistics

Table **13.16**

Types of goods and services bought over the Internet[1], July 2003

Great Britain			Percentages
	Males	Females	All
Travel, accommodation or holidays	62	55	59
Tickets for events	41	38	39
Books or magazines/e-learning/ training material	41	35	38
Music or CDs	40	31	36
Videos or DVDs	36	25	31
Clothes or sports goods	25	38	31
Household goods	21	24	22
Computer software	29	..	22
Food or groceries	16	25	20
Insurance	24	..	20
Electronic equipment	24	..	20
Computer hardware	26	..	18

1 *Goods and services bought in the 12 months prior to interview for personal and private use. Adults aged 16 and over.*

Source: Omnibus Survey, Office for National Statistics

cent of children aged 7 to 11 (Key Stage 2) owned a mobile phone compared with 52 per cent aged 11 to 14 (Key Stage 3) and nearly 70 per cent of children aged 14 to 18 (Key Stage 4 and Post-16).

Another factor which affects mobile phone ownership is income. Ownership within households in the middle income bracket (£17,500 to £30,000 a year) has increased the most in the last few years and in February 2003 were as likely as people in households in the high income bracket (over £30,000 a year) to own a mobile phone (88 per cent and 90 per cent, respectively). Those with lower incomes (less than £17,500) are much less likely to own or use a mobile phone (62 per cent in February 2003).

Over the period April to June 2003, an estimated 11.7 million households (47 per cent of all households) in the United Kingdom could access the Internet from home. Internet access was five times greater than the same quarter in 1998.

In July 2003, 56 per cent of adults in Great Britain had used the Internet in the previous three months: 59 per cent of men and 52 per cent of women. This percentage decreased steadily with age, with 85 per cent of those aged 16 to 24 having used the Internet compared with 39 per cent of those aged 55 to 64. A greater proportion of men than women used the Internet daily. Nearly half of men accessing the Internet did so every day, or almost every day, compared with 35 per cent of women.

Internet access is highest among couple with children households (Table 13.15) The proportion of these households with access to the Internet more than quadrupled in the four years to 2002/03 to 69 per cent. Households containing only people over state pension age are the least likely to have Internet access (only 7 per cent of one adult retired households and 21 per cent of retired couple households).

Household access to the Internet continues to vary across the United Kingdom. The South East, London and the East had the highest proportions of households with access, at just over half of all households in these areas in 2002/03. Wales and Northern Ireland had the lowest proportions, with around two fifths of households in these areas with Internet access.

In July 2003, 83 per cent of adults in Great Britain who had used the Internet in the three months prior to interview used it for email. Similarly 83 per cent said they had used the Internet to search for information about goods and services and 72 per cent to search for information about travel and accommodation. Half of all adults who had used the Internet in the 12 months prior to interview had accessed Government and public authority websites.

Internet shopping is becoming increasingly popular. In July 2003, over half of all adults who had bought or ordered over the Internet in the 12 months prior to interview had used it to buy or order tickets, goods or services. The types of goods and services bought or ordered over the Internet varied between men and women (Table 13.16). In general a higher proportion of men than women used the Internet to purchase goods or services associated with leisure, such as travel, accommodation or holidays, music or CDs, or videos or DVDs. Conversely a higher proportion of women than men used the Internet to purchase clothing or sports goods, and food and groceries.

In July 2003, 28 per cent of adults who had used the Internet in the 12 months prior to interview said that they had not experienced security problems as a result of using the Internet. Forty four per cent stated that they had received too many junk emails and considered this a security problem; 28 per cent had had a computer virus, while 16 per cent had received offensive emails. More men than women reported having taken specific security precautions in the three months prior to interview (Figure 13.17). Over two fifths of men, compared with a third of women, had installed a virus-checking program on a computer and similar proportions had updated virus-checking programs in the period. The majority of Internet users did not use a password to protect their systems; only two fifths of respondents reported the use of a password.

Figure **13.17**

Security precautions taken by adults who have used the Internet[1], July 2003

Great Britain
Percentages

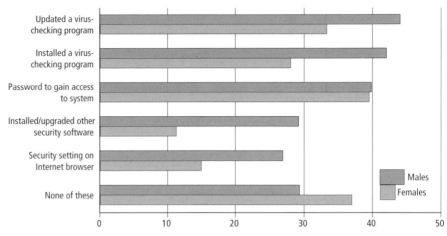

1 In the three months prior to interview. Adults aged 16 and over.

Source: Omnibus Survey, Office for National Statistics

Internet security was one of the reasons given by 12 per cent of adults who had never used the Internet. However, this was not one of the main reasons. Fifty seven per cent said they did not want to use, or had no need for or no interest, in the Internet, 44 per cent had no Internet connection and 39 per cent felt they lacked the knowledge or confidence to use it. (Respondents were able to give more than one reason to why they had not accessed the Internet.)

Ownership and use of technological equipment varies with age. Use of computers and the Internet is high among children up to the age of 18. In autumn 2002, 98 per cent of young people aged 5 to 18 used computers at home, at school or elsewhere – with 22 per cent saying they used computers at school but not at home. For children aged between 11 and 18, the main activities undertaken on a computer at home were school or college work (90 per cent), playing games (70 per cent), and using the Internet (67 per cent) (Figure 13.18). For younger children, 40 per cent of those aged between 7 and 11 who used a computer at home said they did their homework on the computer.

Among parents of 3 to 4 year olds, 64 per cent had a computer at home, and 84 per cent of these parents said that their child used a computer at home.

Holidays and tourism

There are more than 6,400 visitor attractions in the United Kingdom, including leisure and theme parks, museums and art galleries, historic houses and castles, and gardens. Visits to all attractions increased by 15 per cent between 1989 and 2002. Visits to farms and gardens increased the most around 80 and 40 per cent respectively (Figure 13.19). Visits to farms were at the highest level for more than ten years in 2002, showing a recovery from the adverse effects of foot-and-mouth disease in 2001. Visitors to country parks and museums and art galleries increased over the same period by 25 per cent and 20 per cent, respectively. Historic properties and wildlife attractions and zoos attracted around the same number of visitors in 2002 as in 1989.

Among the top tourist attractions in 2002 were Blackpool Pleasure Beach, with over 6 million visitors, and the National Gallery and the British Museum, attracting over 4 million visitors each. Tate Modern, the London Eye (both opened in London in 2000), and the Eden Project in Cornwall (opened in 2001), have established themselves among the country's leading tourist attractions.

In 2002, 102 million trips of one night or more were taken by UK residents within the United Kingdom. This was similar to the level in 2001 and around 4 million lower than in 2000. The South West of England and the Heart of England were the two most popular destinations for trips in 2002, between them accounting for over a quarter of holidays taken (Map 13.20). Scotland was the third most popular domestic destination. Nearly 40 million holidays were taken abroad in 2002. The most popular destinations in 2002 continued to be Spain, accounting for 29 per cent of holidays taken abroad, followed by France at 19 per cent. Outside Europe, the United States was the most popular destination at 5 per cent of holidays abroad.

Figure **13.18**

Activities undertaken on the computer at home by 11–18 year-olds[1], autumn 2002

England
Percentages

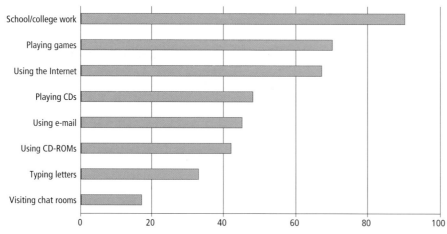

1 More than one reason could be given.

Source: Young people and ICT, Department for Education and Skills

Figure **13.19**

Visits to selected tourist attractions

United Kingdom
Indices (1989 = 100)

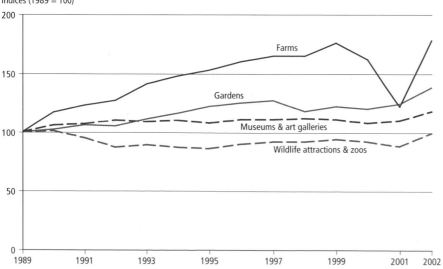

Source: National Tourist Boards

Sporting activities

Sporting involvement can often take the form of a social activity, with many individuals joining teams or clubs to participate in sport. Table 13.21 shows the percentage of people in each age group who had taken part in some kind of sport or physical activity in the four weeks prior to interview during 2000–01. Participation was very high (95 per cent) among the school-age group of 8 to 15 year olds, but fell as people got older, to around 30 per cent of people aged 65 and over. Nearly half of those surveyed had not participated in any form of sport.

Over the past ten years the proportion of boys and girls in England regularly participating in sports activities outside of lessons during term time has stayed constant at around 85 per cent. Swimming and cycling were the most common sporting activities for children in 2002, with around half of those aged 6 to 16 participating in these activities at least ten times in the year leading up to the survey (Table 13.22 – see overleaf). Swimming was the most common activity for girls. It was also popular with boys, although their favourite activity was playing football. The preferences of boys and girls have changed little since 1994. Forty three per cent of all young people in England spent between 1 and 5 hours doing sports and exercise outside of lessons in 2002, compared with 36 per cent in 1999. The proportion of children spending more than 10 hours a week on sports outside of lesson decreased from 24 per cent in 1999 to 19 per cent in 2002.

Social participation

People participate in communities in different ways. Policy makers consider high levels of participation in the community

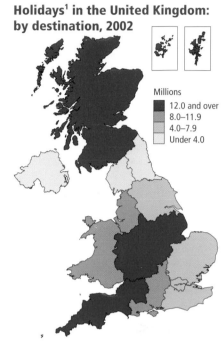

Map **13.20**

Holidays[1] in the United Kingdom: by destination, 2002

Millions
- 12.0 and over
- 8.0–11.9
- 4.0–7.9
- Under 4.0

1 A visit of one or more nights made for holiday purposes by UK residents. Business trips and visits to friends and relatives are excluded.
Source: National Tourist Boards

Figure **13.21**

Participation[1] in a sport or physical activity: by age, 2000–01
United Kingdom
Percentages

1 Percentage reporting participation in the four weeks prior to interview.
Source: UK 2000 Time Use Survey, Office for National Statistics

Table **13.22**

Participation in selected sports by young people outside lessons[1]: by sex, 2002

England   Percentages

	Males	Females
Football	57	18
Cycling	53	45
Swimming, diving, lifesaving	48	55
Tennis	25	20
Roller skating/blading, skate boarding	25	22
Cricket	22	5
Walking: walks lasting more than 1 hour, hiking	21	23
Athletics: track or field	13	13
Cross country, jogging, road running	12	10
Aerobics, keep fit	5	19

1 Those aged 6 to 16 participating at least 10 times in the 12 months leading up to the survey.

Source: Sports England/MORI

Table **13.23**

Attitudes to neighbourhoods: by length of residence, 2001

England & Wales   Percentages

	Under 1 year	1–4 years	5–9 years	10–29 years	30 or more years	All
Definitely enjoyed living in neighbourhood	57	65	67	68	71	67
Thought neighbours definitely looked out for each other	36	40	43	44	45	43
Thought 'many' people in neighbourhood could be trusted	31	31	37	41	48	40
Felt 'very safe' walking alone in neighbourhood after dark	35	38	38	35	25	34
Knew 'many' people in neighbourhood	6	13	25	35	46	30
Believed it 'very likely' that wallet/ purse would be returned intact	9	9	11	11	11	10

Source: Citizenship Survey, Home Office

to be good indicators of healthy and well-functioning communities. Civic participation can include signing a petition, contacting a local councillor or a Member of Parliament, or attending a public meeting or rally. The Home Office Citizenship Survey in 2001 found that in the 12 months prior to interview 3 per cent of people in England and Wales were involved in civic participation at least once a month. The survey also examined levels of informal volunteering and found that a third of people said that they had provided unpaid help to people outside their family at least once a month. A quarter of people had provided unpaid help through groups, clubs or organisations, such as environmental groups, at least once a month in the 12 months prior to the interview.

The Citizenship Survey also examined people's perceptions of their neighbourhood. Two thirds of people in England and Wales said that they definitely enjoyed living in their neighbourhood (Table 13.23). The longer people lived in a neighbourhood, the more likely they were to say that they enjoyed living there. Fifty seven per cent of respondents who had lived in a place for less than one year said that they definitely enjoyed living there. The percentage increased to 65 per cent of those who had lived in a place between one and four years, and 71 per cent of those who had lived there for 30 years or more. People aged 35 and over were more likely to say this than those aged between 25 and 34, who were in turn more likely to say this then those aged between 16 and 24. Belief in the trustworthiness of people also increased with length of residence from just under a third for those who had lived in their neighbourhood for less than 5 years to just under half of those who had lived there for at least 30 years. Overall four out of ten people felt they could trust their neighbours. A similar proportion thought that their neighbours looked out for each other; however only one in ten thought it would be likely that a wallet or a purse would be returned intact.

Religion

In the 2001 Census, 77 per cent of people in England and Wales, 67 per cent in Scotland and 86 per cent in Northern Ireland stated that they had a religion. Some of the variation in these results may be due to the different questions concerning religion that were included in the census questionnaires in England and Wales, Scotland, and Northern Ireland. Around seven out of ten people in England and Wales said they belonged to the Christian faith (Table 13.24). After Christianity, Muslims were the next largest religious group, followed by Hindus, Sikhs, Jews and Buddhists. Fifteen per cent of people in England and Wales said they did not belong to a religion, and nearly 8 per cent did not state their religion.

Table **13.24**

Belonging to a religion[1], 2001

England & Wales

	Thousands	Percentages
Christian	37,338	71.7
Muslim	1,547	3.0
Hindu	552	1.1
Sikh	329	0.6
Jewish	260	0.5
Buddhist	144	0.3
Other	151	0.3
All religions	40,322	77.5
No religion	7,709	14.8
Religion not stated	4,011	7.7
All no religion/ not stated	11,720	22.5

1 The question was voluntary, with tick box options, and asked 'What is your religion?'

Source: Census 2001, Office for National Statistics

Websites and Contacts

Chapter 1 – Population

Websites

Websites	
National Statistics	www.statistics.gov.uk
Eurostat	www.europa.eu.int/comm/eurostat
General Register Office for Scotland	www.gro-scotland.gov.uk
Government Actuary's Department	www.gad.gov.uk
Home Office Immigration and Asylum Statistics	www.homeoffice.gov.uk/rds
National Assembly for Wales	www.wales.gov.uk/keypub
Northern Ireland Statistics and Research Agency	www.nisra.gov.uk
Scottish Executive	www.scotland.gov.uk
The Commonwealth Secretariat	www.thecommonwealth.org
United Nations	www.unfpa.org

Contacts

Office for National Statistics

Chapter author	020 7533 5773
Internal Migration	01329 813872
International Migration	01329 813255
Labour Market Statistics Helpline	020 7533 6094
Population Estimates General Enquiries	01329 813318

General Register Office for Scotland	0131 314 4254
Government Actuary's Department	020 7211 2622
Home Office	020 8760 8280
National Assembly for Wales	029 2082 5085

Northern Ireland Statistics and Research Agency

General Register Office	028 9025 2020
Eurostat	00 352 4301 33298
United Nations Information Centre	020 7630 1981

Chapter 2 – Households and families

Websites

National Statistics	www.statistics.gov.uk
Department of Health	www.doh.gov.uk
ESRC Research Centre for Analysis of Social Exclusion	http://sticerd.lse.ac.uk/case
Eurostat	www.europa.eu.int/comm/eurostat
General Register Office for Scotland	www.gro-scotland.gov.uk
Home Office	www.homeoffice.gov.uk
Institute for Social and Economic Research	www.iser.essex.ac.uk
National Assembly for Wales	www.wales.gov.uk/keypub
National Centre for Social Research	www.natcen.ac.uk
Northern Ireland Statistics and Research Agency	www.nisra.gov.uk
Office of the Deputy Prime Minister	www.odpm.gov.uk
Scottish Executive	www.scotland.gov.uk
Teenage Pregnancy Unit	www.teenagepregnancyunit.gov.uk

Contacts

Office for National Statistics

Chapter author	020 7533 5773
Fertility and Birth Statistics	01329 813758
General Household Survey	020 7533 5444
Labour Market Statistics Helpline	020 7533 6094
Marriages and Divorces	01329 813758

Department of Health

Abortion statistics	020 7972 5533

ESRC Research Centre for Analysis of Social Exclusion	020 7955 6679
Eurostat	00 352 4301 35427
General Register Office for Scotland	0131 314 4243

Home Office

Family Policy Unit	020 7217 8393

Institute for Social and Economic Research	01206 872957
National Assembly for Wales	029 2082 5055
National Centre for Social Research	020 7549 8520

Northern Ireland Statistics and Research Agency

General Register Office	028 9025 2020
Office of the Deputy Prime Minister	020 7944 3303

Chapter 3 – Education and training

Websites		Contacts	
National Statistics	www.statistics.gov.uk	**Office for National Statistics**	
		Chapter author	020 7533 5283
Department for Education and Skills (DfES)	www.dfes.gov.uk	Department for Education and Skills	01325 392754
DfES: Trends in Education and Skills	www.dfes.gov.uk/trends	National Assembly for Wales	029 2082 3507
DfES: Research and Statistics Gateway	www.dfes.gov.uk/rsgateway	Scottish Executive	0131 244 0442
National Assembly for Wales	www.wales.gov.uk	Northern Ireland Department of Education	028 9127 9279
Scottish Executive	www.scotland.gov.uk	Northern Ireland Department for Employment and Learning	028 9025 7400
Northern Ireland Department of Education	www.deni.gov.uk		
Northern Ireland Department for Employment and Learning	www.delni.gov.uk		
Higher Education Statistics Agency	www.hesa.ac.uk		
National Centre for Social Research	www.natcen.ac.uk		
National Foundation for Educational Research	www.nfer.ac.uk		
Learning and Skills Council	www.lsc.gov.uk		
Office for Standards in Education	www.ofsted.gov.uk		
Organisation for Economic Co-operation and Development	www.oecd.org		

Chapter 4 – Labour market

Websites		Contacts	
National Statistics	www.statistics.gov.uk	**Office for National Statistics**	
		Chapter author	020 7533 6174
Department for Work and Pensions	www.dwp.gov.uk	Labour market statistics helpline	020 7533 6094
Department of Trade and Industry	www.dti.gov.uk	New Deal	0114 209 8227
Eurostat	www.europa.eu.int/comm/eurostat/	Jobcentre Plus (Jobseekers direct)	0845 6060 234
Jobcentre Plus	www.jobcentreplus.gov.uk	Eurostat	00 352 4301 33209
National Centre for Social Research	www.natcen.ac.uk		

Chapter 5 – Income and wealth

Websites	
National Statistics	www.statistics.gov.uk
Department for Work and Pensions	www.dwp.gov.uk
Inland Revenue	www.inlandrevenue.gov.uk
Institute for Fiscal Studies	www.ifs.org.uk
Institute for Social and Economic Research	www.iser.essex.ac.uk
Eurostat	www.europa.eu.int/comm/eurostat
Organisation for Economic Co-operation and Development	www.oecd.org
Women and Equality Unit	www.womenandequalityunit.gov.uk
Department of Economics, University of Warwick	www2.warwick.ac.uk/fac/soc/ economics

Contacts	
Office for National Statistics	
Chapter author	020 7533 5757
Effects of taxes and benefits	020 7533 5770
General Household Survey	0207 533 5444
National accounts	020 7533 5938
New Earnings Survey	01633 819024
Regional accounts	020 7533 5809
Retail Prices Index	020 7533 5874
Department for Work and Pensions	
Family Resources Survey	020 7962 8092
Households Below Average Income	020 7962 8232
Individual Income	020 7712 2258
Pensioners' Incomes	020 7962 8975
Inland Revenue	020 7438 7370
Institute for Fiscal Studies	020 7291 4800
Institute for Social and Economic Research	01206 872957
Department of Economics, University of Warwick	020 7652 3055
Organisation for Economic Co-operation and Development	+33 145 248200
Eurostat	
Eurostat Data Shop UK	01633 813369

Chapter 6 – Expenditure

Websites	
National Statistics	www.statistics.gov.uk
National Centre for Social Research	www.natcen.ac.uk
Department of Trade and Industry	www.dti.gov.uk
Department for Work and Pensions	www.dwp.gov.uk
Jobcentre Plus	www.jobcentreplus.gov.uk
Eurostat	www.europa.eu.int/comm/eurostat/
Credit Card Research Group	www.ccrg.org.uk

Contacts	
Office for National Statistics	
Chapter author	020 7533 5130
Household expenditure	020 7533 5999
Expenditure and food survey	020 7533 5752
Volume of retail sales	01633 812713
Retail prices index	020 7533 5874
Harmonised index of consumer prices	020 7533 5818
Comparative price levels	020 7533 5818
Association for Payment Clearing Services	020 7711 6200
Bank of England	020 7601 4878
Department for Trade and Industry	020 7215 3305
Credit Card Research Group	020 7436 9937

Chapter 7 – Health

Websites

National Statistics	www.statistics.gov.uk
Department of Health	www.doh.gov.uk
Department of Health, Social Services and Public Safety, Northern Ireland	www.dhsspsni.gov.uk
General Register Office for Northern Ireland	www.groni.gov.uk
Government Actuary's Department	www.gad.gov.uk
Health Protection Agency	www.hpa.org.uk
Information and Statistics Division (Scotland)	www.show.scot.nhs.uk/isd
Department for Environment, Food and Rural Affairs	www.defra.gov.uk
National Assembly for Wales	www.wales.gov.uk
National Centre for Social Research	www.natcen.ac.uk
Northern Ireland Cancer Registry	www.qub.ac.uk/nicr
Northern Ireland Statistics and Research Agency	www.nisra.gov.uk
Scottish Executive	www.scotland.gov.uk
Welsh Cancer Intelligence and Surveillance Unit	www.velindre-tr.wales.nhs.uk/wcisu
Eurostat	www.europa.eu.int/comm/eurostat

Contacts

Office for National Statistics

Chapter author	020 7533 5081
Cancer Statistics	020 7533 5230
Condom Use	020 7533 5391
General Household Survey	020 7533 5444
General Practice Research Database	020 7533 5240
Life expectancy by social class	020 7533 5186
Mortality Statistics	01329 813 758
Psychiatric Morbidity Survey	020 7533 5305
Sudden Infant Death Syndrome	020 7533 5198

Department of Health

Health Survey for England	020 7972 5718/5660
Immunisation and cancer screening	020 7972 5533
Smoking, misuse of alcohol and drugs	020 7972 5551

Department for Environment, Food and Rural Affairs	020 7270 8547
Department of Health, Social Services and Public Safety, Northern Ireland	028 9052 2800
General Register Office for Northern Ireland	02890 252031
General Register Office for Scotland	0131 314 4227
Government Actuary's Department	020 7211 2635
Health Protection Agency	020 8200 6868
Home Office	020 7273 2084
National Assembly for Wales	029 2082 5080
National Centre for Social Research	020 7250 1866
National Health Service in Scotland	0131 551 8899
Northern Ireland Statistics and Research Agency	028 9034 8132
Continuous Household Survey	028 9034 8243
Northern Ireland Cancer Registry	028 9026 3136
Welsh Cancer Intelligence and Surveillance Unit	029 2037 3500
Eurostat	00 352 4301 32 056

Chapter 8 – Social protection

Websites

National Statistics	www.statistics.gov.uk
Department of Health	www.doh.gov.uk/public/stats1.htm
Department for Work and Pensions	www.dwp.gov.uk
Department for Education and Skills	www.dfes.gov.uk
Northern Ireland Statistics and Research Agency	www.nisra.gov.uk
Department of Health, Social Services and Public Safety, Northern Ireland	www.dhsspsni.gov.uk/stats&research /index.html
Department for Social Development, Northern Ireland	www.dsdni.gov.uk
Scottish Executive	www.scotland.gov.uk
NHS in Scotland	www.show.scot.nhs.uk/isd
National Assembly for Wales	www.wales.gov.uk
Eurostat	www.europa.eu.int/comm/eurostat
The National Centre for Social Research	www.natcen.ac.uk/
ChildLine	www.childline.org.uk/

Contacts

Office for National Statistics

Chapter author	020 7533 5781
General Household Survey	020 7533 5444
Labour Force Survey	020 7533 6094

Department of Health

Acute services activity	0113 254 5522
Adults' services	020 7972 5582
Community and cross-sector services	020 7972 5524
General dental and community dental service	020 7972 5392
General medical services statistics	0113 254 5911
Mental illness/handicap	020 7972 5546
NHS expenditure	0113 254 6012
NHS medical staff	0113 254 5892
NHS non-medical manpower	0113 254 5744
Non-psychiatric hospital activity	020 7972 5529
Personal social services expenditure	020 7972 5595
Residential care and home help	020 7972 5585
Social services staffing and finance data	020 7972 5595

Department for Work and Pensions

Family Resources Survey	020 7962 8092
Number of benefit recipients	0191 225 7373

Department for Education and Skills

Children's services	020 7972 5581
Day care for children	01325 392827

Department of Health, Social Services and Public Safety, Northern Ireland

Health and personal social services activity	028 9052 2800
Health and personal social services manpower	028 9052 2468

Department for Social Development, Northern Ireland	028 9052 2280

National Assembly for Wales	029 2082 5080

National Health Service in Scotland	0131 551 8899

Northern Ireland Statistics and Research Agency	028 9034 8243

Scottish Executive

Children's social services	0131 244 3551
Adult community care	0131 244 3777
Social work staffing	0131 244 3740

Eurostat	00 352 4301 34122

ChildLine	020 7650 3200

Chapter 9 – Crime and justice

Websites

National Statistics	www.statistics.gov.uk
Department of Constitutional Affairs	www.lcd.gov.uk
Court Service	www.courtservice.gov.uk
Home Office	www.homeoffice.gov.uk
Home Office (Criminal Justice System)	www.criminal-justice-system.gov.uk
National Assembly for Wales	www.wales.gov.uk
Scottish Executive	www.scotland.gov.uk
Northern Ireland Office	www.nio.gov.uk
Police Service of Northern Ireland	www.psni.police.uk
Legal Services Commission	www.legalservices.gov.uk
Prison Service for England and Wales	www.hmprisonservice.gov.uk
Scottish Prison Service	www.sps.gov.uk
Northern Ireland Prison Service	www.niprisonservice.gov.uk
Crown Office and procurator Fiscal	www.crownoffice.gov.uk
Northern Ireland Court Service	www.courtsni.gov.uk
Crown Prosecution Service	www.cps.gov.uk

Contacts

Office for National Statistics	
Chapter author	020 7533 5168
Home Office	0870 000 1585
Department for Constitutional Affairs	020 7210 8500
National Assembly for Wales	029 2080 1388
Northern Ireland Office	028 9052 7538
Police Service of Northern Ireland	028 9065 0222 Ext. 24865
Scottish Executive Justice Department	0131 244 2227

Chapter 10 – Housing

Websites

National Statistics	www.statistics.gov.uk
Office of the Deputy Prime Minister	www.odpm.gov.uk
Court Service	www.courtservice.gov.uk
Department for Social Development, Northern Ireland	www.dsdni.gov.uk
Department for Work and Pensions	www.dwp.gov.uk
National Assembly for Wales	www.wales.gov.uk
Northern Ireland Statistics Research Agency	www.nisra.gov.uk
Scottish Executive	www.scotland.gov.uk
Social Exclusion Unit	www.cabinet-office.gov.uk/seu
Council of Mortgage Lenders	www.cml.org.uk
Land Registry	www.landreg.gov.uk

Contacts

Office for National Statistics	
Chapter author	020 7533 5081
Expenditure and Food Survey	020 7533 5754
General Household Survey	020 7533 5444
Office of the Deputy Prime Minister	
Planning and Land Use Statistics	020 7944 5533
Court Service	020 7210 1773
Department for Social Development, Northern Ireland	028 9052 2762
Department for Work and Pensions	
Family Resources Survey	020 7962 8092
National Assembly of Wales	029 2082 5063
Northern Ireland Statistics and Research Agency	028 9034 8243
Scottish Executive	0131 244 7236
Council of Mortgage Lenders	020 7440 2251
Land Registry	0151 473 6008

Chapter 11 – Environment

Websites		Contacts	
National Statistics	www.statistics.gov.uk	**Office for National Statistics**	
Department for Environment, Food & Rural Affairs	www.defra.gov.uk/environment/index.htm	Chapter author	020 7533 5701
Department of Trade and Industry	www.dti.gov.uk/energy/index.htm	Department for Environment Food & Rural Affairs	020 7082 8608
Scottish Executive	www.scotland.gov.uk	Department of Trade and Industry	020 7215 2697
National Assembly for Wales	www.wales.gov.uk	Scottish Executive	0131 244 0445
Department of Environment (Northern Ireland)	www.doeni.gov.uk	National Assembly for Wales	029 2082 5111
Centre for Ecology and Hydrology, Wallingford	www.ceh-nerc.ac.uk	Department of Environment (Northern Ireland)	028 9054 0540
Environment Agency	www.environment-agency.gov.uk	Centre for Ecology and Hydrology	01491 838 800
Environment and Heritage Service (DOE NI)	www.ehsni.gov.uk	Environment Agency	0845 9333 111
European Environment Agency	www.eea.eu.int	Environment and Heritage Service (DOE NI)	028 9023 5000
Eurostat	www.europa.eu.int/comm/eurostat	European Environment Agency	0045 3336 7100
Forestry Commission	www.forestry.gov.uk/statistics	Eurostat	00 352 4301 33023
Joint Nature Conservation Committee	www.jncc.gov.uk	Forestry Commission	0131 314 6337
Northern Ireland Statistics and Research Agency	www.nisra.gov.uk	Joint Nature Conservation Committee	01733 562 626
Scottish Environment Protection Agency	www.sepa.org.uk	Scottish Environment Protection Agency	01786 457 700

Chapter 12 – Transport

Websites		Contacts	
National Statistics	www.statistics.gov.uk	**Office for National Statistics**	
Department of Trade and Industry	www.dti.gov.uk	Chapter author	020 7533 5701
Department for Transport	www.dft.gov.uk/transtat	Census Customer Services	01329 813800
Department of the Environment for Northern Ireland	www.doeni.gov.uk	Expenditure and Food Survey	020 7533 5755
		Household expenditure	020 7533 6001
Civil Aviation Authority Economic Regulation Group	www.caaerg.co.uk	International Passenger Survey	020 7533 5765
		Retail Prices Index	020 7533 5874
European Commission Directorate General Energy and Transport	http://europa.eu.int/comm/dgs/energy_transport/index_en.html	Department of Trade and Industry	020 7215 5000
		Department for Transport	
Scottish Executive	www.scotland.gov.uk	General Queries	020 7944 8300
Strategic Rail Authority	www.sra.gov.uk	National Travel Survey	020 7944 3097
National Centre for Social Research	www.natcen.ac.uk	Civil Aviation Authority Economic Regulation Group	020 7453 6213
		Department of the Environment for Northern Ireland	01232 540807
		Driving Standards Agency	0115 901 2852
		Police Service of Northern Ireland	028 9065 0222 Ext 24135
		National Centre for Social Research	020 7250 1866
		Scottish Executive	0131 244 7255/7256
		Strategic Rail Authority	020 7654 6072

Chapter 13 – Lifestyles and social participation

Websites

National Statistics	www.statistics.gov.uk
Department for Culture, Media and Sport	www.culture.gov.uk
Northern Ireland Statistics and Research Agency	www.nisra.gov.uk
British Video Association	www.bva.org.uk
British Broadcasting Corporation	www.bbc.co.uk
British Film Industry	www.bfi.org.uk
British Phonographic Industry	www.bpi.co.uk
National Reading Campaign	www.readon.org.uk
National Readership Survey	www.nrs.co.uk
Pearl and Dean	www.pearlanddean.com
Policy Studies Institute	www.psi.org.uk
VisitBritain	www.visitbritain.com
Arts Council of England	www.artscouncil.org.uk
British Market Research Bureau	www.bmrb.co.uk
National Centre for Social Research	www.natcen.ac.uk
Sport England	www.sportengland.org
RAJAR	www.rajar.co.uk
Independent Television Commission	www.itc.org.uk
StarUK, the National Tourist Boards tourism statistics website	www.staruk.org.uk

Contacts

Office for National Statistics

Chapter author	020 7533 5168
Expenditure and Food Survey	020 7533 5756
General Household Survey	020 7533 5444
Omnibus Survey	020 7533 5321
UK 2000 Time Use Survey	020 7533 5878

Department for Culture, Media and Sport	020 7211 6409
Northern Ireland Statistics and Research Agency	028 9034 8246
British Broadcasting Corporation	020 7765 1064
British Phonographic Industry	020 7851 4000
British Video Association	020 7436 0041
Cinema Advertising Association	020 7534 6363
VisitBritain	020 5863 3011
National Centre for Social Research	020 7250 1866

References and Further Reading

Those published by The Stationery Office are available from the addresses shown on the back cover of *Social Trends*. Many can also be found on the National Statistics website: www.statistics.gov.uk

General

Regional Trends, The Stationery Office

Social Focus on Ethnic Minorities, The Stationery Office

Social Focus on Families, The Stationery Office

Social Focus on Older People, The Stationery Office

Social Focus on Men, The Stationery Office

Social Focus on Women and Men, The Stationery Office

Social Focus on Young People, The Stationery Office

UK 2004: The Official Yearbook of the United Kingdom of Great Britain and Northern Ireland, The Stationery Office

1: Population

Annual Abstract of Statistics, The Stationery Office

Annual Report of the Registrar General for Northern Ireland, The Stationery Office

Annual Report of the Registrar General for Scotland, General Register Office for Scotland

Asylum Statistics – United Kingdom, Home Office

Birth statistics (Series FM1), The Stationery Office

Census 2001: First results on population for England and Wales, The Stationery Office

Control of Immigration: Statistics, United Kingdom, The Stationery Office

European Social Statistics – Demography, Eurostat

Health Statistics Quarterly, The Stationery Office

International Migration Statistics (Series MN), The Stationery Office

Key Population and Vital Statistics (Series VS/PP1), The Stationery Office

Mid-year Population Estimates for England and Wales, Internet only publication, Office for National Statistics www.statistics.gov.uk/statbase/Product.asp?lnk=601

Mid-year Population Estimates, Northern Ireland, Northern Ireland Statistics and Research Agency

Mid-year Population Estimates, Scotland, General Register Office for Scotland

Migration Statistics, Eurostat

Mortality Statistics for England and Wales (Series DH1, 2,3,4), The Stationery Office

National Population Projections, UK (Series PP2), The Stationery Office

Patterns and Trends in International Migration in Western Europe, Eurostat

Persons Granted British Citizenship – United Kingdom, Home Office

Population and Projections for areas within Northern Ireland, Northern Ireland Statistics and Research Agency

Population Projections for Wales (sub-national), National Assembly for Wales/Welsh Office

Population Projections, Scotland (for Administrative Areas), General Register Office for Scotland

Population Trends, The Stationery Office

The State of World Population, UNFPA

United Nations Demographic Yearbook, United Nations

World Statistics Pocketbook, United Nations

2: Households and families

Abortion Statistics (Series AB), The Stationery Office

Annual Report of the Registrar General for Northern Ireland, The Stationery Office

Annual Report of the Registrar General for Scotland, General Register Office for Scotland

Attitudes towards ideal family size of different ethnic/nationality groups in Great Britain, France and Germany, Population Trends 108, Penn R and Lambert P, Office for National Statistics, The Stationery Office

Birth statistics (Series FM1), The Stationery Office

Birth statistics: historical series, 1837–1983 (Series FM1), The Stationery Office

British Social Attitudes, Ashgate Publishing

Choosing Childlessness, Family Policy Studies Centre

European Social Statistics – Demography, Eurostat

Health Statistics Quarterly, The Stationery Office

Key Population and Vital Statistics (Series VS/PP1), The Stationery Office

Living in Britain: Results from the General Household Survey, The Stationery Office

Marriage, divorce and adoption statistics (Series FM2), The Stationery Office

Marriage and divorce statistics 1837–1983 (Series FM2), The Stationery Office

Population Trends, The Stationery Office

Projections of Households in England to 2021, Office of the Deputy Prime Minister

Recent Demographic Developments in Europe, Council of Europe

Survey of English Housing: Housing in England 2000/01, The Stationery Office

Teenage Pregnancy, Report by the Social Exclusion Unit, The Stationery Office

The British Population, Oxford University Press

3: Education and training

Education at a Glance, OECD Indicators 2003, Organisation for Economic Co-operation and Development, 2003.

Knowledge and Skills for Life, Organisation for Economic Co-operation and Development, 2001.

Learning and Training at Work 2002, IFF Research Ltd, for the Department for Education and Skills, Research Report 399, 2003. The Stationery Office.

Literacy Skills for the World of Tomorrow: Further Results from PISA 2000, Organisation for Economic Co-operation and Development, 2003.

National Adult Learning Survey 2002, National Centre for Social Research, for the Department for Education and Skills, Research Report 415, 2003. The Stationery Office.

Reading All Over the World: PIRLS National Report for England, National Foundation for Educational Research, 2003.

Statistical Volume: Education and Training Statistics for the United Kingdom, Department for Education and Skills, 2003. The Stationery Office.

Statistical Volume: Statistics of Education: Schools in England, Department for Education and Skills, 2003. The Stationery Office.

4: Labour market

British Social Attitudes, National Centre for Social Research

European social statistics – Labour force survey results, Eurostat

How Exactly is Unemployment Measured? Office for National Statistics

Labour Force Survey Historical Supplement, Office for National Statistics

Labour Force Survey Quarterly Supplement, Office for National Statistics

Labour Market Trends, The Stationery Office

Learning and Training at Work, 2002, Department for Education and Skills

Northern Ireland Labour Force Survey, Department of Enterprise, Trade and Investment, Northern Ireland

The State of the Labour Market, Office for National Statistics

What exactly is the Labour Force Survey? Office for National Statistics

5: Income and wealth

Changing Households: The British Household Panel Survey, Institute for Social and Economic Research

Economic Trends, The Stationery Office

European Community Finances: Statement on the 2002 EC Budget and Measures to Counter Fraud and Financial Mismanagement, The Stationery Office

Eurostat National Accounts ESA, Eurostat

Family Resources Survey, Department for Work and Pensions

Fiscal Studies, Institute for Fiscal Studies

For Richer, For Poorer, Institute for Fiscal Studies

Households Below Average Income, 1994/95–2000/01, Department for Work and Pensions

Income and Wealth. The Latest Evidence, Joseph Rowntree Foundation

Individual Incomes 1996/97–2001/02, Women and Equality Unit

Labour Market Trends (incorporating Employment Gazette), The Stationery Office

Low/moderate-income Families in Britain: Changes in 1999 and 2000, Marsh A and Rowlingson K, Research Report, Department for Work and Pensions

Monitoring Poverty and Social Exclusion, Joseph Rowntree Foundation

New Earnings Survey, The Stationery Office

Poverty and Social Exclusion in Britain, 2000, Joseph Rowntree Foundation,

Social Security, Departmental Report, The Stationery Office

Social Security Statistics, The Stationery Office

The Distribution of Wealth in the UK, Institute for Fiscal Studies

The Pensioners' Incomes Series, Department for Work and Pensions

United Kingdom National Accounts (The ONS Blue Book), The Stationery Office

6: Expenditure

Business Monitor MM23 (Consumer Price Indices), The Stationery Office

Consumer Trends, Internet only publication, Office for National Statistics www.statistics.gov.uk/consumertrends

Economic Trends, The Stationery Office

Family Spending, The Stationery Office

In Brief 2003, Payment Markets Briefing, Association for Payment Clearing Services www.apacs.org.uk

Financial Statistics, The Stationery Office

United Kingdom National Accounts (The ONS Blue Book), The Stationery Office

2002/03 Student Income and Expenditure Survey: Students' Income, Expenditure and Debt in 2002/03 and Changes Since 1998/99 www.dfes.gov.uk/research/ DfES Publications, PO Box 5050, Sherwood Park, Annesley, Nottingham, NG15 0DJ

7: Health

The Annual Report of the Registrar General for Northern Ireland, Northern Ireland Statistics and Research Agency

Annual Report on the State of the Drugs Problem in the European Union, 2001, European Monitoring Centre for Drugs and Drug Addiction

Annual Report of the Registrar General for Scotland, General Register Office for Scotland

Cancer Trends in England and Wales 1950–1999, The Stationery Office

Community Statistics, Department of Health, Social Services and Public Safety, Northern Ireland

Geographic Variations in Health, The Stationery Office

Health in Scotland. The Annual Report of the Chief Medical Officer on the State of Scotland's Health, Scottish Executive

Health Statistics Quarterly, The Stationery Office

Health Statistics Wales, National Assembly for Wales

Health Survey for England, The Stationery Office

Infant Feeding Survey 2000, The Stationery Office

Key Health Statistics from General Practice 1998, Office for National Statistics

Living in Britain: results from the 2001 General Household Survey, The Stationery Office

Mortality trends by cause of death in England and Wales 1980–94: the impact of introducing automated cause coding and related changes in 1993, Population Trends 86, Rooney C and Devis T, Office for National Statistics, The Stationery Office

National Food Survey 2000, The Stationery Office

On the State of the Public Health – The Annual Report of the Chief Medical Officer of the Department of Health, The Stationery Office

Population Trends, The Stationery Office

Psychiatric Morbidity Survey Among Adults Living in Private Households 2000, The Stationery Office

Report of the Chief Medical Officer, Department of Health, Social Services and Public Safety, Northern Ireland

Results of the ICD-10 bridge coding study, England and Wales, 1999, Health Statistics Quarterly 14, Office for National Statistics, The Stationery Office

Scottish Health Statistics, Information and Statistics Division, NHS Scotland

Smoking, Drinking and Drug Use among Young People in 2002, Press release, Department of Health (Internet only publication) www.doh.gov.uk/public/spnmar03-smoking.htm

Statistical Publications on Aspects of Health and Personal Social Services Activity in England (various), Department of Health

Trends in life expectancy by social class – an update, Hattersley L, Health Statistics Quarterly 2, Office for National Statistics, The Stationery Office

Welsh Health: Annual Report of the Chief Medical Officer, National Assembly for Wales

World Health Statistics, World Health Organisation

8: Social protection
Annual News Releases (various), Scottish Executive

British Social Attitudes, National Centre for Social Research

Carers 2000, The Stationery Office

Chief Executive's Report to the NHS, Department of Health (www.doh.gov.uk/nhsreport/index.htm)

Community Statistics for Northern Ireland, Department of Health, Social Services and Public Safety, Northern Ireland

General Household Survey, Living in Britain – results from the 2001 General Household Survey, The Stationery Office (www.statistics.gov.uk/lib2001)

Health and Personal Social Services Statistics, Department of Health (www.doh.gov.uk/hpsss/index.htm)

Hospital Activity Statistics, Department of Health (www.doh.gov.uk/hospitalactivity)

ESSPROS manual 1996, Eurostat

Family Resources Survey, Department for Work and Pensions

Hospital Episode Statistics for England, Department of Health (http://www.doh.gov.uk/hes/)

Hospital Statistics for Northern Ireland, Department of Health, Social Services and Public Safety, Northern Ireland

Health Statistics Wales, National Assembly for Wales

Scottish Community Care Statistics, Scottish Executive

Scottish Health Statistics, National Health Service in Scotland, Common Services Agency

Social Protection Expenditure and Receipts, Eurostat

Social Security Departmental Report, The Stationery Office

Social Services Statistics Wales, National Assembly for Wales

Statistical Publications on Aspects of Community Care in Scotland (various), Scottish Executive Health Department

Statistical Publications on Aspects of Health and Personal Social Services Activity in England (various), Department of Health

Work and Pension Statistics, The Department for Work and Pensions

9: Crime and justice
A Commentary on Northern Ireland Crime Statistics, The Stationery Office

Civil Judicial Statistics Scotland (2001), The Stationery Office

Costs, Sentencing Profiles and the Scottish Criminal Justice System, Scottish Executive

Crime and the Quality of Life: Public Perceptions and Experiences of Crime in Scotland, Scottish Executive

Crime in England and Wales 2002/03, Home Office

Criminal Statistics, England and Wales 2002, The Stationery Office

Crown Prosecution Service, Annual Report 2002/03, The Stationery Office

Digest 4: Information on the Criminal Justice System in England and Wales, Home Office

Digest of Information on the Northern Ireland Criminal Justice System 3, The Stationery Office

HM Prison Service Annual Report and Accounts, The Stationery Office

Home Office Departmental Report 2003, The Stationery Office

Home Office Research Findings, Home Office

Home Office Statistical Bulletins, Home Office

Judicial Statistics, England and Wales, The Stationery Office

Legal Services Commission Annual Report 2002/03, The Stationery Office

Northern Ireland Judicial Statistics, Northern Ireland Court Service

Police Statistics, England and Wales, CIPFA

Prison Statistics, England and Wales 2001, The Stationery Office

Prison Statistics Scotland 2002, Scottish Executive

Prisons in Scotland Report, The Stationery Office

Race and the Criminal Justice System, Home Office

Record crime in Scotland 2002, Scottish Executive

Report of the Chief Constable 2002–03, Police Service of Northern Ireland

Report of the Parole Board for England and Wales, The Stationery Office

Report on the work of the Northern Ireland Prison Service, The Stationery Office

Scottish Crime Survey, Scottish Executive

Statistics on Women and the Criminal Justice System, Home Office

The Criminal Justice System in England and Wales, Home Office

Scottish Executive Statistical Bulletins: Criminal Justice Series, Scottish Executive

The Work of the Prison Service, The Stationery Office

Review of Police Forces' Crime Recording Practices, Home Office

Review of Crime Statistics: a Discussion Document, Home Office

10: Housing

A Review of Flexible Mortgages, The Council of Mortgage Lenders

Becoming a Home-owner in Britain in the 1990s – The British Household Panel Survey, ESRC Institute for Social and Economic Research

Bringing Britain Together: A National Strategy for Neighbourhood Renewal, Social Exclusion Unit, Cabinet Office

Changing Households: The British Household Panel Survey, Institute for Social and Economic Research

Department for Transport, Local Government and the Regions Annual Report, The Stationery Office

Divorce, Remarriage and Housing: The Effects of Divorce, Remarriage, Separation and the Formation of New Couple Households on the Number of Separate Households and Housing Demand Conditions, Department of the Environment, Transport and the Regions

English House Condition Survey, The Stationery Office

Housing Finance, Council of Mortgage Lenders

Housing in England: Survey of English Housing, The Stationery Office
Housing Statistics, The Stationery Office

Living conditions in Europe – Statistical Pocketbook, Eurostat

Local Housing Statistics, The Stationery Office

My Home Was My Castle: Evictions and Repossessions in Britain, ESRC Institute of Social and Economic Research and Institute Local Research

Northern Ireland House Condition Survey, Northern Ireland Housing Executive

Northern Ireland Housing Statistics, 2002/03, Department for Social Development, Northern Ireland

On the Move: The Housing Consequences Migration, YPS

Private Renting in England, The Stationery Office

Private Renting in Five Localities, The Stationery Office

Projections of Households in England to 2021 The Stationery Office

Scotland's People: Results from the 1999 Scottish Household Survey, The Stationery Office

Scottish House Condition Survey 1996, Scottish Homes

Statistical Bulletins on Housing, Scottish Executive

Statistics on Housing in the European Community, Commission of the European Communities

The Social Situation in the European Union, European Commission

Welsh House Condition Survey, National Assembly for Wales

Welsh Housing Statistics, National Assembly for Wales

11: Environment

Accounting for Nature: Assessing Habitats in the UK Countryside, Department for Environment, Food & Rural Affairs

Achieving a Better Quality of life, 2002, Department for Environment, Food & Rural Affairs

Agriculture in the United Kingdom 2002, The Stationery Office

Air Quality Strategy for England, Scotland, Wales and Northern Ireland, The Stationery Office

Air Quality Strategy for England, Scotland, Wales and Northern Ireland: Addendum, Department for Environment, Food & Rural Affairs

Bathing Water Quality in England and Wales, The Stationery Office

Biodiversity: The UK Action Plan, The Stationery Office

e-Digest of Environmental Statistics, Internet only publication, Department for Environment, Food & Rural Affairs www.defra.gov.uk/environmental/statistics/index.htm

Digest of United Kingdom Energy Statistics, The Stationery Office

The Environment in your Pocket, Department for Environment, Food & Rural Affairs

Forestry Facts and Figures 2003, Forestry Commission

Forestry Statistics 2002, Forestry Commission

GM Nation. The Findings of the Public Debate, Department for Environment, Food & Rural Affairs

General Quality Assessment, The Environment Agency

Hydrological Summaries for the United Kingdom, Centre for Hydrology and British Geological Survey

Municipal Waste Management Survey, Department for Environment, Food & Rural Affairs

OECD Environmental Data Compendium, OECD

Organic Statistics, Department for Environment, Food & Rural Affairs

Planning Public Water Supplies, The Environment Agency

Pollution Incidents in England and Wales, 2002, Environment Agency

Quality of life counts – indicators for a strategy for sustainable development for the United Kingdom: a baseline assessment, Department of the Environment, Transport and the Regions

Scottish Environment Protection Agency Annual Report 2001–2002, SEPA

Survey of Public Attitudes to Quality of Life and to the Environment – 2001, Department for Environment, Food & Rural Affairs

12: Transport

A New Deal for Transport: Better for Everyone, The Stationery Office

A Strategy for Sustainable Development for the United Kingdom, The Stationery Office

Annual Report, Central Rail Users Consultative Committee

British Social Attitudes, National Centre for Social Research

Driving Standards Agency Annual Report and Accounts, The Stationery Office

European Union Energy and Transport in Figures, 2002, European Commission

Focus on Personal Travel, The Stationery Office

Focus on Public Transport, The Stationery Office

International Passenger Transport, The Stationery Office

National Rail Trends, Strategic Rail Authority

Rail Complaints, Office of the Rail Regulator

Road Casualties Great Britain – Annual Report, The Stationery Office

Road Accidents, Scotland, Scottish Executive

Road Accidents: Wales, National Assembly for Wales

Road Traffic Accident Statistics Annual Report, Police Service of Northern Ireland

Road Traffic Statistics Great Britain, Department for Transport

Scottish Transport Statistics, Scottish Executive

Transport Statistics Bulletins and Reports, Department for Transport

Transport Statistical Bulletins, Scottish Executive

Transport Statistics Great Britain, The Stationery Office

Transport Trends, The Stationery Office

Travel Trends, The Stationery Office

Vehicle Licensing Statistics, Department for Transport

Vehicle Speeds in Great Britain, Department for Transport

Welsh Transport Statistics, National Assembly for Wales

13: Lifestyles and social participation

Annual Report of Department for Culture, Media and Sport, The Stationery Office

Arts in England and Wales: Attendance, Participation and Attitudes in 2001, Arts Council of England

BBC Annual Reports and Accounts, BBC

BPI Statistical Handbook, British Phonographic Industry

British Social Attitudes, National Centre for Social Research

BVA Yearbook, British Video Association

Cinema and Video Industry Audience Research, CAA

Consumers' use of fixed and mobile telephony, Oftel, www.oftel.gov.uk

Cultural Trends in Scotland, Policy Studies Institute

Cultural Trends, Policy Studies Institute

Family Spending, The Stationery Office

Film and Television Handbook, British Film Institute

Internet Access, Households and Individuals First Release, Office for National Statisics

LISU Annual Library Statistics, LISU, Loughborough University

Living in Britain: results from the 2002 General Household Survey, The Stationery Office

The UK Tourist: Statistics, VisitBritain, VisitScotland, Wales Tourist Board and Northern Ireland Tourist Board

Travel Trends, The Stationery Office

UK 2000 Time Use Survey, Office for National Statistics

UK Day Visits Survey, Countryside Recreation Network, University of Wales Cardiff

Visits to Visitor Attractions, English Tourism Council, VisitScotland, Wales Tourist Board and Northern Ireland Tourist Board

Young People and ICT, Department for Education and Skills

Young People and Sport in England, Sport England

Geographical Areas of the United Kingdom

Government Office Regions

ENGLAND

—— GOR boundary

Environment Agency regions

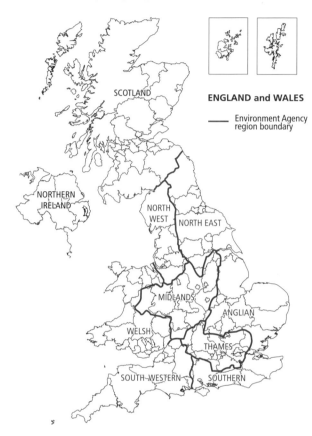

ENGLAND and WALES

—— Environment Agency region boundary

Health areas (from April 2003)

UNITED KINGDOM

—— Health area boundary

Police Force areas

GREAT BRITAIN

—— Police Force area boundary

Tourist Board areas

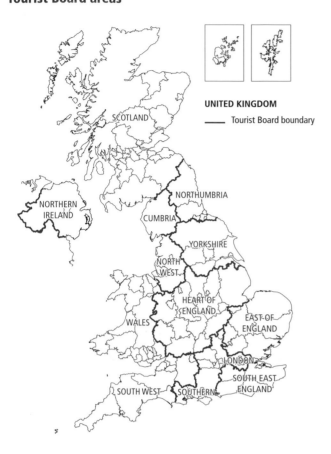

UNITED KINGDOM

——— Tourist Board boundary

Major Surveys

	Frequency	Sampling frame	Type of respondent	Coverage	Effective sample size[1] (most recent survey included in *Social Trends*)	Response rate (percentages)
British Crime Survey	Annual	Postcode Address File	Adult in household	EW	37,000 addresses	74
British Household Panel Survey	Annual	Postal addresses in 1991, members of initial wave households followed in subsequent waves	All adults in households	GB	5,160 households	97[2]
British Social Attitudes Survey	Annual	Postcode Address File	One adult per household	GB	5,644 addresses	61[3]
Census of Population	Decennial	Detailed local	Adult in household	UK	Full count	98
Continuous Household Survey	Continuous	Valuation and Lands Agency Property	All adults in household	NI	4,147 addresses	70
Employers Skill Survey	Annual	BT Database	Employers	E	4,054 interviews achieved	53
English House Condition Survey	Quinquennial	Postcode Address File	Any one householder	E	27,200 addresses	49[4]
European Community	Annual	Various	All household members aged 16 and over		60,000 households	90[5]
Expenditure and Food Survey	Continuous	Postcode Address File in GB, Rating and Valuation lists in NI	All adults in households aged 16 or over[6]	UK	12,096 addresses[7]	57[8]
Family Resources Survey	Continuous	Postcode Address File	All adults in household	GB	38,609 households	66
General Household Survey	Continuous	Postcode Address File	All adults in household	GB	12,223 households	72
Health Survey for England	Continuous	Postcode Address File	All household members	E	12,250 addresses	74[9]
International Passenger Survey	Continuous	International passengers	Individual traveller	UK	255,000 individuals	81
Labour Force Survey	Continuous	Postcode Address File	All adults in household	UK	57,000 households	76[10]
Learning and training at work	Annual	BT Business database	Employers	E	4,010 interviews achieved	62
National Readership Survey	Continuous	Postcode Address File	Adults aged 15 and over	GB	35,871 individuals	54
National Travel Survey	Continuous	Postcode Address File	All household members	GB	5,075 households per year	65[11]
New Earnings Survey	Annual	Inland Revenue PAYE records	Employee	GB	[12]	[12]
National Statistics Omnibus Survey	Continuous	Postcode Address File	Adults aged 16 or over living in private households	GB	Approximately 1,800[13]	66
Survey of English Housing	Continuous	Postcode Address File	Household	E	26,277 households	71
Survey of Personal Incomes	Annual	Inland Revenue	Individuals administrative data	UK	200,000	95
Survey of public attitudes to quality of life and to the environment	Ad hoc	Postcode Address File	One adult per household	E	3,700 interviews	68
UK 2000 Time Use Survey	Ad hoc	Postcode Address File	Adults and children 8 years and over	UK	10,579 individuals	61[14]
Youth Cohort Study	Annual[15]	School records	Young people (aged 16 to 19)	EW	35,000 individuals	56[16]

1 Effective sample size includes non-respondents but excludes ineligible households.
2 Wave on wave response rate at wave eight. Around 76 per cent of eligible wave one sample members were respondent in wave eight.
3 Response rate refers to 2000 survey.
4 The 1996 EHCS response combines successful outcomes from two linked surveys where information is separately gathered about the household and the dwelling for each address.
5 Response rates vary between EU countries.
6 There is an optional diary for children aged 7 to 15 in Great Britain.
7 Basic sample for Great Britain only.
8 Response rate refers to Great Britain.
9 Response rate for fully and partially responding households.
10 Response rate to first wave interviews quoted. Response rate to second and fifth wave interviews 91 per cent off those previously accepting.
11 Response rate for the period January 1999 to January 2001.
12 In the New Earnings Survey employers supply data on a 1 per cent sample of employees who are members of PAYE schemes. For the 2003 sample approximately 239,000 were selected and there was an 88 per cent response, but some 48,000 returned questionnaires were not taken onto the results file for various reasons.
13 Achieved sample size per Omnibus cycle. The Omnibus interviews at one household per sampled address and one adult per household. Data are weighted to account for the fact that respondents living in smaller households would have a greater chance of selection.
14 Responses rate for the household questionnaire.
15 New samples are drawn every two years and each of these cohorts is then surveyed annually over four years.
16 The average across all sweeps for recent chorts.

Symbols and Conventions

Reference years Where, because of space constraints, a choice of years has to be made, the most recent year or a run of recent years is shown together with the past population census years (1991, 1981, 1971, etc) and sometimes the mid-points between census years (1986, etc). Other years may be added if they represent a peak or trough in the series.

Rounding of figures In tables where figures have been rounded to the nearest final digit, there may be an apparent discrepancy between the sum of the constituent items and the total as shown.

Billion This term is used to represent a thousand million.

Provisional and estimated data Some data for the latest year (and occasionally for earlier years) are provisional or estimated. To keep footnotes to a minimum, these have not been indicated; source departments will be able to advise if revised data are available.

Seasonal adjustment Unless otherwise stated unadjusted data have been used.

Financial year – eg 1 April 2001 to 31 March 2002 would be shown as 2001/02

Academic year – eg September 2000/July 2001 would be shown as 2000/01

Combined years – eg 2000–02 shows data for more than one year that have been combined

Data covering more than one year – eg 1998, 1999 and 2000 would be shown as 1998 to 2000

Units on tables Where one unit predominates it is shown at the top of the table. All other units are shown against the relevant row or column. Figures are shown in italics when they represent percentages.

Dependent children Those aged under 16, or single people aged 16 to 18 and in full-time education.

Germany Unless otherwise stated, data relate to Germany as constituted since 3 October 1990.

Ireland Refers to the State of Ireland and does not include Northern Ireland.

Symbols The following symbols have been used throughout *Social Trends*:

    ..   not available

    .   not applicable

    -   negligible (less than half the final digit shown)

    0   nil

Appendix

Part 1: Population

Population estimates and projections

The estimated and projected populations are of the resident population of an area, i.e. all those usually resident there, whatever their nationality. Members of HM Forces stationed outside the United Kingdom are excluded; members of foreign forces stationed in the United Kingdom are included. Students are taken to be resident at their term-time addresses. Figures for the United Kingdom do not include the population of the Channel Islands or the Isle of Man.

The population estimates for mid-2001 are based on results from the 2001 Census and incorporate an allowance for census under-enumeration. The figures for 1982 to 2000 are not consistent with the 2001 estimates, apart from national estimates for the UK, or those for England and Wales combined, where interim revised population estimates are available. All population estimates for 1982 to 2000 may be revised, including the UK and England and Wales interim estimates.

The most recent set of national population projections published for the United Kingdom are based on the populations of England, Wales, Scotland and Northern Ireland at mid-2001. Further details of these can be found on the Government Actuary's Department's website (www.gad.gov.uk).

Classification of ethnic groups

The recommended classification of ethnic groups for National Statistics data sources was changed in 2001 to bring it broadly in line with the 2001 Census.

There are two levels to this classification. Level 1 is a coarse classification into 5 main ethnic groups. Level 2 sub-divides Level 1, and provide a finer classification. The preference is for the Level 2 (detailed) categories to be adopted wherever possible. The two levels and the categories are:

Direct comparisons should not be made between the figures produced using this new classification and those based on the previous classification.

Further details can be found on the National Statistics website:
www.statistics.gov.uk/about/
classifications/downloads/ns_ethnicity_
statement.doc

National Statistics Socio-economic Classification

From 2001 the National Statistics Socio-economic Classification (NS-SeC) has been used for all official statistics and surveys. It replaces Social Class based on Occupation (SC) and Socio-economic Groups (SEG).

The NS-SeC is an occupationally-based classification designed to provide coverage of the whole adult population. The version of the classification, which will be used for most analyses, has eight classes, the first of which can be subdivided. These are:

1. Higher managerial and professional occupations

1.1. Large employers and higher managerial occupations

1.2. Higher professional occupations

2. Lower managerial and professional occupations

3. Intermediate occupations

4. Small employers and own account workers

5. Lower supervisory and technical occupations

6. Semi-routine occupations

7. Routine occupations

8. Never worked and long-term unemployed

For complete coverage, the three categories Students, Occupations not stated or inadequately described, and Not classifiable for other reasons are added as 'Not classified'.

Further details can be found on the National Statistics website:
www.statistics.gov.uk/methods_quality/
ns_sec/default.asp

Level 1	Level 2
White	White
	British
	Irish
	Other White background
	All White groups
Mixed	White and Black Caribbean
	White and Black African
	White and Asian
	Other Mixed background
	All Mixed groups
Asian or Asian British	Indian
	Pakistani
	Bangladeshi
	Other Asian background
	All Asian groups
Black or Black British	Caribbean
	African
	Other Black background
	All Black Groups
Chinese or other ethnic group	Chinese
	Other ethnic group
	All Chinese or other groups
All ethnic groups	All ethnic groups
Not stated	Not stated

Internal migration estimates

At the time Table 1.11 was being prepared for publication, research was ongoing into whether there was a need to revise international migration estimates in the light of the 2001 Census. By the time of publication, the Office for National Statistics will have reported on the necessity and feasibility of producing revised internal migration estimates. Future editions of this publication will reflect any revisions that are made.

Part 2: Households and families

Although definitions differ slightly across surveys and the census, they are broadly similar.

Households

A household: is a person living alone or a group of people who have the address as their only or main residence and who either share one meal a day or share the living accommodation.

Students: living in halls of residence are recorded under their parents' household and included in the parents' family type in the Labour Force Survey (LFS), although some surveys/projections include such students in the institutional population.

Families

Children: are never-married people of any age who live with one or both parent(s). They also include stepchildren and adopted children (but not foster children) and also grandchildren (where the parents are absent).

Dependent children: in the 1971 Census, dependent children were defined as never-married children in families who were either under 15 years of age, or aged 15 to 24 and in full-time education. In the 1991 Census, the LFS and the General Household Survey (GHS), dependent children are childless never-married children in families who are aged under 16, or aged 16 to 18 and in full-time education.

A family: is a married or cohabiting couple, either with or without their never-married child or children (of any age), including couples with no children or a lone parent together with his or her never-married child or children. A family could also consist of a grandparent or grandparents with grandchild or grandchildren if the parents of the grandchild or grandchildren are not usually resident in the household. In the LFS, a family unit can also comprise a single person. LFS family units include non-dependent children (who can in fact be adult) – those aged 16 or over and not in full-time education provided they are never married and have no children of their own in the household.

A lone parent family (in the Census) is a father or mother together with his or her never-married child or children.

A lone parent family (in the LFS) consists of a lone parent, living with his or her never-married children, provided these children have no children of their own living with them.

A lone parent family (in the GHS) consists of a lone parent, living with his or her never-married dependent children, provided these children have no children of their own. Married lone mothers whose husbands are not defined as resident in the household are not classified as lone parents. Evidence suggests the majority are separated from their husband either because he usually works away from home or for some other reason that does not imply the breakdown of the marriage.

Conceptions

Conception statistics used in Table 2.18 include pregnancies that result in one or more live or stillbirths, or a legal abortion under the 1967 Act.

Conception statistics do not include miscarriages or illegal abortions. Dates of conception are estimated using recorded gestation for abortions and stillbirths, and assuming 38 weeks gestation for live births.

True birth order

At registration, the question on previous live births is not asked where the birth occurred outside marriage and at the registration of births occurring within marriage, previous live births occurring outside marriage and where the woman had never been married to the father are not counted. The information collected on birth order, therefore, has been supplemented to give estimates of overall true birth order which includes births both within and outside marriage. These estimates are obtained from details provided by the General Household Survey (GHS).

Part 3: Education and training
Main categories of educational establishments

Educational establishments in the United Kingdom are administered and financed in several ways. Most schools are controlled by local education authorities (LEAs), which are part of the structure of local government, but some are 'assisted', receiving grants direct from central government sources and being controlled by governing bodies which have a substantial degree of autonomy. Outside the public sector completely are non-maintained schools run by individuals, companies or charitable institutions.

Up to March 2001, further education (FE) courses in FE sector colleges in England and in Wales were largely funded through grants from the respective Further Education Funding Councils. In April 2001, however, the Learning and Skills Council (LSC) took over the responsibility for funding the FE sector in England, and the National Council for Education and Training for Wales (part of Education and Learning Wales – ELWa) did so for Wales. The LSC in England is also responsible for funding provision for FE and some non-prescribed higher education in FE sector colleges; it also funds some FE provided by LEA maintained and other institutions referred to as 'external institutions'. In Wales, the National Council – ELWa, funds FE provision made by FE institutions via a third party or sponsored arrangements. The Scottish FEFC (SFEFC) funds FE colleges in Scotland, while the Department for Employment and Learning funds FE colleges in Northern Ireland.

Higher education courses in higher education establishments are largely publicly funded through block grants from the HE funding councils in England and Scotland, the Higher Education Council – ELWa in Wales, and the Department of Employment and Learning in Northern Ireland. In addition, some designated HE (mainly HND/HNC Diplomas and Certificates of HE) is also funded by these sources. The FE sources mentioned above fund the remainder.

Numbers of school pupils are shown in Table 3.2. Nursery schools figures for Scotland prior to 1998/99 only include data for local authority pre-schools. Data thereafter include partnership pre-schools. Secondary 'Other' schools largely consist of middle schools in England, and Secondary Intermediate schools in Northern Ireland. Special schools include maintained and non-maintained sectors, whilst public sector and non-maintained schools totals exclude special schools. The 'All schools' total includes pupil referral units, which account for around 10,000 pupils in 2000/01 and 2001/02.

Stages of education

Education takes place in several stages: nursery (now part of the foundation stage in England), primary, secondary, further and higher education, and is compulsory for all children between the ages of 5 (4 in Northern Ireland) and 16. The non-compulsory fourth stage, further education, covers non-advanced education, which can be taken at both further (including tertiary) education colleges, higher education institutions and increasingly in secondary schools. The fifth stage, higher education, is study beyond GCE A levels and their equivalent, which, for most full-time students, takes place in higher education institutions.

Nursery education

In recent years there has been a major expansion of pre-school education. Many children under five attend state nursery schools or nursery classes within primary schools. Others may attend playgroups in the voluntary sector or in privately run nurseries. In England and Wales many primary schools also operate an early admissions policy where they admit children under five into what are called 'reception classes'. The *Education Act 2002* extended the National Curriculum for England to include the foundation stage. The foundation stage was introduced in September 2000 and covers children's education from the age of three to the end of the reception year, when most are just five and some almost six years old. The 'Curriculum guidance for the foundation stage' supports practitioners in their delivery of the foundation stage.

Nursery education providers covered are nursery schools, nursery classes, reception classess, special day schools and nurseries (which usually provide care, education and play for children up to the age of five), playgroups and pre-schools (which provide childcare, play and early years education usually for children aged between two and five), and combined/family centres.

Primary education

The primary stage covers three age ranges: nursery (under 5), infant (5 to 7 or 8) and junior (up to 11 or 12) but in Scotland and Northern Ireland there is generally no distinction between infant and junior schools. Most public sector primary schools take both boys and girls in mixed classes. It is usual to transfer straight to secondary school at age 11 (in England, Wales and Northern Ireland) or 12 (in Scotland), but in England some children make the transition via middle schools catering for various age ranges between 8 and 14. Depending on their individual age ranges middle schools are classified as either primary or secondary.

Secondary education

Public provision of secondary education in an area may consist of a combination of different types of school, the pattern reflecting historical circumstances and the policy adopted by the LEA. Comprehensive schools largely admit pupils without reference to ability or aptitude and cater for all the children in a neighbourhood, but in some areas they co-exist with grammar, secondary modern or technical schools. In Northern Ireland, post primary education is provided by secondary intermediate and grammar schools.

Special schools

Special schools (day or boarding) provide education for children who require specialist support to complete their education, for example because they have physical or other difficulties. Many pupils with special educational needs are educated in mainstream schools. All children attending special schools are offered a curriculum designed to overcome their learning difficulties and to enable them to become self-reliant.

Pupil referral units

Pupil referral units (PRUs) are legally a type of school established and maintained by a LEA to provide education for children of compulsory school age who may otherwise not receive suitable education. The aim of such units is to provide suitable alternative education on a temporary basis for pupils who may not be able to attend a mainstream school. The focus of the units should be to get pupils back into a mainstream school. Pupils in the units may include: teenage mothers, pupils excluded from school, school phobics and pupils in the assessment phase of a statement.

Further education

The term further education may be used in a general sense to cover all non-advanced courses taken after the period of compulsory education, but more commonly it excludes those staying on at secondary school and those in higher education, i.e. courses in universities and colleges leading to qualifications above GCE A Level, Higher Grade (in Scotland), GNVQ/NVQ level 3, and their equivalents. Since 1 April 1993 sixth form colleges have been included in the further education sector.

Higher education

Higher education is defined as courses that are of a standard that is higher than GCE A level, the Higher Grade of the Scottish Certificate of Education/National Qualification, GNVQ/NVQ level 3 or the Edexcel (formerly BTEC) or SQA National Certificate/Diploma. There are three main levels of HE course: (i) postgraduate courses are those leading to higher degrees, diplomas and certificates (including postgraduate certificates of education and professional qualifications) which usually require a first degree as entry qualification; (ii) undergraduate courses which include first degrees, first degrees with qualified teacher status, enhanced first degrees, first degrees obtained concurrently with a diploma, and intercalated first degrees; (iii) other undergraduate courses which includes all other higher education courses, for example HNDs and Diplomas in HE. As a result of the 1992 *Further and Higher Education Act,* former polytechnics and some other higher education institutions were designated as universities in 1992/93. Students normally attend HE courses at higher education institutions, but some attend at further education colleges. Some also attend institutions which do not receive public grant (such as the University of Buckingham) and these numbers are excluded from the tables.

Figures for higher education students in Table 3.11 are annual snapshots taken around November or December each year, depending on the type of institution, except for Scotland further education colleges from 1998/99, for which counts are based on the whole year. The Open University is included in these estimates.

The National Curriculum

The *Education Act 2002* extended the National Curriculum for England to include the foundation stage. It has six areas of learning namely, personal, social and emotional development; communication, language and literacy; mathematical development; knowledge and understanding of the world; physical development; and creative development. Under the *Education Reform Act (1988)* a National Curriculum has been progressively introduced into primary and secondary schools in England and Wales. This consists of English (or the option of Welsh as a first language in Wales), mathematics and science. The second level of curriculum additionally comprises the so-called 'foundation' subjects, such as history, geography, art, music, information technology, design and technology and physical education (and Welsh as a second language in Wales). Measurable targets have been defined for four key stages, corresponding to ages 7, 11, 14 and 16. Pupils are assessed formally at the ages of 7, 11 and 14 by their teachers and by national tests in the core subjects of English, mathematics and science (and in Welsh speaking schools in Wales, Welsh). Sixteen year olds are assessed by means of the GCSE examination. Statutory authorities have been set up for England and for Wales to advise government on the National Curriculum and promote curriculum development generally. Statutory assessment at the end of Key Stage 1 in Wales in 2002, was by means of teacher assessment only. In Wales the National Curriculum Tests/Tasks were discontinued in 2002 following the outcome of the public consultation on proposed changes to the assessment arrangements contained in 'The Learning Country – A Comprehensive Education and Lifelong Learning Programme to 2010 in Wales'. Northern Ireland has its own common curriculum which is similar but not identical to the National Curriculum in England and Wales. Assessment arrangements in Northern Ireland became statutory from September 1996 and key stage 1 pupils are assessed at the age of 8. Pupils in Northern Ireland are not assessed in science at key stages 1 and 2.

In Scotland there is no statutory national curriculum. Pupils aged 5 to 14 study a broad curriculum based on national guidelines, which set out the aims of study, the ground to be covered and the way the pupils' learning should be assessed and reported. Progress is measured by attainment of six levels based on the expectation of the performance of the majority of pupils on completion of certain stages between the ages of 5 and 14: Primary 3 (age 7/8), Primary 4 (age 8/9), Primary 7 (age 11/12) and Secondary 2 (age 13/14). It is recognised that pupils learn at different rates and some will reach the various levels before others. The curriculum areas are language; mathematics; environmental studies; expressive arts; and religious and moral education with personal and social development and health education. Though school curricula are the responsibility of education authorities and individual head teachers, in practice almost all 14 to 16 year olds study mathematics, English, science, a modern foreign language, a social subject, physical education, religious and moral education, technology and a creative and aesthetic subject.

England	Attainment expected
Key Stage 1	Level 2 or above
Key Stage 2	Level 4 or above
Key Stage 3	Level 5/6 or above
Key Stage 4	GCSE

Social class

Social class is based on occupation and is a classification system that has grown out of the original Registrar-General's social class classification. These are defined in the Classification of Occupations 1990 prepared by the Office for National Statistics. The five categories are:

I.   Professional, etc. occupations

II.   Managerial and technical occupations

III.   Skilled occupations

(N) non-manual

(M) manual

IV.   Partly skilled occupations

V.   Unskilled occupations

For students in Figure 3.13, for those aged under 25, social class is determined by their parents occupation. For students aged 25 and over, social class is determined by own occupation.

Qualifications

In England, Wales and Northern Ireland the main examination for school pupils at the minimum school leaving age is the General Certificate of Secondary Education (GCSE) which can be taken in a wide range of subjects. This replaced the GCE O Level and CSE examinations in 1987 (1988 in Northern Ireland). In England, Wales and Northern Ireland the GCSE is awarded in eight grades, A* to G, the highest four (A* to C) being regarded as equivalent to O level grades A to C or CSE grade 1.

GCE A Level is usually taken after a further two years of study in a sixth form or equivalent, passes being graded from A (the highest) to E (the lowest).

Following the Qualifying for Success consultation in 1997, a number of reforms were introduced to the 16 to 19 qualifications structure in September 2000. Under these reforms, students were encouraged to follow a wide range of subjects in their first year of post-16 study, with students expected to study four Advanced Subsidiaries before progressing three of them on to full A levels in their second year. In addition, students are encouraged to study a combination of both general and vocational advanced level examinations. A new vocational A level is replacing the Advanced GNVQ.

The Advanced Subsidiary (AS) qualification covers the first half of the full A level. New specifications introduced in 2001 are now in place and A levels now comprise of units, normally six for a full A level (now A2) and three for the AS level, which is half a full A level. The full A level is normally taken either over two years (modular) or a set of exams at the end of the two years (linear). The AS is a qualification in its own right, whereas A2 modules do not make up a qualification in their own right.

From 1999/2000 National Qualifications (NQ) were introduced in Scotland. NQs include Standard Grades, Intermediate 1 and 2 and Higher Grades. Pupils study for the Scottish Certificate of Education (SCE)/NQ Standard Grade, approximately equivalent to GCSE, in their third and fourth years of secondary schooling (roughly ages 14 and 15). Each subject has several elements, some of which are internally assessed in school, and an award is only made (on a scale of 1 to 7) if the whole course has been completed and examined. The Higher Grade requires one further year of study and for the more able candidates the range of subjects taken may be as wide as at Standard Grade with as many as five or six subjects spanning both arts and science. Three or more Highers are regarded as being approximately the

equivalent of two or more GCE A levels.

After leaving school, people can study towards higher academic qualifications such as degrees. However, a large number of people choose to study towards qualifications aimed at a particular occupation or group of occupations – these qualifications are called vocational qualifications.

Vocational qualifications can be split into three groups, namely National Vocational Qualifications (NVQs), General National Vocational Qualifications (GNVQs) and other vocational qualifications.

NVQs are based on an explicit statement of competence derived from an analysis of employment requirements. They are awarded at five levels. Scottish Vocational Qualifications (SVQs) are the Scottish equivalent.

GNVQs are a vocational alternative to GCSEs and GCE A levels. They are awarded at three levels: Foundation, Intermediate and Advanced. The Advanced level is being replaced by vocational A levels. General Scottish Vocational Qualifications (GSVQs) are the Scottish equivalent.

There are also a large number of other vocational qualifications, which are not NVQs, SVQs, GNVQs or GSVQs, for example, a BTEC Higher National Diploma or a City and Guilds Craft award.

Other qualifications (including academic qualifications) are often expressed as being equivalent to a particular NVQ level so that comparisons can be made more easily.

An NVQ level 5 is equivalent to a Higher Degree.

An NVQ level 4 is equivalent to a First Degree, a HND or HNC, a BTEC Higher Diploma, an RSA Higher Diploma, a nursing qualification or other Higher Education.

An NVQ level 3 is equivalent to 2 A levels, and advanced GNVQ, an RSA advanced diploma, a City & Guilds advanced craft, an OND or ONC or a BTEC National Diploma.

An NVQ level 2 is equivalent to 5 GCSEs at grades A* to C, an Intermediate GNVQ, an RSA diploma, a City and Guilds craft or a BTEC first or general diploma.

For achievement at GCE A level shown in Table 3.14, data up to 1999/00 are for pupils in schools and students in further education institutions aged 17 to 19 at the start of the academic year as a percentage of the 18 year old population. Data prior to 1995/96 are for school pupils only. For 2000/01, data are for pupils in schools and students in further education institutions aged 18 to 19 at the end of the academic year in England, for those aged 18 in Wales, and those aged 17 to 19 in Northern Ireland, as a percentage of the 18 year old population. In Scotland pupils generally sit Highers one year earlier than the rest of the UK sit A levels. The figures for Scotland relate to the results of pupils in year Secondary 5 as a percentage of the 17 year old population.

Adult education
Academic and vocational courses (schedule 2 courses which generally lead to some form of qualification) are those courses of further education for which the *Further and Higher Education Act 1992* required the then Further Education Funding Council (FEFC), and from April 2001, the Learning and Skills Council (LSC) to secure adequate national provision. Other courses are non-schedule 2 courses and are those courses not included in Schedule 2 to the *Further and Higher Education Act 1992*.

Learning and Training at Work
Learning and Training at Work 2002 (LTW 2002) is the fourth in what is now an annual series of employer surveys that investigate the provision of learning and training at work.

Learning and training information had previously been collected, along with information on recruitment difficulties, and skill shortages and gaps, in the annual Skill Needs in Britain (SNIB) surveys, which were carried out between 1990 and 1998.

The objectives of the LTW 2002 survey were to collect information about:

    the volume, type and pattern of off-the-job training;

    key indicators of employers' commitment to training, such as Investors in people;

    learning opportunities offered; and

    awareness of, and involvement with, a number of initiatives relevant to training.

Part 4: Labour market
LFS Reweighting
The results from the 2001 Census, published in September 2002, showed that previous estimates of the total UK population were around one million too high. As a result, ONS published interim revised estimates of the population for the years 1982 to 2001 which are consistent with the 2001 Census findings. In addition the Government Actuary's Department has published interim national population projections for 2002 onwards. Interim national LFS estimates consistent with the latest population data have now been produced.

The interim mid-year population estimates and projections are available by age and sex

and these have been used to produce interim revised LFS estimates of employment, unemployment and inactivity by age and sex. Other LFS analyses, e.g. full/part-time, have been produced by scaling to this age/sex adjusted data. This scaling has been applied to the existing LFS data and summed to obtain new aggregate LFS totals.

The working age employment rate – the percentage of the working-age population who are in employment – was little affected. Almost all of the population revisions were among men aged 25 to 49. As a result it is the estimates of employment for men in this age group which are most affected. The employment revisions for women are small. Estimates of unemployment and unemployment rates are relatively little affected by the population revisions.

Initial analysis work conducted by the ONS has shown that revisions to the LFS census-adjusted data have a greater impact on levels data than on rates. Generally, revisions to rates are within sampling variability whilst those for levels are not.

ONS will complete a full re-weighting of all series and databases by spring 2004. This will allow the interim revised series to be replaced by final estimates.

For more information, see
www.statistics.gov.uk/cci/ nugget.asp?id=207

Unemployment
The UK definition of unemployment is based on ILO guidelines and refers to people without a job who were available to start work within two weeks and had either looked for work in the previous four weeks or were waiting to start a job they had already obtained. Estimates on this basis before 1984 are only available on an experimental, modelled, basis, as the Labour Force Survey did not then collect information on job search over a four week period.

For more information, see
www.statistics.gov.uk/CCI/ nugget.asp?ID=419

The former GB/UK Labour Force definition of unemployment, the only one available for estimates up to 1984, counted people not in employment and seeking work in a reference week (or prevented from seeking work by a temporary sickness or holiday, or waiting for the results of a job application, or waiting to start a job they had already obtained), whether or not they were available to start (except students not able to start because they had to complete their education).

Following a quality review of its labour market statistics, the ONS have re-labelled

'ILO unemployment' as 'unemployment'. This emphasises that the LFS figures provide the official, and only internationally comparable, measure of unemployment in the UK. Claimant count data will continue to be published monthly to provide further information about the labour market, but these will not be presented as an alternative measure of UK unemployment.

Jobs densities for local areas
Jobs density is the total number of filled jobs in an area divided by the resident population of working age in that area. The total number of jobs is a workplace-based measure of jobs and comprises employees, self-employment jobs, government-supported trainees and HM Forces. The number of jobs in an area is composed of jobs done by residents (of any age) and jobs done by workers (of any age) who commute into the area. The working-age population comprises residents of working age who work in the area plus workers of working age who commute out of the area to work in other areas and those who are unemployed or economically inactive of working age.

For more information, see *'Jobs densities for local areas: a new indicator', pp407–413, Labour Market Trends, August 2003.*

Annual Local Area Labour Force Survey
Estimates coming from the Annual Local Area Labour Force Survey (ALALFS) use data compiled annually from the main LFS together with additional interviews in England and Wales.

The ALALFS data presented here have been weighted to be consistent with the best population estimates available before the results of the 2001 Census were published. Reweighted annual data will be published in spring 2004.

Claimant Count
A complementary indicator of unemployment is the claimant count. This is a count of the number of people claiming unemployment-related benefits. While there is significant overlap between unemployment and the claimant count, not all people who claim unemployment-related benefits are unemployed and not all people who are unemployed claim unemployment-related benefits. For example, unemployment includes women who are often not entitled to claim benefits because their partner is also a claimant. Similarly some people claim Job Seekers' Allowance but carry out a small amount of part-time work and so would not be counted as unemployed. A key strength of the claimant count is that it can provide small area estimates at a lower level of geographic

disaggregation than is possible from the LFS, and it is also more timely. Though they can differ month by month, the unemployment and claimant count measures both tend to move in the same direction over the medium and long term. In times of economic downturn, the claimant count tends to rise faster than the ILO measure so that at the trough of the last recession, in 1993, the two measures were very close together. However, in times of economic upturn the claimant count tends to fall faster than the ILO measure. This is because economically inactive people become more optimistic about their employment prospects, start looking for work and hence become (ILO) unemployed.

Job separations

The job separation rate is the number of working-age people who separated from a paid job in the three months before interview divided by the number of people who said they were in employment for more than three months plus those who had separated from a paid job.

The Labour Force Survey (LFS) asks respondents whether they have left a paid job in the past three months and then finds out the reasons for leaving that job. These reasons are usually grouped into two employee-centric categories: voluntary separations; and involuntary separations to reflect the dynamics of labour supply and demand.

Involuntary separations
Dismissed

Made redundant/voluntary redundancy

Temporary job finished

Voluntary separations
Resigned

Gave up work for health reasons

Gave up work for family or personal reasons

Early retirement/retirement

Other reason

Voluntary redundancy and the termination of a temporary job are seen as involuntary separations as they are symptoms of a contraction in labour demand. Early retirement is a slightly ambiguous category to place in the voluntary group, as in some cases it may also be used by employers as a tool to destroy jobs in times of labour demand contraction. However, it is assumed that in the majority of cases it is the normal retirement age of the organisation which is early and therefore not related to labour demand (for example public sector areas such as the police, civil service, fire brigade, armed forces).

For more information, see *'Job separations', pp121–132, Labour Market Trends, March 2003*.

Labour disputes

Statistics of stoppages of work caused by labour disputes in the United Kingdom relate to disputes connected with terms and conditions of employment. Small stoppages involving fewer than ten workers or lasting less than one day are excluded from the statistics unless the aggregate number of working days lost in the dispute is 100 or more. Disputes not resulting in a stoppage of work are not included in the statistics.

Workers involved and working days lost relate to persons both directly and indirectly involved (unable to work although not parties to the dispute) at the establishments where the disputes occurred. People laid off and working days lost at establishments not in dispute, due for example to resulting shortages of supplies, are excluded.

There are difficulties in ensuring complete recording of stoppages, in particular near the margins of the definition; for example short disputes lasting only a day or so, or involving only a few workers. Any under-recording would affect the total number of stoppages much more than the number of working days lost.

Part 5: Income and wealth
Household sector

The data for the household sector as derived from the national accounts have been compiled according to the definitions and conventions set out in the European System of Accounts 1995 (ESA95). At present, estimates for the household sector cannot be separated from the sector for non-profit institutions serving households and so the data in *Social Trends* cover both sectors. The most obvious example of a non-profit institution is a charity: this sector also includes many other organisations of which universities, trade unions and clubs and societies are the most important. The household sector differs from the personal sector, as defined in the national accounts prior to the introduction of ESA95, in that it excludes unincorporated private businesses apart from sole traders. More information is given in *United Kingdom National Accounts Concepts, Sources and Methods* published by The Stationery Office.

In ESA95, household income includes the value of National Insurance contributions and pension contributions made by employers on behalf of their employees. It also shows property income (that is, income from investments) net of payments of interest on loans. In both these respects, national accounts conventions diverge from those normally used when collecting data on household income from household

surveys. Employees are usually unaware of value of the National Insurance contributions and pension contributions made on their behalf by their employer, and so such data are rarely collected. Payments of interest are usually regarded as items of expenditure rather than reductions of income. Thus from Social Trends 33 onwards, the national accounts data for household sector income have been adjusted to omit employers' National Insurance contributions and to express property income gross of any payments of interest on loans, in order to increase comparability with the data on income derived from household surveys used elsewhere in the chapter.

'Local areas' for statistical purposes
NUTS (Nomenclature of Units for Territorial Statistics) is a hierarchical classification of areas that provides a breakdown of the EU's economic territory.

Within Map 5.2 figures are presented at Nuts Level 3, except for Eilean Siar (Western Isles), Orkney Islands and Shetland Islands and also figures for Caithness and Sutherland and Ross and Cromarty; Inverness and Nairn and Moray, Badenoch and Strathspey; Lochaber, Skye and Lochalsh and Argyll and the Islands. Data for these areas not been estimated separately and are presented as Eilean Siar, Orkney Islands and Shetland Islands; and the Rest of Highlands and Islands, respectively.

Individual income
Net individual income refers to the weekly personal income of women and men after deduction of income tax and National Insurance contributions as reported in the Family Resources Survey. Income is from all sources received by an individual including earnings, income from self-employment, investments and occupational pensions/ annuities, benefit income, and tax credits. Income that accrues at household level, such as council tax benefit, is excluded. Income from couples' joint investment accounts is assumed to be received equally. Benefit income paid in respect of dependants such as Child Benefit is included in the individual income of the person nominated for the receipt of payments, except for married pensioner couples, where state retirement pension payments are separated and assigned to the man and woman according to their entitlements. Full details of the concepts and definitions used may be found in *Individual Income 1996/97 to 2001/02* available on the Women and Equality Unit website www.womenandequalityunit.gov.uk or from the Information and Analysis Division, Department for Work and Pensions.

Earnings and education

The Labour Force Survey provides data on both the earnings levels and the educational attainment of individuals participating in the survey. The research on which Table 5.10 is based uses LFS data for employees in England and Wales pooled over the years 1993 to 2001. An hourly wage rate was computed from the ratio of usual earnings to usual hours in the main job. The methodology then estimates the wage premia associated with different levels of educational qualification, but factors out the variance in wages that arises from differences in age, region of residence, year, decade of birth, having a work-limiting health problem, being non-White, being a union member and marital status. Further details may be found in *'Education, Earnings and Productivity'*, *Labour Market Trends*, March 2003, pages 145-152 or from Professor Ian Walker, Department of Economics, University of Warwick Coventry, CV4 7AL.

Equivalisation scales

The Department for Work and Pensions (DWP), the Office for National Statistics (ONS), the Institute for Fiscal Studies (IFS) and the Institute for Social and Economic Research (ISER) all use McClements equivalence scales in their analysis of the income distribution, to take into account variations in the size and composition of households. This reflects the common sense notion that a household of five adults will need a higher income than will a single person living alone to enjoy a comparable standard of living. An overall equivalence value is calculated for each household by summing the appropriate scale values for each household member. Equivalised household income is then calculated by dividing household income by the household's equivalence value. The scales conventionally take a married couple as the reference point with an equivalence value of 1; equivalisation therefore tends to increase relatively the incomes of single person households (since their incomes are divided by a value of less than 1) and to reduce incomes of households with three or more persons. For further information see Households Below Average Income, Corporate Document Services, Department for Work and Pensions.

The DWP and IFS both use different scales for adjustment of income before and after the deduction of housing costs.

Households Below Average Income (HBAI)

Information on the distribution of income based on the Family Resources Survey is provided in the DWP publication *Households*

McClements equivalence scales:

Household member	Before housing costs	After housing costs
First adult (head)	0.61	0.55
Spouse of head	0.39	0.45
Other second adult	0.46	0.45
Third adult	0.42	0.45
Subsequent adults	0.36	0.40
Each dependent aged:		
0–1	0.09	0.07
2–4	0.18	0.18
5–7	0.21	0.21
8–10	0.23	0.23
11–12	0.25	0.26
13–15	0.27	0.28
16 or over	0.36	0.38

Below Average Income: 1994/95 -2001/02, available both in hard copy and on the DWP website. This publication provides estimates of patterns of personal disposable income in Great Britain, and of changes in income over time in the United Kingdom. It attempts to measure people's potential living standards as determined by disposable income. Although as the title would suggest, HBAI concentrates on the lower part of the income distribution, it also provides estimates covering the whole of the income distribution.

Disposable household income includes all flows of income into the household, principally earnings, benefits, occupational and private pensions, investments. It is net of tax, employees' National Insurance contributions, council tax, contributions to occupational pension schemes (including additional voluntary contributions), maintenance and child support payments, and parental contributions to students living away from home.

Two different measures of disposable income are used in HBAI: before and after housing costs are deducted. Housing costs consist of rent, water rates, community charges, mortgage interest payments, structural insurance, ground rent and service charges.

Redistribution of income (ROI)

Estimates of the incidence of taxes and benefits on household income, based on the Expenditure and Food Survey (EFS), formally the Family Expenditure Survey (FES) are published by the ONS in *Economic Trends*. The article covering 2001–02 was published on

the NS website in October 2003 and contains details of the definitions and methods used.

Difference between Households Below Average Income and Redistribution of Income series

These are two separate and distinct income series produced by two different government departments. Each series has been developed to serve the specific needs of that department. The DWP series, HBAI, provides estimates of patterns of disposable income and of changes over time and shows disposable income before and after housing costs (where disposable income is as defined in the section on HBAI above). The ONS series, ROI, shows how Government intervention through the tax and benefit system affects the income of households; it covers the whole income distribution and includes the effects of indirect taxes like VAT and duty on beer, as well as estimating the cash value of benefits in kind (eg from state spending on education and health care). The ROI results are designed to show the position in a particular year rather than trends in income levels over time, although trends in the distribution of income are given. An important difference between the two series is that HBAI counts individuals and ROI counts households. Also, whereas ROI provides estimates for the United Kingdom, from 1994/95 onwards HBAI provides estimates for Great Britain only.

Indicators of social capital

The summary indicators used in Table 5.24 and their definitions are listed below. More details may be found at **www.statistics.gov.uk/downloads/ theme_social/Peoples_perception_ social_capital.pdf**

Positive indicators

High reciprocity – Answered yes to the following questions: neighbours look out for each other; done a favour for a neighbour, received a favour from a neighbour.

High neighbourliness – calculated from a series of variables relating to neighbourliness, incorporating them into a single scale and calculating a mean score.

Satisfactory friendship network – Saw or spoke to friends at least once a week and had at least one close friend who lived nearby.

Satisfactory relatives network – Saw or spoke to relatives at least once a week and had at least one close relative who lived nearby.

Enjoys living in the area – Answered yes to the question 'would you say this is an area you enjoy living in?'

Feels safe walking alone after dark Answered very or fairly safe to 'how safe do you feel walking alone in this area after dark?'

Feels civically engaged – Felt they were well informed about local issues, felt they could influence local decisions and agreed strongly that local people could affect decisions relating to the neighbourhood.

Negative indicators

Low social support – Had less than three people they could turn to during a serious personal crisis.

Low local facilities variable – Created by incorporating the values for each 'facilities' variable (excluding rubbish collection) into a single scale and calculating a mean score.

High local problems – calculated from a series of 'problem' variables, incorporating them into a single scale and calculating a mean score.

Has been a victim of crime in the last 12 months – Answered yes to 'have you personally been a victim of any of the following crimes in the last 12 months?' The list included crimes that took place in the local area only.

Net wealth of the household sector

Revised balance sheet estimates of the net wealth of the household (and non-profit institutions) sector were published in an article in *Economic Trends* November 1999. These figures are based on the new international system of national accounting and incorporate data from new sources. Quarterly estimates of net financial wealth (excluding tangible and intangible assets) are published in *Financial Statistics*.

Distribution of personal wealth

The estimates of the distribution of the marketable wealth of individuals relate to all adults in the United Kingdom. They are produced by combining Inland Revenue (IR) estimates of the distribution of wealth identified by the estate multiplier method with independent estimates of total personal wealth derived from the ONS national accounts balance sheets. Estimates for 1995 onwards have been compiled on the basis of the new System of National Accounts, but estimates for earlier years are on the old basis. The methods used were described in an article in *Economic Trends* (October 1990) entitled '*Estimates of the Distribution of Personal Wealth*.' Net wealth of the personal sector differs from marketable wealth for the following reasons:

Difference in coverage: the ONS balance sheet of the personal sector includes the wealth of non-profit making bodies and unincorporated businesses, while the IR estimates exclude non-profit making bodies and treat the bank deposits and debts of unincorporated businesses differently from the ONS.

Differences in timing: the ONS balance sheet gives values at the end of the year, whereas IR figures are adjusted to mid-year.

IR figures: exclude the wealth of those under 18.

Funded pensions: are included in the ONS figures (including personal pensions) but not in the IR marketable wealth. Also the ONS balance sheet excludes consumer durables and includes non-marketable tenancy rights, whereas the IR figures include consumer durables and exclude non-marketable tenancy rights.

Part 6: Expenditure

Household expenditure

The national accounts definition of household expenditure, within household final consumption expenditure, consists of: personal expenditure on goods (durable, semi-durable and non-durable) and services, including the value of income in kind; imputed rent for owner-occupied dwellings; and the purchase of second-hand goods less the proceeds of sales of used goods. Excluded are interest and other transfer payments; all business expenditure; and the purchase of land and buildings (and associated costs).

In principle, expenditure is measured at the time of acquisition rather than actual disbursement of cash. The categories of expenditure include that of non-resident as well as resident households and individuals in the United Kingdom.

From September 2003, UK economic growth has been calculated in a different way. Previously the detailed estimates for growth for different parts of the economy were summed to a total by weighting each component according to its share of total expenditure in 1995. The year from which this information was drawn was updated at 5-yearly intervals. This is described as 'fixed base aggregation'.

The new method, 'annual chain-linking', uses information updated every year to give each component the most relevant weight which can be estimated. The new method has been used for estimating change in household expenditure since 1971.

For further details see *Consumer Trends* at **http://www.statistics.gov.uk/ consumertrends**

From April 2001, the Family Expenditure Survey (FES) was replaced by the Expenditure and Food Survey (EFS). This was formed by merging the FES with the National Food Survey (NFS). It continues to produce the information previously provided by the FES.

The Expenditure and Food Survey definition of household expenditure represents current expenditure on goods and services. This excludes those recorded payments that are savings or investments (for example life assurance premiums). Similarly, income tax payments, National Insurance contributions, mortgage capital repayments and other payments for major additions to dwellings are excluded. For further details see *Family Spending*.

Classification of individual consumption by purpose

From 2001–02, the Classification Of Individual COnsumption by Purpose (COICOP) was introduced as a new coding frame for expenditure items in the Expenditure and Food Survey. COICOP has been adapted to the needs of Household Budget Surveys (HBS) across the EU and, as a consequence, is compatible with similar classifications used in national accounts and consumer price indices. This allows the production of indicators which are comparable Europe-wide, such as the Harmonised Indices of Consumer Prices.

Twelve categories are used and in this edition of *Social Trends* they are labelled as food and non-alcoholic drink; alcohol and tobacco; clothing and footwear; housing, water and fuel; household goods and services; health; transport; communication; recreation and culture; education; restaurants and hotels; and miscellaneous goods and services.

A major difference also exists in the treatment of mortgages which were included as part of 'housing' expenditure in the previous editions of Social Trends in the FES coding frame. Mortgage interest payments, water charge, council tax and Northern Ireland rates excluded from the COICOP 'housing, water and fuel' category and are recorded under 'other expenditure items.'

National Statistics Socio-economic Classification (NS-SeC)

From 2001, the National Statistics Socio-economic classification (NS-SeC) was adopted for all official surveys, in place of Social Class based on Occupation and Socio-economic group. NS-SeC is itself based on the Standard Occupational Classification 2000 (SOC2000) and details of employment status. Although NS-SeC is an occupationally based classification, there are procedures for classifying those not in work. The main categories used for analysis in Family Spending are:

1   Higher managerial and professional occupations, sub-divided into:

1.1 Large employers and higher managerial occupations

1.2 Higher professional occupations

2 Lower managerial and professional occupations

3 Intermediate occupations

4 Small employers and own account workers

5 Lower supervisory and technical occupations

6 Semi-routine occupations

7 Routine occupations

8 Never worked and long-term unemployed

The detailed NS-SeC classification can be reduced to four broad classes, as in Chapter 3. The managerial and professional class comprises categories 1 and 2, intermediate comprises categories 4 and 5, the routine and manual class comprises categories 5 to 7 and the never worked and long-term unemployed class consists of category 8.

The long-term unemployed, which fall into a separate category, are defined as those unemployed and seeking work for 12 months or more. Members of the Armed Forces, who were assigned to a separate category in Social Class, are included within the NS-SeC classification. Residual groups that remain unclassified include students and those with inadequately described occupations. For the purposes of *Family Spending*, retired individuals are not assigned an NS-SeC category.

Student expenditure
Living costs for full-time university students refers to costs of some household goods, personal items such as toiletries, clothes, entertainment, some non-course related travel, and other general expenditure.

Housing costs for full-time university students refers to costs of their rent, or mortgage; any retainer fee paid over the vacation; council tax; household insurance; and utility bills.

Participation costs for full-time university students refers to cost of students' personal contribution to fees; the costs of their books, equipment and stationery; and all travel to and from college including field trips.

Retail prices index
The general index of retail prices (RPI) is the most familiar general purpose measure of inflation in the UK. It measures the average change from month to month in the prices of goods and services purchased by most households in the United Kingdom. The spending pattern on which the index is based is revised each year, mainly using information from the Expenditure and Food Survey. The expenditure of certain higher income

households, and of pensioner households mainly dependent on state pensions, is excluded.

These households are:

(a) the 4 per cent (approximately) where the total household recorded gross income exceeds a certain amount (£1,540 a week in 2001/02).

(b) 'pensioner' households consisting of retired people who derive at least three quarters of their income from state benefits.

Expenditure patterns of one-person and two-person pensioner households differ from those of the households upon which the general index is based. Separate indices have been compiled for such pensioner households since 1969, and quarterly averages are published on the National Statistics website, *Focus on Consumer Price Indices* (formerly known as the *Consumer Price Indices (CPI) Business Monitor MM23)* . They are chain indices constructed in the same way as the general index of retail prices. It should, however, be noted that the pensioner indices exclude housing costs.

A guide to the RPI can be found on the National Statistics website, www.statistics.gov.uk/rpi.

Consumer prices index
The consumer prices index (CPI) is the main United Kingdom domestic measure of inflation for macro-economic purposes. Prior to 10 December 2003 this index in the UK was published as the harmonised index of consumer prices and the two shall remain one and the same index.

The methodology of the CPI is similar to that of the RPI but differs in the following ways:

1. in the CPI, the geometric mean is used to aggregate the prices at the most basic level whereas the RPI uses arithmetic means;

2. a number of RPI series are excluded from the CPI, most particularly, those mainly relating to owner occupiers' housing costs (eg mortgage interest payments, house depreciation, council tax and buildings insurance);

3. the coverage of the CPI indices is based on the international classification system, COICOP (classification of individual consumption by purpose). Whereas the RPI uses its own bespoke classification;

4. the CPI includes series for air fares, university accommodation fees, foreign students' university tuition fees, unit trust and stockbrokers charges, none of which are included in the RPI;

5. the index for new car prices in the RPI is imputed from movements in second hand car prices, whereas the CPI uses a quality adjusted index based on published prices of new cars;

6. the CPI weights are based on expenditure by all private households, foreign visitors to the UK and residents of institutional households. In the RPI, weights are based on expenditure by private households only, excluding the highest income households, and pensioner households mainly dependent on state benefits, and

7. in the construction of the RPI weights, expenditure on insurance is assigned to the relevant insurance heading. For the CPI weights, the amount paid out in insurance claims is distributed amongst the COICOP headings according to the nature of the claims expenditure with the residual (ie the service charge) being allocated to the relevant insurance heading.

A guide to the CPI can be found on the National Statistics website: www.statistics.gov.uk/cpi.

Harmonised index of consumer prices
The harmonised indices of consumer prices (HICPs) are calculated in each member state of the European Union for the purposes of European comparisons, as required by the Maastricht Treaty. From January 1999 the HICP has been used by the European Central Bank (ECB) as the measure for its definition of price stability across the Euro area. Further details are contained in an ECB Press Notice released on 13 October 1998: 'A stability oriented monetary policy strategy for the ESCB'. In the UK, from 10 December 2003, the HICP is known as the consumer prices index.

A guide to the HICP can be found on the National Statistics website: www.statistics.gov.uk/hicp.

Part 7: Health
Expectation of life
The expectation of life is the average total number of years which a person of that age could be expected to live, if the rates of mortality at each age were those experienced in that year. The mortality rates that underlie the expectation of life figures are based, up to 2002, on total deaths occurring in each year for England and Wales and the total deaths registered in each year in Scotland and Northern Ireland.

Blood pressure level
On the basis of their blood pressure readings and whether they reported currently taking any drugs prescribed for high blood pressure, Health Survey informants were categorised into one of four categories:

Normal untreated: systolic less than 140mmHg, and diastolic less than 90 mmHg, not currently taking any drug(s) prescribed for high blood pressure.

Normal treated: systolic less than 140mmHg and diastolic less than 90mmHg, currently taking drug(s) prescribed for high blood pressure.

High treated: systolic is 140mmHg or over and/or diastolic is 90mmHg or over, currently taking drug(s) prescribed for high blood pressure.

High untreated: systolic is 140mmHg or over and/or diastolic is 90mmHg or over, not currently taking drug(s) prescribed for high blood pressure.

Blood pressure in the Health Survey was measured using an automatic machine, the Dinamap 8100 monitor. It should be noted that the results may not be directly comparable to readings using a standard mercury sphygmomanometer. Comparison of blood pressure levels from the Health Survey for England with other epidemiological studies which have used different measuring devices is problematic, and should only be done with caution.

International Classification of Diseases

The International Classification of Diseases (ICD) is a coding scheme for diseases and causes of death. The Tenth Revision of the ICD (ICD10) was introduced for coding the underlying cause of death in Scotland from 2000 and in the rest of the United Kingdom from 2001. The causes of death included in Figure 7.6 correspond to the following ICD10 codes: circulatory diseases I00-I09; cancer C00-D48; respiratory diseases J00-J99, and infectious diseases A00-B99. Rates for 2000 are for England and Wales only.

The data presented in Figure 7.6 cover three different revisions of the International Classification of Diseases, and although they have been selected according to codes that are comparable, there may still be differences between years that are due to changes in the rules used to select the underlying cause of death. This can be seen in deaths from respiratory diseases where different interpretation of these rules were used to code the underlying cause of death from 1983 to 1992 and from 2001 onwards in England and Wales and from 2000 onwards in Scotland.

Standardised rates

Directly age-standardised rates enable comparisons to be made over time and between the sexes, which are independent of changes in the age structure of the population. In each year, the crude rates in

each five-year age group are multiplied by the European or World standard populations for that age group. These are then summed and divided by the total standard population for these age groups to give an overall standardised rate.

Immunisation

Data shown in Table 7.9 relate to children reaching their second birthday and immunised by their second birthday. Data for Scotland are for 2002.

Body mass index

The body mass index (BMI) shown in Figure 7.12, is the most widely used index of obesity which standardises weight for height and is calculated as weight (kg)/height (m)^2. Underweight is defined as a BMI of 20 or less, desirable over 20 to 25, overweight over 25 to 30 and obese over 30.

Alcohol-related deaths

The ONS definition of alcohol-related deaths includes only those causes regarded as being most directly due to alcohol consumption. Apart from deaths due to accidental poisoning with alcohol the definition excludes other external causes of deaths, such as road traffic deaths and other accidents

Breast cancer and cervical screening programmes

Screening programmes are in operation in the United Kingdom for breast and cervical cancers. Under the breast screening programme, every woman aged between 50 and 64 is invited for mammography (breast X-ray) every three years by computerised call-up and recall systems. In addition, all women over the age of 64 can refer themselves for screening. In England, the call-up and recall system is to be extended to women aged 65 to 70 by 2004. In Scotland, the extension to women aged 65 to 70 will begin in 2003/04. National policy for cervical screening is that women should be screened every three to five years (three-and-a-half to five-and-a-half years in Scotland). The programme invites women aged 20 to 64 (20 to 60 in Scotland) for screening. However, since many women are not invited immediately when they reach their 20th birthday, the age group 25 to 64 is used to give a more accurate estimate of coverage of the target population in England.

Use of condoms

In the self-completion section of the National Survey of Sexual Attitudes and Lifestyles 2000, informants were asked how long ago their most recent occasion of vaginal sexual intercourse, oral sex and anal sex occurred. The questionnaire also contained a number of questions on condom use asked to those respondents who reported vaginal or anal

intercourse in the last four weeks with a partner of the opposite sex.

Part 8: Social protection

Informal carers

Within the Census 2001, the term 'unpaid care' covers any unpaid help, looking after or supporting family members, friends, neighbours or others because of long-term physical or mental ill-health or disability or problems related to old age.

The definition of carers used within the General Household Survey is a self-defined measure of caring based on respondents' own view of whether there is anyone (either living with them or not) who is sick, disabled or elderly whom they look after or give special help to, other than in a professional capacity (for example, a sick or disabled, or elderly, relative/husband/wife/child/friend/parent, etc.). The definition of care used includes all types of caring task and does not impose limits on the number of hours given to caring.

In-patient activity

Within Table 8.5 in-patient data for England and later years for Northern Ireland are based on finished consultant episodes (FCEs). Data for Wales and Scotland, and for Northern Ireland except acute data after 1986, are based on Deaths and Discharges and transfers between specialities (between hospitals in Northern Ireland).

Finished consultant episodes (FCE)
An FCE is a completed period of care of a patient using a bed, under one consultant, in a particular NHS Trust or directly managed unit. If a patient is transferred from one consultant to another within the same hospital, this counts as an FCE but not a hospital discharge. Conversely if a patient is transferred from one hospital to another provider, this counts as a hospital discharge and as a finished consultant episode.

Operations
Within Table 8.6 FCEs are grouped within broad ranges of main operations. The operation codes are taken from Office of Population Censuses and Surveys tabular list of surgical operations and procedures, fourth revision (OPCS4). The main operation is the first recorded and will normally be the most resource intensive procedure performed during the FCE.

Length of stay
The mean (average) duration of the spell in days. A spell is a period of continuous admitted patient care within a particular NHS Trust, calculated by subtracting the admission date from the discharge date. This involves selecting records which are the last for the spell and therefore carry a discharge date. All

'discharge records' also carry an admission date because, where the spell consists of more than one episode, the admission date is carried forward from earlier episode(s) in the spell. Day cases, which have a length of stay of zero days, are excluded from this calculation.

Benefit units
A benefit unit is a single adult or couple living as married and any dependent children. A pensioner benefit unit is where the head is over state pension age.

Pension provision
In Table 8.13 the 'other' category is all those who are not employed or self-employed based on the International Labour Organisation definition. The table excludes the unemployed, retired people, students, those who are looking after their family/home, those who are temporarily or permanently sick/disabled and those not classified elsewhere.

Benefits to groups of recipients
Elderly people
Retirement pension (including non-contributory retirement pension)

Christmas bonus paid with retirement pension and other non-disability benefits

Winter fuel payments

Over 75 TV licence

Minimum income guarantee (income support)

Housing benefit/council tax benefit

Social fund

Sick and disabled people
Incapacity benefit

Attendance allowance

Disability living allowance

Industrial disablement benefit

Other industrial injuries benefits

Severe disablement allowance

Invalid care allowance

Independent living fund

Motability

Christmas bonus paid with disability benefits

Statutory sick pay

Income support

Housing benefit/council tax benefit

Social fund

Family
Maternity allowance

Statutory maternity pay

Child benefit

Vaccine damage payments

Income support

Housing benefit/council tax benefit

Social fund

Unemployed people
Jobseekers allowance (contribution based and Income based)

Job grant

Housing benefit/council tax benefit

Social fund

Widows and Others
Widows/bereavement benefits

Christmas bonus – contributory paid with widow/bereavement benefits

Industrial death benefit

Guardian's allowance & child's special allowance

Pensions compensation board

New deal 50plus employment credits

Income support paid to people who do not fall within the other client groups

Housing benefit/council tax benefit

Social fund

Part 9: Crime and justice
Types of offences in England and Wales
The figures are compiled from police returns to the Home Office or directly from court computer systems.

Recorded crime statistics broadly cover the more serious offences. Up to March 1998 most indictable and triable-either-way offences were included, as well as some summary ones; from April 1998, all indictable and triable-either-way offences were included, plus a few closely related summary ones.

Recorded offences are the most readily available measures of the incidence of crime, but do not necessarily indicate the true level of crime. Many less serious offences are not reported to the police and cannot, therefore, be recorded. Moreover, the propensity of the public to report offences to the police is influenced by a number of factors and may change over time.

From 2000, some police forces have changed their systems to record the allegations of victims unless there is credible evidence that a crime has *not* taken place. In April 2002, a new National Crime Recording Service (NCRS) formalised these changes across England and Wales.

There have been changes to the methodology of the British Crime Survey. Between 1982 and 2001 the survey was carried out every two years, and reported on victimisation in the previous calendar year. The 2001/02 and 2002/03 surveys cover the financial year of interviews and report on victimisation in the 12 months before the interview.

This change makes the survey's estimates more comparable with figures collected by

the police. Because of these significant changes taking place in both measures of crime, direct comparisons with figures for previous years cannot be made.

In England and Wales, indictable offences cover those offences which must or may be tried by jury in the Crown Court and include the more serious offences.

Summary offences are those for which a defendant would normally be tried at a magistrates' court and are generally less serious – the majority of motoring offences fall into this category. Triable either way offences are triable either on indictment or summarily.

Types of offences in Northern Ireland
In recording crime, the Police Service of Northern Ireland broadly follow the Home Office rules for counting crime. As from 1st April 1998 notifiable offences are recorded on the same basis as those in England and Wales (i.e. under the revised Home Office rules – see above). Prior to the revision of the rules, criminal damage offences in Northern Ireland excluded those where the value of the property damaged was less than £200.

Offences and crimes
There are a number of reasons why recorded crime statistics in England and Wales, Northern Ireland and Scotland cannot be directly compared:

Different legal systems: The legal system operating in Scotland differs from that in England and Wales and Northern Ireland. For example, in Scotland children aged under 16 are normally dealt with for offending by the Children's Hearings system rather than the courts.

Differences in classification: There are significant differences in the offences included within the recorded crime categories used in Scotland and the categories of notifiable offences used in England, Wales and Northern Ireland. Scottish figures of 'crime' have therefore been grouped in an attempt to approximate to the classification of notifiable offences in England, Wales and Northern Ireland.

Counting rules: In Scotland each individual offence occurring within an incident is recorded whereas in England, Wales and Northern Ireland only the main offence is counted.

Burglary: This term is not applicable to Scotland where the term used is 'housebreaking'.

Theft from vehicles: In Scotland data have only been separately identified from January 1992. The figures include theft by opening lock fast places from a motor vehicle and other theft from a motor vehicle.

Drug seizures

The figures in Table 9.7, which are compiled from returns to the Home Office, relate to seizures made by the police and officials of HM Customs and Excise, and to drugs controlled under the *Misuse of Drugs Act 1971*. The Act divides drugs into three main categories according to their harmfulness. A full list of drugs in each category is given in Schedule 2 to the *Misuse of Drugs Act 1971*, as amended by Orders in Council.

Offenders cautioned for burglary

In England and Wales offenders cautioned for going equipped for stealing, etc were counted against burglary offences until 1986 and against other offences from 1987. Historical data provided in Table 9.13 have been amended to take account of this change. Drug offences were included under Other offences for 1971.

Sentences and orders

The following are the main sentences and orders which can be imposed upon those persons found guilty. Some types of sentence or order can only be given to offenders in England and Wales in certain age groups. Under the framework for sentencing contained in the *Criminal Justice Acts 1991, 1993* and *The Powers Of Criminal Courts (sentencing) Act 2000* the sentence must reflect the seriousness of the offence. The following sentences are available for adults (a similar range of sentences is available to juveniles aged 10 to 17):

Absolute and conditional discharge: A court may make an order discharging a person absolutely or (except in Scotland) conditionally where it is inexpedient to inflict punishment and, before 1 October 1992, where a probation order was not appropriate. An order for conditional discharge runs for such period of not more than three years as the court specifies, the condition being that the offender does not commit another offence within the period so specified. In Scotland a court may also discharge a person with an admonition.

Attendance centre order: Available in England, Wales and Northern Ireland for young offenders and involves deprivation of free time.

Reparation Order: Introduced under the powers of *Criminal Courts (Sentencing) Act 2000*. This requires the offender to make an apology to the victim or apologise in person. Maximum duration of the order is 24 hours and is only available to youngsters aged 10–18 in England and Wales.

Action Plan Order: An order imposed for a maximum of three months in England, Wales

and Northern Ireland to address certain behavioural problems. This is again available for the younger age groups and is considered as early intervention to stop serious offending.

Drug Treatment and Testing Order: This is imposed as a treatment order to reduce the person's dependence on drugs and to test if the offender is complying with treatment. Length of order can run from 6 months to 3 years in England, Wales and Northern Ireland. This was introduced under the powers of the *Criminal Courts (Sentencing) Act 2000* for persons aged 16 years and over.

Community Rehabilitation Order: An offender sentenced to a probation order is under the supervision of a probation officer (social worker in Scotland), whose duty it is (in England and Wales and Northern Ireland) to advise, assist and befriend him or her but the court has the power to include any other requirement it considers appropriate. A cardinal feature of the order is that it relies on the co-operation of the offender.

Probation orders may be given for any period between six months and three years inclusive. The probation was renamed in 2000 under the powers of the *Criminal Courts (Sentencing) Act.*

Punishment Order: An offender who is convicted of an offence punishable with imprisonment may be sentenced to perform unpaid work for not more than 240 hours (300 hours in Scotland), and not less than 40 hours. Twenty hours minimum community service are given for persistent petty offending or fine default. In Scotland the Law Reform (Miscellaneous Provisions) (Scotland) Act 1990 requires that community service can only be ordered where the court would otherwise have imposed imprisonment or detention. Probation and community service may be combined in a single order in Scotland. Community Punishment Order came into effect under the powers of *Criminal Courts (Sentencing) Act 2000* when it replaced the Supervision Order.

The term *'community sentence'* refers to community rehabilitation orders, supervision orders, community punishment orders, attendance centre orders, community punishment and rehabilitation orders, reparation orders, action plan orders, drug treatment and testing orders, curfew orders and referral orders. Under the *Criminal Justice and Courts Services Act 2000*, certain community orders current at 1 April 2001 were renamed. Probation orders were renamed community rehabilitation orders, community service orders were renamed community punishment orders and combination orders were renamed community punishment and rehabilitation orders.

Community Punishment and Rehabilitation Order: The *Criminal Justice Act 1991* introduced the combination order in England and Wales only, which combines elements of both probation supervision and community service. Meanwhile, Article 15 of the Criminal Justice (NI) Order 1996 introduced the combination order to Northern Ireland. The powers of *Criminal Courts (Sentencing) Act 2000* brought into affect the Community Punishment and Rehabilitation Order which was known as the Combination Order which requires an offender to be under a probation Officer and to take on unpaid work.

Detention and Training Order: This was introduced for youths aged 10–18 under the powers of The *Criminal Courts (Sentencing) Act*. It is for youths that have committed serious crime. They can serve the sentence at a young Offender Institution or at a Local Authority Establishment, Local Authority Secure Training Centre or Young Offender Institution. The sentence is given from 4–24 months, but sentence can run consecutive.

Imprisonment: is the custodial sentence for adult offenders. In the case of mentally disordered offenders, hospital orders, which may include a restriction order may be considered appropriate.

Home Office or Scottish Executive consent is needed for release or transfer. A new disposal, the 'hospital direction', was introduced in 1997. The court, when imposing a period of imprisonment, can direct that the offender be sent directly to hospital. On recovering from the mental disorder, the offender is returned to prison to serve the balance of their sentence. The *Criminal Justice Act 1991* abolished remission and substantially changed the parole scheme in England and Wales. Those serving sentences of under four years, imposed on or after 1 October 1992, are subject to Automatic Conditional Release and are released, subject to certain criteria, halfway through their sentence. Home Detention Curfews result in selected prisoners being released up to 2 months early with a tag that monitors their presence during curfew hours. Those serving sentences of four years or longer are considered for Discretionary Conditional Release after having served half their sentence, but are automatically released at the two thirds point of sentence. The *Crime (Sentences) Act 1997*, implemented on 1 October 1997, included, for persons aged 18 or over, an automatic life sentence for a second serious violent or sexual offence unless there are exceptional circumstances. All offenders serving a sentence of 12 months or more are supervised in the community until the three quarter point of sentence. A life sentence prisoner may be released on licence subject to supervision and is always liable to recall. In Scotland the *Prisoners and Criminal Proceedings (Scotland) Act 1993* changed the system of remission and parole for prisoners sentenced on or after 1 October 1993. Those serving sentences of less than four years are released unconditionally after having served half of their sentence, unless the court specifically imposes a Supervised Release Order which subjects them to social work supervision after release. Those serving sentences of four years or more are eligible for parole at half sentence. If parole is not granted then they will automatically be released on licence at two thirds of sentence subject to days added for breaches of prison rules. All such prisoners are liable to be 'recalled on conviction' or for breach of conditions of licence, i.e. if between the date of release and the date on which the full sentence ends, a person commits another offence which is punishable by imprisonment or breaches his/her licence conditions, then the offender may be returned to prison for the remainder of that sentence whether or not a sentence of imprisonment is also imposed for the new offence.

Fully suspended sentences: may only be passed in exceptional circumstances. In England, Wales and Northern Ireland, sentences of imprisonment of two years or less may be fully suspended. A court should not pass a suspended sentence unless a sentence of imprisonment would be appropriate in the absence of a power to suspend. The result of suspending a sentence is that it will not take effect unless during the period specified the offender is convicted of another offence punishable with imprisonment. Suspended sentences are not available in Scotland.

Fines: The *Criminal Justice Act 1993* introduced new arrangements on 20 September 1993 whereby courts are now required to fit an amount for the fine which reflects the seriousness of the offence, but which also takes account of an offender's means. This system replaced the more formal unit fines scheme included in the *Criminal Justice Act 1991*. The Act also introduced the power for courts to arrange deduction of fines from income benefit for those offenders receiving such benefits. The *Law Reform (Miscellaneous Provision) (Scotland) Act 1990* as amended by the *Criminal Procedure (Scotland) Act 1995* provides for the use of supervised attendance orders by selected courts in Scotland. The *Criminal Procedure (Scotland) Act 1995* also makes it easier for courts to impose a supervised attendance order in the event of a default and enables the court to impose a supervised attendance order in the first instance for 16 and 17 year olds.

Custody Probation Order: an order unique to Northern Ireland reflecting the different regime there which applies in respect of remission and the general absence of release on licence. The custodial sentence is followed by a period of supervision for a period of between 12 months and three years.

Civil courts

England and Wales: The main civil courts are the High Court and the county courts. Magistrates' courts also have some civil jurisdiction, mainly in family proceedings. Most appeals in civil cases go to the Court of Appeal (Civil Division) and may go from there to the House of Lords. Since July 1991, county courts have been able to deal with all contract and tort cases and actions for recovery of land, regardless of value. Cases are presided over by a judge who almost always sits without a jury. Jury trials are limited to specified cases, for example, actions for libel.

Scotland: The Court of Session is the supreme civil court. Any cause, apart from causes excluded by statute, may be initiated in, and any judgement of an inferior court may be appealed to, the Court of Session. The Sheriff Court is the principal local court of civil jurisdiction in Scotland. It also has jurisdiction in criminal proceedings. Apart from certain actions the civil jurisdiction of the Sheriff Court is generally similar to that of the Court of Session.

Part 10: Housing

Dwelling stock

The definition of dwelling used follows the census' definition applicable at that time. Currently the 2001 Census is used. This defined a dwelling as 'structurally separate accommodation'. This was determined primarily by considering the type of accommodation, as well as separate and shared access to multi-occupied properties.

In all stock figures, vacant dwellings are included but non-permanent dwellings are generally excluded. For housebuilding statistics, only data on permanent dwellings are collected.

Estimates of the total dwelling stock, stock changes and the tenure distribution for each country are made by the Office of the Deputy Prime Minister (ODPM), the Scottish Executive, the National Assembly for Wales, and NI Department for Social Development. These are primarily based on census output data for the number of dwellings (or households converted to dwellings) from the censuses of population for Great Britain. Adjustments were carried out if there were specific reasons to do so. Census years' figures are based on outputs from the

censuses. For years between censuses, the total figures are obtained by projecting the base census year's figure forward yearly. The increment is based on the annual total number of completions plus the annual total net gain due to other housing flows statistics, i.e. conversions, demolitions and change of use.

Estimates of dwelling stock by tenure category are primarily based on the census except in the situation where it is considered that for some specific tenure information, there are other more accurate sources. In this situation, it is assumed that the other data sources contain vacant dwellings also but it is not certain and it is not expected that these data are very precise. Thus the allocation of vacant dwellings to tenure categories may not be completely accurate. This means that the margin of error for tenure categories are wider than for estimates of total stock.

For the 2001 Census, a comparison with other available sources indicated that for local authorities' stock, figures supplied by local authorities are more reliable. Similarly, it was found that Housing Corporation's own data are more accurate than those from the census for the registered social landlords' (RSLs) stock. Hence only the rented privately or with a job or business tenure data directly from the census was used. The owner-occupied data was taken as the residual of the total from the census. For non-census years, the same approach was adopted except for the privately rented or with a job or business for which Labour Force Survey results were considered to be appropriated for use.

In the Survey of English Housing, data for privately rented unfurnished accommodation includes accommodation which is partly furnished.

For further information on the methodology used to calculate stock by tenure and tenure definitions, see Appendix B Notes and Definitions in the ODPM annual volume *Housing Statistics* or the housing statistics page of the ODPM website (**www.odpm.gov.uk**).

Dwellings completed

In principle, a dwelling is regarded as completed when it becomes ready for occupation whether it is in fact occupied or not. In practice, there are instances where the timing could be delayed and some completions are missed, for example, because no completion certificates were requested by the owner.

Tenure definition for housebuilding is only slightly different from that used for stock figures. For details see *Housing Statistics*.

Private rented and living rent free

The 2001 Census definition of private rented accommodation included renting from a private landlord or letting agency, employer of a household member, or relative or friend of a household member or other person. Living rent free could include households that were living in accommodation other than private rented.

Household reference person

As of April 2000 the General Household Survey adopted the term 'household reference person' in place of 'head of household'. As of April 2001 the Survey of English Housing also adopted the term.

The household reference person is identified during the interview and is defined as the member of the household who:

a. owns the household accommodation, or

b. is legally responsible for the rent of the accommodation, or

c. has the household accommodation as an emolument or perquisite, or

d. has the household accommodation by virtue of some relationship to the owner who is not a member of the household.

The household reference person must always be a householder, whereas the head of household was always the husband, who might not be a householder. If there are joint householders, the household reference person will be the householder with the highest income.

Homeless at home

Homeless at home refers to any arrangement where a household for whom a duty has been accepted (i.e. eligible for assistance, unintentionally homeless and in priority need) is able to remain in, or return to the accommodation from which they are being made homeless, or temporarily stay in other accommodation found by the applicant. Such schemes may locally be referred to as: Direct Rehousing, Prevention of Homelessness; Concealed Household Schemes; Prevention of Imminent Homelessness Schemes; Impending Homeless Schemes or Pre-eviction Schemes.

Bedroom standard

The concept is used to estimate occupation density by allocating a standard number of bedrooms to each household in accordance with its age/sex/marital status composition and the relationship of the members to one another. A separate bedroom is allocated to each married or cohabiting couple, any other person aged 21 or over, each pair of adolescents aged 10–20 of the same sex, and each pair of children under 10. Any unpaired person aged 10–20 is paired if possible with a child under 10 of the same sex, or, if that is not possible, is given a separate bedroom, as is any unpaired child under 10. This standard is then compared with the actual number of bedrooms (including bedsitters) available for the sole use of the household, and deficiencies or excesses are tabulated. Bedrooms converted to other uses are not counted as available unless they have been denoted as bedrooms by the informants; bedrooms not actually in use are counted unless uninhabitable.

Poor neighbourhoods

'Poor' neighbourhoods refer to local areas where the English House Condition Survey (EHCS) surveyor visually assessed whether any one or more of the following problems apply:

a. over 10 per cent of dwellings in the local area are visually assessed to be seriously defective;

b. the presence of serious problems related to any of the following: vacant sites or derelict buildings; vacant or boarded up buildings; litter, rubbish or dumping; vandalism; graffiti or scruffy buildings, gardens or landscaping; neglected buildings;

c. very poor visual quality of the local area.

The neighbourhoods themselves are delimited by natural or physical boundaries (eg major roads, railway lines, housing estate dwelling types) observed by the EHCS surveyor in reviewing the area around the sample dwelling.

Property transactions

The figures are based on the number of particular delivered (PD) forms processed by the Stamp Office or District Land Registry. They relate to the transfer or sale of any freehold interest in land or property, or the grant or transfer or a lease of at least 21 years and one day, and therefore include some non-residential transactions. In practice there is an average lag of about one month between the transaction and the date on which the PD form is processed.

Sales and transfers of local authority dwellings

Right to buy was established by the *Housing Act 1980* and was introduced across Great Britain in October 1980.

In England, large scale voluntary transfers (LSVTs) of stock have been principally to housing associations/registered social landlords; figures include transfers supported by estate renewal challenge funding (ERCF). The figures for 1993 includes 949 dwellings transferred under Tenants' Choice.

Scotland includes large scale voluntary transfers to registered social landlords and trickle transfers to housing associations.

Part 11: Environment

Water pollution incidents

Data shown in Table 11.3 relate to substantiated reports of pollution and correspond to categories 1 and 2 in the Environment Agency's pollution incidents classification scheme. For Scotland the term 'significant incidents' is used and compares broadly with all of category 1 and most of category 2 used by the Environment Agency. In Northern Ireland the terms 'high severity' and 'medium severity' are used; these compare broadly with all of category 1 and 2 used the Environment Agency.

The Environment Agency defines four categories of pollution incidents.

Category 1: The most severe, incidents which involve one or more of the following:

1. potential or actual persistent effect on water quality or aquatic life;

2. closure of potable water, industrial or agricultural abstraction necessary;

3. major damage to aquatic ecosystems;

4. major damage to agriculture and/or commerce;

5. serious impact on man; or

6. major effect on amenity value.

Category 2: Severe incidents, which involve one or more of the following:

1. notification to abstractors necessary;

2. significant damage to aquatic ecosystems;

3. significant effect on water quality;

4. damage to agriculture and/or commerce;

5. impact on man; or

6. impact on amenity value to public, owners or users.

Category 3: Minor incidents, involving one or more of the following:

1. a minimal effect on water quality;

2. minor damage to aquatic ecosystems;

3. amenity value only marginally affected; or

4. minimal impact on agriculture and/or commerce.

Category 4: Incidents where no impact on the environment occurred.

Rivers and canals

The chemical quality of rivers and canal waters in the United Kingdom are monitored in a series of separate national surveys in England and Wales, Scotland and Northern Ireland. In England, Wales and Northern Ireland the General Quality Assessment (GQA) Scheme provides a rigorous and objective method for assessing the basic chemical quality of rivers and canals based on three determinands: dissolved oxygen, biochemical oxygen demand (BOD) and ammoniacal nitrogen). The GQA grades river stretches into six categories (A-F) of chemical quality Table 11.4 uses two broader groups – good (classes A and B) and fair (classes C and D). Classification of biological quality is based on the River Invertebrate and Classification System (RIVPACS).

The length of rivers chemically classified in Northern Ireland increased by more than 40 per cent between 1991 and 2001.

In Scotland, water quality is based upon the Scottish River Classification Scheme of 20 June 1997 which combines chemical, biological, nutrient and aesthetic quality using the following classes: excellent (A1), good (A2), fair (B), poor (C) and seriously polluted (D). In 1999 a new Digitised River Network was introduced.

Bathing waters
Directive 76/160/EEC concerning the quality of bathing water sets the following mandatory standards for the coliform parameters:

1. for total coliforms, 10,000 per 100 millilitres; and

2. for faecal coliforms 2,000 per 100 millilitres.

The directive requires that at least 95 per cent of samples taken for each of these parameters over the bathing season must meet the mandatory values. In practise this has been interpreted in the following manner: where 20 samples are taken only one sample for each parameter may exceed the mandatory values for the water to pass the coliform standards; where less than 20 samples are taken, none may exceed the mandatory values for the water to pass the coliform standards.

The bathing season is from mid-May to end-September in England and Wales, but is shorter in Scotland and Northern Ireland. Bathing waters which are closed for a season are excluded for that year.

The boundaries of the Environment Agency regions are based on river catchment areas and not county borders. In particular, the figures shown for Wales are for the Environment Agency Welsh Region, the boundary of which does not correspond to the boundary of Wales.

Forest and woodland
The forestry data shown in Table 11.15 for GB are compiled by the Forestry Commission and cover both private and state-owned land. Estimates are based on the provisional results of the National Inventory of Woodland and Trees for 1995-1999 and extrapolated forward using information about new

planting and other changes. Data for Northern Ireland are compiled separately by the Forest Service, an agency of DARD and also cover both private and state-owned land.

Part 12: Transport
The National Travel Survey
The National Travel Survey (NTS) has been conducted on a small scale continuous basis since July 1988. The last of the previous ad hoc surveys was carried out in 1985-1986.

Information is collected from about 3,000 households in Great Britain each year. Each member of the household provides personal information (for example, age, sex, working status, driving licence, season ticket) and details of trips carried out in a sample week, including the purpose of the trip, method of travel, time of day, length, duration, and cost of any tickets bought.

Travel included in the NTS covers all trips by Great Britain residents within Great Britain for personal reasons, including travel in the course of work.

A trip is defined as a one-way course of travel having a single main purpose. It is the basic unit of personal travel defined in the survey. A round trip is split into two trips, with the first ending at a convenient point about half-way round as a notional stopping point for the outward destination and return origin. A stage is that portion of a trip defined by the use of a specific method of transport or of a specific ticket (a new stage being defined if either the mode or ticket changes).

Cars are regarded as household cars if they are either owned by a member of the household, or available for the private use of household members. Company cars provided by an employer for the use of a particular employee (or director) are included, but cars borrowed temporarily from a company pool are not.

The main driver of a household car is the household member that drives the furthest in that car in the course of a year.

The purpose of a trip is normally taken to be the activity at the destination, unless that destination is 'home' in which case the purpose is defined by the origin of the trip. The classification of trips to 'work' is also dependent on the origin of the trip. The following purposes are distinguished:

Commuting: trips to a usual place of work from home, or from work to home.

Business: personal trips in the course of work, including a trip in the course of work back to work. This includes all work trips by people with no usual place of work (eg site workers) and those who work at or from home.

Education: trips to school or college, etc. by full-time students, students on day-release and part-time students following vocational courses.

Escort: used when the traveller has no purpose of his or her own, other than to escort or accompany another person; for example, taking a child to school. For example, escort commuting is escorting or accompanying someone from home to work or from work to home.

Shopping: all trips to shops or from shops to home, even if there was no intention to buy.

Personal business: visits to services eg hairdressers, launderettes, dry-cleaners, betting shops, solicitors, banks, estate agents, libraries, churches; or for medical consultations or treatment, or for eating and drinking unless the main purpose was entertainment or social.

Social or entertainment: visits to meet friends, relatives, or acquaintances, both at someone's home or at a pub, restaurant, etc; all types of entertainment or sport, clubs, and voluntary work, non-vocational evening classes, political meetings, etc.

Holidays or day trips: trips (within Great Britain) to or from any holiday (including stays of four nights or more with friends or relatives) or trips for pleasure (not otherwise classified as social or entertainment) within a single day.

Just walk: walking pleasure trips along public highways including taking the dog for a walk and jogging.

Road Traffic
The figures from 1993 to 2002 have been produced on a new basis and are not directly comparable with earlier figures. In 2001/02, steps were taken to improve the quality of Department for Transport's major road network database. The net result of these improvements has been little change to the estimates of total motor vehicle traffic for Great Britain for after 1993, but some changes to the composition of the overall figure. In general, from 1993 to 1999 the new motorway traffic estimates are now higher than before, while those for other major roads are lower, with the reverse being true for 2000 and 2001.

Passenger death rates
Passenger fatality rates given in Table 12.22 can be interpreted as the risk a traveller runs of being killed, per billion kilometres travelled. The coverage varies for each mode of travel and care should be exercised in drawing comparisons between the rates for different modes.

The table provides information on passenger fatalities and where possible travel by drivers and other crew in the course of their work has been excluded. Exceptions are for private journeys and those in company owned cars and vans where drivers are included.

Figures for all modes of transport exclude confirmed suicides and deaths through natural causes. Figures for air, rail and water exclude trespassers and rail excludes attempted suicides. Accidents occurring in airports, seaports and railway stations that do not directly involve the mode of transport concerned are also excluded. For example, deaths sustained on escalators or falling over packages on platforms.

The figures are compiled by the Department for Transport. Further information is available in the annual publications *Road Casualties Great Britain: Annual Report* and *Transport Statistics Great Britain*. Both are published by the Stationery Office and are available at: **www.dft.gov.uk/transtat**.

The following definitions are used:

Air: accidents involving UK registered airline aircraft in UK and foreign airspace. Fixed wing and rotary wing aircraft are included but air taxis are excluded. Accidents cover UK airline aircraft around the world not just in the UK.

Rail: train accidents and accidents occurring through movement of railway vehicles in Great Britain. As well as national rail the figures include accidents on underground and tram systems, Eurotunnel and minor railways.

Water: figures for travel by water include both domestic and international passenger carrying services of UK registered merchant vessels.

Road: figures refer to Great Britain and include accidents occurring on the public highway (including footways) in which at least one road vehicle or a vehicle in collision with a pedestrian is involved and which becomes known to the police within 30 days of its occurrence. Figures include both public and private transport.

Bus or coach: figures for work buses are included. From 1 January 1994, the casualty definition was revised to include only those vehicles equipped to carry 17 or more passengers regardless of use. Prior to 1994 these vehicles were coded according to construction, whether or not they were being used for carrying passengers. Vehicles constructed as buses that were privately licensed were included under 'bus and coach' but PSV licensed minibuses were included under cars.

Car: includes taxis, invalid tricycles, three and four wheel cars and minibuses. Prior to 1999 motor caravans were also included.

Van: vans mainly include vehicles of the van type constructed on a car chassis. From 1 January 1994 these are defined as those vehicles not over 3.5 tonnes maximum permissible gross vehicle weight. Prior to 1994 the weight definition was not over 1.524 tonnes unladen.

Two-wheeled motor vehicle: mopeds, motor scooters and motor cycles (including motor cycle combinations).

Pedal cycle: includes tandems, tricycles and toy cycles ridden on the carriageway.

Pedestrian: includes persons riding toy cycles on the footway, persons pushing bicycles, pushing or pulling other vehicles or operating pedestrian controlled vehicles, those leading or herding animals, occupants of prams or wheelchairs, and people who alight safely from vehicles and are subsequently injured.

Part 13: Lifestyles and social participation
Cultural events
Data from 1986–1987 and 1991–1992 in Table 13.9 are taken from the Target Group Index, BMRB International, and data for subsequent years are taken from the Target Group Index Doublebase, BMRB International.

Articles published in previous editions

No.1 1970

Some general developments in social statistics Professor C A Moser, CSO

Public expenditure on the social services Professor B Abel-Smith, London School of Economics and Political Science

The growth of the population to the end of the century Jean Thompson, OPCS

A forecast of effective demand for housing in Great Britain in the 1970s A E Holmans, MHLG

No.2 1971

Social services manpower Dr S Rosenbaum, CSO

Trends in certificated sickness absence F E Whitehead, DHSS

Some aspects of model building in the social and environmental fields B Benjamin, CSC

Social indicators – health A J Culyer, R J Lavers and A Williams, University of York

No.3 1972

Social commentary: change in social conditions CSO

Statistics about immigrants: objectives, methods, sources and problems Professor C A Moser, CSO

Central manpower planning in Scottish secondary education A W Brodie, SED

Social malaise research: a study in Liverpool M Flynn, P Flynn and N Mellor, Liverpool City Planning Department

Crimes of violence against the person in England and Wales S Klein, HO

No.4 1973

Social commentary: certain aspects of the life cycle CSO

The elderly D C L Wroe, CSO

Subjective social indicators M Abrams, SSRC

Mental illness and the psychiatric services E R Bransby, DHSS

Cultural accounting A Peacock and C Godfrey, University of York

Road accidents and casualties in Great Britain J A Rushbrook, DOE

No.5 1974

Social commentary: men and women CSO

Social security: the European experiment E James and A Laurent, EC Commission

Time budgets B M Hedges, SCPR

Time budgets and models of urban activity patterns N Bullock, P Dickens, M Shapcott and P Steadman, Cambridge University of Architecture

Road traffic and the environment F D Sando and V Batty, DOE

No.6 1975

Social commentary: social class CSO

Areas of urban deprivation in Great Britain: an analysis of 1971 Census data S Holtermann, DOE

Note: Subjective social indicators M Abrams, SSRC

No.7 1976

Social commentary: social change in Britain 1970–1975 CSO

Crime in England and Wales Dr C Glennie, HO

Crime in Scotland Dr Bruce, SHHD

Subjective measures of quality of life in Britain: 1971 to 1975 J Hall, SSRC

No.8 1977

Social commentary: fifteen to twenty-five: a decade of transition CSO

The characteristics of low income households R Van Slooten and A G Coverdale, DHSS

No.9 1979

Housing tenure in England and Wales: the present situation and recent trends A E Holmans, DOE

Social forecasting in Lucas B R Jones, Lucas Industries

No.10 1980

Social commentary: changes in living standards since the 1950s CSO

Inner cities in England D Allnutt and A Gelardi, DOE

Scotland's schools D Wishart, SED

No.14 1984

Changes in the life-styles of the elderly 1959–1982 M Abrams

No.15 1985

British social attitudes R Jowell and C Airey, SCPR

No.16 1986

Income after retirement G C Fiegehen, DHSS

No.17 1987

Social Trends since World War II Professor A H Halsey, University of Oxford

Household formation and dissolution and housing tenure: a longitudinal perspective A E Holmans and S Nandy, DOE; A C Brown, OPCS

No.18 1988

Major epidemics of the 20th century: from coronary thrombosis to AIDS Sir Richard Doll, University of Oxford

No.19 1989

Recent trends in social attitudes L Brook, R Jowell and S Witherspoon, SCPR

No.20 1990

Social Trends, the next 20 years T Griffin, CSO

No.21 1991

The 1991 Census of Great Britain: plans for content and output B Mahon and D Pearce, OPCS

No.22 1992

Crime statistics: their use and misuse C Lewis, HO

No.24 1994

Characteristics of the bottom 20 per cent of the income distribution N Adkin, DSS

No.26 1996

The OPCS Longitudinal Study J Smith, OPCS

British Household Panel Survey J Gershuny, N Buck, O Coker, S Dex, J Ermish, S Jenkins and A McCulloch, ESRC Research Centre on Micro-social Change

No.27 1997

Projections: a look into the future T Harris, ONS

No.28 1998

French and British societies: a comparison P Lee and P Midy, INSEE and A Smith and C Summerfield, ONS

No.29 1999

Drugs in the United Kingdom   a jigsaw with missing pieces A Bradley and O Baker, Institute for the Study of Drug Dependence

No.30 2000

A hundred years of social change A H Halsey, Emeritus Fellow, Nuffield College, Oxford

No.31 2001

200 hundred years of the census of population M Nissel

No.32 2002

Children B Botting, ONS

No.33 2003

Investing in each other and the community: the role of social capital P Haezewindt, ONS

Index

The references in this index refer to table and chart numbers, or entries in the Appendix.

A

Abortions
rates, by age — 2.19
teenage conceptions, by age and outcome — 2.18

Accidents
passenger death rates — 12.22
people killed or seriously injured, by road user type and time of day — 12.23
road deaths — 12.24

Accommodation type
by construction date — 10.2
by tenure — 10.5
by ethnic group — 10.12
by household composition — 10.11
dwelling prices — 10.21
temporary — 10.14

Adoptions — 2.8

Agricultural land use — 11.15

Age
abortion rates — 2.19
at divorce — 2.12
at marriage — 2.12
average age of mother
by birth order — 2.21
aged 65 and over, by unitary and local authorities — 1.10
by ethnic group — 1.5
childlessness — 2.20
cohabitation — 2.14
expectation of life at birth, by sex — 7.1
dependent — 1.3
household reference person, by tenure — J.9
immunisation of children by their second birthday — 7.9
low income experienced by people over 60 — 5.23
population — 1.2
sources of gross weekly income — 5.4

Aids — 7.2

Air

See also 'Atmosphere'
passengers at civil airports — 12.21
travel — 12.20

Alcohol
adults exceeding daily benchmarks — 7.13
deaths from alcohol-related diseases — 7.14

Anxiety
prevalence of neurotic disorders — 7.20

Atmosphere
days with moderate or higher air pollution — 11.2
emissions of air pollutants — 11.1

Attitudes
residents views of problems in their neighbourhood — 10.17
to neighbourhoods — 13.23
towards car and bus use — 12.17
towards secondary schooling — 3.5

Asylum Seekers
asylum applications — 1.14

B

Bankruptcies
individual over time — 6.13

Bathing water
compliance with EC bathing water directive — 11.5

Benefits
effect of taxes and benefits on household income — 5.18
household income
composition of — 5.3
composition by age of head of household — 5.4
EU comparison — 5.5
redistribution of income — 5.18

Birds
population of — 11.20

Births — 1.8
adoption register
by date of entry into — 2.8
average age of mother
by birth order — 2.21

caesarean deliveries in NHS hospitals — 8.19
outside marriage, EU comparison — 2.17
population change — 1.7
true birth order — App Pt 2

Blood pressure
high — 7.4

Body mass index — App Pt 7
by sex and NS-SeC — 7.12

Borrowing — 6.12

Breast cancer screening — 7.19

Burglary
recorded crime — 9.1

Bus
attitudes toward use of — 12.17
reasons for infrequent use of — 12.12
travel — 12.16

C

Cancer
breast cancer screening by region — 7.19
death rates from selected — 7.18
incidence: EU comparison — 7.17

Cannabis
use among young adults — 7.15

Car
access
households without — 12.11
number of cars per household — 12.10
trips per person per year by — 12.3
attitudes toward use of — 12.17
driving licence holders — 12.9
travel to work by — 12.13
older people — A.12

Carbon dioxide
emissions of, by end user — 11.7

Caring
communal medical and care establishments, residents — 8.1
home help and home care — 8.2
informal carers by age and sex — 8.3

informal childcare arrangements | 8.15
types of help given by carers | 8.4

Cheques

non-cash transactions | 6.10

Childlessness

By age and year of birth | 2.20

Children

See also 'Families'

ChildLine, calls and letters to | 8.18
child protection registers | 8.17
consultations with an NHS GP | 8.8
death rates, by age and sex | 1.9
dependent population | 1.3
hospital and community health service expenditure | 8.7
immunisation | 7.9
informal childcare arrangements | 8.15
local authority personal social services expenditure | 8.23
looked after children | 8.16
low income | 5.21
mortality, main causes by sex and age | 7.6
social protection benefit expenditure | 8.20
trips to and from school per year | 12.14

Cigarette smoking

by sex | 7.16

Cinema attendance | 13.10

Class size

by region | 3.4

Climate

difference in average surface temperatures | 11.6
winter and summer rainfall | 11.11

Cohabitation | 2.14

attitudes towards, by age | 2.15

Compost

materials collected from households for recycling | 11.10

Computers

activities undertaken on the computer by 11–18 year olds | 13.18
households with selected durable goods | 13.13

Consumers

net borrowing over time | 6.12

Courts

certificates issued on civil non-family proceedings | 9.23

outcome of cases at magistrates' courts | 9.18
prisoners reconvicted | 9.14
writs and summonses issued | 9.22

Credit cards

non-cash transactions | 6.10
spending by type of purchase | 6.11

Crime

British Crime Survey offences | 9.1
concern of | 9.10
crimes committed within last 12 months, by outcome | 9.3
detection rates | 9.16
disorder levels | 9.8
fraud offences | 9.6
involving firearms | 9.5
offenders found guilty of indictable offences by age | 9.12
offenders indictable offences | 9.13
offenders sentenced for indictable offences | 9.17
perception of problems in neighbourhood | 10.17
prison population | 9.19
prison population by ethnic group | 9.21
prison releases on temporary licence | 9.20
prisoners reconvicted | 9.14
reasons for improving home security | 9.9
recorded
by type of offence | 9.2
seizures of selected drugs | 9.7
theft, by region | 9.4
victims | 9.11
writs and summonses issued | 9.22

Crops

land under organic production | 11.16

Conceptions

to teenagers, by age and outcome | 2.18

Coronary heart disease | 7.5

Countryside

frequency of visits to | 11.21

D

Deaths | 1.8

cancer rates, by selected types and sex | 7.18
from alcohol related diseases | 7.14
life expectancy | 7.1
rates | 1.9, 7.6, 7.18
population change | 1.7
suicide rates | 7.21

Debit cards

non-cash transactions | 6.10
spending by type of purchase | 6.11

Debt

net borrowing | 6.12
individual insolvencies | 6.13

Dentists | 8.9

Depression

prevalence of neurotic disorders among older people, by sex and income | 7.20

Development

land changing to residential use | 11.19

Diet

average daily consumption of fruit and vegetables, by sex | 7.11

Disability | App Pt 4

Economic activity status | 4.6

Disposable income | 5.1, 5.14

by area | 5.2
by family type | 5.15
shares | 5.16
sources, EU comparison | 5.5

Divorces | 2.11

attitudes towards, by age | 2.15
rates, EU comparison | 2.13
average age by sex | 2.12

Doctors | 8.9

Driving licence

holders by sex and age | 12.9

Drugs

alcohol consumption | 7.13
cigarette smoking | 7.16
use among young adults | 7.15
perception of problems in neighbourhood | 10.17
seizures | 9.7

Dwellings

See 'Housing'

E

Earnings

average earnings index | 5.7
sources of disposable income, EU comparison | 5.5
effect of a degree level qualification | 5.10
gross hourly earnings, by sex | 5.8

household income, composition of   5.3

by industry   5.9

percentage paid in income tax and National Insurance   5.12

Economic activity

by employment status and sex   4.2

by social economic classification of household reference person   6.3

of disabled people, by sex   4.6

of women by marital status and age of youngest dependent child   4.5

of young people   4.4

rates   4.1, 4.3

Economic inactivity

reasons for, by sex   4.7

Education   App Part 3

See also 'Pupils', 'Qualifications', 'Schools', 'Students'

adult   3.20

effect on earnings   5.10

expenditure   3.21

further   3.11

higher   3.11

Elderly

See 'older people'

Electricity

generation, by fuel used   11.13

generation from renewable sources   11.8

Employees

by sex and occupation   4.15

gross weekly earnings, by sex   5.8

hourly earnings, by industry   5.9

jobs, by sex and industry   4.13

reasons employees look for new job   4.27

trade union membership   4.25

with flexible working patterns   4.18

Employment   App Pt 4

distribution of usual weekly hours   4.17

entering through the New Deal   4.24

jobs density   4.11

population of working age, by socio-economic classification   1.6

rates by highest qualification   4.12

rates by sex   4.9

rates, EU comparison   4.10

self-employment   4.17

voluntarily leaving job   4.23

Energy

domestic consumption of   11.14

electricity generation, by fuel used   11.13

electricity generated from renewable sources   11.8

production of primary fuels   11.12

Entertainment

attendance at cultural events   13.9

cinema attendance   13.10

households with selected durable goods   13.13

interest in television programme type   13.5

music sales   13.7

radio listening   13.6

reading preferences   13.11

video rentals by genre   13.8

visits to tourist attractions   13.19

Environmental Health Officers

noise complaints received by   11.22

Equivalisation

distribution of equivalised income, by family type   5.15

scales   App Pt 5

shares of equivalised disposable income   5.16

Ethnic Group

by accommodation   10.12

by tenure   10.10

higher managers and professionals   4.14

highest qualification held   3.17

low income   5.22

police officer strength   9.24

population, by age   1.5

prison population   9.21

European Union comparisons

asylum applications   1.14

births outside marriage   2.17

comparative price levels   6.18

death rates from circulatory diseases   7.7

demographic indicators

infant mortality, total fertility rate, life expectancy   1.16

electricity generation   11.13

employment rates   4.10

EU expenditure   5.31

EU nationals living in the UK, and UK nationals living in other EU states   1.12

expenditure on education   3.21

expenditure on social protection   8.21

graduation rates

harmonised index of consumer prices   6.17

household expenditure on transport   12.8

incidence of cancers   7.17

income

low income   5.20

older people   A.7

sources   5.5

road deaths   12.24

marriage and divorce rates   2.13

owner occupation   10.8

unemployment rates   4.20

Exclusions from school

by ethnic group   3.8

Expenditure

education

EU comparison   3.21

hospital and community health service expenditure   8.7

government   5.30

household   App Pt 6, 6.1, 6.2

by age of household reference person   6.6

by selected family type   6.4

on selected leisure activities by region   6.7

on selected items as percentage of total   6.8

by social economic classification of household reference person   6.3

on transport   12.7

on transport as proportion of overall   12.8

local authority personal social services   8.23

retail sales volume   6.9

social protection, by function   8.20

social protection, EU comparison   8.21

social security expenditure by recipient group   8.22

credit and debit cards   6.10, 6.11

F

Families   App Pt 2

adults living with parents   2.9

by ethnic group   2.5

children living in different family types   2.4, 2.5, 2.7

contact with relatives

by ethnic group   2.10

distribution of income by family type   5.15

expenditure   6.4

informal childcare arrangements   8.15

lone parent   2.2, 2.4, 2.5, 10.7, 10.11

median individual net income, by sex   5.6

receipt of selected social security benefits   8.14

stepfamilies

dependent children   2.7

social protection benefit expenditure   8.20

social security expenditure 8.22

Fertility rates

by age of mother at childbirth 2.16

European demographic indicators 1.16

world demographic indicators 1.15

Financial assets/liabilities

household net wealth, composition of 5.25

Firearms

recorded crimes involving 9.5

Fish

stocks of 11.17

Forests
App Pt 11

woodland cover 11.18

Freight

goods moved 12.5

Fuels

production of primary 11.12

Further education

Students 3.11

G

GCE A level (or equivalent)

See 'Qualification'

GCSE (or equivalent)

See 'Qualification'

General Practitioners 8.9

Green spaces

frequency of visits to 11.21

Goods

moved by domestic freight,
by mode 12.5

Government

expenditure 5.30

Gross domestic product (GDP)

annual growth 5.28

expenditure on education 3.21

per head 5.1

G7 comparison 5.29

H

Health

alcohol consumption, by sex
and age 7.13

obesity among adults by sex and
NS-SeC 7.12

cancer screening

breast cancer, by region 7.19

cigarette smoking

by age and sex 7.16

contraception

condom use 7.23

diet

consumption of fruit
and vegetables 7.11

drugs

use among young adults 7.15

general 7.3

heart attacks 7.5

high blood pressure 7.4

life expectancy

at birth, by sex 7.1

mental health

prevalence of neurotic disorders
among older people, by sex
and income 7.20

self-reported 7.3

sexually transmitted diseases

HIV and AIDS 7.24

Heterosexual partners 7.22

Higher education

effect on earnings 5.10

graduation rates 3.16

participation rates 3.13

students 3.11

Holidays

in the United Kingdom by
destination 13.20

Home Help

number of contact hours 8.2

Home security 9.9

Homelessness

households in temporary
accommodation 10.14

reasons for 10.13

Housebuilding completions

by construction date 10.2

by number of bedrooms 10.4

by sector 10.3

Household tasks

division of household tasks 13.3

time spent on household tasks 13.2

Households App Pt 2

adults living with parents 2.9

below average income App Pt 5

composition of net wealth 5.25

domestic energy consumption 11.14

by ethnic group of head 10.10

economic status, working age
households 4.8

expenditure App Pt 6, 6.1, 6.2

by age of household reference
person 6.6

by selected family type 6.4

on selected leisure activities by
region 6.7

on selected goods and services
as percentage of total 6.8

by social economic classification
of household reference person 6.3

on transport 12.7

on transport as proportion of overall 12.8

household sector App Pt 5

by household type 10.7, 10.11

income

by area 5.2

children living in low income
households 5.21

composition 5.3

disposable income 5.1, 5.14

shares of equivalised
disposable income 5.16

low income, by ethnic group 5.22

net local taxes as a percentage of 5.13

redistribution of, through taxes
and benefits 5.18

sources 5.4, 5.5

People in households

by type of household and family 2.3

by size 2.1

number of cars by composition 12.10

one person households 2.1, 2.2

by area 2.6

stock of dwellings 10.1

by tenure 10.7

by type of accommodation 10.11

by type of household and family 2.2

without a car or van 12.11

Housing

average property prices 10.21

benefit 10.24

by household type 10.7, 10.11

by tenure 10.6, 10.7, 10.9, 10.10

first time buyers 10.22

moving house

main reasons, by post-move tenure 10.19

mortgages 10.22

loans in arrears and repossessions 10.23

non-decent homes 10.15

sales and transfers of local authority
dwellings 10.20

stock of dwellings 10.1

type of, by construction date 10.2

I

Immunisation   7.9, 7.10

Income

  See also 'Benefits' and 'Earnings'

  by age of head of household   5.4

  by area   5.2

  distribution   5.14

    by family type   5.15

    where people spent the majority
    of their time   5.17

  disposable

    distribution of   5.14

    sources of, EU comparison   5.5

    real household disposable
    income per head   5.1

  household, composition of   5.3

  individual income   App Pt 5, 5.6

  low

    by ethnic group of head of
    household   5.22

    children in low income households   5.21

    EU comparison   5.20

    experience of individuals aged 60
    and over   5.23

    indicators of social capital   5.24

    people below percentages of
    median income   5.19

  older people   A.10

  pensioners and non-pensioners   A.8

  redistribution   5.18

  relative income of older people   A.7

  shares of disposable income   5.16

Income support

  older people   A.9

Industry

  distribution of hourly earnings   5.9

  employee jobs   4.13

  self-employment   4.16

Infant

  mortality   7.2

  mortality, by European demographic
  indicators   1.16

  mortality, by world demographic
  indicators   1.15

Infectious diseases

  notifications   7.8

Inflation   App Pt 6

  Harmonised index of consumer
  prices , EU comparison   6.17

  Retail prices index   App Part 6, 6.14

Insolvencies

Individual over time   6.13

International comparisons

  See also 'European Union
  comparisons'and 'Migration'

  asylum applications   1.14

  demographic indicators   1.15

  G7 comparison of GDP per head   5.29

International travel

  by mode   12.20

Internet

  access by household type   13.15

  activities undertaken on the
  computer by 11–18 year olds   13.18

  goods and services bought   13.16

  security precautions taken for
  internet use   13.17

J

Jobs   App Pt 4

  density   4.11

  reasons employees look for
  new job   4.27

K

Key Stages

  class sizes   3.4

  expected standards   3.6

L

Labour disputes   4.26

Labour force   App Pt 4

Land use

  Land changing to residential use   11.19

  by agricultural and other uses   11.15

Landfill

  Management of municipal waste   11.9

Library

  reasons for visiting   13.12

Life expectancy

  at birth, by sex   7.1

  European demographic indicators   1.16

  World demographic indicators   1.15

Living arrangements:

  older people   A.5

  older people in communal
  establishments   A.6

Local authorities

  sales and transfers of dwellings   10.20

housebuilding completions   10.3

Lone parents   2.2, 2.3, 2.4, 2.5

Low income

  See 'Income'

M

Marital status

  older people   A.4

  changes for older people   A.3

Marriages   2.11

  attitudes towards, by age   2.15

  rates, EU comparison   2.13

  average age by sex   2.12

Maternities

  average age of mother
    by birth order   2.21

  teenage conceptions, by age
  and outcome   2.18

  outside marriage, EU comparison   2.17

Measles

  notifications of selected
  infectious diseases   7.8

Mental health

  prevalence of neurotic disorders
  among older people, by sex
  and income   7.20

Migration   App pt 1 1.7, 1.11, 1.12

  inter-regional   1.11

  settlement grants   1.13

  UK nationals living in other EU states   1.12

Minority ethnic group

  See 'Ethnic group'

MMR   7.9

Mobile phones

  adult ownership   13.14

Mortality

  See 'Deaths'

Mortgages

  loans in arrears and repossessions   10.23

Music sales   13.7

N

Neighbourhoods

  attitudes to, by length of residence   13.23

Neurotic disorders

  prevalence among older people,
  by sex and income   7.20

New Deal 4.24

Noise

complaints received by
Environmental Health Officers 11.22

Non-married couples
See 'Cohabitation'

Non-teaching staff 3.23

NVQ awards 3.15

O

Obesity
among adults, by sex and NS-SeC 7.12

Occupation
employees 4.15
trade union membership 4.25

Obsessive compulsive disorder
prevalence of neurotic disorder, by sex 7.20

Offences
detection rates 9.16
indictable offences
fraud offences 9.6
offenders, by sex, type of offence
and age 9.12
offenders cautioned for, by type
of offence 9.13
offenders sentenced for, by type
of offence 9.17
involving firearms 9.5
recorded by the British Crime Survey 9.1
theft by region 9.4

Older people
See also 'Pensions'
changes in marital status A.3
communal medical and care
establishments, residents 8.1
consultations with an NHS GP 8.8
death rates, by age and sex 7.6, 7.18
dependent population 1.3
experience of low income 5.23
females for every 100 males,
by age A.2
income A.8, A.10
income support A.9
hospital and community health
service expenditure 8.7
living arrangements A.5
living in communal establishments A.6
local authority personal social
services expenditure 8.23
marital status A.4
population, by age 1.2, 1.3, 1.5

population aged 65 and
over, by area 1.10
population by ethnic group
and age 1.5
poverty rates A.7
proportions, by sex and age A.1
prevalence of neurotic
disorders: by sex and gross
household income 7.20
receipt of social security benefits
for pensioners 8.12
relative income A.7
sex ratios A.2
social protection benefit
expenditure 8.20
social security expenditure 8.22
use of personal social services 8.11
with a car A.12

Opinions
of rail services 12.19

Organic
crop production 11.16

Overcrowding, by tenure 10.16

P

Passenger
at civil airports 12.21
death rates, by mode of
transport App Pt 12, 12.22
journeys by bus 12.16
journeys by rail 12.18
transport prices 12.6
transport, by mode 12.1

Pension
income of pensioners and
non-pensioners A.8
pension provision by selected
employment status 8.13
pension provision of older people A.11
receipt of social security benefits
for pensioners 8.12

Phobias
prevalence of neurotic disorders,
by sex 7.20

Police
officer strength, by rank, sex and
ethnic group 9.24
stop and searches 9.15

Pollution App Pt 11
days with moderate or higher
air pollution 11.2
emissions of air pollutants 11.1

emissions of carbon dioxide 11.7
water pollution incidents 11.3
chemical quality of rivers
and canals 11.4
bathing water quality 11.5

Population
See also 'Migration'
age and sex 1.2
aged 65 and over, by unitary and
local authorities 1.10
aged 90 and over, by sex 1.4
change 1.7
dependent, by age 1.3
ethnic group, by age 1.5
of the United Kingdom 1.1
projections App Pt 1, 1.1, 1.2,
1.3, 1.4, 1.7
of working age
by socio-economic classification
and sex 1.6

Poverty rates
older people A.7

Prevention
breast cancer screening 7.19
immunisation 7.9, 7.10

Prices
average percentage change in
retail prices index 6.14, 6.15
comparative price levels,
EU comparison 6.18
of selected items over time 6.16
passenger transport 12.6
percentage change in consumer
prices, EU comparison 6.17

Prison
population 9.19
population by ethnic group 9.21
releases on temporary licence 9.20

Property transactions 10.18

Pupils
by type of school 3.2
expected standards 3.6
reading achievement, G8 comparison 3.7
with statements of Special
Educational Needs 3.3

Q

Qualification App Pt 3
GCE A level (or equivalent)
achievement 3.14

entries by subject 3.12

GCSE (or equivalent)

attainment 3.9

effect on earnings 5.10

employment rate 4.12

highest held 3.17

people working towards 3.10

vocational awards 3.15

R

Radio listening 13.6

Rail

channel tunnel 12.20

journeys by operator 12.18

opinions of services 12.19

Rain

winter and summer 11.11

Reading

reading preferences 13.11

reasons for visiting a library 13.12

Recycling

management of municipal waste 11.9

materials collected from
households for 11.10

Redistribution of income App Pt 5

through taxes and benefits 5.18

Regional comparisons

breast cancer screening 7.19

disposable income 5.2

households where single people
live alone 2.6

inter-regional movements 1.11

local taxes 5.13

population 65 and over 1.10

Religion

belonging to a 13.24

Relatives

See also 'Families'

contact with relatives

by ethnic group 2.10

Renewable energy

electricity generation from
renewable sources 11.8

Rent 10.24

Retail prices index App Pt 6, 6.14
average percentage change
in retail prices index 6.14, 6.15

of selected items over time 6.16

passenger transport prices 12.6

Retail sales volume 6.9

Retired households

See 'Older people'

Rivers

chemical quality of 11.4

Roads

average number of people killed
or seriously injured in accidents 12.23

deaths, EU comparison 12.24

traffic App Pt 12

average daily flow of motor
vehicles 12.15

S

Savings

by household type 5.27

Schools

attitudes towards secondary 3.5

children under 5 3.1

class sizes 3.4

non-teaching staff 3.23

permanent exclusions 3.8

pupils 3.2

teachers 3.22

trips to and from per child per year 12.14

Sea

travel 12.20

Sexual partners 7.22

Sexually transmitted diseases

HIV and AIDS 7.24

Sickness and disability

communal medical and care
establishments, residents 8.1

consultations with an NHS GP 8.8

hospital and community health
service expenditure 8.7

local authority personal social
services expenditure 8.23

NHS in-patient activity 8.5

recipients of disability living
allowance by main disabling
condition 8.10

selected operations in NHS hospitals 8.6

social protection benefit expenditure 8.20

social security expenditure 8.22

Social capital

by household income 5.24

Social class

participation in higher education 3.13

Social security

See 'Benefits'

Socio-economic classification App Pt 1

Population of working age,
by sex 1.6

Students

See also 'Pupils'

expenditure

by type App Pt 6, 6.5

further education 3.11

higher education 3.11

loans and grants 3.2

Special Educational Needs

pupils with statements of 3.3

Sport

participation by age 13.21

participation in selected sports
by young people 13.22

Suicide rates 7.21

SVQ awards 3.15

T

Taxes

household income, composition of 5.3

income tax payable, by income 5.11

net local taxes, by region, 5.13

as a percentage of earnings 5.12

redistribution of income through
taxes and benefits 5.18

Teachers 3.22

See 'Non-teaching staff'

Teenagers

conceptions, by age and outcome 2.18

fertility rates App Pt 2

Television

interest in programme type 13.5

video rentals by genre 13.8

Temperature

difference in average surface
temperatures 11.6

Tenure

by accommodation type 10.6

by ethnic group 10.10

household resident under one year,
previous tenure, by current tenure 10.19

overcrowding 10.16
stock of dwellings 10.5
under-occupation 10.16

Theft
See 'Crime'

Time use
activities 13.1
free time activities of full-time workers 13.4
household tasks 13.2

Trade union membership 4.25

Training
job-related 3.18

Transactions, non-cash
by method of payment 6.10

Transport
attitudes toward car and bus use 12.17
average distance walked by age 12.4
daily flow of motor vehicles 12.15
expenditure
on transport by age of household
reference person 6.6
on transport as percentage of total
household expenditure 6.8
opinions of rail services 12.19
people killed or seriously injured in
road accidents 12.23
prices 12.6
reasons for infrequent bus use 12.12
road deaths, EU comparison 12.24
passenger, by mode
passenger death rates, by mode 12.22
terminal passengers at civil airports 12.21

Travel
bus 12.16
international, by mode 12.20
purpose of 12.2
rail 12.18
to school
trips per child per year, by main
mode 12.14
to work by car or van 12.13
trips
by mode 12.2
car access 12.3

Tuberculosis
notifications 7.8

U

Under-occupation

by tenure 10.16

Unemployment App Pt 4
duration of 4.22
rates 4.19
rates by sex and age 4.21
rates, EU comparison 4.20
social protection benefit expenditure 8.20
social security expenditure 8.22

V

Vaccinations
influenza 7.10
MMR 7.9

Van
See 'Car'

Video rentals by genre 13.8

Violent crime 9.11

W

Walking
average distance per person per year 12.4

Waste
management of municipal 11.9

Water
water pollution incidents 11.3

Wealth
distribution of App Pt 5, 5.26
household sector, composition of 5.25

Whooping cough
notifications of selected infectious
diseases 7.8

Wildlife
population of wild birds 11.20
North Sea fish stocks 11.17

Woodland cover 11.18

Work
travel to 12.13

Work Based Learning 3.19

Working age households 4.8

Working days lost 4.26

Working hours
distribution of usual working hours 4.17
employees with flexible working
pattern 4.18

World
demographic indicators
fertility rates, infant mortality
rates, life expectancy 1.15

Y

Young people
prevalence of recent use of drugs 7.15
economic activity 4.4

182951   167924